THE INSIDE GAME

Ohio History and Culture

Series on Ohio History and Culture

John H. White and Robert J. White Sr., *The Island Queen: Cincinnati's Excursion Steamer*
H. Roger Grant, *Ohio's Railway Age in Postcards*
Frances McGovern, *Written on the Hills: The Making of the Akron Landscape*
Keith McClellan, *The Sunday Game: At the Dawn of Professional Football*
Steve Love and David Giffels, *Wheels of Fortune: The Story of Rubber in Akron*
Alfred Winslow Jones, *Life, Liberty, and Property: A Story of Conflict and a Measurement of Conflicting Rights*
David Brendan Hopes, *A Childhood in the Milky Way: Becoming a Poet in Ohio*
John Keim, *Legends by the Lake: The Cleveland Browns at Municipal Stadium*
Richard B. Schwartz, *The Biggest City in America: A Fifties Boyhood in Ohio*
Tom Rumer, *Unearthing the Land: The Story of Ohio's Scioto Marsh*
Ian Adams, Barney Taxel, and Steve Love, *Stan Hywet Hall and Gardens*
William F. Romain, *Mysteries of the Hopewell: Astronomers, Geometers, and Magicians of the Eastern Woodlands*
Dale Topping, edited by Eric Brothers, *When Giants Roamed the Sky: Karl Arnstein and the Rise of Airships from Zeppelin to Goodyear*
Millard F. Rogers Jr., *Rich in Good Works: Mary M. Emery of Cincinnati*
Frances McGovern, *Fun, Cheap, and Easy: My Life in Ohio Politics, 1949–1964*
Larry L. Nelson, editor, *A History of Jonathan Alder: His Captivity and Life with the Indians*
Ian Adams and Steve Love, *Holden Arboretum*
Bruce Meyer, *The Once and Future Union: The Rise and Fall of the United Rubber Workers, 1935–1995*
Joyce Dyer, *Gum-Dipped: A Daughter Remembers Rubber Town*
Melanie Payne, *Champions, Cheaters, and Childhood Dreams: Memories of the Soap Box Derby*
John A. Flower, *Downstairs, Upstairs: The Changed Spirit and Face of College Life in America*
Wayne Embry, with Mary Schmitt Boyer, *The Inside Game: Race, Power, and Politics in the NBA*
Robin Yocum, *Dead Before Deadline: . . . And Other Tales from the Police Beat*
A. Martin Byers, *The Hopewell Episode: Paradigm Lost and Paradigm Gained*

THE INSIDE GAME

Race, Power, and Politics in the NBA

By Wayne Embry
With Mary Schmitt Boyer

The University of Akron Press
Akron Ohio

All inquiries and permissions requests should be addressed to the publisher,
The University of Akron Press, Akron, OH 44325-1703
Manufactured in the United States of America
First edition 2004

ISBN 978-1-931968-22-5

The Library of Congress has catalogued the cloth edition of this book as follows.
Library of Congress Cataloging-in-Publication Data
Embry, Wayne, 1937–
The inside game : race, power, and politics in the NBA / by Wayne Embry with Mary Schmitt Boyer.— 1st ed.
p. cm. — (Series on Ohio history and culture)
Includes index.
ISBN 1-931968-14-4 (cloth : alk. paper)
1. Embry, Wayne, 1937– 2. Basketball players—United States—Biography. 3. Basketball managers—United States—Biography. 4. National Basketball Association. I. Boyer, Mary Schmitt. II. Title. III. Series.
GV884.E53A3 2004
796.323'092—dc22 2004003605

The paper used in this publication meets the minimum requirements of American National Standard for Information Sciences—Permanence of Paper for Printed Library Materials, ANSI Z39.48—1984. ∞

Book and Cover design by Charles Sutherland

Dedication

For my wife Terri, my children Debbie, Jill, Wayne Jr. and my granddaughter, Little Terri. Thank you for your support. For my parents, Anna and Floyd, and my sister Ruth Ann. For Grandpa Embry and the pioneers who preceeded me.—WRE

For Mollie, who taught me how to tell a good story, and for Gene, who provided the happy ending—MSB

Contents

List of Illustrations

Acknowledgments

A whole team full of relatives, friends, and coworkers encouraged us and supported us. Mentioning each of their names would fill another book. But our heartfelt gratitude goes out to each and every one of them, especially Terri, Debbi, and Little Terri, Wayne Jr., Jill and Gene.

A few people must be singled out, for without them this project would not have been completed.

First and foremost, many thanks to Michael J. Carley, director of the University of Akron Press, for taking a chance on us. David Halberstam made suggestions on structuring the manuscript. Mary's husband, Gene Boyer, suggested the subtitle. Russ Granik, Brian McIntyre, and Carmin Romanelli and his staff at the NBA cleared the way for us to use some of the photos. Bob Price and Bob Zink, formerly of the Cavs, and my former assistant, Judy Berger, greatly helped with our research. Tracy Dodds acted as our first copyeditor and Number 1 cheerleader. Al Attles helped chronicle the events in the book. Robert Miller, Sheila Gabas, and Hilary Hinzmann made suggestions along the way.

Finally, to the attentive staffs of Johnny's and the Union Club in Cleveland, who nourished us, body and soul, and provided us with a place to work.

Foreword

I look at the young, handsome face of a Mr. Wayne Embry. It is on a 1961–62 basketball card I bought at The Locker Room. This card shop is on the island of Martha's Vineyard. And the Vineyard is where Wayne and I see each other at our summer homes.

His hair on the card has waves with a part on the side. I guess that was "fly" back in the day. Turning the $25 card over, it lists his vitals: Center—Cincinnati Royals—6'8"—240—Miami of Ohio—Born in Springfield, Ohio, and "a rough, tough rebounder who last season developed into a stickout scorer." Yes, all of that is true, but thank God for autobiographies like this. You cannot put a human being's complete story on the back of a card. Of course, you can always get the stats. That is how we judge and evaluate the players. As they say, "The numbers never lie." But it has to be more than that. Numbers alone cannot tell the sojourn of a man-child born in a time in the United States of America when a big black man, or shall we say a big black "Negro," was not expected or allowed to rise, to rise up to his human potential in this democratic society.

In this great American story, we witness how Wayne Embry rose up. I may sound corny, but I have come to the belief that black men were of a different stock back then. I often ask him how he views today's black athletes and, like another of my heroes, Jim Brown, they both speak of disgust.

But let us always recognize the great ones who put down the foundation under hardships we can only imagine in our worst collected "American Nightmares." Let us not sleep on their triumphs, their setbacks and disappointments, and the lives that they lived, but rather how they overcame these hurdles.

Wayne Embry gives us, shares with us, his unique perspective, not just into sports but how it all works. And if you are ever so lucky to meet the Big Fella, maybe at a game, airport, or in Martha's Vineyard, maybe he will have time to lecture you on how The Big "O," Oscar Robertson, is the greatest baller of ALL-TIME and not MJ. Wayne says my main man Michael Jordan is answer Number 2.

Spike Lee
Brooklyn, N.Y.
9/3/03

Wayne Embry's first basketball card
(Courtesy of Embry family)

Preface

I wanted to write an important book; important in the sense that people would come to better understand human relationships, what paths people take along the way, and what motivates people to act the way they do.

I wanted this book to appeal to more than just sports fans, and I tried to capture more than just my career as a player. I wanted to talk about my childhood, and its uniqueness insofar as I was the only black student in an all-white environment. I wanted to talk about ideas that were universal in nature—the good and the bad in people, as well as the disappointments we encounter in those we call our friends. I did this by exposing breakdowns in loyalty, which we have all experienced in life, as well as breaches in trust.

I realized that the sports world was no different from the rest of the world, which is constantly growing and changing. I wanted to talk about how those social changes influenced the game of basketball and human relationships in general. In fact, with more than five decades in the National Basketball Association as a player and executive, I learned that each decade was unique in shaping the lives of people and their behavior. I also tried to use my unique experiences to talk about management and leadership—how to be successful through strong character and values, and how to overcome adversity. I talked about how sports now distorts the values of people, which is the opposite of what I experienced when I began my career in basketball.

I have been asked more than once what it was that first drew me to the game of basketball; what motivated me to become the player I ultimately became. I would have to initially point to my childhood, when I developed the drive to play the game. Most of this was because of my feelings of rejection at a very young age. Perhaps this was an offshoot of being black and poor. We never had the best of clothes and, because of my rapid growth, I grew out of the ones I had in a short time. I wore my shoes until they literally fell off my feet. The size of my feet, a size that kept up with my age until I was seventeen, brought even more attention to me. In the seventh grade, I was driven to play basketball on a team because I was seeking a way to gain acceptance. I loved all sports. I was no different from a lot of kids. But it was basketball that stole my heart. I can still remember shooting a ball of rolled-up socks at a clothes hanger and dreaming of making the winning shot in a championship game.

Yet, just making the team was not enough for me. I wanted to be the best. I was driven to be the best on the team because that was the way to be accepted beyond the black community. I was driven to be the best in the classroom because I wanted to be accepted intellectually. No matter how much I was loved and accepted by my family and my church, there always were places I could not go, places I could not feel comfortable. I wanted to eat in the same restaurants as my classmates. I wanted to go to a movie theater and not sit in the balcony. I wanted to retain my dignity. I wanted to belong. I wanted to break down racial barriers.

I believe the message of this book is important to all people. Sports competition provides discipline, teamwork, and values that remain an integral part of one's social and intellectual development. Reading my book will offer insight into my ingredients for success—preparation through education, practice, hard work, and dedication; perseverance through developing mental toughness; perception of opportunities and obstacles that are presented; pride in achievement; persistence in never giving up your dream and passion for that which you seek to accomplish. Even now, five years after my induction into the Basketball Hall of Fame and my subsequent firing, my passion for the game burns as bright as ever.

I miss playing the Inside Game.

Introduction

I walked to the podium in what should have been the proudest moment of my career, and I was a total wreck.

Here I was, about to be inducted into the Basketball Hall of Fame, the crowning achievement for any athlete, a moment of confirmation, and I was never less sure of myself.

I looked out into the audience and saw so many of my friends and family members, my wife, Terri, my children, my father, Floyd, my colleagues. Their faces were beaming, sharing my joy at a moment I never dreamed would come.

I had served as a trustee for the Hall of Fame since 1974, but it never occurred to me that I would be enshrined. Even once I knew I had been nominated, I looked at the other candidates and told myself I would never be among them.

I loved every minute I spent in basketball. It taught me valuable lessons in pride, preparation, perseverance, persistence, and perception, which became my five keys to success. From the time I was a young boy, it had been my passion.

Throughout my career as a player and later as a general manager and president, I always put the game first. I made all my decisions on what was best for the sport.

Now, I was being honored for those decisions and for my contributions to the game. It was an incredible feeling of accomplishment.

And yet, as I stood at the podium and looked out into the sea of expectant faces, one thought kept running through my mind: If I am all that, why did I get fired?

So much had happened before I approached that podium. The past four seasons had been the worst in my NBA career, which spanned forty years as a player or executive.

I was in the midst of the lowest point late one morning in early June 1999, when my assistant, Karen Stewart, burst through the door reading a fax.

"You've been nominated for the Basketball Hall of Fame," she said, handing me the sheet of paper.

"Aren't you excited?"

I guess I was more shocked than excited at that point. Because I was a trustee of the Hall of Fame, I got to see the list of nominees before it was released to the media. As I looked over the other candidates, all of whom were deserving, I did not like my chances of actually being elected. Nonetheless, it was a thrill to be included.

"Yes, I'm excited to just be nominated," I told Karen.

Two days later, I was at the NBA pre-draft camp in Chicago, a round-robin tournament where team executives and scouts get one last look at players expecting to be selected in the upcoming draft. NBA Deputy Commissioner Russ Granik sought me out to inform me that I had been nominated. He, too, was a trustee.

"You certainly are deserving," Granik told me. "Good luck."

I shook his hand. "Thanks, Russ, but the whole list is deserving," I said as we continued to watch the young players.

The news was in the papers the next day, and it was gratifying to receive congratulations from so many of my colleagues. The pre-draft camp is almost like a convention of NBA executives. All the biggest names in the coaching and executive ranks are there, and most of them stopped by to shake my hand.

It was a tremendous boost emotionally, because I was struggling to come to terms with the fact that my career in the NBA was almost over. I was taken aback two years earlier when NBA Commissioner David

Stern greeted me at the league meetings by saying, "You should think about retiring."

Then, on Memorial Day weekend 1999, Cavaliers owner Gordon Gund told me he was not going to retain Mike Fratello as coach and he was replacing me as general manager with Jim Paxson, whom he had hired as our vice president of basketball operations a year earlier. I was to be relieved of my duties as of July 1, even though I had a year remaining on my contract. No explanation was given. It was a rather ignominious end after thirteen years with the organization, the first nine of which had been enjoyable.

While still trying to cope with that, I got a phone call on June 22 from David Gavitt, president of the Hall of Fame, asking me where I could be reached in the next twenty-four hours. He said he expected a report on the election results from the Honors Committee at any moment. I gave him my home, office, and cell phone numbers, and for the next several hours I sat on pins and needles, although I tried to hide my anxiety.

At eleven o'clock the next morning, Karen appeared in the door to my office.

"There's a Dave Gavitt on the phone for you," she said. "He says he is with the Hall of Fame."

I took a deep breath and picked up the phone.

"Wayne, I want to be the first to congratulate you," he said. "You have been elected to the Naismith Basketball Hall of Fame as a contributor to the game of basketball. I can't think of anyone more deserving."

I sat in a stupor for a few seconds before I responded.

Finally, I said, "Thank you, David."

He told me Fred Zollner, Billie Moore, Kevin McHale, and John Thompson also were elected. He told me how the news was going to be released, and he suggested our public relations department arrange a press conference in Cleveland.

When I got myself together, I called my wife and our three kids, my father, and several close friends. The news traveled quickly through our offices, and many coworkers came by to offer congratulations. The owners of the Cavaliers were in town for board meetings, but it was not until we met at two o'clock that any of them acknowledged the honor bestowed on me and, by extension, the franchise. Maybe they did not want to interrupt their business, but they did take a lunch break and still no one sought me out.

When we went in for our meeting, Gordon offered his congratulations and shook my hand. A couple of the others congratulated me with little sincerity, while still others stoically stared into space. Finally, team attorney Dick Watson sneered, "Which is a greater achievement? Being elected to the Hall of Fame or being the recipient of the Double Cross Award at Nisi Prius?" That was an honor I had received a couple of weeks earlier from a local organization of lawyers. It had touched a nerve with Gund and Watson, neither of whom had been so honored, although Gund's father had been a previous recipient. After that awards dinner, Watson and I had an uncomfortable exchange, though I never did understand why he was so upset.

I did not know what to say to him then, and I do not now.

Later, Gordon said to legendary coach Pete Newell, a Hall of Famer who was a consultant to the Cavs, "I understand you're responsible for Wayne being elected to the Hall of Fame," insinuating, of course, that I could not have been elected on my own merits without someone on the inside pushing for me.

"No way," Pete told Gordon, explaining that all the committees involved with the election process are anonymous so there can be no lobbying.

We had a press conference the next day, which gave me the opportunity to share my honor and excitement with my coworkers, the media, and others who had been influential in my life. Despite what I was going through with the Cavs, I expressed my gratitude to Gordon. He gave me the opportunity to extend my career and supported me along the way, which enabled me to do my job effectively and without interference. I have great admiration and respect for him and will always be grateful for his bringing me to Cleveland.

Now, of course, I faced the monumental task of trying to come up with the right words to say at the October induction ceremony. I always watched the enshrinement ceremonies of each of the halls of fame. I shared the emotion of the inductees as they stood at the podium, fighting back tears of joy and humility, acknowledging those who influenced their lives. Each had a different story about how he got there, but there were common themes: sacrifice, dedication, commitment, and hard work seemed to be the constants. Because I was soon to reach the pinnacle of individual achievement in sport, I watched with special interest as Robin Yount, George Brett, Orlando Cepeda, and the rest of the Class of 1999 was inducted into the Baseball Hall of Fame a few months before my induction.

I was overwhelmed by their speeches, and by the flood of congratulatory letters I got from friends—people inside and outside basketball—as well as business associates and fans. The response lifted my spirits. I also found myself flashing back to something my grandfather used to tell me while I was growing up on his farm outside Springfield, Ohio: Always remain humble.

It was not hard to remain humble in this situation, believe me. I could not understand why I was being forced into early retirement at the age of sixty-two. It was hard for me to accept that the NBA no longer needed my contributions, when, just two years earlier, I had been named the league's Executive of the Year for the second time in five seasons. During my thirty-five-year tenure as an executive, I sat on various high-level committees, including the USA Basketball Games Committee that selected the Olympic teams, and I had been a trustee at the Hall of Fame for twenty-five years. I had received many commendations for my contributions to the game, yet induction into the Hall of Fame would be the ultimate recognition for those contributions to basketball and for standing up for what is right in sports.

Athletes grow up dreaming of winning championships and being able to contribute to that effort. What youngster has not gone to sleep thinking about making the winning shot as time expires in the title game? But being elected to the Hall of Fame is beyond all that. It puts you into a select class, the most elite echelon of athletes in your sport.

How did I get here? All summer I reflected on my journey. I realized how blessed I was to have caring parents, grandparents, and other family members who taught me what was right and loved me enough to discipline me. I thought how fortunate I was to have friends who supported me, coaches who pushed me to reach my potential, and fans who appreciated me. I thought about Milwaukee Bucks owner Wes Pavalon's bold move to entrust me with his basketball team at a time when no other African Americans were running sports teams. I thought about all the coaches and players I loved, all the hours spent practicing in hot, dingy gyms or on hard, black-topped playgrounds, or even on the dusty ground around the basket we had erected on the edge of the garden back home. I thought about overcoming all of the "isms" and the "ists": Racism, skepticism, criticism, supremacists, egotists, antagonists. I thought of Detroit center Walter Dukes's elbows, Boston Hall of Famer Bill Russell's blocked shots, and Philadelphia giant Wilt Chamberlain's challenges. I thought of the 2 A.M. phone calls from the nocturnal Wes when I worked for the Bucks. I recalled the battles with agents, most of which ended positively. I thought about the threats on my life for just wanting to do what I loved. I thought about the train wreck that nearly ended my life before I had a chance to start my career. I thought how God had blessed me in so many ways, by being by my side at all times and giving me the strength to persevere.

By the time October came, I was ready. The first weekend of the month is Enshrinement Weekend in Springfield, Massachusetts. It is a time when basketball fans, media, family, and friends of the inductees mingle to share war stories. They lie and argue about who was the greatest or joke about who was the cheapest. The atmosphere is surreal as basketball greats from years past, some moving spryly and some barely moving, gather in one spot for one memorable weekend.

I chose Pete Newell and Al Attles to escort me. I needed as many friends and family members as I could find to keep me propped up through the ceremony. Pete had become a great friend and had helped me learn the ropes of becoming a general manager. Alvan and I had been friends since our playing days, and he tried to keep me loose. At rehearsal he told me there were two things he did not want to see me do—break down during my speech or fall down the steps while returning to my seat afterward.

With that in mind, I made my way to the podium. I thought of Momma, who was looking down from heaven with that loving smile, and of my eighty-six-year-old dad who had made the trip despite the fact he could not get around very well any more. He even endured two

Enshrinement Day at the Basketball Hall of Fame (Courtesy of NBA)

plane rides—the first of his life. My sister accompanied him and said she could not tell if he was more excited about flying or my enshrinement.

I sincerely expressed my thanks to all the most important people in my life—my family, friends, coaches, teachers, and players. I talked about the game and the preservation of the game as we now know it.

"I never wanted to be a taker from the game," I said. "I attempted to always give back to my passion—basketball. It has been and always will be my desire to protect the integrity of the game of basketball, and I ask each of you to join me in this pursuit."

All too soon, my moment in the spotlight was over. Though my voice had cracked, I had not broken down, and I got back to my seat without incident. When all was said and done, the journey from Springfield, Ohio, to Springfield, Massachusetts, had been a successful one. But the trip had taken some strange twists, I can tell you that.

Chapter 1

The Question

Maybe I should have known right from the beginning how it was going to end in Cleveland, and maybe I should have been more prepared. After all, I had come from Milwaukee, where Coach Don Nelson stabbed me in the back after I hired him.

In the fourteen years since becoming the first African American general manager in sports when the Bucks named me to that post in 1972, I thought I had heard almost every racial slur and insinuation. But I was caught completely off guard when, in the spring of 1986, during my very first interview for the general manager position in Cleveland, one of the board members, whose name I did not remember, looked me straight in the eye and asked me, "If you get this job, will you feel compelled to hire a black coach?"

I dropped my head, ran my right hand across my forehead, and paused. Several thoughts ran through my mind, not the least of which was, "What am I getting myself into here?" I knew damn well he would not have asked a white candidate if he would hire a white coach. I felt as if I were right back in Tecumseh High School in Springfield, Ohio, where I was the only black kid in my class.

After a moment, I gathered myself, looked the board member back in the eye and said, "I hope that you would want me to hire the best qualified person. That is what I've been taught and believe. Isn't that the way it should be?"

But the mood in the room had shifted, and some serious doubts had crept into my mind. Maybe I should have listened harder to the little voice in the back of my head.

I had mixed emotions about even interviewing for the position. I was not really looking for a job. I was involved in a manufacturing company that supplied parts to the automotive industry, and I was a part-time consultant to the Indiana Pacers and G. Heilmann Brewing Company. Also, Cavs former general manager Harry Weltman had been a friend, and I was sorry to see him dismissed after doing his best to stabilize the franchise.

On the other hand, there were only twenty-nine of these jobs available and, after spending a lifetime in the sport, basketball still was my passion. Pacers co-owner Herb Simon had made it clear I was not going to become the general manager in Indiana. He had not only given me permission to interview with the Cavs, but had encouraged me to do so. I was originally from Ohio and would be only three hours away from my family. I had grown up a Browns and Indians fan, so being in the same market was appealing.

Plus, after my experience with Nellie in Milwaukee, I had a burning desire to get back to running a team and proving myself to the rest of the league even if, in my mind, I had nothing to prove.

So I agreed to meet with owner Gordon Gund, his brother George and their associates at the O'Hare Hilton during the annual pre-draft camp in Chicago. I was scouting for Indiana, but once word got out I was interviewing in Cleveland, I became the most popular person in the steamy gym at the University of Illinois-Chicago Circle, where every unemployed coach in America sought me out.

I left downtown early, anticipating traffic on the Kennedy Expressway. But I arrived in plenty of time and tried to relax by doing the *Chicago Tribune* crossword puzzle as I waited in the lobby. I was surprised how nervous I was. I knew that the Gunds had talked to legendary Celtics President Red Auerbach, longtime NBA executive Stu Inman, who had been with several teams, and my old friend Pete Newell, and I knew they had gotten good reports from all three.

But it was still with some trepidation that I entered the conference room.

I was met by about six stately men dressed in pinstriped navy or gray suits. Power suits, we called them back then. Of course, I fit right in because I was wearing my power suit, too. I recognized Gordon immediately, because I knew he was blind. I recognized his brother, too. The other men were introduced as associates of Gund Investment Company.

The Gunds, who also owned the Minnesota North Stars, bought the Cavaliers in 1983, rescuing the team from the much-maligned Ted Stepien, whose many personnel blunders forced the league to adopt rules to protect the Cavs from themselves. The team had finished over .500 just three times in its thirteen-year history. The highlight of the franchise came during "The Miracle of Richfield" in 1976, when the Cavs, in their first play-off appearance, knocked off the powerful Washington Bullets in the first round before losing to the eventual champion Boston Celtics in six games in the second round. In their last season under Stepien's ownership, the team finished 23–59.

Three years later, the team was coming off a 29–53 season under Coach George Karl, who was replaced by Gene Littles for the last fifteen games. Major changes were in store, which was what brought me to that interview. But halfway through the process, I wondered if I had made a mistake—or if they thought they had.

Though I continued to answer their questions, my interest in the job had waned after that one troubling question. While I wanted nothing more than to get away from that one guy, a few members of the group were heading downtown for dinner and asked me for a ride, which I grudgingly provided.

When I got back to the gym that night, I felt like the Pied Piper. Wherever I went, I was followed by job seekers. "Did you get the job?" I was asked time and time again. But I shocked all of them by saying I had no interest in the position. I did not offer any explanation.

I got back to the hotel late but I had a hard time sleeping. I tossed and turned all night. Much as I tried to convince myself otherwise, I really wanted the job. I just could not stop thinking about that question about hiring a black coach. I knew some owners were concerned about the increasing number of black players in the league. It was only natural some of those players would pursue careers in coaching. Maybe I was naive, but this was 1986. Why should it matter who I wanted to hire? The Equal Employment Opportunity Commission would have loved this. Finally, I decided I would remove my name from consideration. When I got home and talked to Terri, she agreed with my decision. She could not believe I had been asked that question either.

I called Thaxter Trafton, president of the Cavs, and told him not to consider me for the job. "Was it because of that question?" he asked, not having to specify which question.

I told him yes. I said I did not think I could function in that environment.

"I knew that was going to be a problem as soon as I heard it," Trafton said.

Gordon called the next day and was very apologetic. Then he asked me to reconsider my decision and come for a second interview.

"You're our Number 1 candidate, and I want you to meet one more person," he said. "I promise you that silly question does not reflect my views, or those of my brother, and our views are the only ones that count."

He was convincing enough that I agreed to schedule a second interview in Cleveland. When I walked into the suite at the Sheraton Hotel at the Cleveland airport, I was greeted by Gordon and George and introduced to Dick Watson, a part owner and the team attorney. Dick extended a warm welcome and proceeded to tell me he did not know anything about basketball. But he mentioned he was instrumental in signing the team's star player, World B. Free, flying him in by helicopter and ushering him into the old Coliseum on a red carpet.

"Oh, my," I thought. If he was trying to impress me, he was not doing a very good job.

Then he asked me many questions about my philosophy in building a team.

"I will try to build a team with people who have character and strong values," I told him. "Of course, I'll look for talent. Talent may win games, but it is character that wins championships. I would go so far as to say that talented players without character always will be also-rans."

I have often been criticized for wanting players with character. I have been told choir boys do not win championships. But the people who say that do not understand what I mean by character. By character I mean strength, courage, fortitude, moral fiber, integrity, and the will to win. My family and my coaches instilled character in me using various tools, including the almighty switch, laps around a hot gym, or even sitting me down for a game if I had not done what I was supposed to do. Character helps you overcome adversity. Players with character do not make excuses. Players with character play hurt. Players with character practice self-discipline and restrain from harmful influences. They respect each other and the team above all. Selfish players make it difficult to win. You never know if you can count on them. As a captain on my basketball teams, I have gone to management more than once to report a player who was threatening the unity of our team.

Look at some of the great basketball players: Bill Russell, Jerry West, Oscar Robertson, Michael Jordan, Larry Bird. Each was a man of character. I was looking for players with that kind of heart and determination. I told Watson I did extensive background checks on draft prospects and explained that I did not want any surprises. I always asked prospects what their parents did so I could gauge their work ethic. I asked who had had the biggest influence in their lives and who they would like to be like when they grew up. I found the answers very telling. I also explained that I liked to draft players out of good college programs because I thought coaches with character were likely to instill character in their players.

I am sure my passion on this subject came through, and Dick later told me how impressed he was with my philosophies. He was much less impressed when he asked me to critique their current personnel and I told him the only player on their roster I liked was Phil Hubbard.

"What about World?" he asked, referring to aging star World B. Free. "He is very popular with the fans and the press. He's the only star we have."

I knew the well-traveled World quite well, and I did not think he was a very good fit for the Cavs. Of course, I did not know at the time that Watson had pushed for his signing and dreamed up the idea of delivering him to training camp in a helicopter that landed on a red carpet.

"World is a talented player who likes to score," I said. "In order to score, you have to shoot, and he loves to shoot. If he dominates the ball as he's done in the past, the young players will never develop. You have the eighth pick in the draft, and there's a very good chance Ron Harper will be there. If he is, World can B. Gone. World is a good player, but we need to focus on youth. I also think two or three years ahead as to how good a player will be. I would also be concerned that when the team becomes a contender World will be too old."

I think they liked the fact that I said "when the team becomes a contender," not "if." The review of the current roster continued, and I was asked about Mel Turpin, a beefy center who had just signed a long-term deal with the team.

"We would not have drafted Mel with our late second-round pick," I said, "let alone sign him to the contract you gave him."

Again, I did not realize this had been Watson's idea. But I figured I had nothing to lose at this point so I wanted to be as candid as possible. The job was not going to be worth taking if I was not going to be allowed to build a team the way I wanted. I also explained that personnel decisions would have to be made by the coaches, scouts, and me.

From there, we shifted to the draft. They asked me to rank the players in the order I would draft them. I put North Carolina center Brad Daugherty at Number 1, reiterated my preference for Ron Harper at Number 8, and suggested Dell Curry would be a great alternative. The 1986 draft was a strong one, featuring players like Daugherty,

Maryland's Len Bias, and North Carolina State's Chris Washburn, and with Number 8 and two high second-round picks, the Cavs were positioned to come out of it pretty well.

After a few more hours of philosophical discussions, I was offered the job. I told them I would accept only if I was given the authority that went with the responsibility.

"There are many rewards that accompany this job, but there is also a lot of stress," I explained. "In this job, I expect to be criticized by fans, media, and even people within the organization. But players need to know I am in charge. I don't want players to be able to circumvent my authority, and I don't want other team personnel to bypass my authority. As long as I know I have the authority, I can handle the criticism."

Gordon agreed, though he reserved the right to have the final say on financial issues, which was as it should be. I also informed Gordon that I wanted to report directly to him. This was not meant to offend Thaxter, who was president of the team. But my scouts and I were going to spend most of our waking hours evaluating players, and I wanted the final say, which Gordon granted me.

Perhaps the most important thing Gordon did that day was dismiss my initial fears about the job. He must have told Dick about the question I was asked in Chicago, because Dick was eager to tell me that he did not know I was black until I walked into the room.

That did not do much for my ego. I had been in The League for thirty years. How could he not know I was black? The more I thought about it, I realized it was a lie. I have come to believe it was probably the first thing he knew about me.

I turned the contract negotiations with the Cavs over to my attorney, Gene Smith, and I returned to Indiana to help with the upcoming draft. Herb Simon told me he was going to name Donnie Walsh president and general manager of the Pacers, and he wanted me to report to him. I said I would, but I could not help but wonder why he had chosen Donnie over me, given my credentials. It was nothing against Donnie, who was a knowledgeable basketball man, but he had no front-office experience at the time.

On the Saturday morning before the draft, I met with Donnie. I told him I had agreed to a contract with the Cavs and had a press conference scheduled for the day after the draft. I also told him if he was uncomfortable with me participating in the Indiana draft meetings, I would excuse myself. He assured me he trusted my integrity and valued my input. Indiana had the fourth pick and Cleveland the eighth, so he did not think there would be any conflict. He also said he would expect me to be involved in Cleveland's pick at Number 8. I was flattered by his trust. This might seem unusual to business people not involved in athletics. After all, an outgoing Ford executive is not likely to finish up designing a car before leaving for a new job at General Motors. But this was not an uncommon situation in sports. College coaches routinely coach one team in a post-season bowl game after agreeing to terms with a new team.

Anyway, Indiana had decided to draft Chuck Person, a small forward from Auburn. He was a logical choice, since Clark Kellogg, the Pacers' current small forward, had missed much of the season with knee problems. Still, we spent the weekend researching other prospects, watching videos, and eating the best ham shavings I had ever had, courtesy of the deli next to the Pacers office.

We had decided we needed a back-up plan in case Person was not available, and we were looking at center Chris Washburn from North Carolina State. I had heard there were some character issues with Washburn, as well as rumors of drug use. Pacers coach George Irvine and I decided to fly to High Point, N.C., to interview him. Unfortunately, his agent spirited him out of town to avoid us, which should have been our first clue that something was not right.

We accepted his mother's coffee and cake and talked to her about her son. She assured us none of the bad things we had heard were true. In fact, when we asked her to name the worst thing her son had ever done, she told us about an incident once when he had forgotten to take his lab coat to science class. If she knew about his drug use, she was not going to let on to us.

While we were there, the agent called to see if we had arrived. He said if we wanted to interview Chris, we would have to do so in New York, where he was awaiting the draft. What he did not figure was that, because we had our owner's private plane, we actually could make a trip to New York—and we did. After a short visit, neither George nor I was impressed. We just did not have a good feeling about Chris and, as it turned out, we were right. He was taken third by Golden State and proved to be a total bust. His career lasted just two seasons.

Of course, we did not know that would be the case when we reconvened Tuesday morning in the draft room, commonly called the "war room," in Indianapolis. Person was still our man, and we were positive he would still be there at Number 4. The consensus was that Daugherty and Bias would go with the first two picks. If we could just figure out one more pick, we would be home free. Later in the day, rumors were circulating that Washburn would go third. We were ecstatic, and we started to concentrate on the second round.

While I was in Indianapolis, scouts Ed Gregory and Barry Hecker were in the Cavs war room. I was sure Miami of Ohio guard Ron Harper would be there at Number 8, and in an earlier trip to Cleveland to finalize my contract, I had suggested the Cavs take Johnny Newman and Johnny Rogers with their second-round picks.

After a long day, I headed back to the Embassy Suites, my home in Indianapolis. I was reading the paper when the phone rang.

"Wayne, Gordon Gund," the voice on the other end bellowed.

"Let me get right to the point. We are talking to Philadelphia about trading for the first pick. We will have to give them Roy Hinson and cash. What do you think?"

I could not believe my ears.

"Do it," I said without hesitation.

I could not believe the Sixers really would trade the first pick in the draft, which I felt certain could be used on Daugherty. But I had had enough discussions with Philadelphia officials Pat Williams and Jack McMahon to know they did not like the North Carolina center. I could not understand that. I knew a lot of NBA scouts had labeled him "soft" and did not think he was tough enough or physical enough. But not me. I had watched Brad develop from an underage freshman to one of the best centers in recent drafts. I liked that he had gotten better every year. He was still young and had room for improvement. He would lose the baby fat he carried on his 260-pound frame and be stronger than most centers in the league. He was one of the few centers who had a low-post presence. I was glad no one else felt the way I did.

I slept well that night, confident the Pacers would get their man and that my new team would have a terrific draft, particularly if the trade was consummated. Then mid-morning, several hours before the draft, Gordon called again to tell me the trade was final. But, he said, there was a slight problem.

"We have some mixed views on who we should take," he told me. "Some think we should take Len Bias."

I nearly choked, although I had no way of knowing Bias would be dead of a drug overdose within days. "Gordon, please take Daugherty," I pleaded. "I have some reservations about Bias. I think there are some character issues. Since I'm coming in tomorrow, let's get started on the right foot."

Gordon finally agreed. "Daugherty it will be," he said and hung up.

When we assembled for the draft, I told Herb Simon and Donnie that the Cavs had traded for the first pick. Their main concern was whether the Cavs would take Person, but I assured them that would not happen. The first round went pretty much as expected, although we were surprised to see that Georgia Tech point guard Mark Price was not taken in the first round. He was a player the Pacers wanted to team with Vern Fleming in the backcourt.

Dallas had the second pick in the second round and was shopping it. Herb looked at me and said, "Wayne, you have a good relationship with Rick Sund from your days together in Milwaukee. Call him and see what it would take to get the pick." I made the call and we made a deal. There was euphoria in the room because we had never expected to come out of the draft with Person and Price.

In the midst of a round of handshakes, the phone rang. It was Sund, the Dallas general manager.

"Big Man," he said, using the nickname I had picked up in Milwaukee, "I must apologize. While we were talking, Norm Sonju made a deal with Cleveland for the pick." (Sonju was the Dallas president.)

I shouted into the phone, "Rick, that cannot happen. We had a deal."

All eyes turned to me, and I had to explain what had happened. I was visibly upset, not to mention embarrassed that my integrity was being called into question. But Herb Simon was more upset than I was. He called me outside the room and gave me a verbal lashing the likes of which I had not experienced since growing up on my grandfather's farm. Herb showed me courage and passion. I had witnessed his temper throughout the year as I listened to him and his brother, Mel, go at it. Never did I think I would be the recipient of his wrath.

I could only try to convince him that I had no knowledge of the Cavs' involvement with the Mavericks. In fact, once things calmed down, I called Gordon and asked him to reconsider the deal. He turned me down, and as it turned out, it was one of the better deals in the history of the franchise. I had to eat crow for weeks, but eventually Herb and Donnie were convinced I had nothing to do with the deal.

For a while, they tried to get a draft pick as retribution. The Cavs resisted, insisting they had done nothing wrong. Donnie later wrote a letter absolving all of us. I was glad that chapter was closed.

I was even happier that Mark ended up in Cleveland. In later years, I told Mark that, for a moment, he had been a Pacer. His tenure was not much shorter than mine. I was there a little more than a year. Then we both became Cavaliers.

Chapter 2

Moving to Cleveland

On June 19, 1986, the day after the draft, Gordon introduced Brad Daugherty, Ron Harper, and me to the Cleveland media. He began his remarks by saying this was the most pivotal day in the history of the franchise.

Even though I had yet to actually sign my contract, I followed Gordon to the podium, expressing my happiness at returning to Ohio and having the opportunity to work with Mr. Gund and finish the job Harry Weltman had started. I said our ultimate goal was to build a team that would be a contender for a championship in four years. I added I was looking forward to working with the players selected in the draft, as well as John "Hot Rod" Williams, the talented six-foot-eleven-inch forward from Tulane whom Harry had the courage to draft the previous season, before Hot Rod was cleared of the gambling charges brought against him. I thought the nucleus for a very good team was in place if we had the patience to let it develop.

I told our fans I wanted them to experience the kind of excitement I had witnessed during the seventh game of the 1976 playoff series against the Washington Bullets. I had come from Milwaukee with agent Gene Smith as a guest of his client, Jim Chones, the Cavs center. More than twenty-one-thousand fans crammed into the Richfield Coliseum to cheer their team to victory. It was the largest crowd I had seen at an NBA game, and perhaps the loudest. It was one of the most thrilling games I had seen, as Bill Fitch's young Cavs upset the Bullets on Dick

Snyder's running shot in the closing seconds of the game, which came to be known as the "Miracle of Richfield."

After all the interviews, we adjourned to a room where I finally signed my contract. Talk immediately turned to candidates for our head coaching position, our top priority, as well as a variety of other front-office jobs. George Karl had been released with a few games left in the season, and his assistant, Gene Littles, finished the season. Gene and General Manager Harry Weltman were let go once the season was over. Barry Hecker and Ed Gregory were the scouts and did a good job helping with the draft, but I did not know much about them beyond that. I told Gordon I would like to bring in my own people, and he gave me permission to do so. I was starting much as I had in Milwaukee—with a completely new staff. But this time I had some ideas about whom I wanted to hire.

Lenny Wilkens was the current general manager in Seattle. He was the coach until the Seattle owner bumped him upstairs after a couple of down years. Lenny had been a very successful coach, winning the NBA title in 1979. I recalled a conversation we had a few months earlier when I was still with the Pacers and we were both scouting the Big East tournament in Madison Square Garden. He had approached me at halftime as we were walking up the steps to the refreshment stand, and told me he would be available if I was looking for a coach. He told me coaching was his passion and he longed to return to the bench. I had known Lenny since 1960 when he came into The League as a player. I knew he had a great knowledge of the game when he played. I watched him transfer that knowledge to his players as coach of the Sonics, who beat up on the young Bucks in the 1980 semifinals.

Lenny and I were not what you would call friends. We developed a mutual respect as competitors. Unlike much of the NBA, I would never hire a friend just for the sake of hiring a friend. I did that with Don Nelson in Milwaukee and it was a disaster as far as our friendship was concerned. Emotion must remain out of the decision-making process.

I told Gordon that Lenny was at the head of a very short list of candidates. I gave no consideration to the fact he was black, although, believe me, I had not forgotten my first interview with the team. But, as I had stated at the time, I thought he was the best qualified person available.

After interviewing a number of candidates, Gordon approved my hiring Lenny, and on July 9, 1986, he was introduced as the new coach of the Cavaliers. I could not help but wonder what my questioner, who I learned later was David Prescott, was thinking. But I refused to be intimidated by him. I stuck to my principles, and much later I learned that some board members were worried that I would also sign all black players. How absurd. This was 1986.

Generally speaking, Lenny and I were warmly received, though there was the usual hate mail I had come to expect. Though there were many, many positive responses, I cannot help but remember the one that read, "Mr. Gund, you hired a black general manager, which was bad enough, and he hired a black coach. That is more than I can take. I am keeping my green money."

I hated reading that kind of stuff but, as always, I was eager to prove my critics wrong.

After Lenny was hired, we had to hire two assistant coaches. He wanted to hire Dick Helm, a coach from Wheaton College who had worked with him in Seattle. I recommended he hire one of my former players, Brian Winters, who was Pete Carril's assistant at Princeton. Brian was one of the best shooters in The League as a player, and I had watched him help Quinn Buckner and Junior Bridgeman become better shooters when we were together in Milwaukee. Lenny agreed, and we had our staff.

Next we had to hire a director of player personnel. One of the first calls I got after I was hired was from veteran coach Cotton Fitzsimmons. He was between jobs and I thought he was looking for work. As it turned out, he was not calling about himself but rather about his son, Gary. Actually, Gary already was on my list. I had observed him doing his job while he was with other teams, and I liked his approach. He liked to work, unlike a lot of scouts who just like to socialize. After one interview with Gary, I hired him. I added the well-respected Pete Newell as a consultant, along with Darrell Hedric, an assistant coach while I was at Miami University who became the head coach later, and Ron Michel as regional scouts. Our staff was complete. Now it was time to sign some players and get ready for the season.

In my first meeting with my newly assembled staff, I conveyed my philosophy on building a team. I wanted to use the same template that worked in Milwaukee after we traded Kareem Abdul-Jabbar—building through the draft. Of course, that meant being in a position to get high picks, which usually meant losing. I hate losing, although I can stomach it if it has a purpose. If you lose while playing young players, at least they will gain experience while you gain higher picks in subsequent drafts. As I saw it, there was no need to keep around players who would be over the hill when the team was ready to contend. I knew older players who did not play would become malcontents, and I did not want the young players influenced by them. We also wanted our new group to grow together on and off the court.

Lenny had demonstrated he had the patience to develop young players in Seattle, and he was agreeable to doing the same thing in Cleveland. Most coaches cannot accept losing, no matter what the plan is. Their egos cannot take it. They are also worried about their jobs and their reputations. But Lenny's job and reputation were secure. We were more concerned about where we would be in three years than in our first year together.

That meant we were not interested in extending World B. Free's contract. I planned to make him an offer far below what he expected. I knew it would be an unpopular move, but I knew it was for the best. I explained to his agent, Ron Grinker, that we did not want to tie up World for a long period of time, so we were offering him a one-year deal for the same money he had made the previous season. They were shocked, and after weeks of negotiations, we wound up releasing World so he could sign elsewhere.

This cleared the way for rookie Ron Harper to get the necessary playing time. Playing Daugherty and Price was necessary, too, but they would have to beat out Mel Turpin and John Bagley. Edgar Jones, Dirk Minniefield, Keith Lee, Ben Poquette, Mark West, and Phil Hubbard were the other remaining veterans.

Our first look at our future came during the summer league in Windsor, Ontario, and we liked what we saw. We felt as though we would be good in a couple of years if we continued to build on what we had, remained patient, and stayed the course.

As the summer passed, Gordon, Lenny, and I were establishing a great working relationship. We shared the same values and believed in the same disciplines. This made it easy to establish the principles that would govern our team. I could tell that Lenny was going to be easy to work with because of the mutual respect we had developed over the years as players and executives. I told him I would not interfere with his coaching unless he asked me to comment on things I saw during practice or in games. Our job descriptions were well defined, which made it comfortable to communicate openly.

After a summer of house hunting and getting acclimated to a new city, we were eager for the season to start. We opened training camp with the usual team dinner after a day of physicals. I gave my usual speech about team goals and objectives and the responsibilities each of us had toward achieving those goals. I told them ownership had hired me to create a positive environment so that they could maximize their potential as people and as players. Winning, I told them, was an attitude. I defined character as I understood it and how it related to winning, which was our main objective. I made it clear winning the NBA championship was our ultimate goal. I closed by telling them they should not do anything that would embarrass them, their families, their teammates, or the franchise. Lenny followed with a similar message, and when we were finished, we asked anyone who did not share our vision to leave. Naturally, no one did. We also informed them that in order to get to know them better, we would meet with them one-on-one as training camp went on. I had learned from my earlier experiences that one had to understand the needs of each individual to effectively manage.

It did not take Lenny long to figure out who the keepers were in this bunch. Turpin had reported out of shape, and he did not seem the least bit interested in pushing himself to correct the situation. At the conclusion of every evening practice, Lenny lined up the players on the baseline to run the dreaded suicide drills, an exercise all coaches use for conditioning. The players race against each other or a clock, and the winners are excused from the next round. Mel was always last, just plodding along behind everyone. Finally, Lenny had had it.

"Mel," he said, "you're not even trying to win. Don't you have any pride?"

Mel turned to him and said, "Coach, you can run me long, but you can't run me hard."

Lenny, knowing full well that the terms of Turpin's contract made him all but untradeable, turned to Gary Fitzsimmons and me and said in exasperation, "We have a problem."

Lenny's patience was tested continually. Four days into camp, Edgar Jones had not hit a lick. He spent more time with trainer Gary Briggs than all of the other players put together. He was nursing an injury from the previous season. He occupied a spot on the mats stored along the sidelines during practice. Lenny had just explained a play to the team and, as the players began to execute it, Edgar, clad in sweats, jumped up from his perch and dashed onto the floor shouting, "Coach, that's not how we run that play. Let me show you."

Lenny could not believe his eyes. Neither could the rest of his staff. Those who had been with Edgar before just shook their heads and began to chuckle. After practice, Lenny asked me if we could get rid of Jones. Without hesitation, I said, "Yes, we can." I did not care what the terms of his contract were, we were not putting up with that nonsense.

We opened the season with a win against Washington and compiled a 3–2 record before a seven-game losing streak. Still, there were encouraging signs. Hot Rod Williams was the NBA player of the week during that stretch, which was followed by an 8–7 December, including a 7–3 record at the Coliseum. Ron Harper looked as good if not better than we thought he would, and he was the Rookie of the Month in December. Brad Daugherty continued to impress with his ability to score, rebound, and pass, and he recorded a triple double—double digits in points, rebounds, and assists—in a game against Utah. As John Bagley's backup, Mark Price began to show those who passed on him in the first round that they had made a mistake.

In January, Bagley suffered a severely sprained ankle and Mark had an appendicitis attack. Both spent most of the month on the injured list, while we scrambled for replacements. Grinker came through, letting us beat out several other teams for the services of a CBA guard named Craig Ehlo. A true pro as an agent, Grinker harbored no hard feelings toward us for not signing World. We also signed Tyrone Corbin.

I was loving Cleveland. We moved into a new house in Moreland Hills in December. I was reuniting with some old friends and making many others. I saw my dad often. I was involved in the community. Terri and the kids were happy. The team was performing better than expected. Everything seemed to be falling into place.

Until Judy, my assistant, stormed into my office one day with a letter she had just opened. She was shaking as she handed it to me.

"Who would do such a thing?" she asked, on the brink of tears.

It was an anonymous letter whose author denounced blacks in general and threatened to shoot me in the head or the groin. "Black people should all be dead," it concluded.

I ordered her to pass it along to team president Thaxter Trafton. I really was not too concerned, but I wanted to be safe and pass it on to the authorities. When two similar letters arrived the next day, I started to get a bit more worried. It had been many years since I had seen Ku Klux Klan rallies in southern Ohio, but I should have known they were still in existence. Eventually, the police were summoned. They examined the letters and ordered us to put them in a file and not let anyone else handle them.

A few days later, I was sitting in the press room visiting with the media before a game when one of our security officers appeared in the doorway.

"Wayne, Joe would like to see you in his office," he told me.

Joe Pfeiffer was the director of security, so I knew something was up.

"What's wrong?" I asked as soon as I entered his office. My initial thought was that something had happened to Terri driving to the game.

As I sat down, he reached into his pocket and pulled out an unspent bullet about two inches long.

That got my attention.

"This was found on your seat in your box with a message," he said. He did not elaborate.

I was dumbfounded.

"Is your wife here?" he asked me.

I told him she probably was in the wives room, and I continued to sit speechless when she was brought in and Joe repeated his story. Terri recovered first. After her initial shock, she asked what we should do.

"I want the two of you to go home and stay there until further notice," he said. "We will have a sheriff follow you home. We have advised the Moreland Hills police, and they will put your house under surveillance. We will bring your car inside the building because we can't take any chances on you going out to the ramp. We have details searching the building as we speak."

We sat in stunned silence on the way home, until Terri finally murmured, "Let's get out of this place."

Still shaken, I could not respond. I just kept looking in the rearview mirror to make sure the sheriff's car was still in sight.

We turned onto our street and were greatly relieved to see a police car sitting in our driveway. They briefed us, and then we settled in to listen to Joe Tait broadcast the game on the radio. It did not take long to see why he was so popular.

Roy Jones, vice president of operations at the Coliseum, called first thing the next morning to inform me that a security officer was being sent out to escort me into the office and back home. He told me the process would continue indefinitely.

"Gordon has informed me to do whatever is necessary to make sure you and Terri are safe," Jones said. "We have informed the FBI, and they have begun an investigation. They also have assigned two agents to sit with you at every game for the rest of the season. We have got it all covered.

"Any questions?"

I hardly knew where to begin, and I knew he would not have the answers I was really looking for anyway.

Gordon called, sounding as shaken as we were. He told me everything would be okay. I wanted to believe him.

As it turned out, things got back to normal and for the next nine years in Cleveland, I was as happy as I had ever been. My family was doing well, the team was doing well, and I thought we were on the right track for a long and successful run. But I never really got over that incident. I rarely sat in my assigned seat. I usually stood during games.

Still, I would never have guessed how things would turn out. I did not know at the time that eventually I would have to replace Lenny and hire Mike Fratello, which did not work out too well for either of us. I had a rocky start in Cleveland, and I would have a rocky end, too. But I was able to get through it all with my dignity intact because of the lessons I had learned at my grandfather's knee.

My Grandpa had warned me there would always be some people who did not like me because of the color of my skin. And just as my grandfather refused to let me quit high school in spite of the taunts I received as the only black in my class, these threats were not going to keep me from doing my job, either. I was more determined than ever to succeed at The Inside Game.

Timeout Number One

There were reports that the Klan and other supremacist groups were headquartered in Northeast Ohio and harassed blacks who were in prominent positions. This was why the law enforcement agencies were so cautious with me, although I was still surprised I had been a target. In the 1960s, Cleveland had elected Carl Stokes, making him the first black mayor in America. Frank Robinson became the first black manager in baseball when Gabe Paul tabbed him for the Cleveland Indians. Larry Doby had been the first black player in the American League years before that.

The birth of the Ku Klux Klan came during the period of Reconstruction after the Civil War, when blacks were given the right to vote, among other rights. Originally, the Klan was a group of Confederate veterans led by General Nathan Bedford Forrest. It started as a social group that wanted to preserve white superiority by terrorizing blacks, Jews, and Roman Catholics. There were several major periods of Klan activity after the Civil War, including the 1940s and 1950s, during school desegregation, and again in the mid-1970s, during another major reconstruction period in America in the wake of the Vietnam War and the race riots. At that time, the Klan was protesting the racial equality so many had worked and died to bring about.

I had history on my side. The post-civil rights movement brought radical change to our country between the mid-1970s and the mid-1980s. Corporate America developed affirmative action programs to make it possible for more blacks to enter the mainstream of our capitalistic society. Special grants and loans from the government made it possible for more black business people to become entrepreneurs. It was similar to what happened at the end of the Civil War, when former slaves were promised forty acres and a mule in order to start an independent life away from their former masters, although history showed that few slaves actually received either land or mules. Now, the NAACP, Operation PUSH, and the Urban League were playing instrumental roles in facilitating change. Progress was being made in corporate America, academia, and in sports. The NBA, under the leadership of Larry O'Brien and then David Stern, was well ahead of the NFL and major-league baseball in hiring black coaches and executives. In fact, the complexion of the NBA was changing drastically, causing concern in many of the boardrooms around the league.

Chapter 3

The Hill

We called it The Hill. Some called it Embryville. Population twenty. On weekends the population would increase to thirty-four or more, depending on how many aunts, uncles, and cousins came from town. The Hill was a small, twenty-four-acre farm about five miles outside of Springfield, Ohio. Grandpa and Grandma lived in the big house, a six-room, two-story house they made of wood covered with tar paper nailed onto the frame. There were nine people living there, which made for togetherness. My dad and mom built a house next door, and my Uncle Clint and Aunt Pauline built on the other side of the big house. My Uncle Lou went to prison for shooting the wife of a cousin in a gambling dispute, but when he was released from the penitentiary, he built next door to us. There were several other dwellings. Each house had four rooms and an outhouse, because none of the houses had indoor plumbing. In the summer, most of the men would sleep outside because the houses were so small and crowded. There also were two barns, a chicken coop, a corn crib, and a slaughterhouse. Chickens and other fowl, cows, and pigs also were included in our population, and we also had dogs, cats, and plenty of rats.

William Louis Embry, grandson of a slave, was a sharecropper who packed up his wife, Alice Cunningham Embry, and four children, including my dad, and left Embry Crossroads, Alabama, near Talladega, in 1924. Like many black families and some white families, they migrated north to find jobs when it became impossible to survive working the farms and cotton fields. Grandpa had a brother who had written to tell him about jobs in Ohio. While blacks from the East migrated to New York and blacks from Mississippi and points west of that migrated to Chicago, most people from Alabama headed to Detroit to seek work in the auto plants. Some found work in the coal mines in Kentucky and the steel mills in Ohio. Grandpa made his way north, first by working in the coal mines and, once he had saved enough money, then moving on to a laundry and after that the pump factory in Springfield, where he joined his brother, Savannah. They were happy in Ohio, and the family grew.

Grandpa was the king of The Hill. He was a taskmaster and a strict disciplinarian, and all of us were afraid to step out of line. He believed that hard work and strong character would impress people and would help us have a better life than he did. He also believed in education. He had attended Talladega College, where he studied carpentry, husbandry, and agriculture. He insisted that we use proper grammar, and we were not allowed to swear or use slang. During the day, Grandpa supervised the salvage department at Robbins & Myers, a pump plant in Springfield. All the blacks who moved from the South went to see Will Embry for jobs. Given the times, when "Negro" or "colored" were the nicest things we were called, I am sure that made him a pioneer. He farmed when he got home from work.

Grandma was also a disciplinarian and worked hard. She tended the gardens during the day and did the cooking, canning, and other farm chores. Her biggest challenge was to make sure we kids did the jobs that Grandpa had ordered us to do while he was at work. The water had to be pumped, the cows had to be milked, the hogs fed, the fields plowed, and the hay baled. There was plenty of work for all of us on The Hill.

My father, Floyd, was the third oldest of the thirteen children. He was four years old when the family moved to Springfield. Against Grandpa's will, he quit school after the ninth grade and went to work for Grandpa at the pump factory. He just did not like school. He later became a body and fender repairman. He married Anna Gardner in 1936, and I was born a year later, two years ahead of my sister Ruth Ann.

My mother was a tall woman. She was sweet and gentle, but she could be tough when she wanted us to obey her. She insisted that we be good people with good manners and treat all people with respect. Whenever Ruthie and I left the house, she would tell us to be good. Mom graduated from high school and although my Dad did not, education was a top priority in our family.

My mother, Anna Embry (right), and her friend Mary Kelly (Courtesy of Embry family)

A lanky five-year-old Wayne Embry stands beside his father's car outside their home in Springfield, Ohio, in 1942 (Courtesy of Embry family)

My father was as tough as Mom or Grandpa when it came to discipline. He was raised well. I had my share of whippings with a belt or a switch when I was young. If the weeds were not picked out of the garden, or the grass was not cut, or any other job was not done, the elders showed us no mercy. We would try to hide the switches in an effort to save ourselves, but that did not do any good because there were so many trees on The Hill that replacements were not hard to come by. We also were punished if we disobeyed, or talked back, or did not do our homework. The switch was a great character builder.

Mom and Dad were good athletes. Mom played softball in high school and later played for a semipro team in Springfield. Dad was a baseball player, and many say he could have played in the major leagues if not for the color barrier. Dad also played semipro basketball. Even though Grandpa never cared much for sports, he did allow us time for recreation when the work was done. Dad wanted me to pursue baseball to follow in his footsteps in hopes that the racial barriers would come down.

Because of the social situation at the time, we were more or less confined to The Hill or the surrounding neighborhood. We could not go to movies or eat in restaurants. But with all my cousins around, we always had enough players to chose sides for all games. We also had neighbors who visited The Hill often. In the summer, once we chased away the snakes, we could swim in the creek that ran through our property or the adjacent land. In the fall and winter, we would gather at Grandpa's house and sit around the pot-bellied stove, crack the walnuts that we harvested, and listen to the old folks tell stories about their childhoods in the South; the beatings, the lynchings, the segregation and racism that was a way of life. It was fascinating to learn how they coped in that environment. We would listen to the Friday night fights, particularly when heavyweight champion Joe Louis fought, as well as the usual family-type radio shows. When television was invented, Grandpa saved enough money to get an eight-inch screen. We would crowd around, bathed in the gray light emanating from the little box, and watch shows such as "Howdy Doody," "The Lone Ranger," and "I Remember Mama," as well as the fights. Joe Louis was a hero to millions of black folks. Here was a black man who could beat up a white man and not only not get in trouble for it but get paid big money to do it. He represented all of us who took abuse from whites and did not fight back because of the fear of lynchings, unfair arrests, and further exclusion from mainstream society. We lived vicariously through him. "Save us, Joe," was the cry. I got into many fights at school defending Louis, especially after he had beaten a white opponent. I had learned that if I fought, though, I had better win. If I lost, I would get another beating when I got home for disgracing the Embry name.

Saturday in our house was spent listening to the Metropolitan Opera in the afternoons and The Grand Ole Opry at night. The voices of Ernie Tubbs, Red Foley, and Hank Snow filled the air as Momma straightened Ruthie's hair for Sunday school the next morning. Sometimes Ruthie's cries would fill the air if Momma accidentally burned her scalp. Ruthie and I had no say in what was on the radio; Mom selected the channels. For a time, I actually thought I would be a musician. Like most parents, Mom wanted us to take music lessons. There were two hillbillies Grandpa let stay on the dump at the end of our property who were really good at picking the guitar and singing country songs. My Uncle Larry and I tried to take lessons from them. Larry had an ear for music, so he was successful. I failed.

Sunday was always a great day at Embryville. Sunday school was a must. Aunt Ida would load all the kids in her station wagon and away we went. After Sunday school we would return home to an afternoon of fun and plenty of food. Aunt Thelma and Aunt Mae came out with their families, and we played baseball, basketball, and other organized games. Dinner was a potluck. Grandma would go to the henhouse and kill a couple of chickens for frying, and we had fresh greens out of the garden, corn bread, and plenty of desserts. Everyone loved Momma's pies. Cream pies were her specialty.

We were not rich with money or material things. Despite the fact that my father worked at the car dealer and my mother worked at Wright-Patterson Air Force Base, there was very little money in our family. But we were never going to go hungry. We raised vegetables in the garden, including corn, mustard and turnip greens, and we could pick wild dandelions or watercress out of the yard and fish catfish out of the river. We slaughtered five hogs every Thanksgiving—two for Grandpa and one for each of our houses. The meat was to last all winter. We ate every bit of the pig: pork chops, sausage, shoulder, and even chittlins (or, as the more sophisticated might say, chitterlings). We had many one-pot meals of white beans with corn bread or green beans and potatoes. We would eat Spam, bologna, and wieners with the vegetables. There was always fresh fruit because we had apple, pear, peach, and cherry trees. There were grapevines and berries. The women made pies, and they canned fruits and jam to get us through the winter. I got a reputation of making the rounds. If there was no food at our house, I would go to Grandma's. If there was nothing there, I would go to someone else's place. I was a big boy with an insatiable appetite.

Christmas was my favorite holiday. We were always together. Mom and Dad always found a way to make sure Santa Claus visited our house, but we did not exchange gifts outside our immediate family. It was a tradition to have fried oysters at Grandpa's house on Christmas morning. Then Aunt Ida would give each of us an orange and some hard candy. We were so happy, we did not realize we were poor.

One of many family gatherings featuring (from left to right) my Grandma Gardner, my sister Ruthie, my cousin Donald Craig, me, and my mother, Anna Embry (Courtesy of Embry family)

I had relatives in town, too, and we would go in often to see Grandma Gardner, who raised six kids in a two-story, five-room house. Grandpa Gardner died before I was born, but my mother had three brothers and a sister who lived in town, and we would visit Uncle Doug, Uncle Max, and Aunt Elsie. There were plenty of cousins on that side of the family, too, including Donald Craig, who was my age and loved sports as much as I did. We became very close, and he spent a lot of time on The Hill.

I had other friends, both black and white, in town, too. Some of them were classmates of mine at Rockway Elementary School, which was insulated from the racism around us. Doug McGilvary and I would fight after Joe Louis won his fights, but we were still friends. Jim Slusher and I were best friends. His father owned a restaurant, and he even allowed me to eat there. Tom Journall and I rode our bikes together to Little League. But it was the black families—the Willises, the Williamses, the Webbs, and the Robinsons—we got to know the best.

Anybody who came up to The Hill followed Grandpa's rules. We all had the same discipline. If you did not get it from your parents, you got it from your aunts or uncles or your grandparents. But Grandpa was the patriarch. He had strong values and a strong work ethic. He ruled The Hill. He set the disciplines. We all abided. I remember my Uncle Erbie coming home late from work one day and sassing my grandfather. Grandpa took a two-by-four and hit him across the back. The next day Uncle Erbie joined the navy, even though he was only sixteen. He stayed twenty years.

Grandpa's influence extended beyond The Hill. He was well respected in Springfield. Everybody who knew him respected him. He and I were very close. I was the oldest grandson. I was his helper on the farm. I idolized him because of his work ethic and the way he got along with people. There is a lot of him in me.

My sister and I were close, too. We had to be. We slept side-by-side on roll-away beds in our front room until my junior year in high school, when we added on to the house and finally had indoor plumbing. One morning when I was about six years old, my dad rushed in and woke us up. It was so bright, I thought I was late for school. But a train carrying airplane fuel headed for the Air Force base outside Dayton had derailed and exploded near our property. All of us, no matter how young, had to fight to save The Hill. We formed a human chain from the pump and dumped pail after pail of water on our roofs to keep them from catching on fire. It was one of my earliest lessons in the importance of teamwork.

Although anybody from the outside might have disagreed, we always considered ourselves rich and very fortunate to be able to live and have what we had. What we had was not much, but it was precious to us. Furthermore, we were taught to respect people as people. It did not matter what color their skin was or how much money they had or did not have. We were taught to regard them as people and respect them for who they were.

My Uncle Lou was the perfect example. When I was born, he was in jail, charged with attempted murder in that shooting over a gambling dispute. The numbers racket was alive and well in rural America in the 1930s, and Uncle Lou, the oldest of Grandpa's thirteen children, was an active participant. His cousin's wife, Layunie Cunningham, was a numbers runner. One day Uncle Lou hit the numbers, but Layunie refused to pay him. After a brief argument, he pulled a gun and shot her in the chest in a fit of anger, then realized what he had done and turned the gun and shot himself in the chest. Both of them survived, and Uncle Lou was hauled away to jail with a collapsed lung. Grandpa was upset, but he stood by his oldest son and hired the best attorney we could afford, Lawyer Cobb, one of the few black attorneys in Clark County at the time. Uncle Lou served one year before prison officials determined he was not a threat to society and released him. Once he got out, he started working for my grandfather in the salvage department at the pump factory, where Grandpa served as the supervisor, almost like the overseer of slaves on a plantation. That did not work out too well for Uncle Lou, who did not like to take orders from his father. There were times he thought he would have been better off in jail. So Uncle Lou decided to start his own business. Every year, Grandpa gave each of the families on The Hill a hog. You could fatten it up and then kill it, or you could sell it. Uncle Lou decided he would get a male and a female, mate them, and raise hogs. He would feed them corn or slop, but before long, he had so many pigs he had to hitch a flat bed trailer to his '38 Buick and go around collecting garbage to feed his pigs. I would go along to help him, and he paid me $1.

Eventually, because we had a dump at the end of our property, people started asking him to take other stuff. So he started collecting trash along with the garbage. We would take out anything we could sell—rags, copper, tin—and then dump the rest.

It did not take long before Uncle Lou realized there was money to be made in hauling trash. So he sold the pigs, bought a truck, and started charging folks $1 a week. In addition to getting rid of their garbage, everybody also got a story or a joke from Uncle Lou, free of charge. Like my grandfather, he was able to transcend race and get along with everybody.

He had some tricks, though. He always wore raggedy overalls and an old hat when he went to collect. He saved his new Lincoln and his Panama suits for his Sunday drives with Aunt Jessie.

"Always let them think you're poor," he said of his customers. "Don't let the white folks know what you've got."

As his territory expanded, he needed more, and bigger, trucks. One afternoon, dressed in his grungy old work clothes and with a cigar stub clenched between his teeth, he walked into an auto dealership to ask about buying two trucks. The salesman looked down his nose at my uncle and asked what kind of credit he had.

My uncle said, "There'll be no credit."

The salesman walked away, and Uncle Lou approached another, getting roughly the same treatment.

Finally, he asked to see the sales manager and told him he wanted to buy a truck.

The sales manager asked how he intended to pay for it. That is when

Uncle Lou pulled a wad of cash out of his pocket and started peeling off the bills.

When he died years later, Uncle Lou had more than twenty thousand customers and five 2½-ton trucks. He had done more than prove he was no menace to society. He had demonstrated how one weak moment did not have to ruin a life. Despite being a convicted felon, he was an inspiration to me because of his remarkable recovery, his work ethic, and his will to succeed within the law. Like Grandpa, Uncle Lou was a great storyteller, although he greatly exaggerated whatever small grain of truth was involved. He was so much fun to have around. Now at family gatherings most of the stories we tell are about him.

But he was not the only relative who taught me valuable life lessons and helped me to grow.

My Uncle Larry was only a couple of years older than I. One day when I was twelve, we were milking the cows together in the barn when he started to hit me. After a brutal beating, I went running to the house with a bloody nose and cuts on my chin. When my mother asked him why he beat me up, Uncle Larry told her, "Wayne's got to be tougher." My Uncle Erbie picked on me, too. It was not until I grew to be six feet, eight inches tall in high school that I finally was able to get them back. One day when they came home from the service, I slammed each of them to the ground. It was one of the greatest joys of my life. I had grown up and gotten tougher. From that time on, toughness was one of my main attributes on the basketball court. I was so tough that I usually did not have to prove it. My reputation preceded me. I had them to thank.

I also learned about hard work from them. One day a few years after that beating in the barn, Uncle Larry told me a white man in the nearby town of North Hampton would pay us twenty dollars apiece to dig out a basement for a house. Now $40 to excavate a twelve-hundred-square-foot basement did not seem like a very good deal for us, but that was a lot of money for our family, even though white workers probably would have been paid much more. It was in the middle of August, and it was incredibly hot working in the sun all day. We went up to the house, knocked on the door, and asked the owner for a glass of water. He brought out a pitcher of ice water and some glasses. Boy, did that taste good. But then when we handed the glasses back to him, he threw them in a rock pile and broke them. "We can't drink out of glasses niggers used," he told us.

I had a similar experience baling hay for a neighbor with Eddie Willis, a friend of mine. We got paid $1 a hour. The white workers got $3 an hour. At lunchtime, all the workers went up to the house to eat. We had to stay outside in the yard. "My wife doesn't allow niggers in the house," he told us. So he brought us sandwiches on a plate—and, of course, watermelon—and after we were done, he threw the plate away.

You would have thought I would have been enraged, and maybe I was. But I had learned not to express it. I thought that being bitter about prejudice or discrimination would only impede my progress and hold me back in life.

That was something I learned from my Grandpa. We would go fishing and talk about all sorts of things. When we complained about the discrepancy in pay, he told us, "It's not what you earn, but what you do with it. It's how you work that counts, not how much money you make. Whatever you make is more than you have. If you show a strong work ethic, someone will always want to hire you and one day you will be paid fairly."

He would also tell us not to let anyone else's words or actions keep us from success. "Don't let other people's problems be yours," he would say. He would assure us we were facing a lifetime of challenges. "Your strength will be in your character," he would say. "If you work hard and respect people, you will effect change in the way people treat you. There will be those who never change. Leave them behind," he would say as he put his arms around us.

The only thing I could not talk to Grandpa about was sports, because he did not know anything about them other than boxing. He could not understand why I was out playing ball when I should have been working in the field. This was something he could not relate to at all.

Of course, he loved Joe Louis, Jackie Robinson, and Larry Doby. I was ten years old when Robinson became the first black to play major league baseball after Branch Rickey signed him to play for the Brooklyn Dodgers. Doby joined the Cleveland Indians three months later. Black fans watched with great interest to see how they handled the abuse from players on their team, players on opposing teams, the media, and the fans. It was such an inspiration to watch them handle themselves with dignity while becoming great players. I already followed the Indians, but now I had a special reason to root for them. Plus, like many black families, we also became Dodgers fans, and I always looked forward to our annual train ride to Crosly Field to see the Reds and Dodgers doubleheader. We would sit proudly and cheer loudly for Robinson, who had demonstrated that blacks could excel if they were given a chance.

My own athletic future looked a bit dimmer. My dad tried to push me toward baseball and I played until junior high, but I lost interest after that and wanted to concentrate on basketball.

We hung a peach basket on the barn, but we got shooed away for getting in the way of those who were working. Then we cleared out a space in the garden and put up a basket on a pole. I did not play much organized basketball as a kid. In seventh grade, I went out for the team at Rockway Junior High and I was cut after two days. I was hurt, but I kept at it, working to get better. That is something I do to this day. If someone tells me I cannot do something, I am more determined than ever to do it.

I never was sure why I did not make the team in the first place. I was big, and I thought I was good. Was race a factor? That is the unknown. I cannot say.

Coming up in the 1940s and '50s as an African American, you often were rejected. You started from so far behind that even when you caught up, sometimes that still was not good enough. In order to get ahead you just had to work that much harder. Grandpa told me that being as good was not good enough. I had to be twice as good, and sometimes that still was not going to be enough. So I always worked to be the best at what I did, whether I was digging ditches or baling hay. I also kept growing.

One day, after someone got hurt or dropped out, the seventh-grade coach asked me back. We had a game the next day. I was very excited. I went home, tried on my uniform, and started practicing late into the night. I was so wound up I lost track of time, and I did not do my English homework. It was for my last period, and when my teacher, Miss Hannabery, found out the next day, she said I could not go to the game, even though I was an A student in English. I was devastated. But it helped me realize that academics were more important than sports. That never happened again. My final two years at Rockway, I was an A student.

But there did come a day not too long afterward when I did not care about academics or sports.

Coach Frank Shannon (circa 1950) had a huge impact on Wayne Embry during his years at Tecumseh High School (Courtesy Springfield News Sun)

When it was time for high school, I had two choices. I could have gone to Springfield High School, which was more diverse, but my parents and my junior high school coach were more familiar with the situation and Coach Frank Shannon at Tecumseh High School. So on my first day of class, I walked down our driveway, turned left, and got on a bus heading west on US 40 for Tecumseh. Fifty years later, Ohio Governor Robert Taft signed a bill naming that stretch of road Wayne Embry Way.

Back then, it felt like a dividing line. Mamie Robinson, the only other black student in our class, and I sat together, wondering what kind of reception we would get. I had lived a sheltered life on The Hill. We did not go where we were not welcome. But we had to go to school.

Our reception was mixed. We hung out with the kids we knew from Rockway, but we did not know anyone else in the school. We got a lot of strange looks, and heard a lot of whispers, and it occurred to me that the other students probably had never seen a black person in real life. I heard the word "nigger" more than once.

I could not wait for the day to be over so I could get back to The Hill. Mamie evidently felt the same way. When we got on the bus, she told me she was not coming back. I did not believe her. But the next day, she was gone. Now I was the only black kid in the school. I was scared to death. This was a whole new world for me. I was a big, awkward kid. I always had to sit at the big desk in the back of the class. I was shy, and very self-conscious about myself, my clothes, and my shoes. I was a target, and I was not strong enough at the time to take it. I also got it from my black friends at Springfield High School, who accused me of acting as if I were white.

After four or five days, I had had enough. Some teachers, like Frank Shannon, and classmates had gone out of their way to welcome me, but others were downright mean. I remember getting off the school bus crying. I walked up to The Hill, and my grandfather was up in one of the fields on his tractor. I told him I was not going back. He listened to me, but he made it clear he was having none of it. He told me I was going back to school, not just to learn the subjects but to learn how to get along with people of all kinds and to effect change by the way I conducted myself. This was training in diversity way back then, before it was known by this term.

He told me to give it a chance. He told me only cowards quit and the Embrys were not cowards. He told me not to let anyone take my identity. He wanted me to respect the Embry name and make sure it stood for something.

"All people are not bad," he said. "You can't let the bad ones run you off."

I started to whimper. "I can't go back," I said.

Up until this point, he had been very gentle with me. But he never wanted to hear us say, "I can't," or "I don't care." Suddenly his voice got louder, and I knew he was reaching the breaking point. I did not want to get a whipping from him. So I dropped the subject.

But I had made up my mind. I went home to wait for my parents. The minute they walked through the door, I told them: "I am not going back to school."

Mom and Dad were not pleased with my announcement. That was an understatement.

"What do you mean you're not going back to school, boy?" Dad shouted.

Mom was more inquisitive.

"What's wrong?" she asked, noticing that I was upset about something.

Both were puzzled because they knew I had always loved school.

Finally, I blurted it out.

"Some kids called me a nigger," I said, breaking down as the word left my lips.

They understood then, but they did not change their minds.

"You are going to school tomorrow," Dad insisted. "Don't make me get the switch."

Even though I was fourteen, I had not outgrown the switch, which was a branch cut from the limb of a tree. As I got bigger the switches got bigger with more knots on them from where the leaves were cut off. They were usually four or five feet long. Mom used the shorter ones, and it always looked as if it really did hurt her more than us when she used them. Dad used the longer ones, and he would yell at us while he was using them on our bare bottoms. "Stop that crying," he would say. That was a real test, because they really hurt. Hickory ones had more whip to them, but oak ones were stronger. Naturally, we did not care for either one! And we were in even more trouble if we tried to hide them. I would call them the ultimate character builder. We learned not to talk back or fib. We learned to do our chores and homework. We learned to be home before dark. We learned to respect our elders.

With the threat of the switch lingering in the air that particular night, we continued to talk about school over dinner. They tried to convince me to give it a chance. They told me my fears were unwarranted. They told me if I respected my classmates I would have friends for life. The discussion was closed, from their point of view.

"Now get in there and do your homework," Dad said. It did not matter that he had dropped out. Like most parents, he wanted better for his children.

Ruthie was scared I was headed for a whipping, so she urged me to obey.

The walk down the driveway the next morning was one of the longest of my life. As I boarded the bus my buddies began to laugh.

"We did not expect to see you," Slusher teased me. Actually, he knew I would be there because he knew my folks.

It was an anxious thirteen-mile ride to Tecumseh. There was more good-natured ribbing, but my childhood friends on the bus convinced me that my fears were unfounded and that the rest of the students viewed me as one of them.

When I walked into school that day, instead of noticing the kids who made me feel like an outsider, I noticed how many kids smiled and said, "Hi, Wayne." It was quite heartwarming. With my new outlook, I started to relax and be myself, and as the day went on, I was really enjoying myself. I even was sorry to see the end of the school day, but I also could not wait to get home and tell Grandpa and my parents that they were right.

Each day got better for me. I was meeting more and more people and making more and more friends. I kept thinking how silly I had been for overreacting and prejudging the situation. But I was shy and I had something of a persecution complex as a result of some of my early childhood experiences off The Hill. Now I could see that this would be a great opportunity for me to make a difference and, as always, basketball played a key role.

Coach Shannon made arrangements for the gym to be open after school so those interested in coming out for the team could play. Olive Branch High School was the county champion and was favored to repeat, but Coach Shannon was regarded as one of the best coaches in the state, and he had most of his team returning from the previous season. I had listened to the games on the radio, hoping, praying, that someday some play-by-play announcer would be saying my name over the airwaves after I made a shot to win a game.

I was happy to start working out with the team because this was another way to ease my transition, and it allowed me to express myself in a different way and make more friends. We played in the gym every day after school, and on weekends we played in Bill Burkhart's barn. He had a full-court gym in his barn—a long way from the basket hanging on the outside of ours.

School had become fun by now, and I could not wait to get there. But when basketball practice started, I was facing a new challenge. I really wanted to make the team, but I was not sure that I was good enough. I had played with the guys all fall, and they were talented. I was a big, clumsy kid with bad hands, which meant I had my work cut out for me. At six feet, four inches, I was the biggest guy trying out, so Coach definitely wanted to keep me around. He approached me after a practice and assured me I was going to make the team. But he told me how much I played would be up to me.

With that, he handed me a jump rope and told me he wanted me to use it every day before and after practice. He had one of the student managers throw me a medicine ball before and after practice. I had never worked so hard, but with every jump, every catch, every breath and drop of sweat, I fell more and more in love with the game. I loved all sports, but I had found my niche.

I finally felt as if I belonged. Everything was falling into place. The teachers were warm and caring, and the students went from being classmates to friends. I made good grades, and I made the team! Coach told me I probably would not play much because of all the returning upperclassmen, but he wanted me to get some experience and he warned me he would be demanding. He was not kidding.

It meant more rope jumping, more medicine ball, and endless laps around the hallway if he thought I was not playing up to my potential. Jim Schildknect and Don Radar were the upperclassmen who played center, and they had no mercy on me during the scrimmages. I was timid, and they knew it. They wanted to toughen me up, and they knew Coach would not stop them from pounding on me. I had always been taught to fight back, and one day I had had enough. I threw a retaliatory elbow into Schildknect's chest. He charged me, but the other players grabbed him. The last thing I wanted was a fight. As the only black kid in school, I did not like the odds: four hundred to one.

Calm was restored, and we both apologized after practice. Coach was not unhappy to see me get riled up. It was a sign I was willing to compete.

We cruised through the regular season and we were seeded Number 1 for the tournament. I was about to play in a game that actually would be broadcast on the radio. After all those nights I had dreamed about that, it was about to come true.

My playing time had increased as the season went on, and Coach told me he thought I could be a big help during the tournament, which was played in the Wittenberg Fieldhouse in Springfield. We left school for a morning practice at Wittenberg before our first game. It was a forty-five-minute trip, and we were not going to get back for lunch. After a ninety-minute practice, we headed to the Velvet Dairy, known for great hamburgers and malts.

I had an anxiety attack. I had been there before, and I knew I was not going to be welcome. I was the last to get off the bus, stalling, and it was obvious I did not want to go in. Everybody else raced in and began to order. First, there was a round of milk shakes, followed by orders for hamburgers.

Basically, I was ignored, except for the stares I got from the customers. Some of them got up and left. I was scared, but I hoped that because I was there with white people, I would get served, too.

I was wrong. I overheard the manager tell the coach he would not serve niggers and that I had to leave. But Coach was great. "If he has to leave," he said evenly, "we all will. Let's go guys."

At that exact moment, a waitress came out with a tray full of hamburgers. I wish I had a picture of the look on her face. It was priceless. Then the manager came running out yelling, "Who's going to pay for all this food?"

"You pay for it," Coach said, and we walked out as the remaining patrons sat in amazement.

If I had any doubts that I belonged, they were erased that day. It also served as a sociology lesson for my teammates who had never witnessed racism. There would be more.

We were still coming together as a team. We won the county but lost the first game in the district tournament and were eliminated. That was a downer, but Coach told us that we should look forward to next year. We had a good nucleus returning, and we were going to be big. Phil Semler was six feet, four inches, and Herm Schiller was six feet, three inches. They would be the only seniors on the team. I was six feet, four inches and still growing. Donnie Barnhart, who was in my class, was an outstanding point guard. There was a reason why Coach Shannon had good teams. Basketball was a way of life at Tecumseh. We played every night throughout the spring, either at school or at the barn. Coach insisted that I continue my regimen of jumping rope and working out with the medicine ball. He even enrolled me in a dance class.

The lessons Coach Frank Shannon taught his athletes at Tecumseh High School in the 1950s went beyond the basketball court (Courtesy Springfield News Sun)

My basketball career got a big boost on my fifteenth birthday when my dad surprised me with a car. He bought a junker that had been totaled. Under normal circumstances, the car was beyond repair, but somehow he managed to fix it up for me. I passed the driver's test and got my license, so now I could drive to Burkhart's barn and to the blacks' YMCA (they were segregated back then) to play during the summer.

Friday night was basketball night at the YMCA. Alonzo Moss was the director there, and he was like a surrogate father to all of us. I played with my cousin Donald and several players from Springfield High School—Al (Caro) Cohill, Waddell (Oats) Warfield, Darrell (Moody) Trimble, Kent Browning, and Clarence Carter, (who much later became the father of record-setting NFL wide receiver Chris Carter and NBA coach Butch Carter). I had grown up with these guys. They would have been my teammates at Springfield, so they were disappointed when I opted for Tecumseh. But we were still good friends, and although we were still in high school, when we played together at the Y we would beat older guys like Bobby Bronston, Boo Ellis and Chink Hutchins, who had played on the Springfield High School state championship team. After our workouts, we would all go over to the skating rink in Urbana, where Friday nights were reserved for black folks. I was the only one with a car, so I was always the designated driver.

When school started again, I went out for football. Coach Shannon thought it would make me tougher for basketball. I had always been a football fan. I listened to the Cleveland Browns and the Ohio State games on the radio, and I watched the Springfield High games. I had grown three inches over the summer, so I was now six feet, seven inches and 225 pounds, the perfect size for a tight end. I wound up as the team's leading scorer and made the all-county team. I had a great time, but I still could not wait for basketball to start.

I had improved considerably since my sophomore year, and we had a very good team in spite of the fact that Tecumseh had grown to 480 students, which meant we moved up into Class A from Class B. Still, we finished the season 19–1 and were the top seed in the district tournament in Troy. We won the district and had to go to Cincinnati for the regional. This was the first time I was going to stay in a hotel, and that provided all of us with another of those sociological experiences.

In 1953, the hotels in Cincinnati were segregated, and Coach searched for one that would let us stay together. I had mixed feelings about this. Although I was feeling persecuted, I did not want to be a burden. But Coach assured me that I was part of the team and that the team did things together. He also reminded me my family wanted me to make a difference.

We wound up staying in the Alms Hotel. I put up with some strange looks, as well as being banned from the dining room and limited to ordering room service. But I tried to put it all behind me and concentrate on the tournament.

After winning our first game in the regional, we lost to a very good Middletown team, which went on to win the state tournament. The fact that we advanced to the regionals was an accomplishment because it was our first year in Class A. Even once basketball was over with, I still loved going to school. I kept up my grades and kept making lots of friends. In fact, I was flattered to be voted "most popular" my junior year. This was quite a comeback after my first few days.

Senior year, I told Bob Warner, the football coach who stood all of five feet, seven inches, I was going to concentrate on basketball. This did not go over well, since I had led the football team in scoring. The football coach did not care for Frank Shannon, and he accused Shannon of telling me not to play. But the simple truth was that I wanted to devote all my time and energy to basketball because I thought I might have a chance to play for the University of Dayton.

Even though I was still the only black student in school, I was elected vice president of the senior class and I was widely regarded as a leader. My grades were still good, and my basketball skills had improved immeasurably. Coach admitted he had received some inquiries from colleges about me, but he wanted me to concentrate on the high school season and not think about college. Nowadays, students often have selected a college by their junior years.

After an undefeated season, we advanced to the district tournament in Troy again, seeded Number 2 behind Springfield, which had played a tougher schedule. We both advanced to the semifinals, setting the stage for a classic Friday night matchup. It was the first time a county school played Springfield, which was three times as big and had won the state title several years earlier. Naturally we were the underdogs, so all of Clark County was pulling for us. I had an added incentive: All of my cousins and plenty of my friends attended Springfield so the outcome of this game would determine bragging rights for the summer.

Both schools held huge pep rallies the night before the game, and most of the county attended ours. Tickets were scarce, so many people had to listen on the radio, but those fortunate enough to crowd into

Hobart Arena saw a thriller. It was a close game all the way, but we won, 59–51. It was like David beating Goliath. It felt great and, yes, part of the reason was because I had beaten my buddies.

Our celebration was short-lived, because we had to prepare for the regionals against Portsmouth, a team in the same conference as Springfield. We lost a close game, and so my high school career ended on a down note. We really thought we were going to win the state championship that season. I knew Tecumseh would continue to have good teams. Donnie Barnhart, Bill Burkhart, Don Culp, and I were seniors, but the rest of the team would return, including Dave Zellers, who would later play with the Cincinnati Royals. But at that moment, all I had was an empty feeling.

I also was unsure of my future. I knew nothing of the recruiting process, and the less I knew the better. I had grown up listening to the University of Dayton games on the radio, and that was the only place I wanted to attend. I was familiar with their program, and it was only twenty miles from The Hill and my family and my friends at Tecumseh, which had become like a security blanket for me. Dayton had great teams and played a good schedule, and Coach Tom Blackburn was a close friend of Coach Shannon's, so I thought I had it made. But I learned it was not going to be that easy.

Coach screened the schools and set up visits, starting with his alma mater, Wittenberg University, which just did not strike me as a major college. Next was Ohio State. I loved listening to the Buckeye football games on the radio, but I knew nothing about the basketball program, except that it featured the nation's leading scorer, Robin Freeman. I visited the campus three times with Coach Shannon and Charlie Frye, a local businessman and alumnus. Lee Williams, a Springfield native and All-American football player for the Buckeyes, tried to persuade me to attend. I even met Woody Hayes, the legendary football coach. When he shook my hand, he was so impressed with the size of it that he told me if I came to Ohio State I would be an All-American football player. But I wanted no part of Columbus. It was just too big. I could not see going from a school of four hundred to a school of forty thousand. So I turned down their offer.

Bobby Bronston was another Springfield native who played football at Miami University, and he called to tell me Miami wanted to recruit me. I knew nothing about the school. I did not even know where it was. But Coach Bill Rohr called Coach Shannon to set up a visit. I was terrified to learn Coach Rohr wanted to come to my home. Mom always said she was embarrassed to have company, so I told him no. But I actually was quite impressed that he wanted to meet my family, something no one from Ohio State was interested in doing.

Eventually, Mom relented and Bill Rohr came to call. I sat on the front porch waiting for him, half eager and half scared. I saw a gray Oldsmobile pull up and stop next to the little wooden bridge that crossed the creek that ran through our property. A man got out, walked across the bridge, looked under it, checked a couple of boards and, deciding it would hold his car, got back into the vehicle and continued up to the house. After introducing himself, Coach Rohr asked if anyone ever drove off the bridge. We laughed and told him no. No one had ever asked that before. Of course, not many strangers came to visit.

He spent the next forty-five minutes telling us what a fine academic institution Miami was. He asked me about my "major." I really did not know what he was talking about, so I told him I wanted to be a lawyer. I just picked that out of the air. I had no idea what I wanted to be, although I had entertained the notion of playing for the Harlem Globetrotters after seeing them play in Cincinnati Gardens. My favorite was Goose Tatum, who could palm the basketball. Because of the size of my hands, I could do it too, so, naturally, I was nicknamed "Goose."

Anyway, I did not think Coach Rohr wanted to hear me talk about the Globetrotters, so we continued to talk about school. He mentioned that Miami's business school was nationally ranked and that perhaps I should consider that. He told me I would qualify for an academic scholarship because of my grades, which made my mother happy. The school would pay my tuition, but I had to work in the dining hall for my room and board, and I had to buy my books. This was a lot different offer from the one from Ohio State, where everything was paid for and I would earn $90 a month for studying in the state treasurer's office.

He never mentioned a word about the basketball program until I asked. He said they were the Mid-American Conference champions and he thought they had a chance to repeat. He said they played in Florida, New York, and California, which definitely piqued my interest. After having a piece of Momma's banana cream pie, he suggested I visit his campus the following weekend.

Meanwhile, letters were still coming in, but there was nothing from Dayton. I still had my heart set on playing there, so I asked Coach if he had talked to Coach Blackburn. He told me that he had not. I was puzzled because Coach told me that he and Blackburn had a deal that if Coach ever had a good prospect, he would send him to Dayton. I could not understand why every other college in Ohio wanted me and Dayton did not. I remained hopeful.

In the meantime, I got in my '47 Chevy and headed out Route 40 for the eighty-mile drive to Oxford. I kept thinking it would be nice to have this decision behind me. Other than Grandpa, no one on The Hill had been to college, so I had no point of reference. I thought about turning around and going home, but I did not want a repeat of my first days in high school. I was not going to disappoint my proud parents and grandparents.

As I approached campus, I could tell it was going to be very different from Ohio State. The campus was surrounded by farms, and the buildings were red brick. The leaves were starting to open on the trees and the grass was getting green. Spring definitely was in the air, and the coeds were adorned in sundresses and shorts. I fell in love with the campus immediately.

I followed the directions to Withrow Court, where Coach Rohr was waiting in his office with upperclassmen Larry Glass and Harley Knosher. After introductions and a brief chat, they gave me a tour of the building, and we met more people along the way. We interrupted a meeting of the football coaches, who were preparing for a spring practice. After shaking hands with Coach Ara Parseghian, he asked if I had ever played football. I told him I had played one year.

Coach Parseghian turned to Coach Rohr and said, "Billy, I can make him a helluva tight end."

Coach Rohr hustled me out the door, laughing and saying, "You ain't gettin' this one."

The hallways outside the coaches' offices were covered with pictures of former coaches who had gone on to do great things. It was quite impressive to see photos of Paul Brown of my favorite football team, the Cleveland Browns, Woody Hayes of Ohio State, Weeb Eubanks of the Baltimore Colts, Paul Deitzel of Louisiana State, Sid Gillman of the University of Cincinnati, Red Blaik of Army, and the manager of my beloved Dodgers, Walter Alston.

As an advocate for academics, Coach Rohr gave me a tour of the business school and some other classrooms. He also pointed out some of Miami's famous landmarks, like the Beta Bells and Slant Walk.

I was totally hooked. The rural setting was perfect for me. The campus was beautiful. I loved those red brick buildings. The people were great. And with a student body of six thousand, I felt more comfortable than I did drowning in the forty thousand at Ohio State.

Instead of going to a fancy restaurant for dinner, Larry and Harley took me to a dorm dining room. I got to sample the food but also saw a demonstration of the job I would be doing. The waiters in their white jackets were athletes, as were the dishwashers. They seemed to have a sense of pride in the jobs.

After a morning pickup game with some of the varsity players, we watched the spring football game.

While sitting at the game, Coach Rohr told me he wanted to offer me a scholarship. Before he even finished talking, I accepted.

"Don't you think you should talk to your parents?" he asked.

"I will when I get home," I told him.

I was afraid he would change his mind, so I wanted to make a commitment as quickly as possible. When I got home, I assured my family I had made the right decision.

Unfortunately, without knowing I had made up my mind, my mother agreed to let Bowling Green Coach Harold Anderson visit the following Friday. He was going to bring Boo Ellis, one of his players who starred at Springfield High. I had played against Boo many times in our pickup games at the Y.

I did not have the heart to face him and tell him I was going to Miami, so as they were winding their way up our driveway, I ran to the barn and hid behind several bales of hay. Despite the fact that my mother was calling me and others were searching for me, I stayed there until I could see them pulling away.

When I came down, my parents scolded me.

"What on earth is wrong with you?" my mother asked. "You've embarrassed the entire family."

My father told me if I had just have been honest with Coach Anderson, he would have understood. He ordered me to write a letter of apology before dinner. I felt very guilty and had no problem writing the letter.

Spring was a fun time at Tecumseh. Seniors skipped school occasionally to work on the farms, or go fishing or mushroom hunting. We either participated or watched spring sports—anything to keep from going to class. With only a few weeks left, our schoolwork was done. Our grades were established unless we failed the final exams. We wanted to enjoy each other as much as possible since we were going in different directions after graduation. Pat Hopkins was my only other classmate who was going to Miami. I was still hoping Donnie Barnhart would because we had become good friends.

One afternoon Coach Shannon called me to his office.

"I've got some good news," he told me as I took a seat in a chair facing him. "You've been selected second-team All-State by the Associated Press. And you've been invited to play in the Kentucky-Ohio All-Star game in June. There will be one game in Middletown and one game in

Lexington, Kentucky. I was asked to inform you that you can only play in the game in Ohio. You, Norm Lee, and Alex Ellis, are not welcome in Kentucky."

He did not have to tell me why.

But he figured this was as good a time as any to get something else off his chest.

"Dayton did not recruit you because of your color," he told me. "I tried to convince Tom Blackburn to change his mind by describing your experiences here, but he just said no and that was the end of it. I guess he felt his team played too many games in the South and there would be problems."

"I understand," I said. And I did. But I could not help but wonder when all this would change and what I could do to speed that change. I wished all my friends who had accused me of thinking I was white because of where I went to school could have heard this conversation. There was no way I ever thought I was white. There were daily reminders that I was not.

None of that news marred graduation day. It was a joyous time, but also a sad one. There was a lot of hugging and kissing; tears and laughter; talking with teachers, parents, and friends. We were left with so many fond memories. It was a great experience for me, one that shaped the way I would live the rest of my life as I continued to try to co-exist in America. I will forever be grateful to Coach Shannon for helping me grow as a person and protecting me against the ignorance of society. I will cherish the friendships of my teammates and classmates forever. I think of them every time I drive past the school on my way home to visit my family.

Chapter 4

Vowing to Become Great

I was eager to start college, but I was apprehensive as well.

After a summer of working on a gravel truck for the county engineers, I had saved enough money to buy clothes for college. The university guide gave me some idea as to what the bare necessities were. I would have to settle for those, because I had no money to spare. My parents told me they could afford to send me $10 a week for an allowance to pay for laundry and other miscellaneous expenses, but there would be no more. I just told myself I would make it work.

Sunday morning I packed all the clothes I owned in a suitcase I bought at a secondhand store. Before our noon departure, I wanted to make the rounds to say goodbye to Grandpa and Grandma, Aunt Pauline and Uncle Clint, Aunt Jessie and Uncle Lou, and all the other relatives who had come to The Hill to see me off.

Uncle Lou dug into the pockets of his overalls, pulled out a wad of cash, and peeled off ten twenty dollar bills.

"Here's a little going-away present," he said.

Aunt Jessie grumbled her objection under her breath. She had never forgiven me for the time she had asked my cousin, Donald Craig, and me to pick a bucket of blackberries for Uncle Lou's favorite cobbler. While picking the berries, we had killed a big black snake and coiled it in the bucket with the blackberries. When Aunt Jessie took off the lid, she let out a scream, dropped the bucket, went to the bedroom, and came back brandishing a silver .38 pistol that we had never seen before. Donald and I took off up The Hill and hid under the porch.

I had found those kinds of memories flooding my mind as I prepared to leave The Hill, not knowing whether I would ever live there again. I would miss Grandpa and his words of wisdom, but I knew the character he instilled in me through his disciplines and values would guide me forever.

My aunts and cousins gave me boxes of brownies and other homemade goodies.

"No tellin' when you'll get another home-cooked meal," Grandma said, pressing a package into my hand.

Uncle Clint, who loved playing with us kids, wanted one more game of one-on-one down on the basketball court that we had made at the end of the garden.

After the big send-off, Mom, Dad, Ruthie, and I piled into Dad's old Cadillac and headed down Route 40 to Oxford. As we passed Tecumseh High School, I was overcome with emotion. Memories of the good times surfaced again. I vowed that I would come back for games as often as I could. Despite my shaky start, I knew I would always be proud to have graduated from Tecumseh.

As we approached campus, I directed Dad to Reid Hall, which was to be my home for the next year. It was the first time they had seen Miami's campus and, like me, they were impressed with its beauty. A hostess told me where I could pick up the key to my room, and Dad followed with my meager belongings as we proceeded down the hall.

The door to my room was open, and we found my roommate-to-be unpacking with the help of his parents.

"Hi, I'm Barry Kent, and this is my mom and dad," the redhead said, extending his hand to shake mine. "I'm your roommate."

After the brief introductions, I looked around the room and was shocked to see a small bed against the wall. There was no way I could sleep in it. I had grown another inch over the summer to six feet, eight inches, and the bed was a twin size.

Before I had any more time to fret about it, a resident adviser came to inform me that Coach Rohr had requested an extra long bed. He told me there was one available down the hall in a single room.

I turned to Barry. "It was nice knowing you," I told him, secretly pleased that I would have a room to myself. On the other hand, I appreciated the fact that he did not seem to have a problem rooming with me.

Mom, Dad, Ruthie, and I took a drive around campus, and then they left for home. I returned to Reid Hall, and Coach Rohr was waiting. He wanted to introduce me to the housemother, who was also in charge of the dining room where I would be working.

Mazie Minor was a tiny lady who looked to be in her late fifties. She did not weigh eighty-five pounds. She had curly gray hair, beady little eyes and was all business.

She came right to the point. "You will wash dishes," was her greeting.

She continued to give instructions about when to report and where to find my work schedule and the rules of her dining hall, which were many. As she talked, I just kept saying, "Yes, ma'am." Washing dishes was nothing new to me. Every night Ruthie and I fought over who was going to wash and who was going to dry.

When Miss Minor finished, we headed over to Withrow Court for a meeting with the other members of the 1954 recruiting class. On our way, Coach Rohr let me know what I was in for with my new "boss."

"She has fired more athletes than anyone else on campus," he told me. "She is very strict. She takes pride in her dining rooms being the cleanest on campus."

By the time we got to Withrow, the other players were waiting, having spent the time bragging about their high school exploits. Coach made some brief introductions, then told us a little bit about himself and what he expected from us.

Bill Rohr came to Miami from Portsmouth High School, where he had coached for years. He had played for Paul Brown at Massillon High School and then later was an assistant coach for Brown, who had coached football and basketball at Massillon and then Miami before becoming coach of the Cleveland Browns. Rohr was quick to tell us how much he admired Brown's coaching philosophy and style, which meant that he, like Brown, was a strict disciplinarian. That had always been Brown's recipe for success.

He reminded us that we had come to get a degree and that we were to earn it in four years. That was his, and our, Number 1 priority.

"I don't want anyone skipping class," he said. "If you're having trouble in a class, I want to know about it so I can talk to your professor.

"And I don't want anyone getting fired from his job."

I gulped. I was about to go to work for someone who had a reputation for firing people for the least little thing.

But Rohr was not finished. He told us how he expected us to conduct ourselves on and off campus. We were not to embarrass our families, the basketball program, or the university. After all this, he released us and told us he would see us when basketball practice started in October.

It seemed like a long time away, but I had a lot to learn before then. Later that day, fifteen hundred freshmen crowded into Withrow Court for orientation. President John Millett, a distinguished man with gray hair, spoke for forty-five minutes.

"We are Miami, and we are proud," he told us. "Miami's mission is to teach you to become leaders in your chosen fields. Miami will build character in its students, and that will help you become leaders."

He spoke of Miami's tradition and its standard of academic excellence. He also said he was proud of the athletic tradition, and I was pleased to hear that he was interested in sports.

After orientation, I went back to the dorm to finish unpacking before reporting for work. I had an empty feeling because this was the first time I was going to be away from home for an extended period of time.

Cars were not allowed on campus, which meant that there was no way I could go home if I got homesick unless I hitchhiked. I did not have enough money to waste on a bus ticket. In other words, I was there to stay until Thanksgiving.

I was jolted back to reality when I walked into Mazie's kitchen.

"Here's your apron," she said. "When the waiters clear the tables, you will scrape the plates and run them through the dishwasher. And I don't want to hear a sound."

She pointed to the sinks and a shiny stainless steel counter. "In the meantime," she said before walking through the double doors to the dining room, "get your dinner."

While I was still pondering how to wash dishes without making any noise, the cooks warned me that I was in for a hellacious experience.

"She is downright mean," Leroy, the head chef, told the other dishwashers and me as we ate dinner. "You'll be lucky if you last the week."

I kept thinking about what coach had said about getting fired, and I was determined I was not going to be the first to go. It also occurred to me that if I did not work in the dining room, I would not eat.

My coworkers were local hired hands and football players who also were on scholarship. The football players did not seem the least bit intimidated, but most of them were waiters. One football recruit, Dick Kinkoff, was going to wash dishes with me. We assumed our positions behind the counter awaiting the onslaught of dirty dishes. We did not wait long. Suddenly, the waiters/football players burst through the doors slinging dishes our way as if they were throwing mud in the faces of opposing linemen.

They were followed immediately by Mazie.

"You're making too much noise," she screamed at the top of her voice. "Stop it."

I snapped to attention as she made a beeline right for me. Her ranting did not seem to faze my coworkers. In fact, the football players, proud of their macho demeanor, seemed to relish it.

She sneered at us. "I will fire all of you if you don't quiet down," she said as she turned to hurry back to the dining room. But the rest of the evening passed without incident.

The next day was spent registering for classes and talking with my adviser. I had twelve hours of required classes and six hours of electives. Since I was majoring in business, I had first-year classes in accounting, economics, and business. I also registered for an English class and a psychology class to get me to eighteen hours.

I got quite a shock in my first psychology class. The first words out of the professor's mouth were, "If there are any athletes in this class, please leave." I thought she was kidding. Then she repeated, "All athletes please leave."

I stood, embarrassed, and saw two other big guys who looked to be football players standing, too. We met up in the hallway outside class, trying to figure out what had happened and whether this was an indication of what was in store for us. We had no idea why she asked us to leave. It was not a racial issue as there were both black and white athletes involved. When I related the experience to Coach Rohr that afternoon, he said he had forgotten to tell us that not everyone on campus was excited about athletics. It was one of the early lessons I learned at Miami.

But lessons were not on everyone's mind the first week of school. Instead, most of our time was spent getting to know our classmates and the traditions of the school. We played cards and told stories about our high school exploits. And we wrote letters home to our families and sweethearts.

At 11:30 every night, an old school bus converted into a traveling kitchen showed up outside the dorm, sounding a siren upon its arrival. I joined the rest of the crowd fighting for a place in line to sample the hamburgers and french fries sold by the Sangy Man. The food was tasty, but the operation gave new meaning to the term "greasy spoon." Not that it mattered at the time. But eventually I would pay the price for such indulgences.

It did not take long to learn about the other diversions on campus. One of the best places to meet people—or grab face time, as we used to say—was the library, known as "The Lib." That was for serious students, which we all were supposed to be. For the more socially inclined, there were "The Res," which stood for The Reservation, and the steps outside Tuffy's coffee shop, which sold the best toasted rolls in Oxford.

A toasted roll is one of the greatest snacks known to man and is unique to Miami. A sheet of Danish pastry is cut into squares, which are then sliced in half, buttered, grilled, and served with powdered sugar. The finished product is served in sandwich form, preferably with peanut butter in the middle and two scoops of ice cream on top. We were so eager when we ordered that "toastedrollwithpeanutbutterandicecream" came out like one word. One of these four-by-six-inch beauties contained a day's worth of calories and about a week's worth of fat grams. It was the best thing I had eaten since Momma's cream pies and, like the Sangy Man, it caused a problem for me later.

There were a couple of bars, The College Inn and The Purity, for those who enjoyed three-two beer, but that was the extent of the alcohol served in Oxford. It did not matter to me. I had never had the urge to drink because my parents and coaches told me drinking was bad for me if I wanted to be good at basketball.

"The Res" was a gathering place for students between classes or at night. Most of the white students would socialize at fraternity houses or sorority suites. In fact, Miami was known as the Mother of Fraternities because several fraternities were founded there. There were black Greek organizations on campus, but they were not allowed houses or suites. Instead, the sparse black population socialized at "The Res" playing bridge or bid whist, a form of bridge. "The Res" claimed many casualties; students who spent more time there than "The Lib" often did not make the grades to stay in school.

I could have been one of the casualties, as I did my share of hanging out there, and my grades reflected it: I had a 1.4 for the first term. My parents were enraged, and Coach Rohr was not happy either. Like many freshmen, I assumed my grades would come as easily as they had in high school. I was wrong. I received warnings from my adviser and my coach that I had better spend more time in "The Lib" or studying in the dorm if I was going to survive.

In mid-October basketball practice started. The first week, the freshmen practiced with the varsity. It was a good test for me to play against the juniors and seniors. It did not take long for me to realize that I had a long way to go if I wanted to play college basketball. Dick Klitch, a senior center, and Buzz Ellis and Ron Albers, both sophomores, outplayed me. Coach Rohr watched my progress with great interest. He had conveyed to the Roundball Club of boosters that he expected me to become better than Dick Walls, the wide-bodied All-American who set scoring and rebounding records at Miami. But after watching my performance in the freshman-varsity game, it was obvious I had a long way to go. In fact, one of the Roundballers told Coach he had wasted a scholarship on me. There was other criticism, too, and all of it got back to me. Right then and there, I vowed I would become the best player in the history of Miami University.

John Pont, who was a fierce All-American football player at Miami, was the freshman basketball coach. He was also on Ara's football staff. John's jersey is the only football jersey retired at Miami. But I could not help but wonder how a running back who was five feet, seven inches tall was going to teach me how to play basketball. To this day, John takes credit for teaching me the hook shot. His strength as a coach was instilling confidence and providing motivation. Coach Rohr told him to work me hard because he also wanted to prove the critics wrong.

John Powell clearly was the best player on the freshman team. He was a six-foot guard from Franklin. I got to know him when we were teammates in the Ohio-Kentucky All-Star Game. John had trouble adjusting to college life and quit school on several occasions. Darrell Hedric, a senior guard on the team who also was from Franklin, made many trips back home to bring John back to campus. It seemed as if John quit school at least once a week, but he and I became good friends once he settled in as a student.

His background was similar to mine. The only money he had was what he was able to save from his summer job. He received nothing from his family, but he always remembered that my $10 allowance came every Tuesday, and he was there to meet me at the mailbox every week. The money provided us with movie fares and Sangy Man wares until it ran out. As we got more familiar with campus life, we learned there were lots of card games going on. I had never played cards, but John was a shark and he taught me. We accepted invitations to join poker games and all sorts of other gambling games John knew, and we were able to substantially increase our income.

Despite the card games and socializing, I managed to improve my grade point average to 1.7. But this was still unacceptable to my parents and Coach Rohr, who summoned me to his office one afternoon.

"Basketball is enough of a burden," he told me. "You need to cut out the socializing and spend more time studying."

I gave up "The Res" but John and I could not give up the card games. Jimmy Wespiser, the son of a local businessman and a manager for the basketball team, was responsible for increasing our net worth, but he almost was responsible for the fact that John and I nearly flunked out of school. Some of the best card games on campus were in the basement of his parents' house.

The year was flying by. Before I knew it, it was spring, and springtime in Miami was something special. The buds were coming out on the trees, the flowers were blooming, and the grass was getting green. The Bluffs and the golf course were full of young lovers, or those who thought they were in love. The joke on campus was: "Don't kick a bush on the golf course; it might kick back at you."

Of course, none of this meant anything to me. I had not had a date all year. Part of it was because I was shy. Part of it was because I was concentrating on basketball.

I was not happy with my freshman season. John was our leading scorer, an honor that I wanted to achieve. So before spring practice started, I went in to do some extra work. Because the freshman team practiced at night, we never observed Coach Rohr in action. He had a reputation as quite a tyrant, and he was going to preside over spring practice.

Precisely at four o'clock, he walked through the door, all business as usual. A slightly built man with graying hair and piercing blue eyes, he watched us for a while and then asked us to sit against the wall.

"I want you to work hard this week, so I can determine who comes back next fall," he said. "We want to defend the Mid-American Conference championship, so I want you to think about that this summer."

As I listened to him, I could hear the voice of Paul Brown. But it did not take very long before I would hear the full wrath of Coach Rohr.

Ten minutes into practice, we were running through the lay-up line and I happened to glance up at the clock hanging on the wall above Rohr. A whistle sounded at once.

"Gaaddammit, Embry!" he shouted in the manner of a drill sergeant. "Why are you looking at the clock? Do you have to be somewhere?"

I froze. He came over and continued his verbal assault while we were standing toe-to-toe. You could have heard a pin drop in the gym. Everyone had stopped in their tracks completely astonished.

"Start running laps until I tell you to stop," he ordered.

After twenty-five laps around the gym, I resumed practicing with the rest of the team. After practice, I sat in front of my locker, totally bewildered. Harley Knosher and Larry Glass came over to comfort me, knowing that I was shaken.

"Coach did that because he likes you," Larry said in a soothing tone.

"If he did not care about you and your future, he wouldn't have said anything," Harley added.

I took my shower and headed back to Reid Hall feeling very tired, beat up, and hungry. We did not have to work when we practiced, but I was really happy to see Mazie, who had become a second mother to me.

When the week of spring practice was over, I fully understood what Coach Rohr wanted of me. He wanted me to be another Dick Walls, and he wanted me to silence the growing number of critics. What he did not know was that I wanted to silence them more than he did.

Coach called me aside after the last practice and asked me, "How good do you want to be?"

I knew that I wanted to be better than Dick Walls because I was sick of hearing his name.

"Here's what I want you to do over the summer to improve," Coach told me, handing me a typewritten list.

I finished my freshman year with a 2.0 grade point average, a surrogate mother, and a serious workout schedule that included jumping rope, as well as shooting and agility drills. I was eager to get back to The Hill and my family, because I had not been home since the holidays. I had my summer job with the county again, and I continued to help Grandpa with the little farm work he was doing.

I followed the regimen Coach had given me. I did all the drills, jumped rope until I thought I would drop, and played in the usual Friday night pickup basketball games at the Y. My old friends and I still took trips to the skating rink in Urbana, and all of us compared notes about our freshman years.

Summer passed quickly, and soon it was time for Mom and Dad to drive me back to Oxford and Reid Hall. Mazie had claimed me as her own, so I would not think of working at another dining hall. My coworkers could not wait to get reassigned, and they could not understand how I had become her pet. I treated her with respect and would say, "Yes, ma'am," or "No, ma'am" when she addressed me. She often used me as an example to the others of how to act.

"Wayne had good upbringing," she would tell folks. She was right about that.

It was different being a sophomore. No longer were you under the scrutiny of the upperclassmen. Furthermore, you had the right to scrutinize the incoming freshmen. The football players, adorned in the famous white T-shirts with "Miami" stamped in block letters across the front and "Athletic Department" on the back, were permanent fixtures at the prime locations for scoping out freshmen co-eds. The T-shirt, issued by athletic equipment manager Watson Kruszeski, was a football tradition. Of course, the right size was two sizes too small, allowing their muscles to bulge out and (hopefully) impress freshmen girls. Other athletes pleaded to get the shirts, to no avail. Watson favored the football players.

But it was fun seeing all the old and new faces. All the favorite spots were ready to welcome the students back for the fall term. Our advisers warned us that the classes would be more difficult. Instead of freshman-level courses, we would be taking sophomore-level business courses and electives. I was determined to work harder to improve my cumulative grade point average, not get fired by Mazie, and be a better player than Dick Walls.

Despite my first experience in that psychology class, sports were important to most of those at Miami. Our football program was nationally recognized at the time, having played in the Sun Bowl. Ara upheld the tradition of his distinguished predecessors by beating Big Ten school Indiana in Bloomington. The standard for the athletic department was established by Paul Brown, Woody Hayes, and the rest of the coaches who passed through on their way to national acclaim. George Rider was one of the best track coaches in the country, and John Brickels, the basketball coach before Rohr, was the athletic director. He was a pain for the coaches because he was so demanding.

That was the backdrop for my sophomore season. The veterans started playing pickup games in the late afternoons at Withrow, with Coach watching—unofficially, of course—from the bleachers. Ron Ellis and Ron Albers were juniors, and I would have to beat them out if I was going to start. Bill Kennon, a Springfield native, was the lone senior on the team and he was named captain for the 1955–56 season. The nucleus of the Mid-American Conference champion team had graduated. If we were going to repeat, Powell and I had to step up.

The first day of official practice started with the usual meeting at which Coach Rohr reminded us of our objectives and what he expected from each of us. The clock experience was never far from my mind, so I kept my eyes on Bill and listened to every word he said. He passed out a list of rules and told us anyone who broke any of them would be in serious trouble. Discipline was important to him. Being on time for practice, acting like a gentlemen on and off the court, and respecting the university were standard. We had to wear a hat during the season. We could not skip classes or get fired from our jobs.

He reminded us of our priorities: getting a degree, winning the MAC, and beating Cincinnati, Dayton, and Xavier, our natural rivals. Of course, I had my own reason for wanting to beat Dayton.

Don Barnett, an all-conference guard, and I were the only blacks on the team. Color had no relevance in the athletic department. Everyone was treated the same. This was the case everywhere at Miami except for a few students and Dr. Joyner, a history professor from Mississippi who was still fighting the Civil War. A few athletes belonged to fraternities, but the greatest alliance was in the athletic department. All the coaches were concerned about our well-being. We supported each other.

The work that I did over the summer and fall was not enough. I still was not good enough to win a starting job. I did play off the bench, but that was not good enough for me and it was not good enough to prove to the Roundball Club that Bill had not made a mistake by recruiting me. I had a flashback to my early years as a basketball player and my grandpa telling me, "You've got to be twice as good."

Midway through the season, I began staying after practice to work on my weaknesses. The experience of playing against varsity competition helped me to realize how good I had to be. If you do not know how good you have to be, you do not know how hard you have to work. I decided then that I did not want to be better than Walls. I wanted to be one of the best in college basketball.

Rohr became more demanding as the season progressed. After winning our first game against Kent State, we lost four of our next six. According to the upperclassmen, Rohr was worse than he had ever been. I could not believe his yelling and screaming, and I was his whipping boy.

Later in the season, we lost a Friday night game at Kent and had to travel to Chicago to play Loyola the next night. During the eight-hour train ride, captain Bill Kennon sat in the seat next to me and began to talk.

"Wayne, you have to loosen up and just play basketball," he told me. "You seem uptight."

I told him, "Bill, I don't know how much more I can take of the constant yelling. You know my background and why I would be overly sensitive. Most black people have a low tolerance for any white person yelling at them."

Bill told me he understood what I was saying, and he told me he would talk to Coach Rohr.

When we boarded the team bus in Chicago, Coach interrupted our usual word game and asked me to come and sit with him.

As I crowded into the empty seat next to him, he smiled and said softly, "I have been pushing you because I believe you can be the best player in the history of Miami University and the Mid-American Conference," he said, his voice more sincere than I had ever heard it. "I am going to start you tonight, and I want you to have fun and play basketball. I am going to loosen you up before every game from now on."

That night as I was sitting in front of my locker with a more solemn than usual game face, he approached me and slapped me on the cheek saying, "Get rid of that Joe Louis frown." (Joe Louis always had an intimidating frown on his face as he sat in his corner waiting for the bell to start his fights.)

This was the turning point in my college career. I began making a positive contribution to the team's winning. We beat Loyola and won the next four games, including victories over Cincinnati and Xavier. We finished second in the conference, so there was no NCAA appearance. That meant our season was over, except for our breakup meeting and the traditional pastry party held each spring at the Rohrs'.

Dick Walls actually was responsible for the party. While in Kalamazoo to play Western Michigan, the team visited a bakery and loaded up on pastries for the trip back to Oxford. This was against Bill's rules, so the players hid the pastries under their coats in the overhead racks on the bus.

Western Michigan upset Miami, earning a tie for the conference title.

Rohr was irate after the game and told the bus driver to drive straight home and not even stop to let the players eat. The athletic director and trainer protested, because that meant they could not sit in the bar and drink while the players ate.

Bill finally relented, and the driver stopped. When Bill turned to address the team, he noticed a couple of players eating the pastries they had stashed.

"Gaaddammit," he screamed at the top of his lungs, using the one mispronounced epithet he permitted himself because he never cursed. "Whoever has pastries, hand them over. And heaven help the SOB who holds out on me."

Eleven terrified men started to hand over the goods. Bill took the bags of goodies and threw them out the door into the pile of snow next to the bus. Unfortunately, Walls tried to keep a cake hidden under his seat. Bill was tempted to smash the cake in his 270-pound center's face, but thought better of it and threw the cake out the door with the rest of the treats.

To make up for it, Bill had a party at his house every spring, and his wife Mary Ellen, who loved to bake, made an assortment of pastries to go along with the Sloppy Joes. Attendance at the party was mandatory, and each player had to bring a date. When I started going to the parties, this was a major problem. Through my sophomore season, I had not had a date, and I dreaded having to find one. But I knew I could not fake being sick, so I finally asked a girl from one of my classes. The news spread like wildfire, and many of my friends would not believe I had actually asked someone out. I secretly cursed Rohr every day until the party was over.

For the rest of the semester, I focused on my classes and the pickup games at Withrow. I wanted to build on my modest success and I wanted us to get back to the NCAA tournament. I was shooting hook shots one afternoon when a guy approached me and asked if he could rebound for me. Eventually, he challenged me to go one-on-one. His name was Bob Miller. He was much smaller and quicker than I was, and he was an excellent ball handler—the first player I had seen go behind his back with his dribble. Of course, that would never fly with Rohr, but playing with Bob did help me improve my quickness and agility.

When we finished up, Bob said he would see me the same time the next day. Eventually, he filled me in on his background. He was a transfer from Brown who loved basketball and hoped to make the team the next season. He knew a lot about the NBA, whereas I knew nothing about The League. The Globetrotters was the only pro team I followed. When Bob told me he had been a counselor at Bob Cousy's camp, I was unimpressed since I had never heard of Cousy. The only great players I knew had played at Dayton or with the Globetrotters.

One afternoon just before I left for home, Coach Rohr called me to his office and took me down to the training room. Trainer Jay Colville was standing at the sink washing a batch of mushrooms he had picked that afternoon.

"Wants some mushrooms, Emry?" he asked, mispronouncing my name the way he always did.

"He doesn't need any food," Rohr said and told me to get on the scale. It read 280 pounds.

"I want you back at 240," he said. "You played the entire season overweight. That's why you struggled."

Those nightly visits to the Sangy Man, the toasted rolls, and all that food in Mazie's dining room had taken its toll.

My junior year was a transition year for me. I had not concentrated on academics the first two years, and I knew I had to get more serious about my studies if I wanted to graduate on time and get a decent job. I also decided I wanted to join the long line of Miami graduates coaching at major colleges, in high schools, and even in the pros. That meant I would have to transfer to the school of education, and I would have quite a load in my last two years. But I had developed better study habits by sacrificing the late night card games and bull sessions.

The year got off to a promising start. While scouting the incoming coeds, I spotted the girl I would eventually marry. Theresa Jackson was in "The Res" sipping a Coke with her roommate. One of my teammates, Eddie Wingard, dragged me over and introduced us, and my shyness disappeared. We started dating right after that, although the first time I called to ask her out, she thought it was Wingard playing a joke because she knew how shy I was. But Terri was shy, too, and as we walked down High Street to the movies on our first date, we did not say much. After we got into the theater and sat down, she asked me what I was going to do with my legs. I had no response and, in fact, not much else was said the rest of the evening. She told me later that asking that question embarrassed her. We still laugh about that.

In general, everything was going well for me. I felt as though I knew where I was headed, and I had a plan to get there. Most jocks struggled with their grades during the season because of the practices, the emotions of the games, the travel, and the pressures of winning. But our coaches demanded that we excel in the classroom as well as on the court. Tutors were available for those who needed help. The coaches never breached the integrity of education, which explained why they were all so successful.

I found the best way to prepare for exams was opening the books and studying, as well as taking good notes in class. As time went on, I found there were other ways to prepare. For one thing, I learned fraternities kept files of the previous exams because often professors did not alter their questions from year to year. That was one more advantage to belonging to a fraternity. I could not belong, but I spent a lot of time at the Sigma Chi house because several of my teammates belonged.

The fraternity of jocks also had access to exams. Marv Pollins, affectionately called "Weasel," was a student trainer and a protege of head trainer Jay Colville. He had learned some tricks from the master. He became very popular with the athletes, and not because of the way he taped ankles. Marv realized that after professors prepared their dittos to mimeograph for exams, they would throw away the carbons, which eventually found their way into the trash bins. He made a habit of frequently searching the dumpsters outside the class buildings around exam time. As a testimony to his success, many jocks got good grades and graduated. People who held doctorates were supposed to be smarter than their students, and they were as far as book smarts were concerned. But Marv introduced street smarts into the equation. Naturally, he charged a fee.

When basketball practice started, I reported at a svelte 240 pounds. A summer of running three miles a day and cutting down on Momma's pies worked to perfection. I dominated the scrimmages because I was quicker and more agile. I also saw the benefit of the two hundred hook shots and jump shots that I took every day. Bill acknowledged my improvement, but he continued to get on me if he felt I was letting up. He told me he did not ever want to see me fat, dumb, and happy again.

He did not say anything about being scared out of my wits. But just before the season started, I had a car accident, and I am still not sure how I survived.

I had hitchhiked home for Thanksgiving, and I had gone out in my car on Friday evening. It was a rainy night, and the fog was hanging low. I was driving home, approaching the railroad tracks about fifty yards from The Hill. I inched the car ahead toward the crossing. There were no lights or gates, and the brush had grown up making it nearly impossible to see. Making matters worse, there was a bend in the road just before the tracks.

I crept forward. Then BAM. The train smacked the front third of the car, lifting it fifteen feet into the air and turning it a full 360 degrees before depositing it right back down, on all four wheels, on the other side of the tracks. I banged my knee, hard, against the dashboard. Of course, that seemed like nothing compared to what might have happened. There was no doubt in my mind God was with me that night.

The car was totaled, so I walked the rest of the way home. I was a complete wreck when I got there and told my parents what happened. I called Coach and told him about my knee, and we agreed to keep it quiet so it would not get into the papers. That night, when I went to bed, I lay awake, wondering why I had been spared and what God had in mind for me. It would be awhile before I figured it out.

When I got back to school, the season was about to begin. I was the starting center for good and I never looked back. Bill kept up the screaming and yelling. That was just who he was. He also was one of the most compassionate and moral people I ever knew and he was a man of the highest integrity. I took the advice of the veterans and ignored his tirades. I even got to the point where I thought if he did not get after me at least a little bit I felt as if something were wrong. Eventually, we started to mimic him and laugh at his idiosyncrasies.

He did have ways of loosening up practice. One day he got mad at Ken Babbs, a free spirit who paid very little attention to Coach. He was an A student who was not very serious about basketball, and his attitude showed it. He was always last in drills, sprints, and laps. In the middle of practice one afternoon, Bill blew his whistle and brought us to a halt. Jimmy Rohr, his twelve-year-old son, was dribbling a ball along the sidelines.

"Babbs," he barked. "I bet even I can beat you in a race to the wall and back."

With Jimmy Rohr cheering at the top of his lungs, "Beat him, Daddy, beat him," Coach and Babbs took off. We stood on the sidelines wanting to laugh but afraid what might happen if we did. The race was close, but Babbs extended his stride and finally eked out a victory, thank goodness.

We all got serious when the season started. Eddie Wingard, Jim Thomas, and Billy Brown joined John and me as starters, and we went on to win the conference by posting an 11–1 record. We still did not own bragging rights in southwestern Ohio because we went 1–4 against our chief rivals, but we did finish the season with a 17–8 record. We qualified for the NCAA tournament and lost in the first round to Notre Dame.

Terri and I were still dating, so I had no anxiety about the pastry party. In fact, I looked forward to it with a new confidence. But an unexpected meeting the following week caught me off guard. When I walked into Bill's office, I could tell by the look on his face that this was going to be more than the usual spring meeting. He was visibly shaken.

"I have accepted a job as head basketball coach at Northwestern University," he said in an unusually soft voice. "I wanted you to know before everyone else."

I was stunned. I did not cry, but I felt as if I could. When he told the team, the rest of the players were equally emotional, and there was a round of heartfelt hugs and handshakes before they left. I lingered a bit.

As No. 23, I grabbed many rebounds at Miami (Courtesy of Miami University)

"Goose, you are special," Coach murmured, and a tear formed in his right eye. He explained it was a tear of joy as well as sadness. "You have come so far as a basketball player and person," he said. "I'll regret not being here your senior year to see you end your college career, but I'll be watching."

I had an empty feeling as I began to think about our first visit on The Hill. I started to realize how much I appreciated his recognizing my potential and driving me so I could realize it.

"Bill, I want to thank Dick Walls, the Roundball Club and most of all you for being the person you are," I said and we both laughed. "Thanks for bringing me to Miami and all you've done for me," I said sincerely.

"We showed them, didn't we?" he responded.

He praised me for my work ethic and told me he knew that I was going to be special. He reminded me of a game at Western Michigan we won by 5 points. He told me after that game he had never seen anyone play as hard as I did in that game. He loved to talk about how I fought for rebounds with blood streaming out of my nose and mouth. Even though I was getting beaten up, I had 34 points and 22 rebounds.

"It was in that game that you learned how to compete," he said as we walked out of his office. "You would not let us lose."

As I walked back to the dorm, I vacillated between being angry with Bill and being happy for him. I was angry because he was leaving before I graduated. I was happy because he had the opportunity to go to a Big Ten school. Ara had gone to Northwestern the previous year, and Bill merely followed the pattern established by Weeb, Woody, and the other Miami coaches who had moved on.

It was not the only loss I would suffer that year. Shortly afterward I got a call from my father.

"Pop has been transferred to the County Sanitarium," he said. "It does not look good. You had better come home."

Grandpa had been in and out of the hospital since January with what had been diagnosed as tuberculosis. My dad was proud of being the father of the oldest grandson, and he knew how much I loved Grandpa and how much I respected him and the influence he had over The Hill. He knew how much I needed to see him.

I hitched a ride to Springfield after classes on Friday. I got home too late to visit him that night, but I spent the evening talking to Grandma about his condition. She kept telling me how proud Grandpa was to see the Embry name in the headlines. She told me he was thrilled to see how I was representing our family. I told her I had taken his advice to heart and wanted to keep his legacy going.

I was not entirely prepared to see him the next day. He was extremely thin, and he was in tremendous pain. Aunt Thelma and I tried to comfort him. All he wanted to do was talk about me. It made me uncomfortable, but it seemed to make him feel a little bit better.

"You did good, boy," he said, his weakened voice a whisper.

"Only because of you," I told him.

"You keep it up, and don't let 'em get to you," he said.

I had flashbacks to the many conversations we had had doing our chores or peeling apples on the front porch. So many of his words stuck in my mind: "Bring no embarrassment to the Embry name. Don't let anyone take your dignity. Always remain humble."

I had a surge of strength as I sat next to his bed with my left hand over his hands, which were folded over his chest.

"Grandpa, what you need is a steak to fatten you up," I said, trying to lighten the mood.

"Now you've gotten to be high fa-lootin', talkin' about steak," he said, trying to sit up. "You never had a steak before you ran off to school."

He was not entirely right. We did not do it very often, but we did kill cows and eat beef. We just never called the portions "steak." We just called it "meat."

Of course, I was not going to argue with him. We stayed awhile longer, and when he fell asleep we left, knowing he was not going to last much longer.

I returned to school Sunday evening to prepare for final exams. I also was eager to talk to our athletic director to see who was going to succeed Rohr. I had heard that Coach Shannon was the leading contender. He had turned down a couple of college jobs, waiting for the right one. The Miami job was the one he wanted. It would have been great for me to reunite with my high school coach. But it was not to be. Although Frank had been led to believe he was going to be offered the job, Miami hired Dick Shrider, a high school coach from Fairborn. I was extremely disappointed, because I knew Frank and I did not want to adjust to a new personality and a new system in my senior year. I also thought Frank deserved the job.

I did not have much time to pout about it. On the morning of May 31, 1957, William Louis Embry died at the age of sixty-eight. The cause of death was lung cancer, not tuberculosis, which was a surprise to the family. I stood over his casket remembering him and the influence he had on those whose lives he touched. His legacy would live forever in my mind and in the minds of the Embry family. He was a black man who was respected by all people, which was unusual in the time in which he lived. Hundreds of whites came to pay their last respects and talk about how he inspired them. I listened with great pride as they told their stories, and I was even prouder when they said I reminded them of him. Although he was not an eloquent speaker, his words of wisdom inspired more people than I realized.

Things were changing in every aspect of my life. Grandpa was gone, Bill Rohr was leaving, and Frank Shannon was not going to replace him. Three of the people who helped me grow up were gone, but each of them left a little bit of themselves with me. Bill always said part of growing up was learning to adapt to change. Change was to be the central theme of my senior year.

I spent the summer working construction in Oxford and taking classes so I would graduate on time.

Switching majors left me a little behind. I continued playing basketball every day, either at Withrow or going to Middletown to play pick-up games at Sunset Park, where all the college players from the area gathered. That was where I first saw local high school phenom Jerry Lucas. He played well beyond his years, and actually outplayed most of the college players.

After a summer of working at another dining hall, I was eager to get back to Reid Hall and Mazie. I decided to try working somewhere else the second semester of my junior year. Mazie was devastated, but she seemed to know I would be back. Why would I not want to work and eat in the cleanest kitchen on campus? Not much had changed. She had a new group of athletes to break. When they learned I had been there all but one semester, they could not believe it.

"How do you put up with her?" I was asked repeatedly.

I explained the difference between mediocrity and excellence. I told them she demanded perfection, and she had inspired me to seek the same. That was why I was still there.

John and I were roommates again. Jim Hamilton, a point guard who was moving up to the varsity, was our third roomie. John and I thought he was a mole who told the coaches everything that went on, so we were going to make him pay. We like to think we coined the term "go-fer."

It was customary that roomies flipped a coin to determine who went to the Sangy Man when he arrived each night. John and I would determine sometime during the day whether we would toss heads or tails that night so we would be synchronized. Since there were three tossing, the odd man out was the loser. Jim lost forty-five straight days until he got wise. To no one's surprise, he was voted "Most Gullible" at our athletic banquet.

Dick Shrider was no Bill. I missed Bill's yelling, but it did not matter because we were going to be a good team. Jim Hamilton replaced Curt Gentry and joined John, Jim Thomas, Billy Brown, and me as starters. Our team objectives remained the same: win the Mid-American Conference and beat Dayton, Cincinnati, and Xavier.

My college days were swiftly passing, but there was still a lot to be done. Class work was a breeze. Between my new study habits and the wizardry of Marv Pollins, I made my way onto the dean's list. Terri and

I were still dating. We were winning basketball games and I was on my way to becoming a serious All-American candidate. In fact, I was fourth in the country in scoring, trailing Oscar Robertson, Wilt Chamberlain, and Elgin Baylor.

We breezed through the conference, 12–0, becoming the only team in the history of the league to go undefeated. We split with Dayton and Xavier, but lost twice to Cincinnati. Robertson, of course, was the reason for those losses. The highly touted Indianapolis product had moved up to the varsity, becoming the first black player at Cincinnati. Though only a sophomore, he led the country in scoring and already was being proclaimed the best ever to play the game.

By winning the conference, we qualified for the NCAA tournament. We opened with Pittsburgh at Northwestern. How ironic it was to open the tournament in Coach Rohr's presence. He beamed with pride as he talked to reporters about my success.

We beat Pittsburgh and advanced to the regional in Lexington, Kentucky, along with a field that included Kentucky, Indiana, Michigan State, and Notre Dame. We drew Kentucky, with legendary coach Adolph Rupp. The Kentucky team, featuring Adrian Smith, was not integrated and vowed not to be as long as Rupp was the coach. In fact, because they played most of their games in the South, the Wildcats had not even faced many integrated teams.

Even though it had been four years since I was in high school, it was obvious that racism was alive and well in Lexington in 1958. Wingard and I had to eat in the kitchen or in our rooms at the hotel, and when we went to the movies, we had to sit in the balcony. I learned Rupp had absolutely no sympathy for us or our situation.

We lost to a Kentucky team that went on to win the national title. In the closing minutes of the game, we were down by 20 points with no chance of coming back to make the defeat respectable. Shrider cleared the bench to let the subs finish the game. Much to my surprise, I received a standing ovation from the sold-out fieldhouse as I walked off the court. That was an incredible gesture considering the racial climate.

In my mind, it offered hope that through sports we just might be able to overcome racism.

My final game as a collegian was in a losing effort to Indiana in the consolation game of the tournament.

This spring was different from the rest. It was my last as a student. I had concluded that I wanted to become a teacher and coach high school basketball, following in the footsteps of so many of Miami's graduates. I was confident I would be the latest member in what would become known as the Cradle of Coaches. In an effort to do so, I planned to take courses in the summer toward my master's degree and then enroll in graduate school in the fall. To pay for this, I was hoping I could become a graduate assistant to Coach Shrider like so many of my teammates had done. I set up an appointment with him to discuss my plans.

After some small talk, I popped the question. "Have you decided on a graduate assistant yet?" I asked.

"Not yet," he said.

"I would like to apply for the job," I said. "I've decided I want to become a coach."

I nearly fell off my chair when I heard his response.

"I can't hire you," he told me. "It would hurt my recruiting. There has never been a colored graduate assistant at Miami."

I knew that was not true. Donald Roach, a physics major who was black, had just been hired as a graduate assistant in the physics department. I pointed this out to Dick.

"That's different," he told me.

Suddenly, I heard my grandpa's voice: "Remain humble."

That was not hard. This was a tremendously humbling experience and a reminder that although I had just anchored an undefeated season in the Mid-American Conference, a feat that has never been duplicated, set scoring and rebounding records, been selected as Miami's first basketball All-American and been named the best basketball player in the history of Miami, I was still black, and I still faced discrimination.

Simply stated, I was rejected again because of the color of my skin. Although temporarily stalled, I vowed to keep focused on my goal.

I returned to the dorm, set the tables for dinner, and returned to my room. The phone rang.

"You have a call from Marty Blake of the St. Louis Hawks," the operator said.

"Who the hell is Marty Blake?" I asked. I knew nothing about Blake and very little about his league, the National Basketball Association. I had heard of Bob Cousy and Bill Sharman and the Celtics because Bob Miller talked about them all the time. I knew Bill Russell, the great center from San Francisco's two-time NCAA championship teams, was a Celtic. But that was the extent of my knowledge.

Nonetheless, I took the call. Marty told me the Hawks had drafted me in the third round. He promised to call me later with the details. I tried to be excited, but I really had no idea what it meant. I knew of the Harlem Globetrotters, and I remember my folks telling me about the New York Rens, the first black professional team that barnstormed around the country because they could not play in a league. Even though I had dreamed of playing for the Globetrotters, I knew that was not going to happen because I was not invited to play in the annual tour between the college All-Stars and the Globetrotters. I did, however, play in the North-South All-Star Game in Raleigh, North Carolina. It was the first time I was south of Lexington. I hoped it would be the last.

Marshall star Hal Greer and I were the only black players on the North team. Southern schools were still segregated, and no one from the traditionally black colleges had been invited to play. I was petrified the entire weekend. Our DC-3 plane had to stop at the Tri-Cities airport in eastern Tennessee to refuel. We were told we could get off if we liked, but I declined even though I was starving and had to use the restroom. Fear dictated my behavior and my decision to remain where I was.

In Raleigh, much to the chagrin of our coach, the legendary Joe Lapchick of St. John's, Hal and I were asked to stay in a black hotel apart from the rest of the players. Coach Lapchick tried to remedy the situation but he could not. Some good came out of this. After watching me play, Coach Lapchick told the Knicks to draft me. He told me he thought I could have a promising career. Word spread, and it was not the Knicks but the Hawks who selected me.

Before I could think about the pros, I had to finish up my schoolwork. But the week before finals, I received more disturbing news. I opened a letter from home that seemed thicker than the usual note that accompanied my $10 allowance. It was a letter from Dad, explaining that he and Mom were separating. Mom was going to move in with Grandma Gardner. He went into great detail about their relationship after I had gone to college. He even talked about considering blowing his brains out with the .38 revolver I knew he had.

I sat paralyzed by the news. I had no idea what to do. I had seen arguments while I was growing up, usually about money or the lack of it. But they were so supportive of Ruth Ann and I. They would come to all my games in high school and college, and I knew they had made many sacrifices to raise us properly.

After I got myself together, I called my mother and told her I loved her, hoping to cheer her. I called my dad, too, to tell him I had received his letter. He tried to elaborate, but I kept cutting him off. The one thing they both said was that they wanted to make sure my sister and I got through college before they split up. My love and respect for them grew even more because of that, and I vowed to make sure their sacrifices were not in vain.

They did come to Oxford for my graduation, and both were proud of my accomplishments. I thought about how special this was, that parents could do these kinds of things despite simultaneously confronting their own personal problems. As they sat there during the ceremony, bursting with pride, my thoughts kept flashing back to The Hill and the four-room shack we lived in. I thought about the good times and the bad times, but I realized that the most important thing was the disciplines and values they had instilled in my sister and me, despite their problems.

One of the proudest days of my life was when I received my college diploma from Miami President John Millett (Courtesy of Embry family)

Commencements are always highly emotional experiences. It is the time to say goodbye to classmates, faculty, and friends you have made over the past four years. It is also a time for change. You are no longer dependent on your parents. Although I did not have the faintest idea where I was going, I was ready to meet the challenge of being an adult. I had fallen in love with Terri, and I knew I wanted to marry her when she finished school. I hoped I would not be too far from her while she finished her degree.

I took to heart the words of Dr. John Millett. In his commencement speech he told us that because we had spent the previous four years at

Miami, we were better prepared to meet the challenges of society than any other college classes graduating in 1958.

"We have provided you with intellect, and we have taught you character, two necessary components for success," he said. "Use them to make a difference when you leave this campus."

I certainly learned the meaning of character while I was there. Bill Rohr was responsible for most of that, but Ara Parseghian and John Pont also contributed to character building in those of us fortunate enough to have been influenced by them. They were just the latest in the long line of coaches whose pictures lined the hallway at Millett Hall. Even today, when one walks into Millett Hall, there is a sense of wonder at the accomplishments of all those athletes and a pride of being part of the great athletic legacy.

Way back then, I knew I wanted to be part of that tradition of excellence.

Chapter 5

Becoming a Pro

After graduation, I spent a week at home helping Momma adjust to her new life apart from Dad and talked to Dad about what was going on with him. Both seemed to be adapting reasonably well, and I made sure they knew how much I loved and appreciated both of them. I especially appreciated the fact that they had stayed together until my sister and I were on our own. That unselfish act of responsibility made a world of difference in our lives. I vowed not to choose one over the other, and I promised myself that on my future trips home I would divide my time between the two of them.

As I had not heard from the Hawks since that one phone call from Marty Blake, I was unsure of my future. But I had signed up to take some summer school courses toward my master's degree, which I figured I would need if I was going to become a coach.

For the second summer, I moved into the Quonset hut behind Withrow with the same football players, who were setting school records for length of time it took them to pass bacteriology. Despite the tutoring of Dolly Hendricks and the efforts of our well-connected student trainer Marv Pollins, Pat Orloff and some of the other footballers still could not grasp the subject matter.

In between classes, I took a crash course on the NBA. I knew that the Hawks had won the 1958 championship by beating the Boston Celtics. I learned about Bob Pettit, Cliff Hagan, and Charlie Share, and I also learned there were no black players on the team. I assumed that was not a problem since they had drafted me. But I was very wrong in that assumption.

The next time I heard from Marty Blake it was to tell me he had traded me to the Cincinnati Royals. I was not sure exactly what that meant, but before I could figure it out, I got another call from a Pepper Wilson, who identified himself as the general manager of the Royals.

"Welcome to Cincinnati," he said.

"What does it mean to be traded?" I asked him.

Pepper explained that the Hawks traded the rights to me and Jim Palmer, along with three other players, to the Royals for Clyde Lovelette. Five players for one. It did not do much for my confidence right off the bat. In fact, the only reason they really wanted me and Palmer, who had played at the University of Dayton, was because they thought we would have local appeal. They were not even planning to spend any money to bring the other three in.

On the other hand, playing in Cincinnati meant I would be close to Terri in Oxford and my family and friends in Springfield.

The Royals were coming off a tough season. They had been eliminated in the first round of the 1958 play-offs by the Detroit Pistons, but they had suffered a far greater loss.

Maurice Stokes was a powerful six-foot-seven-inch All-American forward from St. Francis College in Loretta, Pennsylvania. I recalled hearing about his heroics during the radio broadcast of St. Francis's overtime loss against Dayton in the semifinals of the 1955 National Invitation Tournament. He had 43 points in the 79–73 loss and was named the tournament's Most Valuable Player. He averaged 23 points and 22 rebounds as a senior, using his muscular body, quickness, and positioning to become a rebounding force.

Stokes was the Royals' best player. He had been the NBA Rookie of the Year in 1955–56, when he averaged 16.8 points and led the league averaging 16.3 rebounds. In the final regular-season game of his third season, 1957–58, he drove to the basket in a game in Minneapolis, got bumped, fell to the court, and banged his head. He was knocked unconscious for several minutes but, after smelling salts were administered, he came to and eventually returned to the game. Three days later, he had 12 points and 15 rebounds in the play-off opener at Detroit. After the game, he and his teammates had a few beers in a bar in the Detroit airport while waiting for their flight to Cincinnati. He complained of dizziness while boarding the flight, and he continued to complain on the short flight, despite the flight attendants trying to comfort him. Upon landing, he was taken to a nearby hospital, but he lapsed into a coma. Maurie, as his teammates called him, remained in the coma for several weeks, and when he finally emerged, he was paralyzed from the neck down and was unable to speak. At first he was treated for encephalitis. Eventually, though, he was diagnosed with post-traumatic encephalopathy, a brain injury that damaged his motor-control system. The injury was traced back to the fall at Minneapolis.

Not only did the team lose Stokes; veterans Dick Ricketts, Jim Paxson, and Richie Regan also chose not to return to the team for various reasons. The only veterans who returned were Jack Twyman, the University of Cincinnati great who was the Royals' leading scorer and Dave Piontek of Xavier—both of whom I had played against in college—and Tom Marshall. Si Green, the Duquesne All-American, was returning from the army. Archie Dees, the six-foot-eight-inch forward from Indiana, was the Royals' first-round draft pick. I had played against Archie in the consolation game in Lexington six months earlier. Arlan Bockhorn from Dayton was the team's second-round pick and the rest of the draft choices were from nearby colleges. The strategy at that time was to have as many local players on the team as possible in an effort to attract a local following. So far, since moving from Rochester to Cincinnati in 1957, that had not happened. The local college teams all drew better than the Royals.

Bobby Wanzer, a former guard for the team, was the coach. He did not have much to work with, and I thought making the team would be fairly easy. Making the champion Hawks would have been much more difficult. While I was thankful Marty Blake had drafted me, I also was thankful he traded me.

For most of June and July I played ball at Withrow, and I still made my trips to Sunset Park in Middletown. But in early August I got a call from Jack Twyman, inviting me to play at the University of Cincinnati gym, where many of the Royals played against college players from Cincinnati and Xavier. The main attraction was Cincinnati phenom Oscar Roberton, aka "The Big O" or, as I came to call him, "The Large O." This was an opportunity to get acquainted with some of my new teammates and play against the best competition in the district.

The rules were standard for pickup games: The winners kept the court. I quickly learned that if you were not on Big O's team, you did not play long. His team never lost. He either beat you himself or inspired the others to play over their heads. The only time his team did not win was if he got tired. Though he was only a sophomore, it was clear he was going to be a special player. I had played against his team in college, but watching him practice and play every day gave me a greater appreciation for his talent. The NBA had a territorial draft at the time, which meant that in two seasons, he would be joining the Royals. No matter how bad things were, we always saw that light at the end of the tunnel. We knew "The Big O" would continue his excellence as a pro and make us a better team.

After one of our workouts, Pepper Wilson pulled me aside and asked me to stop by his office to sign my contract. The very next day, I walked into his office, tucked away on the third floor of the Cincinnati Gardens. I was greeted by two elderly men dressed in business suits. Wilson introduced me to Tom Woods, the owner of the team, and Tom Grace, the president of the team.

"Are you ready to sign?" Pepper asked me.

I actually did not know. Neither Grandpa nor my dad had ever talked to me about this, and neither did Frank Shannon or Bill Rohr.

I answered quickly, "I guess so." Just as when I signed Rohr's offer from Miami, I was afraid if I did not do it right away, the offer would be rescinded.

Pepper handed me the contract to read while he cleared a spot on his desk so I could sign it. In the second paragraph, $6,300 already was typed in. It was a one-year, make-good contract, which meant I had to make the team to get paid.

I looked at the three men in business suits. "I guess there's no negotiating, is there?" I said.

"We can't pay you any more than that," Pepper said.

"Okay," I said. "Where do I sign?"

Way to play hardball, huh?

After I signed, they all congratulated me and told me they were happy to have me. Mr. Woods owned an insurance agency and told me I could have a job in the off-season if I needed one. That made the $6,300 more palatable. In truth, it was more than starting teachers made and almost the same as entry-level accountants and other business school graduates would make.

Twyman was terrific. Right away, he started teaching us the ropes of pro ball. He would talk to us before and after our workouts. He wanted us to know what to expect when we reported for training camp. Not only was he a great mentor, but he was a great humanitarian as well. Because Maurice Stokes had no relatives in the state of Ohio, Jack volunteered to become his legal guardian, taking full responsibility for his affairs, which included signing all documents and raising money to offset hospital costs not covered by insurance. For all of this, Jack was flooded with letters from racists around the country who could not understand how a white man could care for a black man. I always thought the letters strengthened Jack's resolve.

Before long, it was time for training camp. My first was held at Lockbourne Air Force Base outside of Columbus. The Royals had rented the gym and the use of one of its barracks, which consisted of two rows of cots and a john. We ate in the mess hall with the military personnel or in the noncommissioned officers club. It was hardly the Ritz.

One morning I had a swollen Achilles tendon and was unable to practice. As I lay on my bunk reading, the door flew open and I was approached by two uniformed men so stiff it looked as if they had ironing boards strapped to their backs. The braid on their billed hats and the adornments on their chests made it apparent they were important.

"Don't you salute officers?" one of them asked me. "Who is the OD?"

"Sir, I am not in the service," I told him. "I don't know what an OD is."

I explained why I was there, but neither one was impressed. They had never heard of the Cincinnati Royals.

"This place looks like a pigsty," the other officer said. "Find out who the officer of the day is and get this place cleaned or get these guys out of here."

This was my introduction to pro ball. I sat there, embarrassed, wondering which was worse: pro ball, the Air Force, or Mazie's kitchen.

In a way, it was only too fitting that we were "stationed" at an Air Force base for training camp because the two-a-day practices were war. Fifteen men were competing for twelve jobs. It was like musical chairs with hand-to-hand combat.

Almost all of us were on make-good contracts, except Jack and Si Green, who sat in the bleachers smoking cigarettes while we beat our brains out. Si told us he was saving himself for the season and did not want to be part of the mess he was watching. I confess, it was a mess.

With only four players who had any NBA experience and the rest of us literally fighting on every play, not much was accomplished. I recovered quickly from my Achilles injury because I realized if I did not get back into shape quickly I might be forgotten.

I was the only legitimate center. Archie played center in college, but he wanted no part of the punishment of the inside game in the pros. At six feet, eight inches, Jim Palmer was the only other person who had any size, but he was more comfortable at forward.

I was somewhat timid, at least until Arlan "Bucky" Bockhorn got my attention by running through a pick and belting me in the midsection on the way past.

"Damn, Bucky," I yelled.

"You've got to be tough out there, big boy," he shouted back.

Bucky epitomized intimidation. Whoever took his job was going to have to fight him for it. Literally. Bucky was a six-foot-four-inch guard who may have been the oldest rookie in the history of the NBA. No one ever knew his real age. We knew he was in the army for two years before his four years of college.

Somehow the twelve of us survived. After beating each other up, we were more than ready for our first exhibition game against the visiting Detroit Pistons. Then we were to load into four cars and travel to New England to play the Celtics seventeen times in eighteen days before finishing up with a game against the Minneapolis Lakers in Charleston, West Virginia. My head was spinning. We were going to play nineteen games before the season even started. We played only twenty games in an entire season in college.

I was immediately christened into the inside game. Walter Dukes, a gangly seven-footer from Seton Hall, was the Pistons' center. Words cannot describe him. He was relentless going to the offensive boards, and he led with his bony elbows. Even George Yardley, who was only six-foot-four-inches tall, took his shots at my broad anatomy. I was getting an old-fashioned whipping. All that was missing was Grandpa's switch.

During a timeout late in the game, my teammate Dave Piontek told me, "Wayne, you won't last long in the NBA if you don't fight back." I made up my mind then and there that if I had to take any punishment, I was going to dish some out, too. I could not rely on Joe Louis to do my fighting for me any more as I had done when I was a kid.

The next morning, four of us piled into each car and headed east to the turnpike on our way to New England. "Is this how they travel in the NBA?" I asked myself. "Couldn't we at least afford a bus?"

Automobiles were not the most comfortable mode of transportation for men our size, especially when the trip took fourteen hours. But somehow we managed. Everyone showered and used plenty of deodorant, and there was an ample supply of breath mints. Today's players, with their sushi and Caesar salads on their chartered flights, would not have believed this whole scene as it existed for me. But I cannot help but wonder if toughing it out like this would not have done them some good. We got to know each other as people, not as just basketball players. We had plenty of time to get to learn more about each other, tell college war stories, and brush up on our knowledge of the NBA. Jack raved about the team we were about to face for the next two and a half weeks. He told us the only reason the Celtics lost to the Hawks was that Bill Russell missed two games with a sprained ankle. The Celtics definitely were favored to win the title this season. Very soon, I found out why.

In a high school gym in Keene, New Hampshire, I made the acquaintance of one Bill Russell, unquestionably the best center in the NBA. He was an intimidating presence, with his long, wiry-strong body and his signature goatee. His game face was stoney, and the aura around him regal.

During the pre-game warm-up, I found myself watching Russell and his teammates in awe. Each one exuded confidence as they trotted through the layup line. Cousy. Sharman. Heinsohn. Loscutoff. Ramsey. And the Joneses—K. C. and Sam. There were a couple of rookies, too, and Gene Conley was to join them when the baseball season ended. This was the team Bob Miller had talked to me about while we played one-on-one back at Miami. This was THE BOSTON CELTICS.

It did not take me long to figure out my baby hook shot was not going to make it. Russell practically stuffed the first two down my throat. Meanwhile, the Celtics' famed fast break was working to perfection. Russell rebounded, Cousy passed, and Sharman or Heinsohn shot. They killed us.

As I tried to wash off the defeat in the shower, I turned to Twyman and said, "These guys are really good. And we have to play them sixteen more times."

Jack smiled. "Not sixteen. Twenty-five. We'll play them nine times in the regular season, too."

Now there was something to look forward to.

Despite the beatings we were taking, we enjoyed the trip because we got to know each other on and off the court. We stayed in the same hotels (imagine that) and so we were able to socialize while eating, drinking, or just hanging around in the lobbies. I was impressed by how friendly all the players were—at least off the court. Once they got on the court, they were all business and losing was unacceptable.

I will never forget meeting Gene Conley in the lobby of the hotel as he arrived once the baseball season was over. We talked for a while and then he went to his room to get ready for the game. I remember thinking how friendly he was. A few hours later, we were engaged in my first fight as a pro.

We battled for a rebound, and I forcefully pulled it away from him. Gene had quite a reputation as a feisty baseball player, and he was no different on the basketball court. He threw a punch at me. Before I could retaliate, the referees broke it up. I could not believe this was the same guy I was chatting with a few hours earlier.

But that was how it went. All friendships ceased once we stepped onto the court. We played and fought our way through Maine, Vermont, New Hampshire, and Connecticut, places I never dreamed of going. We were awful, the Celtics were great, and pro ball was fun. Red Auerbach never had to worry about firing up his victory cigars. He could have lit some of them before the games even started. It was a sight I got to know well in the years to come.

Twelve travel-weary players and a coach headed back to Cincinnati for a couple of days rest before we opened the season at Minneapolis. Practices were cut to one a day, although they were every bit as intense because there was still one cut to be made.

I did not want to be one of the final cuts. Even though I had held my own in the preseason games, I did not radiate confidence. I was hoping that because I was a local product I would have an edge, so I tried to act as if I was going to be there, even if I was not completely convinced.

With the start of the season approaching, players were looking at housing options. Most of them took apartments in Swifton Village, which was across the street from our home court in the Cincinnati Gardens. When I asked the real estate agent if I could look in the same complex, she suggested that I look in Avondale. That, she informed me, was where the colored people lived. I got the message, a message that had been sent to me only too often, no matter how hard I tried or how successful I hoped to be. It was a message that never ceased to hurt each time I heard it, but one I vowed would never defeat the spirit inside me.

I wound up staying at the Manse Hotel, a black-owned hotel, until I finally rented a room in Avondale with a schoolteacher named Ann Brummitt, whose son had moved away. She was a great cook, which was a blessing since not many restaurants served blacks. As an added attraction, Don Newcombe, one of my Dodger heroes, lived downstairs. He had been traded to the Reds. But black baseball players were not any more welcome in segregated Cincinnati than black basketball players.

Avondale was about thirty-five miles from Oxford, and most evenings I made the drive to see Terri. I was not at all worried about our relationship. I was worried about making the team, however. I was not sure I was good enough.

It was not until two days before the 1958–59 season started that Coach Wanzer made his final cuts, reducing the roster to ten. I had survived. Elated, I called Terri, Momma, and Dad to tell them the good news: I made the NBA.

The League was twelve years old at that point, and it was made up of eight teams. The Celtics, the New York Knicks, the Syracuse Nationals, and the Philadelphia Warriors were the Eastern Conference. The Royals, the Minneapolis Lakers, the St. Louis Hawks, and the Detroit Pistons were the Western Conference. Maurice Podoloff, a Russian immigrant who went to Yale and became a lawyer, was the commissioner, and The League's headquarters were in the Empire State Building in New York City. I still remember the phone number: Bryant 9–1535. Haskell Cohen was the public relations man, Connie Maroselli was the comptroller, Pat Kennedy was in charge of officials, and Zelda Meyer (later Spoelstra) was in charge of everything else. Nat "Feets" Broudie was a part-timer who was responsible for clipping articles out of the newspapers and filing them.

Those who played or worked for the NBA in any capacity referred to it as "The League." We would say, "I made The League." Or we would ask questions like, "Did you play in The League?"

The League followed the steps first taken by baseball by integrating in 1950. That year, Celtics owner Walter Brown drafted Charles Cooper out of Duquesne in the second round. Washington drafted Earl Lloyd in the ninth round, and the Knicks bought the contract of Nat "Sweetwater" Clifton from the Globetrotters. Cooper was the first drafted, Clifton was the first to sign, and Lloyd was the first to play in a game. But even eight years later, there still were very few black players in The League.

Our opening night roster had two, me and Si Green, and he was soon to be traded to St. Louis, leaving me, once again, as the only black player in the group. The rest of the roster included Jack Twyman, Dave Piontek, Archie Dees, Jack Parr, Jim Palmer, Larry Staverman, Arlan "Bucky" Bockhorn, Tom Marshall, and Vern Hatton.

We flew to Minneapolis the day of the game, arriving late in the morning. After a short nap, several of us met in the lobby so we could find a restaurant for our pre-game meal. Being a rookie, I left it up to the veterans to lead the way. I knew it had to be some place cheap, because we had only $7 a day in meal money. The frugal Piontek asked the bellman for the nearest Tad's Steakhouse. We all followed along to Tad's for the $1.39 special—a steak, baked potato, and salad. On the way back to the hotel, Dave promised to show us how to live on $7 a day.

As excited as I was, I knew we were not a very good team. How could we be when our best player, Maurice Stokes, was back at home? Stokes was third in assists and rebounding and averaged 16 points a game in the 1957–58 season. Twyman was the only legitimate returning starter. Piontek and Marshall had played sparingly.

Of course, the Lakers had won only nineteen games in 1957–58, finishing last in the Western Conference. That gave them the first pick in the draft, which they used on Elgin Baylor, the Seattle star who led his team to the Final Four. Aging veterans Slater Martin, Vern Mikkelson, and Jim Pollard remained from the great Lakers teams of the past.

I remembered the time when I was starting my career, did not do my homework, and could not play in my first game. That was exactly how I felt when I opened my gym bag before my first game as a pro and realized I had forgotten my road uniform. I had my shoes, and my warm-ups, and nothing else. At first I thought someone might have been playing a joke on me, but I had not left my bag unattended for a single minute. Then it hit me. I had left my blue, red, and white jersey and shorts on the bed back home.

I had absolutely no idea what to do. Wanzer walked over and said, "Aren't you getting dressed?"

"Yeah," I mumbled, turning several shades of red, no small feat for a black guy. My teammates started to laugh and joke. I turned to Jack and admitted I had forgotten my uniform.

"What do I do now?" I whispered urgently.

Jack sent a locker room attendant over to the Lakers, who sent back one of their blue road uniforms, which I wore inside out. I said a silent prayer thanking Laker center Larry Foust for being as big as I was.

Actually, I was hoping I would not play at all, so I would be spared the embarrassment of modeling the Lakers' uniform. But just before the game, Wanzer told me I was starting.

Off came my warm-ups and on came the heckling—not just from the fans, but from the Lakers, my teammates, and the referees. The night ended as badly as it had started as we lost, 99–79. This was not how I envisioned starting my career in The League.

I learned two things that night. The first was to double-check the contents of my bag. The second was that Baylor was great and the Lakers were going to be tough to deal with in the 1960s.

Three nights later, we beat the Lakers in our home opener, 110–94, before thirty-three hundred fans at the Cincinnati Gardens. Of course, we lost the next seven games. It got to be pretty depressing losing night after night. In fact, it got so bad that on off nights we would hold a victory party because we had not suffered another defeat.

But then we shocked everyone by beating the Celtics at home after losing to them big in Boston the night before. Of course, we went on to lose six of the next seven, but I would not trade that one victory over Boston for anything. The Celtics were to become basketball's greatest dynasty.

After losing to the Lakers again at home, Wanzer asked me to stay after the game. I could not imagine why, but he did not waste any words. "Em, I have decided to cut you," he told me with no remorse. Although I had been in and out of the lineup, I never expected to get fired. It was not as if I was a bum, as Billy Rohr would call guys who could not play.

I took the news hard. After stopping at Frisch's to get my usual postgame Big Boys hamburgers, I went home to ponder my future. I was so upset I could not eat, which did not happen often. I sat on the edge of the bed wondering who I should call first—Terri, my parents, or Coach Rohr. I was so embarrassed I could not call any of them. Basketball had become my passion. Surely there was something else I could do. I wondered if I would get picked up on waivers. I thought about playing in the semipro Eastern League. Or maybe I would just go back to school, get my master's degree, and coach. All of those thoughts were running through my mind as I fell into a fitful sleep.

The next morning the phone rang. I looked at my watch. It read 8:05.

I fumbled around for the phone. As I picked up the receiver I heard Pepper's voice.

"Wayne," he said, "I want you to stop by the office before practice."

I was more than a little puzzled. "Didn't Wanzer tell you he cut me?" I asked.

Pepper sounded embarrassed. "That's what I want to talk to you about," he said.

Practice started at 10 A.M., but I left the house in plenty of time to meet with Pepper. When I walked into his office I knew something was up. Steve Hoffman, the public relations director, was sitting at his typewriter pounding away on the keys, totally ignoring me.

Pepper had a sheepish grin on his face. "You are not cut," he told me. "As a matter of fact, we just fired the coach. Now get to practice."

I thanked him and, without much more conversation, did an about-face and strode out the door, down the hall, and to my car. On the drive to practice at Xavier, I reviewed each stage of my career—junior high, high school, and college, and how they had all followed a similar pattern. I thought about what I had done each time I had a reprieve. Suddenly, I heard my grandfather's voice as clear as day: "You have to be twice as good," he said, as he had time and time again.

I told myself I would never be cut again. For the rest of my career, I was going to get to practice early, stay late, work hard, and take no prisoners at practice or in the games. God had blessed me with a second chance, and I was not going to let Him down. I was not going to let Grandpa down. I was not going to let my parents down. I was not going to let Pepper down. And I was not going to let down the new coach, Tom Marshall, a former player for the Royals. It did not make any difference in the big picture. Neither did several roster changes. We continued losing, finishing the season 19–53 with very few bright spots.

The only positive thing was that we were gaining experience. I still felt sorry for Jack Twyman. He was a great player and deserved better than to play with a bunch of rookies and journeymen. Nonetheless, he was second in The League in scoring, averaging almost 26 points per game.

I appreciated how he encouraged the rookies by keeping us focused on the future. He taught us how to be pros—how to approach the game, how to dress, and how to conduct ourselves at home and on the road. I will say this about Jack: He never saw a shot he did not like. I had to get used to him intercepting passes into the post and shooting without blinking an eye. Of course, he could do that because none of the rest of us could score.

In addition to playing experience, we also were getting to know the ins and outs of The League—the players, the characters, and the cities. The NBA was still in its infant stage and was not very popular in most cities. There was no television and very little radio. Although there were All-Americans on most rosters, many of the teams played before sparse crowds. The games were incredibly competitive, largely because of pride and honor, but also because few players had guaranteed contracts. We all played hurt because if you missed a game, someone might take your job. Fights were common for the same reason. The stars were targets, but every team had an enforcer, which was another reason why Jack had befriended me. The average salary was less than $20,000 and the total payroll did not exceed $100,000. Most teams carried the minimum number of players, and very few of them were black, certainly no more than one per team, except in rare instances. Most front offices had fewer than five employees. There were no assistant coaches. Trainers did not travel.

That was The League as I joined it. But I was still proud to be a part of it, and I enjoyed learning my way around the cities. Well, most of them, anyway.

Boston was by far the best team in The League, and one of the better cities to visit if you liked history. There was so much to do and see, although playing the Celtics was an attraction in and of itself.

Red Auerbach's shrewd deal to acquire Bill Russell from the Hawks for Ed Macauley and the draft rights to Cliff Hagan will go down as the best trade in the history of the NBA, unless you are a Hawks fan. Russell was to dominate the game like no other, and, combined with the other

Signing autographs during a clinic in Cincinnati (Courtesy of Embry family)

future Hall of Famers on the team, the Celtics were destined to create a dynasty. Imagine the backcourt of Bob Cousy and Bill Sharman with K. C. and Sam Jones, Jim Loscutoff, and Tommy Heinsohn at the forwards and Frank Ramsey playing both positions. There was greatness at every position. It would have to go down as the greatest team in the history of the game. Red controlled the game, his players, and the officials.

Before every game in Boston, Russell would invite us to his Reading home for our pre-game meal. This was a common practice among black players in those days because so many of the restaurants were still segregated. Rose Russell, Bill's wife, laid out as many steaks as you could eat, baked potatoes, greens, and some sweets. We would fill up—maybe that was the idea—while Russ ate very little, perhaps because he threw up before every game.

The Boston Garden was a Boston landmark, maybe even a national landmark. There was a lot of character in that old barn, not to mention a lot of characters. It was the only arena with a parquet floor. The fans were loud and boisterous and not very kind to me. Announcer Johnny Most was as popular as the players. Howie McHugh was Mr. Do It All and Jock Semple was on loan as our trainer.

Probably my favorite city to play in was New York. New York was considered the Mecca of basketball, and Madison Square Garden was its shrine. Ned Irish, who owned the team and the arena, ruled the roost, and the Knicks main players were Kenny Sears, Carl Braun, Richie Guerin, Willie Naulls, Sweetwater Clifton, Ray Felix, and Charley Tyra.

I think every kid growing up dreams of playing in the Garden. Located on the corner of Eighth Avenue and 48th Street, it was in the heart of downtown Manhattan. More championship fights were held there than any other arena. It had the best indoor track meets, tennis matches, and college basketball games. It was the home of the National Invitation Tournament, at that time the premier post-season collegiate tournament. All of us wanted to shine in the Garden because we were performing before great writers such as Milton Gross, Leonard Lewin, Leonard Koppett, Red Smith, and Sam Goldaper, as well as legendary announcer Marty Glickman.

The Garden staff was unique, too. There were some real characters behind the scenes—Feets Broudie, PA announcer John Condon, and

John Goldner, who did a little bit of everything, including scoring tickets for some of the championship fights.

The New York fans claimed to be the best in the world, and they were not necessarily Knicks fans. The team was not that good in the 1950s and early 1960s but the seats were always filled. Jack told me the reason was that most of the fans were betting on the game. That was news to me.

We stayed at the Manhattan Hotel on Eighth Avenue. I stayed close to Jack and Piontek because I had never been to New York before and it seemed like a strange place to me. They warned me about getting taken for "long" rides by the cabbies. They told me to tip the drivers well. Mostly, they told me to try to blend in. They told me definitely not to look up at the skyscrapers.

I was amazed at how much the fans, particularly the kids, knew about me and how much they loved basketball. Going in and out of the employees' entrance was a hassle because of all the autograph seekers. They had magazines, photo albums, and who knows what else for us to sign. After the game, kids from all over the city waited outside the door and begged to carry our bags to the hotel. I had never considered myself a celebrity until I came here.

The toughest thing about New York was trying to stretch that $7 a day meal money. One meal usually was a bologna sandwich to go from one of the city's famed delicatessens, at least until Jack introduced me to Ed Mosler of the Mosler Safe family. Ed was a great sports fan and he loved to entertain us on our trips to New York. We were his guests at Broadway plays or for dinner at his favorite steak house, Jim Downey's. Ed introduced me to the culture of the theater.

We actually spent a great deal of time in New York because doubleheaders were scheduled at the Garden. If we played the Knicks on a Saturday and were part of the doubleheader on Tuesday, we would stay in New York the whole time. I loved going to the jazz clubs to see some of my favorite musicians: Miles Davis at Birdland, Otis Redding at the Apollo, John Coltrane at the Village Gate, and Sammy Davis at the

Copacabana. While we were uptown, we would catch Nipsey Russell at the Baby Grand before a late dinner at Frankie's and then head over to Small's Paradise, where athletes and entertainers rendezvoused for a late-night jam session.

It would be interesting to check the records of the teams that stayed over from Saturday until Tuesday. I will bet not too many won that second game, which I am sure the gamblers noted. We were all for having a good time, but as we would tell each other: There are eight million stories in the Big Apple. Do not be one of them.

Another one of my favorite stops was Philadelphia, the City of Brotherly Love—unless, of course, you were there as an opponent. The team was called the Warriors in 1958. The owner was Eddie Gottlieb, who also made up the league schedule. Despite the fact that the Warriors were champions in 1955–56, the team of Paul Arizin, Woody Sauldsberry, Joe Graboski, Tom Gola, Guy Rodgers, Neil Johnston, and Andy Johnson finished last in the Eastern Conference. Things would change the next season, when a savior in the person of Wilton Norman Chamberlain arrived.

Philadelphians would disagree that New York was the Mecca of basketball. They claimed the best ball was played in the Palestra, where the Big Five colleges played their games, or the Convention Center, where the Warriors played, or Sonny Hill's Baker League, where the best high school players competed in the summer.

Philadelphia's Andy Johnson, a six-foot-five-inch forward, was one of the toughest guys in The League. He resembled Jack Johnson, the fabled heavyweight champion in the 1900s, and he was every bit as mean. Twyman hated that matchup. On the nights we played the Warriors, Jack would stick close to me. Invariably, there would be a fight or two, and he wanted to make sure I had his back. The fans would get into it, too. There was very little security in those days, and you could count on some trouble when you passed through the crowd on the way to the elevator that took us to the locker room. In fact, sometimes we had to fight the security guys, too.

Among the characters in Philadelphia were Harvey Pollack, the legendary public relations man and statistician, and announcer Dave Zinkoff. Harvey always would give you an extra rebound or two, while Zinkoff always gave you a kosher salami to help stretch that meal money.

After the games, there were great jazz clubs, including Pep's and the Show Bar. Before the games, history buffs could always take in the Liberty Bell and Constitution Hall.

Detroit was one of my least favorite trips. Fred Zollner was the owner, and the team had just moved from Fort Wayne, Indiana. The players included Gene Shue, a great shooter; George Yardley, a future Hall of Famer; Earl Lloyd, Walter Dukes, and Dickie McGuire. Shelley McMillan was a rookie.

The Pistons played in Olympic Arena, which was the coldest building in The League. The Pistons had eliminated the Royals from the playoffs the previous season, so there was some animosity going into the 1958–59 season.

I hated playing the Pistons because of Walter Dukes and his sharp elbows. I finally got to the point where I blocked him off the boards by taking a boxer's stance—with my fists up—and I found it necessary to use them on more than one occasion. It did not matter, because you could give Walter your best punch and he took it. There was no way to intimidate him. My only hope was that he would get into foul trouble early, which he usually did. Eventually, he would foul out of the game, and take his elbows with him. I was never sorry to see him, or them, go. Players would lobby the referees to keep an eye on him, but that never seemed to help. He also never stopped running, so even if you somehow managed to avoid his elbows, you were exhausted anyway.

Earl Lloyd, the first black to play in an NBA game, was a great mentor to me and the rest of the black players. He felt obligated to take us under his wing and teach us how to cope in the predominantly white league. He told us where we could eat in each city, what clubs we could visit, who we could trust. He told us the one, sure way to get cut or traded was to date a white woman. He was tough, but he also was a gentle giant.

Detroit was called the Motor City because the big three auto makers were headquartered there, but it became better known as Motown with the emergence of some of the more popular musical artists. We would go to the 20 Grand nightclub to hear Stevie Wonder, Marvin Gaye, the Temptations, and Martha and the Vandellas long before they became famous. A trip to Detroit was never complete without one of the cheeseburgers from Kayo's Bar behind the Sheraton Cadillac. They were the best burgers in The League.

Of course there were cities I did not get to know as well, like Syracuse, home of Danny Biasone's Nationals. Biasone was best known as the creator of the 24-second clock and his team featured Dolph Schayes, Johnny Kerr, Larry Costello, and Hal Greer. The fans were nearly as avid as Philadelphia's, but there was always too much snow for me. The city holds the record for teams not being able to get out of town. I also hated the flight from Cincinnati—a milk run that included stops in Cleveland, Buffalo, and Rochester. Minneapolis, home of the powerful Lakers with George Mikan, Jim Pollard, and Elgin Baylor was so cold we often did not leave the hotel. In fact, I would go hungry sometimes if the hotel restaurant was not open because I was not about to go outside.

St. Louis, the Gateway to the West, was not one of my favorites, either. Ben Kerner was the owner, Marty Blake was the general manager and Alex Hannum was the coach. The defending champions were a very good team. Bob Pettit was one of the better players in The League and a future Hall of Famer, as was Cliff Hagan. These two were the prime scorers and demanded the ball. Players who did not recognize that did not stick around very long. Hagan had a variety of shots, and he cherry-picked more than Twyman did on my team. Clyde Lovelette was a crafty inside player, and I understood why Marty wanted him more than me. Charlie Share was getting older, and if the Hawks were going to repeat as champions, they needed the veteran Lovelette. Slater Martin and Jack McMahon completed the starting five.

Si Green, traded from Cincinnati, was the only black to play in St. Louis at the time. (Chuck Cooper was a Hawk when the team was in

Milwaukee.) The city was not integrated, and we relied on Ted Savage of the St. Louis Cardinals and his friends, Bill Baldwin and Levester Cannon, to ease our visits. Until Marty Blake convinced the Sheraton Jefferson to put us up, we could not stay in any downtown hotels. We still could not eat in any of the restaurants, so we had to settle for room service or go across the tracks to the black-owned restaurants.

I was just as proud when Terri graduated one year after I did (Courtesy of Embry family)

The fans did not hesitate to express their biases, either. They were crazy about their Hawks, and they were hard on all the visitors, but they took extra pains to taunt the black players, especially if one mistreated Pettit or Hagan. Kiel Auditorium was another place you had to almost literally fight your way through the crowd to the elevator that took you to the locker room.

That was The League in 1958–59. Although we often lost, I was learning how to be a pro, both on and off the court. I improved as a player and grew as a person. Coming from a very sheltered existence in Springfield, Ohio, I had never been exposed to big cities like New York, Boston, and Philadelphia. I was exposed to new culture, new arts, and new people. Considering I had not traveled out of Ohio except to play games in Kentucky, Michigan, West Virginia, and North Carolina, I thought I learned the ropes rather quickly.

I learned I had to get a lot better as a player if I was going to contribute to a winning team. I learned Jack Twyman was not only a great player but a great mentor who knew all the tricks of surviving in the NBA. When we grew tired of Tad's, we looked for friends and relatives who would trade a home-cooked meal for tickets. I learned never to sit in the middle of the backseat in a taxi. That person was always the last one out and got stuck paying the bill.

The main thing I learned was that I had much more to learn. I respected the players in The League, and I knew I had to get tougher, both mentally and physically. I wished the Lakers would move out of Minneapolis, and I wished Walter Dukes would do something about those elbows.

But I did not just want to survive The League. I wanted to make a difference. Now that I knew how good I had to be and how much work I had to do to get there, I needed to spend time in the gym over the summer. But I also needed a job, because Terri and I planned to marry in June.

Mr. Woods, owner of the Royals, had mentioned selling insurance in the off-season, which meant taking an exam. But Pepper had a different idea. He offered Larry Staverman and me jobs selling season tickets for the team. At first, I was not real keen on working for the team in the off-season, but I needed the money and I realized that if I helped the team increase its revenues I had a better shot at getting a raise on my new contract. Not only would I help make money for the Royals, but I saved them money because they did not have to hire a real sales staff. Furthermore, it would allow me to network with the business community, which could not hurt in the long run, and it did not hurt to let the ticket holders get to know the players they were supporting. So Larry and I agreed to work for the club for $100 a week, plus commissions and gas.

It was difficult to create a positive sales campaign considering our record, and we were not nearly as popular as the University of Cincinnati team, which featured the great Oscar Robertson, or Xavier University. Making cold calls and being rejected constantly was not much fun. I got a list of Miami alumni and thought maybe they would support one of their own, but I was not having much luck there, either.

Finally, we came up with a different approach. Tickets were hard to come by at UC, and the games were not televised. Oscar was going to be a senior, which meant he was a year away from playing for the Royals, thanks to the territorial draft. UC also had several great recruiting classes, attracting George Wilson, the best player ever to play high school basketball in Chicago, as well as Tom Thacker and Ralph Davis, each of whom would follow Oscar to the Royals. Miami, Xavier, and Dayton had good teams, and Jerry Lucas, who may have been the greatest high school player in the state of Ohio, was at Ohio State. So Larry and I got smart and started selling the future: Buy seats now to guarantee your spot for the 1960–61 season. It actually worked.

We were continuing our nightly workouts at UC, and the Big O still dominated. I never told him he was part of our marketing campaign for fear that he would want my commissions. It was too bad we could not sell tickets to those workouts, because they would have been worth the price of admission. As it was, the curious fans who filled the stands got quite a show.

All the basketball stuff came second that summer, though, because Terri and I were married on June 6. Her family loved me, although her grandmother was not sure how I was going to take care of Terri without a real job. We spent our honeymoon in New York, enjoying the theater and fine dining as a guest of our good friend Ed Mosler. We moved into an apartment in Oxford. Terri continued school, and I commuted to Cincinnati to sell tickets and play basketball.

If Pepper was satisfied with our sales effort, he did not show it by his contract offer. Despite all my begging, I signed a nonguaranteed contract for $8,600, a $2,300 raise. I tried convincing him that I deserved combat pay or a special bonus for each time we played Detroit, but he did not buy it. He would have understood it better if he had ever been on the receiving end of one of Dukes' elbows. Even Grandmother Jackson could see how hard I was working if she took in a Pistons' game.

We returned to Lockbourne again in September with pretty much the same team. Bob Boozer was our first draft pick, but he decided to play in the AAU league, which allowed him to play on the 1960 Olympic team. We had added Phil Jordan, a six-foot-ten-inch center from Whitworth College. Marshall wanted a bigger center, which meant that I was going to have to beat out Jordan. Bockhorn still intimidated the competition in the backcourt, and Twyman was shooting more than ever. We added veterans Win Wilfong, Med Park, and Phil Rollins. Piontek was gone.

It was hard for me to believe we could be worse than we were my rookie year, but we were. In 1959–60, we finished 19–56; The League had added three more games, and we lost them all. Twyman was our only star. He scored 59 in one game and finished the season averaging more than 31 points per game, second only to Wilt Chamberlain, who certainly lived up to his reputation by averaging more than 37 points and 27 rebounds as a rookie. Wilt was seven feet, two inches tall but relatively thin, and he took a lot of punishment from stronger opponents, including my old pal Walter Dukes.

I did not have as good a season, primarily because my minutes had been cut with the acquisition of Jordan. We shared the post position early in the season, but I knew I would eventually beat him out. I would always play against the Pistons, because Phil was afraid of Dukes. He would either foul out on purpose or refuse to play altogether.

I remember starting one game in Detroit and coming out for a rest after about eight minutes. Marshall put Jordan into the game, but I knew he was in no shape to play basketball against anyone that afternoon. Watching him getting dressed, we could tell he had been drinking. He was not in the game two minutes before referee Jim Duffy came over to the bench to tell Marshall he should take Jordan out before he got hurt. Marshall ignored Duff until Phil was fouled and went to the line to shoot the free throws. His fifteen-foot shot went about four feet. It was the craziest thing I had ever seen. Twyman, who was thoroughly disgusted, ushered him to the sidelines and told him to sit down.

That game aside, there was another reason I did not think Phil would be the center of the future for the Royals. He lacked that one ingredient essential for success in The League—heart. He was not an inside player because he did not like the punishment that accompanied the inside game. I do remember him squaring off with Woody Sauldsberry in a game against Philadelphia. Woody was a tough six-foot-seven-inch forward who feared no one. He also knew he had ample backup in Andy Johnson and Wilt. As Woody moved forward, Phil, who was of Native American descent, went into a tribal war dance. Woody took one look and fled to the locker room. The rest of us looked on in bewilderment.

Despite the comic relief such moments provided, losing was not fun. We convinced ourselves if we were going to lose, we had to lose with a purpose. We needed to try to improve and gain experience while awaiting the arrival of the Big O.

Oscar Robertson was a six-foot-five-inch, 210-pound guard who might have been the best basketball player I ever saw on any level. He was the 1956 Mr. Basketball in the state of Indiana, where he led Indianapolis's Crispus Attucks High School to an 87–6 record in his three seasons on the varsity. The team won its first state title in 1955 and followed it up with an undefeated season in 1956, the first undefeated season in the history of Indiana high school basketball. He averaged a record 28 points his senior year, and his career average of 24 points per game was another record. He had 38 points in the 1956 state tournament final against Lafayette Jefferson. At the University of Cincinnati, he led the Bears to a 79–9 record his three seasons on the varsity (freshmen were ineligible for the varsity back then), won three national scoring titles and was the NCAA's all-time leading scorer at the close of his career, averaging 33.8 points per game, which now ranks third in NCAA scoring history. He set fourteen NCAA records, was a three-time All-American and three-time college Player of the Year and co-captain of the 1960 U.S. Olympic team, which won the gold medal. There was no doubt he was going to help us.

If Oscar was the source of our hope, Maurice Stokes was the source of our inspiration. Although he was engaged in an extensive rehabilitation program, he had not made much progress and was still completely paralyzed. We visited often and were heartened by his smile and his promise to return. Hall of Famer Bobby Wanzer, our former coach who had also played with Stokes, believed Stokes would have been one of the top ten players of all time if the accident had not happened.

"Don't let the losing get you down, I'll be back soon," Maurie would tell us through a complicated communication process. We would recite the alphabet and when we got to the letter he wanted, he would grunt. In that painstakingly slow manner, he was able to spell out words and messages to us. After those visits, winning or losing did not seem quite so important anymore, and all of our troubles seemed trivial. I tried to visit at least once a week or more often if I felt I was losing my perspective. Here was a gifted athlete facing the biggest challenge of his life just to return to normalcy, and he never complained once. He never said, "Why me?" His attitude never failed to inspire me, and others, too. When Stokes died in 1970, New York Post columnist Milton Gross wrote, "Stokes lived as a symbol of the best that a man is, despite the terrible things which can happen to him. He was a beautiful man who believed that surrender was not the way, even though he couldn't walk, couldn't talk except agonizingly. And he laughed when he should have cried."

With my second season behind me, I looked toward the off-season with joy and a chance to spend time with our new baby, Deborah Lynn. Of course, now that my family was growing, it was even more important to make some money during the off-season. With Oscar set to join the team, it was much easier to sell season tickets. People were calling the office begging for someone to take their orders. Often, it was me, and I enjoyed the experience. I met a variety of professional and business people, and I learned something from each of them. I also got some insight as to how the front office functioned, which would come in handy later, even if I did not know that at the time.

Good days in Cincinnati with Oscar Robertson (left) and Coach Charley Wolf (center) (Courtesy of Embry family)

The summer seemed to fly by, and we headed to training camp knowing things were about to turn around for the Royals. Besides Oscar, Bob Boozer, another Olympian, joined what was now a veteran team. It became apparent quickly that we were much improved, although many other teams could make that same claim. Jerry West was joining Elgin Baylor and the Lakers, who had moved from frigid Minneapolis to sunny Los Angeles. Lenny Wilkens was going to St. Louis. Wilt, upset after getting pushed around by opposing centers, spent the summer in the weight room and added several pounds of muscle. He arguably became the strongest person ever to play in the NBA, and the added strength made him even more effective. Al Attles, a six-foot-one-inch brute, also joined the Warriors, which made them an intimidating team. The Celtics added defensive specialist Tom Sanders, and they were not about to concede, either.

Tom Marshall resigned as our coach and was replaced by Charley Wolf from Villa Madonna College in Covington, Kentucky. Charley lacked NBA experience, but it did not matter because Oscar made us a better team. His impact was felt immediately. He was much better than we thought. His big frame made it impossible for other point guards to play him, and off guards had their hands full, too. Even forwards and centers did not like matching up with him because of his strength.

We started the season by winning four in a row and six of the first nine before collapsing. We did win nine of our last sixteen, finishing the season 33–46, one game out of the play-offs. Naturally, we were all disappointed at not qualifying for post-season play, but we figured this would be the last time that would happen. The Celtics beat the Hawks, 4–1, for the NBA title, and Wilt led The League in scoring, averaging more than 38 points per game, and rebounding, with more than 27 per game.

Oscar was Rookie of the Year and first-team All-NBA, and he averaged almost a triple double (double digits in points, rebounds, and assists) with more than 30 points, 10 rebounds, and almost 10 assists per game. He also was the MVP in the All-Star Game. Jack Twyman continued his fine play and was fifth in The League in scoring. For the first time, I made the All-Star team, too.

But I knew our success was because of Oscar. The most telling attribute of a great player is how he affects winning. It is not just his statistics, but how he makes his teammates better. There was no question, Oscar made us all better. He was a great passer and very unselfish. If you were open for a better shot, you got the ball. But you had better not blow it, because he would let you know in no uncertain terms that you let him down. He would either let you have it verbally with a barrage of expletives or give you that famous look of disgust and roll his eyes. His greatness inspired the rest of us to strive to become better. He raised the bar. Even though he had the ability to dominate a game, he encouraged all of us because he knew we all had to be effective for us to be a truly good team.

Oscar and I were roommates and we spent a lot of time with Boozer, especially on the road, where we searched for places that would serve us or for friends to take care of us. Oscar and I had much in common. He grew up in rural Tennessee before moving to Indianapolis. We had similar personalities, shared the same values, and liked the same foods. He loved to needle guys, especially Boozer. Bob had a wide variety of quirks, most of them relating to his car.

The major difference between Oscar and me was that he loved to watch television and watched it late into the night while I liked to sleep. Nothing interfered with my sleep. This annoyed Oscar sometimes when he wanted to talk.

I also got some insight into what made him so great. He would often bring a ball with him to bed, and he would practice shooting the ball into the air.

"Big Fella, you've got to make sure you've got a perfect release if you want to be a good shooter," he would tell me, spinning the ball off his finger tips.

I wondered if he was trying to tell me something. Not that he had to. I knew I had to become a better shooter because Russell and Wilt were eating me up inside. I was going to have to learn to play outside and shoot facing the basket. I knew I had to get stronger, too, after going against Wilt all season. I knew this was going to be a long, hard summer. My work was cut out for me.

Chapter 6

An Era of Change

The 1960s were an important time for our country, as well as our league.

The young and dashing John Fitzgerald Kennedy had been elected president, and we would put a man on the moon, but tensions were growing on a number of fronts. We were worried about Vietnam and the Cold War overseas, the Cuban Missile Crisis and the Civil Rights movement closer to home.

Dr. Martin Luther King Jr., Ralph Abernathy, James Lowery, and Malcolm X became familiar names in the news as they organized sit-ins and marches in the South to protest the discrimination that existed in our country.

Even The League was not exempt. Though the number of black players was growing, there was the perception that there could not be more than three per team and that less talented white players were paid more.

Still, there was an air of change as we embarked upon the 1961–62 season. Owners had survived the 1950s on a shoestring, but the influx of new stars like Oscar and Jerry West brought more stability to The League. That was certainly the case on our team.

I had worked out hard all summer, and with Terri expecting our second child, I had taken a job as a marketing representative doing promotional work with Coca-Cola. I actually had an offer of $7,500 to play football for the New York Giants, but I turned it down. I thought big things were in store for the Royals, and two weeks after Jill Mari was born, I left for training camp.

Adrian Smith, who had been on the 1960 Olympic team with Oscar and Bob Boozer, was out of the army and joined us that season, and we began to mature as a team. Though we played only .500 ball most of the season, we won nine of our last thirteen games to make the play-offs after a three-year absence. Oscar continued his brilliant play by doing something no one else had ever done: He averaged a triple double for the season—30.8 points, 12.5 rebounds, and 11.4 assists per game. Twyman averaged 22.5 points per game, and I improved to 19.8 points and 12.0 rebounds a game. I thanked Big O for my improvement, which netted me a second All-Star berth.

We had perfected the most effective pick-and-roll play in the game. I used my wide body to set jarring picks for Oscar, and he was either free for a wide open jump shot or I was free to roll to the basket if the defense switched onto him. Because he was such a great passer, Oscar would either zip a pass through the defenders or throw the ball up near the rim. I knew I had better go up and get it or I would get the evil eye from him. When defenses adjusted to stop our two-man game, Oscar would find someone else open on the weak side.

We did not last long in the play-offs, losing to a bigger Detroit team in four games of the best-of-five series. But we established ourselves as a team to be dealt with in the future. We got a taste of the play-offs, and experiencing that for the first time made us determined to return. The play-off competition, we learned, was much more intense, but that made it much more fun, too. We might not have been ready to dethrone the Celtics at that point, but no one else was either, and they won their fourth straight championship, beating the Lakers in seven games.

At the end of the season, The League approved divisional realignment, moving us into the Eastern Division with Boston, Syracuse, and New York. The Warriors moved from Philadelphia to San Francisco, which made all the players happy. Fisherman's Wharf, Chinatown and, especially, North Beach were a welcome change. Teams now spent at least a week in sunny California, playing two games in Los Angeles and two up north, which was a nice break from the snow and cold at home. The expansion Chicago Zephyrs also joined The League.

I was happy to see Wilt make the move West, because that meant the only true superstar center in the East was Russell. Syracuse was still a contender, but Dolph Schayes, Johnny Kerr, and Larry Costello were aging, and we felt as if we were gaining on them. With Oscar and Twyman leading the way, we won our last four games to finish the 1962–63 season with a 42–38 record.

We still were the underdogs as we ventured to Syracuse to open the play-offs, but we split the first four games, setting up a Game 5 showdown in Syracuse in what would prove to be the final NBA game played there. We won in overtime, and then had to fight our way through a hostile crowd to the locker room. I got sucker-punched in the head by a middle-aged man half my size. I was too stunned to even think about retaliating. I just could not believe people would come down out of the stands to relieve their frustrations, but the fans were almost as tough as Kerr, Alex Hannum, and Lee Shafer had been in the game. One fight had broken out during play, and Alex charged off the bench yelling at me, "You big bear. You big bear." I just told him to get back to the bench.

We survived only to move on to the challenge of facing the defending champion Celtics, who had beaten us nine times in twelve close regular-season meetings. But we got their attention right off the bat by winning the first game in Boston. Of course, they came back and beat us on our home court the next night, but we kept trading road victories and so we came back to Cincinnati, leading three games to two, and had a chance to pull off a major upset. Because of a scheduling conflict in the Cincinnati Gardens, we had to play Game 6 at the Xavier University Fieldhouse. We lost and headed back to Boston for the deciding Game 7, hoping against hope that we would tire out the older Celtics.

The Celtics feared us, because they knew Oscar would be ready. Sam Jones was so nervous he walked the streets of Boston all afternoon. In the end, the Celtics were up to the challenge, beating us, 142–137. Sam Jones bested Oscar in an old-fashioned shootout, 47–43.

Although the season ended on a disappointing note, we thought we had something to build on. Plus, we had the territorial rights to another All-American and Olympian, Jerry Lucas, the very same Jerry Lucas we had discovered on the playgrounds in Middletown during the summers, and who went on to star at Ohio State.

Wayne Jr. was born later that month, easing the pain of getting bumped from the play-offs. In addition, I drew strength from my visits with Maurie, who continued to work so hard on his rehabilitation despite the fact that he was making little progress. After months and months, he could feed himself, but he could not talk. Of course, that did not keep us from taking him to the Stokes benefit game at The Kutsher's Resort in the Catskill Mountains. Jack made arrangements to use a private plane owned by Dayton friend and businessman Milt Cantor to fly Maurie to the game, which featured many of the players he should have been facing. It was an ordeal getting him from the ambulance to the plane, and it took six of us to lift his 280 pounds. But all the bumping and banging getting him on and of the plane was worth it as we saw his face light up watching us playing the game he loved. We could not help but wonder how good we would have been with him in our lineup.

There was much going on besides basketball in the summer of 1963. The march on Washington and Dr. King's "I Have a Dream" speech electrified the civil rights movement and spurred the freedom marches in the South. Much to the dismay of many white owners, we joined the protests when we could. But we still thought the best way to narrow the gap between the races was to demonstrate how blacks and whites could work together to achieve a common goal. For us, sports provided that opportunity.

Much to our surprise, Charley Wolf resigned as coach and was replaced by Jack McMahon, a veteran NBA player who was a guard on the Hawks' championship team. It took him only two weeks to realize he was coaching a special team. Lucas was every bit as good as his reputation, and he was joining a lineup that was among the best in The League and was poised to challenge the Celtics and the new Philadelphia 76ers, who had been the Syracuse Nationals.

Not only did we have great chemistry on the court, but we also got along great off the court. Most of our travel time was spent playing bridge in the airports, on the planes, and in the hotels. Play-by-play announcer Ed Kennedy and I claimed bragging rights, but the partners of Jack and Oscar and Lucas and Bud Olsen put up a good fight. Lucas also liked to impress onlookers with his ability to recite portions of the phone book after a quick glance. He had other skills besides his photographic memory and he loved to entertain us with his tricks.

Adjusting to Lucas and our new coach, we started the season slowly, straddling the .500 mark through the first month of the season. We also were distracted by the goings-on in our society, including our increasing involvement in Vietnam and the struggles of the freedom marchers.

On November 22, 1963, we had a home game scheduled against the Celtics. I picked up Russell from his hotel to take him to my tailor, Tom Simon, in downtown Cincinnati before bringing him out to our house for dinner. We stopped at Simon's office, and while we were there a secretary opened the door and, fighting back tears, told us President Kennedy had been shot in Dallas. With our hearts in our throats, we turned on the television to watch the news. Not a word was spoken for a long, long time. The silence grew deeper with the announcement of the president's death.

How could this happen? Amid our prayers for the president's family, we wondered about the future of our society. John Fitzgerald Kennedy had offered so much hope for bringing our country together, and we were not sure Lyndon Johnson, a Texan, would carry the torch.

Our game that night was postponed, but the schedule resumed the next day, despite the fact that we were mourning just like the rest of the country. At least we were somewhat comforted by the fact that we were coming together as a team. In fact, by the All-Star break, we were 30–15. Oscar, Lucas, and I had been selected to play in the 1964 All-Star Game in Boston. I was especially looking forward to it, since illness had kept me out the previous year.

We beat the Pistons at home before a sparse crowd on a Sunday evening. One of the worst snowstorms in history hit the East Coast that weekend, making travel uncertain. It even took me hours to get our babysitter home, and I got a flat tire in the process. Once I finally walked in the door at 3:00 A.M., I felt the full force of Terri's wrath, which was almost as bad as the storm. Then she informed me instead of leaving at 10:00 A.M., Jerry, Oscar, and I had to leave at 7 A.M. because the airport in Boston was closed. We had been rerouted through Minneapolis—which I found highly ironic—but once we arrived in Minnesota, we found that the airports in the East were still closed. In fact, there was concern that Tuesday's game would be canceled because of the weather. None of us wanted that. But we also were supposed to be meeting Monday evening with Larry Fleisher, a New York lawyer who wanted to talk to us about getting the owners to recognize our union and improve our benefits.

Well, the three of us spent Monday night in Minneapolis and on Tuesday morning we flew to Washington. When the Boston airport still was not open by noon, we took the train north, arriving at 5 P.M., three hours before tipoff. Union president Tommy Heinsohn met us in the lobby of the Park Plaza Hotel and informed us that the players were meeting in the Celtics locker room to discuss what had transpired in our absence.

"The agenda is very short," he told us. "Some of us have been negotiating with the owners for a players' pension plan, and we're going to take a vote on whether we should play tonight if the owners won't commit to address our demands."

We three weary travelers just looked at each other. We did not know it at the time, but the next few hours would be a critical time for the future of The League.

As it turned out, it was the most important pre-game meeting in the history of the NBA.

At 6 P.M., two hours before tipoff of the nationally televised All-Star Game on January 14, 1964, twenty-four players in the uniforms of their respective teams came together as one in the crowded Celtics locker room.

Heinsohn stood to speak. "We have not made any progress with the owners," he said. "What do you want to do?"

Most of us were worried about what would happen if we did not play. If the owners refused to budge, we would be out more than pensions if we went on strike. Our jobs would be on the line, and none of us could afford not to get paid. The networks would never televise another game. The League could be in jeopardy.

In the tense ninety minutes that followed, Heinsohn and Fleischer negotiated with Commissioner Walter Kennedy and Celtics owner Walter Brown. Heinsohn would give us periodic updates as we anxiously awaited any news. At 7:30, there was no movement. We took a strike vote: It was 22–2 to strike. Lenny Chappell and Wilt were the dissenters. Fear was the reason. Lenny was afraid he would get cut, and Wilt was afraid The League would not survive.

When Kennedy was informed, he stormed through the locker-room door. He was sweating profusely and his face was beet-red as he yelled, "You sons of bitches. You had better play this game or else."

We tried to look as if we did not care at all, but our insides were in knots. Still, there were some pretty good poker players in that room, and it was a matter of bluffing and waiting . . . and waiting . . . and waiting. The Commissioner left the room for another caucus with his owners. We sat and waited some more—and tried to figure out Wilt.

At 7:55 the Commissioner came through the door. He looked like a man who had been through hell. "The owners have agreed to a pension for you guys," he said. "Now get your asses out there and play ball."

It was the biggest victory any of us had ever celebrated. So great was the relief that, with no warm-up, we treated the puzzled crowd to one of the greatest games ever, with the East winning, 111–107. Oscar scored 26 points to win the MVP. I was in the game at the end, grabbed the last rebound, and dribbled out the clock. On the way back to the hotel, I passed through North Station and was booed by a crowd of obnoxious fans, who informed me that by dribbling out the clock instead of trying to score, the East failed to cover the spread.

Whatever they lost on the game was nothing compared to what we might have lost had the owners not met our demands. Even so, most of us anticipated some sort of reprimand from our owners when we got home, although Pepper Wilson just told us we were nuts and that The League could not afford a pension plan.

We went right back to business on the court and won twelve straight games in February to push our record twenty games over .500. The League and the fans were taking notice. We were playing to near capacity crowds at home, and expectations had risen to such a level that we were favored to win the East. We won fifty-five games, finishing four games behind the Celtics, but we beat Boston in seven of twelve matchups.

As so often happens, the play-offs were a different story. We beat the Sixers, three games to two, but the Celtics blitzed us, four games to one, en route to their sixth straight championship. All we could do was marvel at their dynasty. They always seemed to rise to the occasion in the play-offs. It did not matter how they performed during the regular season, they always played at a different level in the post-season. Three or four of their players would be wearing bandages, giving the impression they were hurt or injured in some way. But that never mattered during the play-offs. They played like they were kids again.

Despite our play-off failures, Oscar was named the Most Valuable Player again after nearly averaging a triple double—31.4 points per game (second in The League), 9.9 rebounds, and 11.9 assists. Jerry Lucas was the Rookie of the Year and second team All-NBA. With these two superstars, the future seemed bright, even with an aging Twyman. Once again, I could not help but wonder how good we would be if Maurice Stokes had been able to play. The territorial draft was good to us again, as we added George Wilson and Tom Thacker, two of the stars on the University of Cincinnati's NCAA championship team. We continued our usual off-season preparation knowing we would eventually overcome the Celtics.

But then something happened we had not foreseen: Wilt was traded back to Philadelphia. Now both conferences had three tough teams—Boston, Philadelphia, and Cincinnati in the East and the Lakers, St. Louis, and Baltimore (formerly the Chicago Zephyrs) in the West.

I was the captain of the Royals again, as I had been since the 1961–62 season, and I sensed some friction between my teammates. Midway through the season, I found out I was right. Oscar angrily approached me after a game.

"Do you know what Mac (Coach McMahon) said to me?" he asked. "They want me to pass the ball more. Can you believe that?"

I did my best to calm him down by telling him I would talk to the coach. But, in reality, I could not believe it. After all, he was averaging 12 assists a game, so he had to be throwing the ball to somebody. He was one of the most unselfish players in the game, and he always played to win, which meant he gave the ball to the open man or to the guy with the hot hand. Why, just ask Bockhorn, who knocked down 13 straight shots one night, many of them off feeds from Oscar.

On the other hand, Luke was very conscious of his stats. Every time a player flung up a shot at the end of a quarter, Luke would chase down the rebound as it rolled on the floor and then go to the scorer's table to make sure it was recorded as an individual and not a team rebound. Once in a game against the Sixers, he shouted to me to block out his man so he could get more rebounds. In other words, he was asking me to block out a 350-pound Wilt Chamberlain and a 270-pound Luke Jackson.

"Jerry, I can't block out 600 pounds of muscle so you can boost your rebounding average," I yelled back. "Damn your stats. Let's just worry about winning the game."

I did not like what was happening with our team. The internal feuding was undermining our hopes of beating the Celtics in the play-offs.

It was crucial that we made our run this year, because Twyman was contemplating retirement, and I was beginning to feel the wear and tear on my knees. The tendinitis was so bad that I had to take shots of cortisone every two weeks, which made me less effective.

But perhaps it should not have been surprising that what was going on in the country was spilling over into our teams. As much as we tried to foster a sense of teamwork and dependency on each other, it was only natural that, given the heightened focus on race relations, problems should crop up. More and more black players were being signed to play in The League, which did not always sit well with some fans in some cities. Much of white America was nervous and upset about the growing number of protests in many of the major cities in our country, North and South. The marches in the South were all over television, and the country watched as blacks were beaten or dispersed by whites spraying them with fire hoses. President Johnson sent a Civil Rights bill to Congress, but Southern politicians tied it up with filibusters. Black leaders were becoming more vocal in the fight for equality. Jails throughout the country were filling with Civil Rights protesters, both black and white. White America began to show contempt. The passage of the Civil Rights Act did not help in that regard, nor did it appease blacks.

As black players, we were sympathetic to what was going on, and we often talked about the situation amongst ourselves and with other players in The League. But management encouraged us not to get involved for fear that attendance would drop. In fact, owners became even more sensitive to the composition of teams, except in Boston, of all places, where Red Auerbach started five black players. Of course, since there were no black owners, general managers, or coaches, there really was no one in a position of authority who could understand our position.

Although we were not able to be as active as we would have liked, there were no such restrictions on our wives. Oscar and I were in our hotel room in Philadelphia, watching the evening news on March 20, 1964, when the telephone rang. I answered it. Terri was on the other end. "Yvonne and I are going to Selma to join Dr. King's march to

Montgomery," my wife told me. "Don't tell Oscar. Yvonne will call him as soon as we get off the phone."

I could not help myself. "Are you crazy?" I asked her. "Have you been watching the news?"

She assured me she had and that, in fact, that was precisely why she wanted to join the protest.

"We are going," she said firmly. "We'll be all right."

I hung up, and told Oscar to expect a call from his wife. Before the words were out of my mouth, the phone rang again.

"Okay, Yvonne," were the only words I heard him say.

Though we admired their courage, we were worried. We could not keep from thinking about "Bloody Sunday" on March 7, when troopers beat demonstrators with clubs and hoses. This march, from Selma to Montgomery, was to protest the fact that blacks were denied the right to vote in Alabama and throughout the South, and it had the potential to spawn the same sort of violence.

The next day we traveled to Boston to finish the season. As was our custom, Oscar and I went to the Russells' for our pre-game meal. But when we got there, we sat in the den with our eyes glued to the television set, watching for news of our wives and the march.

The coverage did nothing to allay our fears. In fact, it confirmed our worries. We saw thousands of determined blacks and whites orderly marching down Route 80, which was lined by armed National Guard units. There appeared to be an equal number of whites throwing rocks and sticks and anything else they could get their hands on.

Somehow we managed to drag ourselves away from the television and head to the arena, where, not surprisingly, we were distracted and lost to the Celtics. When we got back to the hotel, we got a call from our wives, but instead of calming us, it only served to further worry us. They could not talk, they said, because they were at a pay phone in a dangerous area. All they told us was that they were due to return to the Cincinnati airport shortly after we were to land.

That was one night I stayed up to watch television with Oscar. We were saddened to learn that Viola Liuzzo, a white civil rights activist from Detroit, was killed by a sniper's bullet on her way back from the march. We knew we would not rest until our wives were safely back home.

It was a long wait at the airport the next day until their chartered DC-3 landed and two familiar but weary faces appeared on the jetway. Although visibly exhausted, both mentally and physically, they were eager to tell us about the horrible experience. They told us they had walked hand-in-hand singing verses from "We Shall Overcome" and other spiritual songs while the angry mobs shouted racial epithets and threw things at them. They had to lie flat under blankets in the back of a truck in order to get to the airport safely. Both said the experience changed their lives because they had never been exposed to that kind of violence or hatred.

With that as a backdrop, somehow basketball just did not seem quite as important. That was just as well, since we finished the 1964–65 season 48–32 (not as good as last season) and lost to Wilt and the Sixers in four games in the first round of the play-offs.

It had been a disappointing year. With four All-Stars in Oscar, Lucas, Twyman, and me and our other talented veterans, we had been picked to dethrone the Celtics, but the chemistry was not what it should have been and we played like a team in turmoil. Despite my attempts as captain to bring unity, cliques developed and the rift between Oscar and Lucas was apparent. There would be many great examples of superstars who got along on teams—Cousy and Russell in Boston, for example—but there remained friction between our two superstars.

Both were great players who had led their teams to victory at every level. Both were proud, fierce competitors. But they came from different backgrounds, and Oscar and I and the other black players felt that management and the coach desperately tried to make it Lucas's team for marketing purposes. Instead, management and marketing destroyed us, although that certainly was not the first nor the last time that would happen.

Why did they have to turn it into a black-and-white issue? I do not believe the players viewed it that way. We just wanted to win and hoped our contributions would be acknowledged. We thought we could make a difference in how blacks were perceived and serve as an example of how blacks and whites could get along and accomplish a common goal. If they had just left it up to us, we would have succeeded.

Lucas was a great player at every level, and we respected his ability. Oscar may have been the best player ever to play the game, and he was extremely proud. Ordering him to look for Lucas to enhance our performance was the wrong thing to do. Lucas did not need anyone to help him be great, and Oscar did not need anyone to tell him how to play the game. In a time when black leaders were preaching to us to be proud of our heritage and fight for equality, any blatant attempts to suppress our efforts were regarded as being insensitive.

Like all black players in the 1960s, Oscar was driven to be the best. This was the only way we thought we would be accepted. Late in the 1965–66 season, I recall being in New York for a game with the Knicks. I woke up from my pre-game nap to find Big O sitting at the desk with a pen, a pad of paper, and the New York Post opened to the sports page.

"Big Fella, I know they want Jerry West to outscore me again this season," he said, figuring out exactly what he would have to average the rest of the season in order to prevent that from happening. He looked over at me and smiled. "Set some good picks tonight."

He and West had become friends when they played on the 1960 Olympic team, but they were intense rivals. Oscar went out and scored 48 that night and wound up averaging 31.3 points that season, tying West for second place behind Wilt's 33.5.

Despite that, and the fact that Oscar and Lucas were first team All-NBA and Adrian Smith was the MVP of the All-Star Game, we failed as a team, losing in five games in the first round to the same Celtics we were supposed to beat.

The dissension had continued, and management lost confidence in my ability to compete against Russell and Wilt. They thought I was too small at six feet, eight inches. They tried to find a replacement for me, through a trade or the draft, but were unable to do so. No player they brought in could survive the punishment I dished out during training camp. They did acquire Connie Dierking in a trade, and we split time at center, but neither of us was very effective. Twyman had come back for one more season, but his age was showing. Injuries forced Arlen Bockhorn into retirement, and his toughness and defense was missed. After years of facing players so much bigger, my knees were aching more and more and my body started to break down. In addition, I was not having much fun. I was having a terrible season as a player and as the captain as our chemistry was even worse. There was more friction between newcomer Happy Hairston, a fine rebounder, and the rest of the team. I think we set a record for team meetings, but we never were able to resolve the social issues that plagued our team. When the season ended prematurely again at the hands of our nemesis, there were many, many questions that accompanied the loss.

I was not going to be around to search for the answers. I decided to retire and pursue a career with Pepsi-Cola as a regional marketing representative.

I was ready to start my life after basketball, but I was not sure I was adequately prepared to meet the challenge. I had competed for most of my adult life, and I figured I could be competitive in my new world. I just had to convince consumers that Pepsi tasted better than Coke. I was excited about the challenge. Since my days at Miami, I had tried to dispel the "dumb jock" label and prove I could be successful at things other than sports.

Though I was not playing any more, I still traveled quite a bit. I was assigned to the Midwest, but I made frequent trips to New York to meet with the corporate vice president of marketing. The whole notion of marketing fascinated me. I wanted to learn what made the consumer choose one brand over another.

Even in my new life, I kept in touch with my teammates and continued to visit Maurie, who had not made much progress. Still, seeing him kept me grounded, and attending the funerals of friends who had died in Vietnam made me realize how fortunate I had been.

Growing up on The Hill, I was too young to understand the meaning of war, even though two of my uncles, Lew Minny and Woody Hood, served in Europe during World War II. I was four years old when the Japanese bombed Pearl Harbor and seven when the liberation of France began with the D-Day invasion. Now that I was older, I still was not sure why we were sending our best and brightest to the battlefields of Vietnam. Surely, it did not seem right to be doing something we loved, like playing basketball, while our friends were off in an unknown country fighting a war none of us understood. I kept thinking that if the marines had not rejected me for being too tall, I would have been right there fighting alongside many of my classmates.

Instead, I was at home attending funerals for boys like Ronnie Jones, a high school track star who had just graduated and gone to work at Dino's, one of my favorite clothing stores. Ken and Evelyn Jones were good friends of ours, and we shared the same concerns about what was going on at home and abroad. Our concerns were heightened when Ronnie announced he was joining the army instead of attending the University of Cincinnati. He wrote letters telling us not to worry and talking about how proud he was to be serving our country. Several months later, the Joneses received the call telling them that Ronnie had been killed while on patrol in the jungles of Vietnam. Not long after that, we learned of the death of Lieutenant Walt Williams, an outstanding football player at UC who had played basketball with us during the summer. Although he had been drafted by the NFL, he had to fulfill his ROTC requirement by serving two years on active duty in the army.

There was trouble closer to home, too. Later that summer, Terri got a phone call about a riot developing in nearby Avondale. Despite pleas from me and our neighbor, Leonard Smith, she bolted out the door in an effort to try to work to calm the situation. She did not return until late that night, by which time I was nearly paralyzed with fear for her safety. News bulletins on television reported that black youngsters were throwing rocks and fire bombs at passing white motorists. I knew that if the police were called, they would be on the lookout for all blacks. They were not going to distinguish between the peacemakers and the troublemakers.

With all that going on, basketball had taken a backseat—although I wished I could find some way the ideals it embodied (teamwork, unity, working toward a common goal) could be used to bring our country together. All of the protests were going to either unite us or completely rip our country apart. Civil unrest was spreading to every major city in America, and antiwar demonstrators were becoming more hostile.

As concerned as I was, I remained on the sidelines; Terri was the activist in our family. I was still hoping some team would pick me up, and I knew becoming active in the Civil Rights movement would not help my chances of signing with a new team. So I pursued my new career in business and played basketball when I could. I realized I had not really lost any of my passion for the game, and I was starting to have some second thoughts about my future in the business world. I had a hard time accepting the fact that no team could find a place for me.

Chapter 7

The Chance to Be a Champion

Late in July 1966, I got a call from my friend and former nemesis, Bill Russell, who invited me to play golf with him while at the annual Maurice Stokes benefit game in August in the Catskill Mountains. He told me he wanted to discuss something with me.

When I arrived at The Kutsher's Resort, Bill was waiting for me in the lobby of the hotel. I thought it strange that it was just the two of us, but it was not long before I figured out what was going on.

After several holes of golf, Bill asked me if I was serious about retiring. Despite my fears, I insisted I was because it was a great opportunity for me to have a life after basketball. I could not help wondering why he was being so inquisitive, but then he got to the point.

Russ told me that Red Auerbach was retiring as coach and becoming general manager of the Celtics. Russ was going to take over as player-coach, becoming the first African American head coach in the NBA. He told me he needed a center to back him up and asked if I would be interested.

"Hell, no," I told him.

We debated for a while before he suggested that I talk to Red, who was waiting back at the hotel.

We finished our round of golf and went back to Red's room. Red told me he had made a trade for me and wanted me to sign a contract that afternoon. I told both of them that I had to talk to my family before I could make a decision. Red really started to pressure me for an answer. He asked all the right questions and said all the right things.

The one thing he said that stuck in my mind was, "You've had a great career, but you never played on a championship team. Now is your chance."

I asked him if he could guarantee that, fully realizing there were no guarantees in life. Even so, I knew history was on their side. I had read that Tommy Heinsohn had announced his retirement, along with a couple of other players. Russell convinced me that is why they needed me.

I returned to Cincinnati and discussed the idea with Terri. It was not well received. Terri had just started a job with a social service agency, and she did not want to move. So I told the Celtics no.

Later that evening, Bill called to talk to Terri. He had a way of charming people. Whatever he said to Terri worked, because when she hung up, she looked at me and told me to do whatever I wanted.

Red called shortly thereafter and we talked about money. He offered me $20,000. I told him I was going to make more than that with Pepsi. He reluctantly raised it to $25,000, and also mentioned the certainty of play-off money and a championship ring. I was sold, so I agreed.

It turned out to be one of the better decisions I had ever made. It gave me my first real chance to be a champion, a lifelong dream for anyone who plays sports. Our greatest Cincinnati teams could not beat the Celtics. Now I had a chance to join them instead.

I learned more than I could ever have imagined. I thought I knew the Celtics from playing against them so many times as an opponent. But it was different being on the inside. Being with Red and the Celtics was equivalent to getting a master's degree in social science, psychology, management, finance and history—all skills I would use later on in life.

Red was the dean, the patriarch. Owner Marvin Kratter made each of us rub a good luck stone during our warmups. That had no bearing on the outcome of games. Red did. Bill was important, but Red was in charge. Many people, including several former players and coaches, have written about this great dynasty, which epitomized what character meant to me.

First there was Arnold "Red" Auerbach. Red was the ultimate team builder. He was a master at managing people. He was a great motivator because he made an attempt to know and understand each person. He knew the needs of his players emotionally and mentally. He respected each player and his family and welcomed all of us to the Celtics. He had great compassion and created a family atmosphere.

He understood chemistry. He would take players who failed elsewhere and make them winners by restoring their confidence. There were a number of players who were cut from other teams who became stars and major contributors in Boston. He taught me things about people that were universal in nature, about qualities in people that all of us hold dear and close to our hearts to this very day. Red may not have been the best X-and-O coach. He ran only six plays, although there were options off those plays. But he believed if you competed, concentrated, and executed, you could win.

When I joined the Celtics, Red knew that my confidence had been destroyed. He told me, "I want you to do what you do best when you are on the court and don't try to be something that you are not." He went on to say that he would determine when and how my talents would be used. After every game, he came around and said something positive to each of us. He would find a way to compliment you whether you played five minutes or forty-five minutes. He made each of us feel as if we were important, as if we were all needed.

He never said a bad word about any of his players, regardless of ability. "You never know when you might need him," he would say.

Even though Bill was the coach, Red was always around to help or raise hell when necessary, although he seldom interfered. I do recall one particularly bad practice Red stormed in and ordered us to sit down. He really was furious. He proceeded to scold everyone, even Russell, which was a rarity. I was waiting for my turn, but I could not imagine why he would get on me. I had not played that much. He knew I was still struggling to regain my confidence, so he ripped me indirectly. He jumped all over the trainer, Joe Delauri, saying, "Look how fat you let Embry get. I want his ass in shape—and soon." I got the message at poor Joe's expense, and I realized Red was a master psychologist. He was feisty, but he also was a very caring person. He often asked about your family members and he always gave them big hugs when he saw them. The wives appreciated that he made them part of the team. One mark of a great leader is how those he touches fare in later life. A leader always leaves a piece of himself with them. Red certainly did that. He produced twenty-eight Hall of Famers during his tenure as coach and general manager of the Celtics. Red's greatest attribute—his ability to manage people—could apply to any business.

William Felton Russell was affectionally called "Russ." Some called him "The Lord." Sam Jones called him "Russh" or "Russell," never "Bill." Russ affected winning more than anyone who has ever played the game. He had a huge passion for winning. He will not be known as the best player, but if I were going to start a team, he would be the first player I would want. He was not a good shooter, but when the game was on the line he made shots. When the team needed a rebound, he got it. He will be remembered as the best shot blocker to play the game. Just call him a winner. He really enjoyed playing and wanted to be regarded as the best. When he was in college, his University of San Francisco teams won two NCAA championships. He was on a gold medal Olympic team, and he won eleven NBA championships in thirteen years. His greatest attribute was his intelligence. It was what allowed him to make the most of his abilities.

Making Russell the first black coach in the NBA was a bold move by Red, considering the civil unrest in Boston and the rest of the country. Russ accepted the challenge and, as in everything else he did, he wanted to excel. He struggled at first. He tried to be the great player that he was and also prove that he could coach. He wanted to do it all by himself, even though he had a veteran team. He became a much better coach after his first year. In his second year, he appealed to us to help him.

Although Sam Jones was a member of the NBA's 50 Greatest Players, he was still underrated. Sam possessed speed and quickness and he loved to compete. He hated to lose, whether you were playing cards, shooting pool, or bowling. He was a great shooter with a great first step. He was not only a jump shooter, but he also had mastered the two-handed set shot. Sam had a way of keeping the locker room loose. During one of Russell's redundant pre-game speeches—he gave the same speech every game for two years—he told Sam he wanted him to assert himself more as a leader on the court.

Sam told him he could not do that.

"Why not?" Russell wanted to know.

"Because I don't have any authority," Sam told him. He loved to mess with Russ.

Some called John Havlicek "Hondo" because he looked like John Wayne. Tom Thacker called him "Bomba." I called him "Perpetual Motion" because he never stopped running.

No matter what you called him, he was a great basketball player. A member of Ohio State's 1960 NCAA championship team, he was drafted by the Celtics and by the Cleveland Browns football team. In fact, he was one of the last cuts, beaten out by Chris Collins, who went on to become an All-Pro receiver. Fortunately for the Celtics, he decided to focus on basketball. He succeeded Frank Ramsey as the Celtics' fabled sixth man. It did not matter whether John started or came off the bench, he was one of the most productive players in the history of the game.

John will forever be remembered for the steal he made against the Sixers in the 1965 play-offs. Celtics fans will go to their graves hearing Johnny Most's gravelly voice screaming, "Havlicek stole the ball. Havlicek stole the ball. The Celtics win. The Celtics win."

John was an engaging person who made sure everyone felt a part of the team. On the road, he made sure we all shared time together, regardless of color or status. Because of changes in our society and culture, this is seldom seen today.

John knew I had been offered a contract to play for the New York

Giants of the NFL, so in order to satisfy his football craving and to keep me loose, we would hit as football players do before games, ramming our shoulders together.

Tom Thacker, otherwise known as "Doggie," was a key player on the 1962 and 1963 NCAA championship teams while at the University of Cincinnati, and he also was a former teammate of mine on the Royals. He was a role player at best in the pros. At six feet, five inches, he was neither a guard nor a forward. He was wiry strong with long arms. He was quick and could jump out of the gym. But he was only a fair shooter, which kept him from being a better pro. He was a very good defender, and this is what kept him in the NBA and the ABA. He is the answer to the basketball trivia question: Who is the only player to play on an NCAA, NBA, and ABA championship team? Tom played very little while a member of the Celtics, but he was considered an integral member of the team. He was a good practice player, and he was always ready when called upon in games.

Tom was a free spirit who drove Russell crazy with his carefree attitude. When Tom came to Boston, he was on a very strict budget. He did not have a car, and he often relied on teammates to pick him up and drop him off. When Red found this out, he offered to sell Tom an old compact car. After Tom got the car, he started being late for practice. One day, he arrived about twenty minutes into our warm-ups, and Russell went nuts. "Don't you have an alarm clock?" the coach yelled.

"Yeah, I got an alarm clock," Thacker yelled back. "But that lemon Red sold me won't go into reverse, so I have to find a parking spot I can pull into where no one will park in front of me."

Russ had no comeback for that one.

Another time we were in New York dressing for a game against the Knicks. Russell turned to Thacker and asked, "What were you doing walking around Times Square at 5 this morning?"

Thacker alertly responded, "How do you know I was up at 5?"

"I saw you," Russell said.

"Doesn't our curfew apply to you?" Thacker asked.

Russ did not answer, but he did not drop the subject, either.

"Did you get laid?" he asked. "Because if you did not, I'll have to fine you."

Thacker was not sure where this was going. Neither did the rest of us, but we were enjoying it nonetheless.

"Why would you ask me that?" Thacker, a bachelor, demanded.

"If you did not get laid," Russell told him, "I figure you were up all night trying and did not get any sleep. That's why I asked, and that's why I would have to fine you."

Before a key Sunday afternoon game in the 1968 play-offs, we were waiting for Russell to deliver his canned pre-game speech. We had lost the first two games in Philadelphia, so we were wondering if Russell might actually come up with a different speech. He did not, and when he got to Doggie, he started telling him what he wanted him to do when he got into the game. With the sun shining brightly through the windows, Doggie interrupted him and said, "If it rains one more day, I'm going to buy me a pair of goulashes." The whole place went up for grabs. Even Russell had to laugh. We often wondered if Doggie did that on purpose to loosen us up, because we did go on to win the game.

We called Bailey Howell "Bails." Sometimes we tried to imitate his accent and called him "Baaaaleeeehowwelll," all one word with a Southern drawl. Bailey was a perennial All-Star with the Detroit Pistons and a great player. We never could figure out how Red was able to get him. Not only could Bailey score, but he was a great rebounder, particularly on the offensive end. He never saw a rebound he did not like. In practice, we wanted to put a bell around his neck so we could tell where he was and get out of his way. He had no fear when he crashed the boards, and he ran over whoever got in his way.

Because Bailey was from Mississippi, the black players wondered how he would fit into the team. But he fit in great and was well-liked by all of us. Bails loved to get on Russell and Russ loved it when he did. There was one tense moment for Bailey. We had returned from a long trip and Russ needed a ride to his car, which was parked several miles from the airport. Bailey's wife, Mary Lou, and his daughters, Beth and Amy, came to pick up Bailey. Bails offered Russ a ride, and Russ settled himself into the backseat. As they started to drive away, Beth started to cry and asked her father, "Do I have to sit on the black man's lap?" Bails broke out into a cold sweat and told his daughter, "Beth, you hush your mouth."

Russ broke out into that cackle he called a laugh, and pretty soon everybody, including Beth, was laughing. Bailey loved to tell that story.

I roomed with Satch Sanders for a while, and he had some strange quirks when it came to hotel room security. In fact, he was downright obsessed with the fear of someone breaking into a room. He would lock all the locks on the door and then slide the desk in front of it to make sure no one could get in. If he could not move the furniture, he would tie a rope across the base of the door way to trip any intruder or set up other contraptions that would alert him to the presence of someone who should not be there. I will say this. No one ever did set foot into our room. Of course, walking through all the booby traps to the bathroom in the dark was a real adventure.

We called Larry Siegfield "Siggy" or "Siggy Darling." Siggy was another player no other team wanted. But Red liked his toughness and his knowledge of the game. Siggy played on the NCAA championship team with Havlicek at Ohio State. He was a tough, hard-nosed player. Although he was slow, he found a way to score, and he would knock your head off on defense. He was a winner.

But Siggy used to give Russ headaches. There were times during the season that Larry would come to Russ before a game and say, "I can't give it to you tonight, Russ." When Russell would ask why, Siggy would say, "Because." That was it. No other reason. What happened was that Siggy played so hard in practice and the games, there were times he just got burned out. Russ thought it was better Siggy did not play than play poorly.

Although we loved Siggy, he would occasionally annoy us. One time after we lost a game in Cincinnati, we were on Marvin Kratter's plane back to Boston. Russ and the owner played gin in the front of the cabin, while the rest of us sat in the rear of the cabin, reflecting on the fact that we were struggling and needed to turn things around. Each of us was critical of Russell's coaching and his play. Of course, we tried to be as quiet as possible for fear Bill would hear us. The next day at practice, we were still playing poorly. Not long after the start, Russ ordered us back downstairs. As we started to get undressed, he told us to sit down, shouting, "What in the hell is going on here?"

It got very quiet. No one uttered a word. All of a sudden, Siggy started repeating what each of us had said about Russell the night before: "Wayne, you were bitching about your playing time. Sam, you wanted more plays called for you. Bailey, you said Bill needed to get the lead out of his ass." He spared no one.

Russ got that pensive look on his face. He asked if anyone had anything else to say. By that time, everything already had been said. On the way to the showers, we vowed never to say anything when Siggy was around. But I will say this: Things started to turn around after that.

A similar situation came up later in the season. We were in San Diego, and things were going badly again, so Russell wanted to air things out. He asked us if we had anything to say. We all sat tight-lipped. Finally, Siggy started to say something, but he just stuttered and could not get it out.

Russell waited and then asked Siggy if he had said it yet. The whole room broke up. Once again, things got better after that.

Those were some of the players as I got to know them. Together, they sustained the great Celtic tradition, keeping the greatest basketball dynasty in the history of pro sports alive.

Certainly there were greats before us. There was Bob Cousy, who was one of the better ballhandlers of all time. He also was a great passer, particularly on the fast break. There was Tom Heinsohn, a fierce competitor who never met a shot he did not like. He had a wide assortment of shots, and he would take them from anywhere on the court. He shot hook shots from anywhere, but he will be best remembered for his slingshot jump shot. There was Jim Loscutoff, the enforcer who protected

Russell and the rest. Whenever a fight broke out, Loscutoff was there. At six feet, five inches and 255 pounds, he was extremely strong, and he loved a good fight. There was Frank Ramsey, the prankster, better known as instant offense. He was the sixth man on the early championship teams. He was six feet, five inches and played guard or forward. Through Ramsey, Red made the sixth man as important as the starters. Gene Conley was another member of the Celtics championship teams. He also was a great pitcher for the Milwaukee Braves and once decked Billy Martin when he charged the mound after Conley threw at his head. One punch and Martin was out. Bob Brannum was the original tough man.

I mention all these players because they were always around offering support. Heinsohn and Cousy became broadcasters, and the others attended most of the home games. These guys set the standard we had to live by. They were there to give us inspiration and tips on how to play certain players. They sometimes played the games from their seats.

I spoke of Conley and how he loved a fight. Even in his retirement, he felt compelled to assist when a fight broke out during a game. Once against our great rivals, the Sixers, a fight broke out between Siggy and Wali Jones. Both benches cleared, and to everyone's surprise, Conley left his seat well up in the stands to join in the brawl.

That was the atmosphere surrounding the Celtics—all for one and one for all. Now I was part of it.

My first experience as a Celtic was a memorable one. We were staying at the Lenox Hotel during training camp at Babson College in the fall of 1966. I knew I had my work cut out for me, because I had ballooned up to 285 pounds, thirty pounds over my playing weight. I always reported to camp in shape when I played in Cincinnati, but I would let myself go when I was planning to retire.

I wanted to make a good impression, so I knew I had to get in shape fast. I brought a rubber sweat suit to wear over my practice gear and a regular sweat suit.

With all my layers on, I joined the others who had arrived early to get in some extra work. We all wondered what Russell would be like as a coach. We wondered if he would try to emulate Red or whether he would try to establish his own identity.

It did not take us long to find out. All of a sudden, Russell appeared at the door to the gym. He was standing in his stocking feet. I had heard that Russ did not practice all the time, but I never dreamed he would miss his own first workout.

Apparently, that was not his plan.

"You sons of bitches are going to pay for the SOB who hid my sneakers," he screamed.

And we did. It was absolutely the most grueling practice of my entire career. We practiced for two and a half hours, nonstop, without a basketball. We did sprints. We ran laps. We did calisthenics. Then came more sprints and more laps until all of us were ready to drop.

My work station looked like Boston Harbor. Periodically throughout practice, I would lift the top of my sweat suit and the water just flowed out and created a huge puddle. After those two and a half hours, I went to the locker room, peeled off my clothes, and stood on the scale. I had lost twenty-eight pounds. I felt so weak I thought I was going to pass out. The trainer told me to drink some water, so I stood under the shower head and just let the water flow into my mouth.

I took my time getting dressed as we all tried to figure out who took Russell's sneakers. There were no confessions, for fear of retaliation. Siggy was the prime suspect, though he denies it to this day. Another theory was that Russell hid them so he would not have to go through what he was putting us through.

Somehow, we all made it back for the second practice that day. It was not nearly as hard, and Russ joined us this time.

As the week progressed, I began to appreciate why the Celtics were champions. There was complete focus and everyone was serious about his job. The words used most often were "execute" and "concentration." The plays were simple. There were only six, and it did not take long to learn them because I had played against them for eight years. Nothing had changed. The Celtic philosophy was that if you executed, the plays would work, even if the opponent knew them. Of course, there were options off the plays, which confused the opposition.

Within a few practices, I began to fit in with the rest of the team and started to acquire the same Celtic arrogance that I and the rest of The League had always hated. I started to feel the great mutual respect for each other and how each depended on the other on and off the court. They actually liked each other. No one was more appreciative of his teammates than Russell. He often says today how much he enjoyed the locker room. We were his extended family.

Bill also was establishing himself as a coach. He worked hard enough to get in shape but he also took time to observe what the rest of us were doing. Red was around, but he kept his distance. I was surprised.

The two-a-days were over, and we were to start our exhibition season, which included four intrasquad games. I was glad to have the opportunity to play against someone else. Playing against Russ every day was no joy.

Our first exhibition game was in Puerto Rico against Atlanta. My first trip with the Celtics started off badly. I overslept and missed the plane. It was not exactly the best way to impress my new coach, not to mention Red.

I had to make my own arrangements to get to Puerto Rico. I got a flight that would arrive shortly after the team's plane. I was pissed that I missed the plane, and I wondered what I was going to tell Russ. But I was in for a shock. When I boarded my plane, my assigned seat was right next to Red's. I never wanted to see that look on his face again. He asked what happened, and I told him the truth. Once he calmed down, I got a three-hour lesson on the Celtic lore. I started to think missing the plane might not have been the worst thing that could have happened to me, because I was learning so much from the master.

After the plane landed and we got to the hotel, his mood changed in a hurry and I saw his fiery temper up close. When Red got his room, he realized it was a regular room and not the suite he expected. When he asked what happened, he was told Russ got the suite because he was the coach. Red went berserk, but then he calmed down and accepted the room.

When we met to board the bus for the game, all hell broke loose. First, Russell chewed me out for missing the plane. That did not last long, though, because Red came along and screamed at Russ for taking the suite. Even the veteran Celtics said they had never heard Red yell like that. I was perfectly happy to let him go on, since it took the focus off me. But Russ settled the argument by reminding Red that the coach always got the suite on the road. It was another reminder of the change in Red's status, and he did not like hearing it.

Each day of being a Celtic became more enjoyable. The players were helpful in so many ways and made the newcomers feel part of the team. They made us feel as if we were important to winning another championship. Bailey was key, because he was to replace Heinsohn. He moved right into the starting lineup. I was there to be Russell's backup. Russ was accustomed to playing the entire forty-eight minutes. The only rest he would get during a game was in a timeout or, occasionally, on the offensive end of the court. Often he would not run the court after getting a rebound because the Celtic fast break was so efficient.

By the time the exhibition season was over, I felt as if I had been in Boston my entire career. I played a lot and began to get my confidence back. I played particularly well against Bill in the intrasquad games. So good that after our last practice before opening night, I suggested to Coach Russell that I had beaten him out as the starting center. Russ looked at me and broke out in his famous cackle.

"You will not start," he said.

"Why not?" I asked. "I clearly outplayed you."

"That doesn't matter," he said, "I am the coach."

I was not surprised, and I certainly was not displeased with the way things were going. My teammates became my family, because Terri had decided to stay in Cincinnati. She had a job she liked, and she wanted to make sure we were secure once basketball was over. I continued to stay at the Lenox Hotel. The rates were cheap, and it was convenient to the Cambridge YMCA, where we practiced, and to Boston Garden. That was my first home in Boston. I quickly learned my way around the city and was welcomed by the fans. There were many well-wishers and many who expressed their delight that I was there. I, too, was happy because I remembered, as an opponent, being booed by the very same people.

Johnny Most, the Celtics play-by-play announcer, had labeled me a dirty player when I was on the other side, but that changed when I started playing for the Celtics. He began referring to me as "Wayne the Wall." The nickname stuck with me my entire time in Boston. Wherever I went in Boston, that is what the fans called me. But the famed *Boston Globe* columnist Bob Ryan renamed me. Ryan loved the Celtics, and there is no one outside the Celtics who knows more about them than he does. In fact, he knows more than the current players ever will. After my retirement, as my weight went up, Ryan renamed me, "Wall to Wall."

The Celtics had few disciplines. Being on time was the one that was essential. We also had to wear a suit or coat and tie for all home games. Appearance was important. Red would insist that we look, act, and be like champions. We were to be at home games two hours before game time—and not a second later.

Our opening night game was against the San Francisco Warriors. I got to the Garden very early to make sure I would not be late for my Celtic debut in the fabled Boston Garden. A new state-of-the-art dressing room had been built with Celtic green carpeting and the shamrock in the middle, shiny wooden stalls, and a nice new bathroom and shower. It was quite different from the dingy dressing room we used before. The training room was twice the size. As you walked in the door, there was a plush coach's office. There had never been a coach's office before, and Russ loved it.

It was fitting that the office have a name and, in remembrance of the controversy over the hotel suite in Puerto Rico, which we later learned was the Ponce de Leon suite, we thought that would be the perfect name. I took a wide piece of tape from the training room, wrote "Ponce de Leon" in big letters and taped it on the office door. When Russell arrived, he saw the sign and yelled, "Who's the wise guy?" We all started to laugh, including Red. Thus the office had been christened, and I was about to start my first season as a Celtic.

My jersey number was 28. I had worn 15 in Cincinnati, but Heinsohn wore that number and it was to be retired. I had a feeling of accomplishment just slipping that jersey over my head. I felt like a champion even though I was not one yet.

There were so many stories about the Celtic myth. I wondered about the superstitions and rituals, and I was not entirely sure there was not a leprechaun that helped win all those championships. The first ritual I learned about was that every player had a designated place in line as we left the locker room, beginning with K. C. Jones and ending with Russell. I was assigned the eleventh spot. Russell was last because of his own pre-game ritual. He threw up before every game. No one ever knew why.

There was another ritual I knew nothing about. After we had started our pre-game warm-ups, Marvin Kratter, the proud new owner, came to courtside to insist we rub a polished stone. He said it would bring us luck. Not wanting to embarrass him, everybody rubbed the stone—except Russell. After the game, Kratter came into the locker room and asked Russ why he would not rub the stone.

Russell told him two things: The Celtics had won eight straight championships before Kratter and his stone came along, and the owner was not allowed in the locker room.

Kratter was outraged, and he left the locker room to look for Red. But Red backed Russell. Obviously, Kratter still was not pleased with Russell, so Red asked him, "Do you want me to trade him?"

That pretty much ended the discussion. Red was not going to trade Russell and he was not going to fire him as coach, so Kratter was going to have to learn to live with him.

So did we. Russ practiced very little. He did just enough to keep his timing in sync with the rest of the team. There were several reasons he did not practice. He was the best shot blocker in the game, and if he practiced the way he played, he disrupted things. We could not be hesitant to shoot in practice because that would carry over into games. We also were fierce competitors, and there was always the risk of his getting hurt. I like to think he did not like having to go against me every day. But Russ played forty-eight minutes a game. His body needed to recover. Nobody wanted Russ tired or hurt.

The players accepted the fact that Russ did not practice until the day Howie McHugh brought him coffee and doughnuts along with the newspapers. As we were out practicing hard, he sat drinking coffee and reading the papers.

After winning our first four games, we were to play the 76ers in Philadelphia. This matchup was one of the greatest rivalries in sports.

This game was always a classic because of the matchup between Russ and Wilt Chamberlain. It was Bill's quickness and savvy against Wilt's power. But there was more to the game than that. The Sixers had a powerful team with Chamberlain, Chet Walker, Luke Jackson, and Billy Cunningham up front and Hal Greer and Wali Jones in the backcourt. They also had a good, deep bench.

I had never seen the two greatest centers in the game go head-to-head, so I was eagerly awaiting tipoff. My competitive juices were flowing because I was there to help Bill if necessary. I kept thinking this was as good as it got. I even would have paid to see this game. Both teams exemplified greatness.

But the Sixers wanted to make sure we knew this was their year, and they beat us convincingly. Of course, we had them coming to our place three games later, so we had a chance to respond quickly.

At practice, Russ told me I was going to play more to give him a rest. Naturally, I could not wait for the challenge. I had held my own against Wilt for eight seasons.

In the locker room before the game, it was very quiet. I had finished putting on my warm-up jacket when Ronnie Watts approached me and suggested that I take the two green pills in his open hand. "These will give you energy," he said. "We need you tonight. This is an important game." Well, I knew that, so I took the pills and did not think twice. As we were warming up, I felt completely energized. This was a totally new feeling. I got called on early in the second quarter, and Wilt and I got after it right away. But it was not until the fourth quarter that things really got crazy. Wilt and I squared off, and both benches emptied. Sam Jones quickly grabbed an empty chair and came running toward Wilt. The referees intervened, and they were able to restore order. We went on to win the game, but the message was clear. It was not going to be a cakewalk to the tenth championship.

I also was concerned about the pills I had taken. I learned they were commonly used pep pills referred to as "greenies." Ronnie had gotten them from his roommate, who was a doctor. After the game, we went to a bar and had a few beers and I wanted to fight the whole bar. I could not sleep that night. It was terrible. I told Ronnie I did not want any more. Besides the fact they were prescription drugs, illegal unless prescribed by a physician, I did not need to be getting into fights with Wilt or anybody else.

I was enjoying the winning, and my teammates were special. Boston became even more enjoyable as I got more involved in the community. I loved seafood, and the North End had the best Italian food in the country. There was always good entertainment available, and I never tired of visiting the many historical sights.

But my real purpose in being in Boston was to play basketball and win the elusive championship ring. We finished the 1966–67 season 60–21, good enough to win the conference in most seasons. But this season, we finished second to the Sixers, who set an NBA record with their 68–13 record. By finishing second, we lost the homecourt advantage for the play-offs.

After beating the Knicks, three games to one, we opened the series against Philadelphia. We were in deep trouble. The Sixers were on a mission. Their confidence was high because they had come close a year ago, and they won the season series against us.

We lost the series, four games to one, and the string of consecutive championships was over. I was surprised at the reaction in the locker room. There were no feelings of remorse, and Russ thanked us for our efforts. This was a new experience for him, because he had won championships since his junior year in college, except for 1958, when the Hawks beat the Celtics when Russell was hurt. All the post-game comments were respectful of the Sixers. We congratulated them and wished them well in The Finals.

Not only did the Celtics win with class, I thought, but they lost with class, too. Our meeting the next day was upbeat as well. I felt bad for Bill losing in his first season as coach. And I still did not get the ring they had promised me. As we said goodbye for the summer, all of us had our sights set on next season.

First, though, I made a goodwill trip to South America, joining some other NBA players for games against the national teams of Brazil and Uruguay. This was not my first such trip. Two years earlier I had been on a team that played games in Italy and Yugoslavia, becoming one of the first teams invited to play in a Communist country. I thought the Yugoslavian fans were tough, but the fans in South America were every bit as intense.

Richie Guerin, an ex-marine who had become a rugged player in The League, was our coach. We won the first game at the buzzer on a Friday night before a raucous crowd of ten thousand. A reception was scheduled at the U.S. Embassy for Saturday night, but apparently the fans did not take the loss too well, because a bomb threat was called in to the Embassy, so the reception was moved to a nearby hotel. In the middle of the evening, I was standing with some teammates when I looked over to see Richie in a heated discussion with some of the officials from the Uruguay basketball federation. Suddenly, his voice rose above the noise of the party.

"Hell, no," he shouted. "You've got to be crazy."

Guerin looked as if he would explode he was so angry as he made his way back to us.

"Those SOBs asked us to tank the game on Sunday," he said. "They offered to pay us to let them win so the team would gain some confidence heading into the Pan American Games. Can you believe it?

"We're going to kick their asses."

Sunday's game was a sell-out, and we were primed. We did not need a pre-game pep talk from Richie. We charged onto the court ready for war. The fans were primed, too, screaming and whistling and throwing coins at us. The game was extremely physical. As I drove hard to the basket, I got hit across the bridge of the nose, and the blood started pouring. I looked at the referee for a call, but he only smirked and shrugged his shoulders. As he turned to run back down the court, I cupped my hand under my nose, collected a handful of blood and dumped it on the back of his uniform as I ran past him. He immediately ejected me, but I got in one more lick before I left. On my way to the locker room, I looked for the guy who hit me and threw an elbow that sent him four rows into the seats.

We won the game convincingly, but it was a battle. As I think back, it was one of the early signs that the world was ready to challenge us at our own game.

When I got back to the United States, I did some consulting work for Pepsi and worked out every day with my former Cincinnati teammates to make sure that I reported to training camp in shape. There would be no more rubber suits for me. Although I loved my former teammates, I was now a Celtic, and being a Celtic meant the rest of The League hated you. They were envious that I was playing on a team that had a chance to win it all, while their team was on its way down.

The summer passed, and Terri and our three kids and I were off to Boston for the 1967–68 season. We rented a house in Newton not too far from some of the other players. The wives welcomed Terri, which helped to ease her anxieties.

Training camp started with the usual team meeting. Russell reflected on the past season, assured us that we were champions, and promised we would prove it. He admitted he tried to do too much in his first season as coach and that he needed our help to be successful. We were a veteran team, and there was no reason he could not trust our opinions. He agreed he could not always know when a player was tired or when the plays broke down. We developed an honor system that seemed to work. There was a wealth of experience on the team.

There were a couple of new players, and K. C. Jones had retired to become coach at Brandeis University. Mal Graham, the first round draft pick out of NYU, was to take his place. Mal's career started out on a bad note. He was the first Celtic to bring an agent to Red. Of course, that got him nowhere, other than on Red's bad side. Red kicked Mal and the agent out of his office. Ricky Weitzman, a local star out of Northeastern, was another rookie. He and Johnny Jones and I anchored the bench and called ourselves the "weenies." Red made a deal for my former Cincinnati teammate Tom Thacker. But Toby Kimball and Jim Barnett were gone.

We had a routine exhibition season as we could not wait for the season to start. We won our first four in a row, and then came the matchup we had been waiting for—the game against the Sixers. Russ had nothing to say to us. We were all keyed up for this one. We needed to make a statement. But we won the game by only 6 points. That was hardly a statement. The Sixers looked as strong as ever. It was going to be another challenge to regain the championship.

Although we were starting to show our age, we were still considered a contender. Detroit with Dave Bing was getting better and the Knicks were coming on with Willis Reed and Walt Bellamy. Every practice was like a game. Bill still was not practicing, but we did not care. We were determined to get the homecourt advantage and beat the Sixers every game. We did continue to win, and the season was even more fun than the previous one.

We also got to see Red chew out Russ another time. A Noreaster came up unexpectedly, and the snow began to accumulate quickly. It was almost impossible to drive. I happened to be in the Back Bay and started home at four o'clock to get Terri. After going a block, I turned around and headed toward the Garden. It took three hours to make a trip that usually took twenty minutes. Surprisingly, the Warriors got there and all of the Celtics made it except Russell. Several of the players had to walk two miles to make it.

Without Russ, Red had to coach and I had to play forty-five minutes against Nate Thurmond. This was no picnic. I had not played extended minutes in nearly two years and it showed. Much to the delight of the fans who had braved the weather, we did win the game. When we got to the locker room, Russ was sitting there, fully dressed in his street clothes.

"Nice game guys," was all he got out before Red lit into him. When Red finished, I took my turn for having to play all those minutes.

The conference was better than last year because of the emergence of Detroit. Dave DeBusschere, Dave Bing, and Eddie Miles were solid. New York was getting better as was Baltimore. Cincinnati was still competitive. It would still come down to the Sixers and the Celtics in the East. Of course, the defending Western Conference champion Warriors and the Lakers with Elgin Baylor and Jerry West were still factors. It was going to be more difficult for us to reclaim the title, but it was still fun trying. It was always fun when the team won. We were winning at a fifty-game pace during the regular season, but we did not know if we could win enough to get the homecourt for the play-offs.

Each game with the Sixers was a war because each team knew the significance of the outcome. The rivalry grew with each game. There were fights or near fights every game. The working staff, the media, and the fans in both buildings got into the games. You really had to beat more than the players. It was not uncommon to see the ushers come onto the floor to assist in a fight. The games were more than the Russell-Chamberlain duel or the Sam Jones-Hal Greer duel. The pride of both cities was at stake.

We finished the 1967–68 season 54–28, still not good enough to beat the Sixers and get the homecourt if we were to play again in the play-offs. We had split eight regular season games. The stage was set for another classic series, but we had to get past the Pistons first. We were careful not to look past them and won the series, four games to two.

The regular season games between the Celtics and the Sixers were like play-off games, so I wondered how we could raise the intensity for the play-offs without getting too wound up. But we were confident and ready and could not wait to get it on. My playing time had increased during the season, and I felt as if I were making a contribution. I was wired without the help of the "greenies" or the "gobies" as they were also called. Practices were like games. We actually had to temper them. Russell practiced just enough to stay sharp. God forbid he get hurt, although the Celtics played hurt as long as there were no broken bones.

We were all business getting ready for the series, but then something happened that pushed basketball into the background.

On April 4, the world was stunned by the assassination of Dr. Martin Luther King Jr. in Memphis. As the news spread, we were all in disbelief. Bill and Wilt and some of the other players had participated in the famous march on our Capitol in 1963 and had a personal relationship with Dr. King, but all of us mourned his death.

The country was put on immediate alert for fear of retaliation in the streets of the major cities. Despite the fact that Dr. King was an advocate of nonviolence and had done much to calm the unrest while working for equal opportunity, there already had been civil disorders throughout the country.

The series against the Sixers was to open the next day in Philadelphia. The League had considered postponing the start of the series until after the funeral. No one was in any mood to play. But after conferring with the mayors of both cities, The League decided to proceed with the set schedule. The Philadelphia police chief and safety director believed that the game would take the focus off of what had happened and keep people occupied. There would be seventeen thousand people in the Spectrum with millions more watching on television or listening to the radio. It proved to be a good idea.

We won the game in a typical war, but there was no celebration. We needed three more victories, and the Sixers were not going to let up.

There was a moratorium for several days as the country mourned Dr. King's death. After his funeral, we resumed play, and Philadelphia won the next three games rather handily. We had to regroup and refocus if we were going to reclaim the title. Losing was unacceptable. We won the next two games to tie the series at three games apiece. The seventh game was in Philadelphia.

We had a light practice on the eve of the game. The mood was mixed. I detected a defeatist attitude, which was uncharacteristic of the team. I knew that some of the writers were skeptical. As we were leaving the Garden floor, Cliff Keane, the legendary columnist for the *Globe*, told Havlicek and me, "They can take the floor up today. It won't be needed until next year." As we headed to the locker room, I said to John, "Let's prove old Cliff wrong."

John was the captain of the team and I was the captain of the scrubs. We wanted to do something to get the team's attention. So we went into the locker room and wrote on the blackboard: PRIDE. DETERMINATION. We added a small dollar sign.

After a restless night, we went to Philadelphia. When we arrived at the hotel, a band was playing in the lobby. It was loud and very annoying. Russ asked that they stop, but he got no satisfaction. It was a deliberate attempt to distract us, and it worked because it was impossible to sleep, although we were all very nervous anyway.

Finally I told my roommate, Don Nelson, that I could not sleep and I was going for a walk. On the way out, Russ grabbed me. "Big Red," he said using a nickname I had picked up for no apparent reason, "be ready tonight. I've noticed you play Wilt pretty good, so I'm going to use you a lot of minutes. Chet has hurt us, so I'll try and contain him. Stay out of foul trouble."

I thought it was a brilliant idea, and I was even more psyched. I was not the only one who was restless. Sam and Bailey joined me, and we walked the streets, taking as many side streets as we could to avoid the Sixers fans. It worked a little.

Five o'clock came quickly. As we boarded the bus for the Spectrum, there were several Sixers fans to greet us. We fought our way through the crowd and were on our way. There were more fans when we got to the arena. I thought about how it was going to be after we won the game. No team had come from being down three games to one to win a series.

Nobody went out to shoot early because we wanted to avoid the abuse and preserve our energy. When we did go out, you could feel the tension. This is what we all played for. The fans were louder than ever. Harvey Pollack, the legendary public relations man for the Sixers, strutted the sidelines. He tried to make conversation, but no one was very talkative.

The horn blew to clear the floor, and both teams came to the sidelines to await the introductions. As I sat down next to the scorer's table, a rather large man approached me. "Here, this is for apes," he said as he handed me a banana. I drew back my right fist to throw a punch, but Red was there to intercept it.

"Show him on the court," he told me.

I always prayed during the national anthem. I still do. I pray for America and for peace and harmony among people. I pray that we compete to the best of our abilities. I pray no one gets hurt. I thank the Lord for the privilege of playing in the NBA. Since Dr. King's death, I prayed that his dream come true.

On this night, I prayed for the strength to outplay Wilt and that if the physical pattern continued I wanted Him to protect the two of us.

Zink, the public address announcer, did his best to incite the capacity crowd. His introduction of us was more condescending than usual, and he dragged out each of the Sixers' names as long as he could: "Now starting at guard for the WORLLLLD CHAMPIONNNNNS, Hal GREEEEEEEER. And at the other guard, WAAAAAALLIIII JOOOOOONES. At center, DIPPPPPPPPERRRRR DUUUUUUUNK. At forward CHET WAAAAAAALKERRRRRR. At the other forward, LUUUUUUUUUUCIOUS JACKSONNNNNNN." There was only one Zink.

The game started with all the fervor that was expected. It was going to be a nail biter all the way. I got my call early in the second quarter. I went to Wilt and Russ covered Chet. Russ had put into our offense the pick-and-roll play that Oscar Robertson and I ran so effectively in Cincinnati. We went right to it. Sam and Havlicek were great shooters, and we knew my picks would get both of them open shots. Wilt hated having to switch out onto a smaller player. It was effective, and I could hear Sixers coach Alex Hannum yelling in his high voice, "Switch, Wilt, switch." Wilt would not, and I could sense Wilt was getting mad. He was getting more and more physical, and I knew it was only a matter of time. He pushed me to establish a low post position. I pushed him back to take the foul. I might have pushed a little excessively. He came toward me with a raised fist, and I lunged at him. Quickly, veteran referee Mendy Rudolph jumped between us and things calmed down. Thank God. He answered my prayers.

Wilt kept threatening me the rest of the quarter. I had been here before. Finally, when play stopped, I went to him and said, "You know, Wilt, we don't know how you take a punch. And I am going to get one in, believe me." There were no more problems between us.

I played nearly the entire second half. Wilt was not much of a factor after a decent first half. It was not my great defense, as I learned later. Wali was on fire at the close of the first half and at halftime Alex instructed the team to keep feeding the hot hand. Wilt followed instructions.

I could feel victory midway through the fourth quarter. Momentum was on our side. I liked being in the game at crunch time. It was like old times. With a four-point lead and the clock running out, Wilt took a fadeaway jump shot and missed. As fate would have it, I got the final rebound. I nearly squeezed the air out of the ball as I looked up at the scoreboard that read: Visitors 100, Sixers 95. What a tremendous feeling. The locker room was rather quiet. It was almost like it was when we lost a year ago. Russ came over and complimented me on my effort, and Red stopped puffing on his cigar long enough to tell me I was the difference. The Celtic way of doing things was not to celebrate until you had won the whole thing. According to them, you had not won anything until you won the championship.

Out in the West, the Lakers beat the Warriors in four straight, setting up what by then seemed normal—a Boston–L.A. Finals. These two teams had dominated the play-offs in the 1960s. The games were always competitive, but the Lakers just could never get it done, despite Elgin Baylor's heroics and Jerry West's clutch play. Still, they were confident coming into the Finals this time. They thought the Philadelphia series had taken its toll on our aging team. This time, the Lakers were more determined than ever.

We split the first four games, then won the fifth game in overtime in Boston, so we took a three games to two lead back to Los Angeles, one game away from regaining the championship. With a title so close, we were all focused on the upcoming game. We wanted to end the series. We did not want to take it back to Boston.

But we were a little concerned about Bill. After our workouts, he would disappear to Hollywood. He wanted to be an actor when he finished playing basketball, and he had done a bit part in the *I Spy* television show with Bill Cosby and Robert Culp.

Bill loved to talk about his acting, and we played along. Havlicek was kidding him after practice one day.

"Bill, what do the directors say about you?" Havlicek asked.

"They say I have 'presence,'" Russ would say. That was all he would say, although he reminded us to make sure to watch the show.

Most of us did, which led to more razzing the next day.

"Russ," I cracked, "did you have the 'presence' to put your legs together when you were lying on the floor unconscious after you were hit in the head with a gun and the villain was tying you up?"

The room broke up. Even Bill laughed.

"You weren't supposed to notice that," he said.

Mal Graham said, "I hope that he's got 'presence' tomorrow night."

Bill had 'presence,' and we won the sixth game and the championship easily. I was ecstatic and ready to celebrate, as were the others who had never been here before. But there was no celebration on the floor. Okay, I figured, we are just running off the floor so we can celebrate in the locker room. But there was no celebrating there either. No champagne. No nothing.

"What the hell?" I thought.

Then I realized this was the tenth championship for the Celtics. They had been here before, and they acted like it. It was no big deal. They expected to be champions. So while there were congratulations and hugs from Russell, who had won his first title as coach, the rest of the post-game was fairly formal. Red and Marvin congratulated us, and Red came over to me and thanked me for my contributions. He was happy for me. I gave him a big hug and thanked him for making me a part of all this. After all those years of the Royals chasing the Celtics, I finally had my ring. Bailey was in the same boat, and Red and Bill—and I—were happy for him, too.

Our trainer, Joe Delauri, got permission from Red to organize a victory party back at the hotel. He got a room and some beer, but there still was no champagne. Before long, Thacker, Ricky, Mal, and I went to the hotel bar to celebrate on our own. As captain of the bench squad, I took charge and ordered champagne. I had never tasted the stuff before, not even at my wedding. Terri and I could not afford champagne, so we drank lemonade. But that night I wanted to drink champagne, as all champions do.

When the bartender gave me the bill, I told him to run a tab. He asked me whose room to bill. I gave him Red's room number. We began to celebrate and, before long, the whole bar was celebrating with us. I never did find out what the final bill was.

From the hotel I joined Nellie and Havlicek at a bar on Century Boulevard. We continued to celebrate until the early morning hours. When we finally made our way back to the hotel, we were in pretty bad shape. I went to my room but I could not get the key to work, so I just slumped to the floor and fell asleep. Nellie woke me up the next morning, but I did not recognize my surroundings. Sometime during the night, he had helped me into Red's room. Red had taken the red-eye back to Boston. Nellie and I flew back that day, and we continued to celebrate the whole six-hour flight.

The next night we all gathered at Lenny's, a jazz club north of Boston. The Cannonball Adderly quintet was playing. We had gotten to know him and Nat over the years, and he was a Celtics fan. His pianist, Josef Zawinul, had written a song called, "Mercy, Mercy, Mercy," and it was just released and soared to Number 1 on the Billboard charts, so we all had something to celebrate. And boy did we.

I was so happy to be part of a championship team with Red Auerbach (front row, third from left) and Bill Russell (front row, second from right). I'm in the back row (No. 28), next to Don Nelson (No. 19) (Courtesy of NBA)

An athlete waits his whole career for this moment. Everything I had been through, from Springfield to Oxford to St. Louis to Cincinnati and then Boston, prepared me for this and made me appreciate it all the more. I thought my career was over. Little did I know, it was just beginning.

Chapter 8

A New Direction

The NBA had announced it was expanding to Milwaukee and Phoenix, and the expansion draft was to take place shortly after the Finals. Citing the fact that I was thirty-two years old, the Celtics had left me unprotected, which was my first indication that my tenure with the team was over. Red, Bill, and I tried to discourage both teams from taking me, but Richard Block, the new owner of the Phoenix franchise, told me in Los Angeles he was going to select me.

I was playing golf on the day of the expansion draft, and after nine holes I called Terri to ask her if I had been drafted. Her response caught me off guard.

"You were taken by Milwaukee," she said.

Milwaukee? What the hell happened to Phoenix? I had played in Milwaukee in college, and all I remembered was how cold it was. I had been to Phoenix, too, and I remembered how warm and sunny it was. That memory of Phoenix made Milwaukee seem all the colder.

Now I had another decision to make. My family had joined me in Boston, and we were getting adjusted to the city. Debbi, Jill, and Wayne Jr. liked their new school and had made new friends.

Because of my age, I did not feel secure about Milwaukee. I did not want to uproot my family again, move for a year, and then have no place to go after that. Ray Patterson, a former star player at the University of Wisconsin, was the president of the Bucks. Former University of Wisconsin coach John Erickson was the general manager, and Larry

Costello, a former NBA player with Philadelphia and Syracuse, was the coach. I knew Larry from playing against him, and we were teammates on a squad that toured Europe one summer. The three of them called me the night of the draft to welcome me to the Bucks. I was not very enthusiastic, and they knew it. Larry told me they needed me for my leadership because they had drafted a lot of young players. He thought my experience would help jump start the franchise. But I remained non-commital.

After much deliberation and discussion with Terri, I decided I would go to Milwaukee if the Bucks doubled my salary. Then I turned the negotiations over to my agent, Bob Woolf.

I had met Woolf through Earl Wilson, the Red Sox pitcher who had become a good friend of mine. Bob was a tort lawyer who handled insurance claims, but with players starting to hire agents to represent them in their contract negotiations, Bob was trying to branch out into that area. He would invite us to his house nearly every Sunday for Chinese food, and he would always encourage me to bring other Celtics along so he could get to know them, too. He and his wife, Ann, were great hosts.

But no matter how much Chinese food I ate, there was still a huge void in my life that summer. I was caught between two franchises, and I already missed the Celtics tremendously. I worked at Camp Milbrook for Jerry Volk, who was a friend of Red's. Red held his camp there when the kids went back to school. I lectured at all the players' camps and, because Celtics were always in great demand, I also made speeches all over New England. It was fun, and I made a little money, but the hardest part was knowing I was not going to training camp with the Celtics in the fall.

I knew I would miss the tradition and the camaraderie. The Celtic players were very close, and we had gotten to know the front office and staff. We were very much a family. We ate together on the road and sometimes at home. We hung out together on the road and at home. I would miss the daily arguments about who was the tightest with his money. I think Havlicek holds that distinction since I am quite sure he still has the first dollar he ever made.

Russell and I had been friends for many years, and I knew that would continue. But I also knew I would miss watching him dominate on the court. The only thing I would not miss was his one lame pre-game talk. I would miss the Garden and the fans, even the one guy in the nosebleed seats whose distinctive voice could be heard above the din yelling, "Embry, yer a bum."

Above all, I would miss Red's words of inspiration. There were many reasons the Celtics were a dynasty. The players played the game better than any other team, and much of the responsibility for that went to Red. It was not so much his ability to pick talent as it was how he managed the players he had. He wanted good people on his teams. I left the Celtics with a championship ring, but the most important thing I took with me was an education in management skills I could apply to whatever I did after my playing days.

And at that point, I was not sure how many more playing days I had left. It was September 1968, and I still had not signed a contract with the Bucks. I had been approached about a job as the director of recreation for the city of Boston, which still was an option if I decided to retire. Whenever I asked Bob how negotiations were going with Milwaukee, he was extremely vague.

The truth was, he had had little contact with the Bucks. He had acquired Red Sox baseball player Ken Harrelson as a client. Ken had great flair and was very popular in Boston. He was to become a national icon. Bob seized the opportunity to get recognition as Harrelson's agent and had basically ignored my needs.

So I called Ray Patterson to try to work out a deal. I was trying to make a killing with this contract. Time was running out on my playing career, so I wanted to maximize my earnings, and I thought I had the leverage to do so. I finally agreed to a one-year deal for $40,000. It was a decent amount of money, though it fell far short of doubling my salary from the year before. I had made $30,000 in Boston. But the thrill of playing with the Celtics and winning a title was priceless.

Now I had to put that all behind me. I flew to Milwaukee, where Eddie Doucette, the new play-by-play announcer, picked me up at the airport to take me to Beloit College, where we were to train. Eddie had been a disc jockey at a local radio station and was never at a loss for words. For two hours I listened to him tell me a little about Milwaukee and the Bucks and a lot about himself. He asked me a zillion questions about the NBA and the Celtics, and he could tell I was not happy about leaving.

We arrived just in time for a team meeting. After checking into the hotel, I went to meet with Ray Patterson, John Erickson, and Larry Costello. They all extended warm welcomes and told me how happy they were to have me and how much they were looking forward to taking advantage of my leadership skills. I still could not express much joy.

I got my practice gear, and Eddie and I walked over to the gym. The other players were getting dressed when I arrived in the locker room. All the veterans, former opponents of mine, stopped to welcome me. Guy Rodgers was happy just to see someone his age. The rookies looked at both of us in awe. I could not believe it when one of them actually asked me for my autograph. Guy and I looked at each other and thought this was going to be an interesting year.

Expansion teams are made up of aging veterans and young players who have not yet developed. Throw rookies into the mix and you have a mishmash of players who are destined to lose—something I had not done much of for eight years. No wonder I was having such a hard time getting excited about this.

We left the locker room thinking we were going to the court. Larry came out in his coaching attire, along with his assistant, Tom Nissalke. Both were laden with loose-leaf binders. "Everyone over here," Costello called, and he ushered us into a small room off the court. Then he and Tom started passing out the binders. Each one had a name on it. I remember wondering what on earth these were until I got mine: It was

Larry's play book. There were twenty or more pages of offensive and defensive sets, along with a list of team rules and a history of The League. I had played ten years and won an NBA title, and I had never seen anything like it. I was inclined to dismiss the whole thing as non-sense until Larry told us, "I expect you guys to know everything in this book, and I will give you periodic quizzes and an exam midway through the season."

While we were still in shock, he asked us to introduce ourselves to the group and tell a little about our background. I knew Jon McGlocklin, Bobby Weiss, Len Chappell, John Eagan, and Guy Rodgers because I had played against them. Jon and I were roommates in Cincinnati. I had never heard of the rest of the guys, but all together we were the new Milwaukee Bucks.

After the meeting, we went out onto the court to start practice. Larry took off his warm-ups, and his skin was so pasty white it was obvious he had not been outside in months. He must have been working on that play book. During our first break, I eased over to Jon and made reference to how pale Larry looked while everyone else was sporting their summer tans. From then on, we referred to him as "Casper the Friendly Ghost."

Though we teased him, Larry Costello was as dedicated a basketball person as I have known. I got to know him on the tour we took to Europe. He dispelled the ill-conceived perception that he was a racist by hanging out with Nate Thurmond, Hal Greer, and me, and he was perfectly comfortable in our company. Hal was a teammate of Larry's in Syracuse and Philadelphia. I could see he was going to coach the game as he played it. He was a hard-working, no-nonsense player, and early indications were that he would be the same as a coach. As we went through our first workout, you would have thought we were going to challenge the Celtics for the championship. There was no humor or frivolity, just work. I saw nothing wrong with this approach, but the younger players were a bit mystified. Although I felt like a senior citizen, I really enjoyed training camp and my new teammates. I was in reasonably good condition and was having fun acting as a mentor to the young guys.

I had to take a short break from basketball to focus on Terri and the kids. We decided that we would move to Milwaukee even though we planned to return to Boston after the season. They were holding the job in the recreation department for me, and Terri had a job waiting in the redevelopment authority. With that in mind, it made sense to look for temporary housing and avoid a long lease. The search was eased because Marvin Fishman, one of the early investors in the Bucks, owned an apartment complex in Oak Creek, a suburb on the south side of Milwaukee. I knew nothing about the city or where to live, so we accepted his offer of a short lease in one of his apartments.

Thus started my education on the city that was to become my home. The year 1968 was an election year. Governor George Wallace of Alabama decided to run for president, thinking he would appeal to white America in the wake of the civil disturbances that had plagued so many cities, including Milwaukee. His motto was: "Segregation yesterday, segregation today, and segregation tomorrow." Catchy, huh? Wallace was running as an Independent against the Republican candidate, Richard Nixon, and the Democratic candidate, George McGovern.

As usual around election time, there were campaign posters everywhere. Milwaukee, a hard-working, blue-collar city, was heavily Democratic, so the McGovern posters clearly outnumbered the Nixon posters, except in our neighborhood. I will never forget the look on Terri's face when we turned into our apartment complex, our new home, and saw a huge truck with a "Wallace for President" sign taped on its side.

Welcome to Milwaukee.

That sign was bigger than life, but it was not the only one we saw. As we drove to our apartment, we saw more lawn signs endorsing America's foremost segregationist. Terri's eyes grew wider and wider.

"Where on earth have you brought me?" she asked.

She remembered what she saw when she went to Selma in 1965. I had to spend the rest of the night trying to calm her. If there was anyone who hated racism more than I did, it was Terri. She was worried about being there alone with the kids while I was traveling the country playing basketball. I told her everything would be fine and that I would call the Oak Creek Police Department to make sure. That was not exactly the right thing to say. We had seen policemen, sheriffs, and other law enforcement officials beat and turn the hoses on African Americans in Alabama. The only thing that made her feel better was the fact that four of the other black players and their families moved in near us. We were hoping there would be safety in numbers.

I went back to training camp in Beloit and Terri had the unenviable task of enrolling the kids in school. She had to go alone because all the other players' kids were babies. When I called her that night to see how things had gone, I got an earful. She told me our kids were the only black kids in Edgewood Elementary School and might be the only black kids in the entire Oak Creek school system. We were not pleased about it, but we did not have much choice. I just figured the kids would get the same lesson in perseverance that I had gotten. In fact, my son still vividly remembers being the only one left out when all the other kids exchanged presents at Christmas time.

There was more. When Terri went to the grocery store, a white woman approached her and asked her if she took in laundry.

I related our experiences to some of the Bucks officials. They were empathetic and assured us they would make other accommodations if things did not work out. I also called Marvin and told him of our fears. He was concerned, too, and told us he and his wife would look in on our wives and families whenever the Bucks were out of town.

That was going to be soon, because training camp was coming to an end and the exhibition season was upon us. I had held up better than I thought. I had the usual muscle soreness, but that was about it. I had very little pain in my knees, which was good news, especially after going against rookie Dick Cunningham every day in practice.

Dick was six feet, ten inches, 270 pounds, and strong as a bull, although he actually was rather timid, until I taught him how to use his size and strength. At first, he told me he had too much respect for me and did not want to hurt me. But Larry told me he wanted me to take Dick under my wing and teach him the inside game. This was quite an assignment. He had two left feet and a shooting touch like a blacksmith. He was never going to be Bill Russell by any stretch of the imagination. But the Bucks projected him as their center of the future. When they told me that, I laughed and told them they had better hope they were lucky enough to win the coin flip next spring to determine the Number 1 pick in the draft, which was sure to be UCLA's standout seven-foot-two-inch center, Lew Alcindor.

That was months away, though. Now it was time to catch up with Terri and the kids. According to her, there had not been any unusual incidents in the neighborhood, just the usual stares. The kids were adjusting in school, and Terri was making friends with the other black wives. There was very little contact with the whites who lived in the complex. But one Sunday afternoon, Terri was cooking one of our favorite meals—pork chops, candied yams, and collard greens. The smell of the collard greens cooking floated through the building, and before long there was there was a knock on the door.

When I opened it, a redhead greeted me with a Southern accent. "Here we go," I thought. But she introduced herself and told me she and her family had just moved from Georgia. She said she had smelled the greens and wondered where we got them, since her family loved soul food but did not know where to get any in Milwaukee. Terri told her she would never find any soul food on the south side, that the only place she could get soul food in Milwaukee was on the north side, where most of the blacks lived. Terri promised to bring some extra greens back the next time she went shopping. That was how we met Pat Truax. She and her family became good friends of ours, and her daughter, Karen, became our babysitter.

Things were shaping up at home and on the team, too. Our roster was down to twelve. Many of the older players were waived or traded because the coach had an eye toward the future and wanted to develop younger players. Eddie Doucette became famous for the nicknames he gave players, and here was how he saw the inaugural Milwaukee Bucks:

Jon McGlocklin was "Johnny Mac." Greg Smith was "Captain Marvel." Dick Cunningham was "The Cement Mixer." Sam Williams was "Soup." Guy Rodgers was "Cooty Brown." Lenny Chappell was "Tyrone," short for Tyrannosaurus Rex, not Tyrone Powers. Bob Love was "Butterbean." Charlie Paulk was "Rook." Freddie Hetzel was "Money." Bobby Weiss was "Smoothie." And I was "The Wall."

We were to play in the strong Eastern Conference, where Baltimore, led by Gus Johnson, Earl Monroe, Jack Marin, Kevin Loughery, and rookie sensation Wes Unseld, emerged as the team to beat. New York, with new coach Red Holzman and Rhodes Scholar Bill Bradley, Walt Frazier, Phil Jackson, and the newly acquired Dave DeBusschere and an aging Boston were still considered contenders.

I looked at those teams and thought we would be lucky to win fifteen games. But Larry and Tom and I, as the team captain, had higher goals. I tried to convey to the young players that we could win more, and we should try to do so.

I was astounded by the reception we got opening night from a sold-out crowd in the Milwaukee Arena. It was not much different from the reception the Celtics received in Boston. It was almost as if we were the world champions. Milwaukee always had the reputation of being a great sports town, and the fans were eager for a new team to cheer after the Braves moved to Atlanta. The Packers were sacred, but they were based in Green Bay, two hours north, and played only a few games a season in County Stadium.

Despite the warm welcome, we lost our first game, and four more, before we got our first win. In the process, we played in Boston Garden, and returning there was a special moment for me. I received a standing ovation when I was introduced as the Bucks' starting center. After the introductions, much to my surprise, Red, Russ, and the rest of the team gathered around me at center court and handed me a replica of the championship flag that we had won in May. I was overwhelmed as Red informed the fans this was to acknowledge my contribution to that title, and the fans responded with another standing ovation. By the time the game started, I was so touched I could barely keep my emotions in check. After the game, they held a reception in my honor at the exclusive Board and Blade Club in the Garden. I was told it was the first time a person of my color had entered the room.

Wilt Chamberlain made even me look small (Courtesy of NBA)

We won our first game against the Pistons. I scored 30 points and was beginning to feel rejuvenated. I continued to lead the team in scoring, and we remained competitive even though we were losing. I actually was having fun, except for the losing. I was enjoying the questions from my inquisitive young teammates, but I did not enjoy getting beaten up by Cunningham every day in practice. He just did not realize how strong he was. I finally had to tell him that he did not have to do everything I did, especially against me, his mentor. Dick got the respect of all of us one day at practice when he and Lenny Chappell were jawing at each other. Dick finally had enough of Lenny physically and mentally abusing him. As they squared off, Dick shouted at Lenny, "Give it your best shot, Big Boy," and he stuck out his jaw. Lenny punched him and,

A classic battle against Bill Russell and the Celtics (Courtesy of NBA)

to our astonishment, Dick did not flinch. Lenny was stunned. He could not believe that punch did not even phase Dick.

Dick sometimes got carried away with his ability and often needed a reality check. We were about to face the Lakers for the first time, and as we dressed, I was trying to explain to Dick how good and how strong Wilt was.

"Hey, man, he puts his pants on the same way I do," he responded.

As the others laughed, all I could say was, "I admire your attitude, but let's not get carried away."

During the game, he very nearly did get carried away. He tried to stiff arm Wilt and Wilt almost threw him into the basket with the ball.

Players were coming and going as the season progressed. We were getting used to Larry and his many plays. I passed his midterm exam and was ready to close out the season. I was averaging close to 20 points a game midway through the season, but that ended when we traded for Flynn Robinson, who hit the ground shooting. It did not take long for Eddie Doucette to label him with the nickname "The Electric Eye." Between Flynn and fan favorite Johnny Mac, there were not enough shots left over to satisfy the rest of us.

I started to break down physically as the season was nearing a close, and I was sure this would be my last year. I still provided leadership, both verbally and by example. I played just as hard in practice as in games, even though my playing time was being reduced to allow Dick to gain experience.

I also acted as the team jester, and we needed that. It was necessary to keep everybody loose because Larry felt we should be fighting the front-runners for the conference title. The practices got longer with every loss, and our team meetings increased.

We were on our final road trip of the season, which happened to be to the West Coast. While in San Francisco, we liked to visit our favorite Big Man's store. Lenny, who was a character, bought what appeared to be a new wardrobe and, believe me, he needed one. I had noticed he wore the same black turtleneck, black pants, and mustard-colored blazer every day. Anyway, he carried his garment bag full of new clothes with him, but he never opened it.

We got up at 5 A.M. to fly to Phoenix, arriving at 9 A.M. Before we could get to our rooms, Larry called another team meeting, which was strange since we had only two games left. While sitting there waiting for Larry, I turned to Lenny and asked him, "How many more days are you going to wear that awful outfit? Why in the hell don't you wear your new clothes and get rid of the fox you're wearing?"

The room broke up and, just then, Larry appeared in the doorway. He thought we were laughing at him, until I told him what had happened. Lenny told us he was saving his new clothes so his wife could see them before he wore them. Wasn't that sweet?

We wound up winning twenty-seven games, not bad for an expansion team. I formally announced my retirement. I had a job waiting for me in Boston. Terri could not wait to get back there, in part because one night when she was driving home to Oak Creek from visiting a friend on the North Side, two men in a car followed her and tried to force her off the road. She left town the next day, vowing never to return.

I drove back a few days later, arriving in time to see the gutty Celtics, who had finished fourth in the Eastern Conference, tie the championship series with the Lakers at three games apiece, forcing Game 7 in L.A. Lakers owner Jack Kent Cooke was so confident his team would win that he had purple-and-gold balloons ready to drop from the rafters at the end of the game. Instead, Red was able to light one more victory cigar in spite of the fact that his team had not had the homecourt advantage in a single series. I could not help but wonder whatever happened to those balloons.

That would mark the end of the Celtics era. Russell announced his retirement, capping the greatest run in the history of the NBA. Life would take some new turns for all of us.

Timeout Number Two

The decade of the 1960s was one of the most turbulent in our country. Sports were not immune from this. Many of the athletes were students on college campuses during antiwar protests and demonstrations. This culminated in a cultural revolution that changed our nation forever. The 1960s ushered in the drug culture and left America a different nation. Whites and blacks collaborated during this time and came together for the common goals of protesting Vietnam, racial issues, and injustice.

One of the biggest reasons for all the trouble was the TET offensive in Vietnam. Our military leaders were duped into thinking that we were close to a cease-fire as both sides had agreed to a temporary truce around the lunar New Year.

Unfortunately, they were wrong—again.

At 3:00 A.M. on January 31, 1968, the North Vietnamese Army and the Viet Cong waged an all-out offensive on American military bases and charged the American embassy in Saigon. Other major cities in South Vietnam also were targeted in what proved to be one of the greatest campaigns in military history. We were now in a full-scale war. America deployed more than five hundred thousand troops to Vietnam.

Antiwar protests escalated throughout the country.

College campuses became havens for "peace-niks" and districts like Haight-Ashbury in San Francisco sprang up in every major city. A new culture developed in America. Young adults, black and white, had their causes.

The whites, known as "flower children" or "hippies," became rebellious and defiant of all authority figures, including their parents. They grew their hair long and donned blue jeans and army jackets. Many ran away from home and took refuge in parks or communes. The universal symbol of peace became the V formed by raising the index and middle figures, and round peace symbols were sewn on clothing or drawn on walls and sidewalks. Rock stars and folk singers who supported the cause, like Bob Dylan, Sly and the Family Stone, and the Grateful Dead, became popular. They traveled the country holding concerts and antiwar rallies before hundreds of thousands of young sympathizers.

The militant Black Panther Party was formed and names like Bobby Seales, Huey Newton, H. Rap Brown, and Angela Davis became prominent. The Panthers held rallies in many major cities advocating Black Power, and a raised, clenched fist became their symbol. Blacks began wearing African dashikis in honor of their heritage and, instead of straightening their hair, they grew it out into afros—the bigger the better.

The country was coming apart at the seams, despite the efforts of elected officials and other leaders to keep order. The military was getting younger and younger, and many of the young soldiers, like the young protesters, did not understand what we were doing in Vietnam. Thousands of young men of draft age fled to Canada to avoid being drafted. Soldiers who returned home after their tours of duties told of the horrors they had seen and joined in the protests.

Many who returned home wounded were vilified by friends and neighbors protesting the war.

Kenny Babbs, my old teammate at Miami, had joined the movement. He had been a Marine Corps chopper pilot in Vietnam, but when he got home he became a Ford Fellow and was attending Stanford University. I had not seen him since graduation and did not recognize him one night when he sneaked onto the court during a game against Golden State and assumed the role of ball boy. I came out of the game late in the fourth quarter and headed toward the end of the Celtics bench. A bearded man with hair below his shoulders handed me a towel and said, "You still sweat like a pig." I knew the voice, but it took me a few minutes to see past the beard, the hair, the fatigue jacket, T-shirt, softball pants, combat boots, and red bandana around his neck. Kenny sat on our bench until the end of the game. I think he was hoping Russ would call his name.

Afterward, he introduced me to another student, Ken Kesey, and we all went for a late dinner in Haight-Ashbury. It was a memorable evening as I sat listening to their views on what was wrong with our country. Both became successful authors. Kesey is best known for his book, *One Flew Over the Cuckoo's Nest.* Together, they created the traveling troupe known as the Merry Pranksters.

Lord knows we could have used a good laugh. But there seemed to be no end to the troubles facing our country. President Lyndon Johnson had such a low approval rating because of the war that he decided not to run for reelection. Robert Kennedy, the brother of the late president, was gunned down while campaigning for the California primary. Later that summer, during the Democratic Convention in Chicago, America watched in horror as riot squads from the Chicago Police Department beat angry protestors in the streets outside the convention. Young Americans had become disillusioned and hopeless, and increasing numbers were turning to drugs like marijuana and LSD. That was just the start of what would become a major problem for our country and our society.

Athletes and other celebrities were encouraged to join the protests, and many did. We had dual responsibilities of providing leadership while also addressing the injustices that existed. We admired the courage of John Carlos and Tommie Smith, who lifted their clenched fists to protest racism as they stood listening to the "Star Spangled Banner" on the medal stand at the 1968 Summer Olympics in Mexico City. They were immediately put off the team.

Many future NBA stars were involved in protests on their campuses and in their hometowns. All of this would have an impact on The League as we moved into the 1970s. Commissioner Walter Kennedy and The League's owners had no idea what was in store for them in the next decade. I did not know what was in store for me as I was about to begin my new career as the director of recreation for the city of Boston. But the Bucks knew greatness was in store for them: By finishing last in the Eastern Division, they entered into a coin flip with the Phoenix Suns, who finished last in the West. The Bucks won the coin toss for the Number 1 pick in the draft, which meant franchise player Lew Alcindor, the UCLA center, was headed for Milwaukee. I did not think I could beat him out, so I retired.

Chapter 9

Big Plans

Life outside of basketball was . . . interesting. At least the life I chose was.

After I retired from the Milwaukee Bucks as a player in 1969, I moved back to Boston. Mayor Kevin White had saved a position for me when I left the Celtics in 1968—director of recreation for the city of Boston. Let me assure you, it was no walk in the park. This was back in the days of forced busing, which was a very volatile issue in Boston. My appointment did not sit too well, either, and it became highly political. Then there was the matter of my having a white driver as part of the job, but that was a whole other issue. As in every other part of my life, however, I was determined to persevere, to change people's minds. I had to start in my own backyard. Literally.

Now that I was a city employee, I had to live within the city limits. For us, that meant the Moss Hill area of Jamaica Plains. There was no welcome wagon. Instead, on the day we moved in, during a downpour, our white next-door neighbor erected a six-foot-high fence between our houses. This was the same neighbor who got into a fight with our real estate agent for finding us the house in the first place.

On the second day of school, a bomb threat was phoned in.

Fortunately, things settled down after that. Chuck Daly was the head coach at Boston College back then, and he lived right around the corner, so that helped ease our transition into the area. I also had become good friends with Eunice Kennedy Shriver and became very involved working with the basketball program in Special Olympics, which did my heart good.

The job was another story. It really was a rocky year—all for $18,500. I did color commentary on the Celtics broadcasts to supplement my income.

My appointment was controversial for a number of reasons, not the least of which was that I was black. I later learned several of my former Celtics teammates had to convince the mayor to go through with the hire because I had not come through the proper channels. I was an outsider who had not spent years in the department. Promotions usually were based on years of service and the scores on civil service exams, with preference given to veterans and disabled veterans. I was neither of those. I had tried to enlist as a senior in college, but the marines would not take me because I was too tall.

Anyway, the mayor did not think there was a qualified person for this job within the department, and he wanted someone with some new ideas. Jack Warner, the parks commissioner, wanted to bring in reform. Both of them had higher political aspirations. I was hired as a result of all that.

The protests started almost immediately. I got so much hate mail I feared for my children. There were weekly editorials and letters to the editor criticizing me. But I wanted to stick it out. I wanted to make a difference. I took the job seriously, which I soon found out made me a minority in a completely different sense. I started holding organizational meetings and weekly staff meetings. I also decided to tour all the facilities to see how they operated.

We started in the South End. We pulled up to the first recreation center about 7 P.M. The doors were locked, and it looked totally deserted. We started pounding on the doors until somebody finally came around to see about all the noise. I asked where the director was. "Well, he has a job down the street tending bar," I was told. When I asked why the center was locked up, I was told, "If we open the doors, all these kids will come in."

That's me (third from left) with Wayne Jr. in a parade during my days as Director of Recreation in Boston (Courtesy of Embry family)

It was the same thing at the other centers we visited that night, and for many nights afterward. Of course, there were some centers that were open and were doing some very good things. But far too many of them were being run (or not) by directors not at all interested in anything but their paychecks.

My first reaction was to fire all those directors. Of course, I found out they were civil servants and I could not fire them. That was my introduction to patronage.

Despite those drawbacks, I came up with an idea to start the Boston Neighborhood Basketball Association (BNBA), and I am proud to say it is still in existence today. Together with Jeep Jones of the Boston Youth Authority and Kenny Hudson of Coca-Cola, we lined up some corporate sponsors, including Coca-Cola, the *Boston Globe*, and television station WBZ, and it became a huge success. I had much assistance running it. Vinnie Costello, a former Boston College player, was the commissioner; Tom Sanders represented the Celtics; and Alfreda Harris was the assistant director of recreation.

In the wake of the riots over busing, I thought this would be a way to bring harmony to the city and get kids to cross some boundaries as the result of sports. While the kids all started playing games in their own neighborhoods, by tournament time, they had to go across town for the championship. It took off like crazy, and it was really rewarding to see these kids getting along. It also brought neighborhoods together. It was just great.

Of course, I still had moments where I wondered what I had gotten myself into. I remember on Christmas Eve, my driver, John Gallagher, from South Boston, came to me and said, "C'mon, let's go for a ride. We're not going to work today."

He headed toward Southie, the scene of some violent protests against forced busing and integration. Pretty soon he stopped at a bar. I said, "John, I can't go in there." And he said, "You're with me." So in we went.

Well, every eye in the place turned toward the door, and it got so quiet you could have heard a pin drop. After a couple of seconds—two of the longest seconds in my life—I heard someone whisper, "It's Wayne the Wall." I had never been so thankful I had worn that Celtics green. Before you know it, everybody is buying us drinks. In fact, eventually, I had to drive John home. But that one afternoon helped me build courage for some later challenges.

I lasted through the spring and into the summer. White was running for governor, while Warner was going to run for mayor. I remember walking through Public Gardens with him one day, and it seemed like everyone we passed said hello to me.

I looked at Warner and joked, "Maybe I should run for mayor."

He told me, "Don't get any ideas."

In reality, I knew I did not belong in the world of politics. I thought I had done some good. The basketball league was so popular, they created a similar one in hockey. But the system was not going to change, and I did not really fit into the political scene.

I had been following the Bucks, and I had kept in touch with Wes Pavalon, the owner. Late in the summer of 1970, Wes came to a tennis tournament outside of Boston to visit his good friend Arthur Ashe.

Let me explain about Wes. We first met in 1968, when I was taken by the Bucks in the expansion draft. I was not going to go to Milwaukee, but I changed my mind after I met the Bucks' owner.

Wes was born in Chicago and grew up in one of the city's poor neighborhoods. He loved playing basketball, but he did not pursue it because he had to work to provide for his mother and brother. As an adult, he made his fortune by developing Career Academy, a school that trained people for skilled jobs that did not require a college degree.

His love for basketball never waned, though, and when the chance arose to buy the expansion Bucks, he jumped at it. He never wanted to be referred to as the owner, though, because he disliked the notion that any one person owned any other. He was a very compassionate man, a sympathizer who had championed many unpopular causes. After the riots in Milwaukee, he took to wearing dashikis and giving the Black Power sign and handshake. He had supported such diverse groups as Native Americans and the Puerto Rican FALN. I loved him because of that compassion, even if, as a night owl, he would often call me at 2:00 A.M. to discuss one thing or another.

He was very sensitive to the perception of African Americans in and out of sports. He had made incredible friends. One of them was Alex Haley, author of the groundbreaking *Roots*, which was later turned into a popular television miniseries, and another was Ashe. And while he had come to see Ashe play in the tennis tournament, he had come to talk to me, too. He came out to the house on a Saturday afternoon, and it did not take long for him to broach the subject of my returning to Milwaukee.

"For what?" I said.

"An assistant to the president," he said, referring to Ray Patterson.

The Bucks general manager, John Erickson, was leaving, and Wes told me I would be responsible for player personnel and scouting. He was offering me a salary of $25,000.

At that point, I was not a pioneer. This was a front-office job without a lot of responsibility. There was one hitch, though. Wes wanted me to convince my old teammate Oscar Robertson to come to the Bucks.

He asked me if I thought that was a good idea.

"It's an instant championship," I told him. "It's a no-brainer. Short of giving up Alcindor, do whatever you have to do."

At the time, they were squabbling over $15,000, which seemed ridiculous even then. I convinced Wes to pay the money, and I told Oscar he should accept a trade from Cincinnati.

"You're the greatest player ever to play the game, but there's one thing you haven't achieved," I told Oscar. "You deserve a championship ring."

I told him I had decided to take the front-office job, so this would be a chance for us to reunite. Once Oscar agreed, I knew we would have something really special. We traded Charlie Paulk and Flynn Robinson to get him and never gave it a second thought.

Larry Costello had devised an offense that made it impossible to double-team Lew Alcindor, and that made us tough to stop. That team came together perfectly. We won sixty-six games in the 1970–71 season. We had a six-foot-four-inch power forward in Greg Smith. Bobby Dandridge was a very underrated player. Jon McGlocklin was one guard, and Oscar was the other. It was a very special group of guys, a lot of fun. We just kept winning. If we lost a game, Larry took it as if we were a sub-.500 team. But we were way ahead of everybody in the conference.

Players hung out together then. Alcindor was a loner, but overall there was more dependency on each other. It was more of a family atmosphere. They respected Oscar. They had a greater appreciation of the game. Not that any of that really mattered. We were just better than everybody else that season. We beat San Francisco in the conference semifinals, four games to one, beat Los Angeles in the conference finals, four to one, and then swept Baltimore in the four games of the NBA Finals.

It was nothing like the championships now, with all the media and television exposure and games in prime time. You had to be a fan of the Bucks or Bullets to really know when the games were being played.

After we won, for some reason our plane was delayed, so we went back to the hotel in Baltimore and threw a huge party. We stayed up celebrating and it got pretty wild. When we were getting ready to board the bus for the airport the next morning, one of the reporters—Bob Wolf of the *Milwaukee Journal*, a World War II veteran who had lost his arm—was nowhere to be found. He had roomed with the other beat writer—Rel Bochat of the *Milwaukee Sentinel*. They were the original odd couple. Eventually, Rel came downstairs. "You're not going to believe this," he told us. "Wolfie lost his arm."

The missing prothesis finally was found under the bed, and we were on our way. Back home, we had another party at another hotel.

Wes was so excited, he was like a little kid. I finally had to tell him, "Stop hugging me."

But it was a great day for him, for the team and for the city of Milwaukee, which had not won a world championship since the Braves won the World Series in 1954.

Little did we know it would be the last major professional title for the city in the century, although Al McGuire did lead Marquette University to the NCAA title in 1977.

But the Bucks were not able to repeat as champions. Winning the championship in the third year of our existence was quite a feat, and because most of the players, except for Oscar, were young, it appeared a dynasty was in the making. But the rest of the league continued to get stronger.

In Chicago, general manager Pat Williams and coach Dick Motta had put together a powerhouse built around the considerable skills of Chet Walker, Jerry Sloan, Norm Van Lier, and Bob Love, a former Buck. In Golden State, the Warriors had a dynamic pair in Nate Thurmond and Rick Barry and an excellent coach in Al Attles. The Lakers were still potent with Chamberlain, Baylor, and West. In the East, Baltimore was still good, but New York and Philadelphia were coming on and Boston had retooled and was good again. Any of those teams, along with the Bucks, was capable of going all the way.

We started the 1971–72 season the way we ended the 1970–71 season. Every game against the West was like a play-off game. The Bulls became our main rivals largely because of proximity and the relationship between the two competitive coaches. In Los Angeles, the Lakers were on a roll. Gail Goodrich had come over from Phoenix to join West in the backcourt, and they had hired Bill Sharman, the former Celtic great, as coach. Wilt was physically sound, and Jim McMillan was no longer a rookie. The Lakers went on a thirty-three-game winning streak, breaking the record of twenty straight we had set the year before. But we did have the pleasure of snapping that streak with a 120–104 victory at Milwaukee on January 9, 1972.

Five teams won fifty or more games, led by the Lakers' sixty-nine and our sixty-three. Chicago won fifty-seven, Boston fifty-six, and Golden State fifty-one. The stage was set for an incredibly competitive play-offs, and we knew it was going to be extremely tough for us to defend our title.

In the first round, we lost the first game at home to Golden State but then won the next four games. The Lakers beat Chicago in four straight to set the stage for a showdown between the two teams with the best records in The League as well as four of the biggest stars. The individual matchups between Lew Alcindor and Wilt, and Oscar and Jerry West, were absolute classics.

We won the first game in Los Angeles, but with Oscar nursing a leg injury, we lost the series in six games. The Lakers went on to beat the Knicks in five games to win the 1972 championship.

The big news after that season would come off the court.

Chapter 10

Making History

On March 6, 1972, the course of my life was changed forever.

It was a Monday morning. I was sitting in my office preparing for the draft when Ray Patterson came in and dropped the first bomb.

"I'm going to Houston as general manager starting next week," he said. Pete Newell had left the Rockets to return to the Lakers, which created the opening for Ray.

I was stunned. I also wondered where this left me in the Bucks organization. I did not have to wait long to find out. Ray told me Wes Pavalon wanted to see me in his office that afternoon.

After several anxious hours, I went to see Wes, and I was surprised to see several of the board members of the Bucks sitting with him. I knew something was up, but I did not know it concerned me.

Wes got right to the point. "We are naming you general manager of the Milwaukee Bucks this afternoon," he said with a big smile. "Congratulations." He added that Bill Alverson was going to be president of the team, and the franchise was in our hands.

I stood speechless as everyone started shaking my hand and patting me on the back. They were looking for a response from me. All I could do was sit down.

Wes took note of my state and asked gently, "Do you have any questions?"

I could not tell him my Number 1 question was, "What in the hell just happened here?" I could not articulate the other questions running around in my brain: "Am I ready? Can I do this? Will I be accepted?"

This was 1972 in Milwaukee, which had a reputation as one of the more segregated cities in the country. The city was only a few years removed from the race riots. As much as I grew to love it there, it was hardly the most progressive of communities, and this was a groundbreaking move. There were no other African American general managers in professional sports at the time. I was the first.

Believe me, I had plenty of doubts and misgivings. But as I sat there in a stupor, my grandfather's voice came through loud and clear. This was no different from when he made me go back to high school when I wanted to quit. I could almost picture him on The Hill that afternoon telling me, "Give it a chance. Only cowards quit and the Embrys were not cowards. Don't let anyone take your identity. Respect the Embry name and make sure it stands for something."

I snapped out of it and looked at Wes. He told me my salary would go from $27,000 to $32,000. I was sure my colleagues in similar positions made more, but I was not going to make an issue of it. Actually, that was one of my least concerns. The questions I finally was able to ask had more to do with job description. I wanted to make sure I had the authority that went with the responsibility. He assured me I did and made it clear Larry Costello and the coaching and front-office staffs reported to me.

It started to register just how big an undertaking this was going to be. In addition to scouting and the draft, I was going to negotiate all the contracts, oversee ticket sales and all the other business operations, and manage a budget. I had some experience in some of these areas. I sold season tickets during the off-season during my first two years with the Royals, and I had managed four hundred people as the director of recreation in Boston. I had also taken a Dale Carnegie management course, thank goodness. And I had a great mentor in Red Auerbach.

I was still somewhat in shock when I got home and told Terri. She congratulated me and wondered why I was not more excited. I told her

I just wanted to stay low-key and take it one step at a time. In truth, I was still worried about the reaction I would get.

A press conference was scheduled for noon the next day so the afternoon paper would get the story. We were able to get through the night without a leak, which was extremely unusual. As we filed into the room and took our places at the head table for the press conference, I could see the reporters really had no idea what was about to happen.

Wes did not waste any time. "We are happy to introduce Wayne Embry as the new general manager of the Milwaukee Bucks," he said. A jolt went through the room. Some reporters scrambled out the door looking for phones; others stayed to ask questions.

I stood to address the throng, but I kept my remarks short. I thanked Wes and the board for having confidence in me and promised to do my best to keep the team in contention. I said I wanted to build on the great job Ray had done. (He was being introduced as the new general manager in Houston at about the same time.)

Then I asked for questions. The very first one was, "How does it feel to be the first black general manager in professional sports, and do you think that it is significant?"

I thought for a moment. "It is significant," I said, "only if others think it is significant."

Clearly, others thought it was, although interestingly enough, the *Milwaukee Journal* story that day made no mention of race. I had become a familiar figure in town, and I think my promotion generally was viewed as a natural progression.

In a column in the *Journal* the next day, Terry Bledsoe wrote, "Embry's ability, not his color, earned him this job, and Embry's ability will determine his success in it."

Nonetheless, the coverage was extensive, and the headlines around the country focused on my being a pioneer. Of course, that brought added pressure. I could not fail, because it would be a setback for blacks. Forget the fact that hundreds of white general managers had been fired and no one thought twice about hiring another one. What I tried to get across was that we as blacks should be given the same opportunity to fail as whites. That would be significant, but it would be more significant if I succeeded—as Jackie Robinson did.

In almost every interview I did, I was asked if I felt added pressure because of my color. I always said I did not, and I would bring up my grandparents and parents raising families when the racial climate was much more tense. That was pressure. I would bring up how Robinson broke the color barrier in baseball. That was pressure.

Because of his liberal tendencies, Wes was accused of appointing me as window dressing in response to the civil rights movement. But he dispelled that theory by pointing out my qualifications and experience, and he told anyone who would listen that I had all the authority and support I needed to do the job.

It did not take long for the mail to start pouring in. A lot of it was congratulatory. A lot of it was not. Wes actually kept the worst hate mail from me, but I knew what was going on. Terri and I discussed it, but we decided quitting was not an option now, just as it had not been an option in high school.

I was worried there might be a mass exodus of season ticket holders and sponsors, but Wes assured me that would not happen and would not make him change his mind if it did. With that sort of support, I started to look forward to the opportunity and the challenge, and I used all the negative reaction as motivation. Whenever doubt started to creep in, I would think about what Jackie Robinson or Dr. Martin Luther King had experienced. They were great inspirations to me. I could not allow their struggles, nor those of so many blacks, to go to waste.

So, I was about to start my career in management, something that had never entered my mind, even as a remote possibility, at any time. Remember, when I left Miami, I wanted to be the newest member of the Cradle of Coaches. I knew I would have to draw on everything I had learned in every aspect of my life if I was going to be successful. Expectations were high, although they had less to do with me and more to do with the presence of Kareem and Oscar. But I had expectations for myself, too. I wanted to be the best.

There was no time to celebrate my appointment. I learned two days later that Ray was taking half our staff to Houston, leaving me without a public relations director or ticket manager. Three other support staff people quit, so I was left with a staff of four out of eleven. I tried to persuade my good friend Jim Foley to stay on in public relations, and I asked ticket manager Cathy Bartley to stay on also. But Ray had promised them substantial raises in Houston, so I had office positions to fill immediately, and later I had to hire an assistant coach.

We had lost assistant coach Tom Nissalke to the ABA's Dallas Chaparrals. We had gone without an assistant in 1971–72, but Larry recommended one of his Niagara College teammates, Duke assistant coach Hubie Brown, as a replacement for the 1972–73 season. I had interviewed Hubie while scouting the Big East tournament in New York. Actually, if the truth be told, he had interviewed me. This was the first time I had crossed paths with someone from the Five-Star camps, a sort of unofficial basketball fraternity in which Brown played a key role. He was only too happy to brief me on the Five-Star lore. In spite of that, I hired Hubie, hoping his experiences on the university campus would help Larry better understand the college athlete.

Larry was old school. There was nothing wrong with that, but society was changing and the young people of the 1970s, including the athletes, were products of those changing attitudes. Because of the war and other current events, young people had grown distrustful of adults and resented authority of any kind—even on the basketball court. We had to find a better way of communicating with our players.

I had made more hires off the court. I moved John Steinmiller, a former intern who had just graduated from the Marquette University School of Journalism, from a part-time job to full-time director of public relations. John was extremely bright, and I had no reservations about promoting him. I also named Cathy's assistant, Bea Westphal, as our ticket manager. They proved to be two of the best hires I ever made. I named Larry Reed, a coach of the minor-league Milwaukee Muskies, head scout. Comptroller Ted Herpel chose to stay. This inexperienced crew set about running a franchise that had won the championship a year earlier.

I was standing at the bar in the Crown Room, a popular spot in the classic Pfister Hotel, when a stranger approached me to offer congratulations on my appointment. He introduced himself as Ed Damgaard, whose daughter Kim was my daughter Jill's best friend at Oak Creek Elementary School. He asked me about staff openings, and I told him I did not think I had anything for him.

"Oh, it's not for me," he told me. "It's for my ex-wife." He was looking to relieve some of the financial burden he had assumed since their divorce.

The following Saturday morning Jean Damgaard showed up for an 11:00 A.M. interview. She was as nervous as I was. We chatted about our daughters to relieve the tension, and she told me she had worked as a secretary at their school. She also informed me that we had accepted a dinner invitation to her home and then stood her up. I felt terrible, mumbling something about a miscommunication. Then I offered her a job as my secretary.

She started on Monday morning, and if I thought she was nervous on Saturday, she was a basket case on Monday. The sixty words a minute she claimed she typed was more like thirty words a minute, and she did not take dictation as I had been led to believe. She was afraid I was going to fire her after one day, but instead I called her in and told her, "Relax, Jean. We'll learn this job together."

On the court, we were in much better shape. I welcomed the chance to work with Larry Costello. I admired his work ethic. In fact, I often thought he worked too hard at the job. The players also thought he worked too hard and, as a result, overworked them. Still, I guarantee that no team was better prepared.

Now that I was in charge, we had to go through a little role reversal. But we had a great deal of mutual respect for each other and thought we could work well together because of our passion for winning. He quickly learned to trust my judgment on players and my knowledge of the game in general.

The next adjustment I had to make was to de-playerize myself. To be the boss, I realized that I had to discard the player mentality. I had to establish a different relationship with them. No longer could we hang out and party together. This was a difficult transition for me. Oscar and I had roomed together for six years in Cincinnati, while Jon McGlocklin and I had been roommates in Cincinnati and Milwaukee. They had become good friends of mine, and we had fought many wars together, both on and off the court.

But I could no longer be one of the boys. It was difficult to explain to them how my responsibilities had changed. As a player, I had joined in the fight to make as much money as possible with little regard for the profitability of the club. Now I had to keep an eye on the bottom line as well as protect the integrity of the club.

Most of all, I wanted to establish a relationship of trust and mutual respect. I promised them I would always tell them the truth, even if it was something they did not want to hear. I knew honesty was essential in keeping their respect. As a player, I never wanted to be lied to by management or the coach, particularly when it impacted my family. I decided I would always treat them the way I had wanted to be treated as a player. I knew I could not treat everyone the same, because each had different needs, but I resolved I would be fair to everyone. I had learned from Red Auerbach that it was important to understand players as people.

This was another test of my management and leadership capabilities. I dug out my notes and manuals from the Dale Carnegie management course I took while director of recreation in Boston, and I tried to brush up on some of the skills I had learned.

There were external relationships I had to manage. I had to overcome skepticism from the fans and the media. The question I was most frequently asked was how could a thirty-two-year-old former player assume the responsibility of running the franchise. There had been coaches my age, but Jerry Colangelo of the Phoenix Suns was the only person my age running a team. I had to establish a rapport with agents, who were becoming increasingly prominent. It was necessary to develop relationships with my colleagues in the field and the league office. I also made it a point to network with college coaches, who were interested in getting their players drafted because it helped their recruiting. I had been taught by my family and by the coaches at Miami that relationships were built on trust. I had been taught you should never lie to anyone. My coaches at Miami were emphatic in telling me never to lie to the media. This proved to be valuable advice. These were the basic qualities I needed, but as time passed, I learned there were many other attributes that I needed. I was about to be tested in more ways than I could imagine.

It was imperative that I earn the respect of the players as quickly as possible, since I was going to be drafting them and signing them. I had to prove to the skeptics that I could handle the responsibility of the job. Early on, I thought drafting the most talented players was the way to build a team, but I learned there was more to it than drafting talent.

In fact, I learned there was more to everything than I thought at first.

With the changing society and the threat of the rival American Basketball Association, managing in the 1970s was going to be quite a challenge. I had learned from Ray that because we were a small-market team, the Bucks could not compete with New York and Los Angeles for the top players. The Milwaukee Arena was the smallest in The League. We could not charge the same ticket prices as the larger markets, and we could not expect the same revenues from radio, television, and sponsorships. Therefore, it was crucial that we stay within our budget, which determined what we paid for draft picks and other players. This left us vulnerable to losing players to the ABA, which was not going away. With Kareem and Oscar making top dollar—for Oscar, that meant $275,000 at his peak—we tried to get the best players we could with what was left.

Milwaukee Pro Sports was a public corporation, which meant we had an obligation to our shareholders. We were competing in a league in which most of the owners were entrepreneurs who could spend whatever they wanted on players in the days before the salary cap. We set our budget for player personnel based on potential revenue, and we did not exceed it. Because of our limited resources, we received considerable criticism for not signing players. Some of that criticism came from Kareem and Oscar, who, understandably, wanted good players to complement them. But we made every decision with an eye on the bottom line. We believed profitability was the key to success in Milwaukee. Nonetheless, we still wanted to win and satisfy our fans, who had been spoiled by the success of the great Green Bay Packer teams.

By winning the NBA title in the third season of our existence, we raised expectations. At the same time, with Kareem, Oscar, and a bona fide star in Dandridge, who had become one of the best small forwards in The League, we thought we had a dynasty in the making. Lucius Allen, Jon McGlocklin and Curtis Perry rounded out our top six players. Now I had the chance to add to that core.

The 1972 draft was my first as general manager. After losing to the Lakers in the play-offs, it was apparent that we needed more depth. I had watched Russell Lee as a six-foot-five-inch high school standout in Boston. He dominated his opponents in high school and was a great college player at Marshall. He attended many of the basketball camps in the Boston area, and he always held his own when he played against the Celtics players. I drafted him with the sixth pick in the first round, which we had acquired in a trade. With our own pick, Number 12, I drafted Julius Erving from the University of Massachusetts, who was playing in the ABA. Though he became a legend, he was not all that well known at the time.

I first met Julius in August 1968, when I was invited to speak at a basketball camp in Schroon Lake, N.Y. I drove down from Boston and arrived in the evening. I was supposed to talk to the coaches that night and address the campers the next morning. But, with my first training camp with the Bucks fast approaching, I wanted to get in a workout before I met with the coaches. I was going to run a couple of miles and then do some work on the court. The coaches asked me if I wanted to play a game, but I did not really want to beat up on their counselors, so I declined. Then they told me they had a high school kid who would play me one-on-one. I was doubtful, but I agreed.

"Go get Julius," somebody said.

This skinny, timid-looking kid showed up. I told him I wanted to work on my outside game, so I promised I would not shoot within the free-throw line. I was afraid I might hurt him. I told him he could use the whole court. Well, he proceeded to turn me every which way but loose. We were supposed to play to eleven and, right off the bat, he scored the first seven points. I scored a couple of points to make it respectable, but he was the first to eleven. We were going to play the best-of-three, so he said, "Mr. Embry, you can play regular basketball against me." I said, "Okay, but I'll be easy on you." I still thought I would hurt him. So I am trying to practice my hook, but he was blocking my shots all over the place. He totally dominated me. That was my introduction to Julius Erving.

The next time I saw Erving, he was at UMass playing against Marquette in the NIT in Madison Square Garden. He scored 12 of the first 14 points and Marquette Coach Al McGuire was fit to be tied.

"Who is that skinny kid?" he screamed at Assistant Coach Hank Raymonds.

"That's Julius Erving," Raymonds said.

"Who the hell is Julius Erving?" Al yelled, looking right at New Yorker Dean Meminger.

"That's the Doc," Meminger said, using the nickname Erving had earned because of the way he operated on the court.

"Why isn't he playing for us?" McGuire wanted to know.

No one had an answer for that, but it was a question I kept asking myself in 1972.

Erving had come out after his junior year in college and signed with the ABA's Virginia Squires. He averaged 27.2 points in 1971–72. After we took Lee, I told my staff we were taking Erving with Number 12.

"What do we know about him?" they asked me.

I said, "Trust me, he's good. I don't know if we can get him out of the ABA, but there's nothing wrong with having his rights."

We could not pry Erving out of the ABA, and of our ten draft choices, only Lee, Chuck Terry, and Mickey Davis, another ABA player, made the team. Obviously, none of them was exactly the kind of help Kareem and Oscar sought. I knew we still had work to do if we were going to recapture the title in an improving league.

In addition to trying to improve our team on the court, my management skills were tested in off-the-court events as well.

Until the summer of 1971, Kareem, who had converted to the Muslim faith some years earlier, had gone by the name Lew Alcindor, the shortened version of the name he was given at birth, Ferdinand Lewis Alcindor Jr. But before taking a State Department tour of Africa with Oscar and Larry Costello and their wives, he made it known he preferred to be addressed by his Muslim name, Kareem Abdul-Jabbar. Roughly translated, it meant "generous servant of Allah" and "powerful."

Given that Milwaukee was not the most progressive city, there was an undercurrent of concern as people assumed he was part of Elijah Muhammad's controversial Black Muslims. In fact, Kareem belonged to the Hanafi Madhab sect, which believed in a literal interpretation of the Koran.

The difference between the two sects was not driven home until tragedy struck. On January 18, 1973, seven persons, including five children, were slain execution-style in a Washington, D.C. home that Abdul-Jabbar had purchased and donated to the Hanafi sect. With the rival Black Muslims believed to be responsible, there was concern Kareem or his family might be targets, so he was assigned round-the-clock security. The security was beefed up for our games in Chicago, home of the Black Muslims, and Kareem even skipped the 1973 All-Star Game, which was held in Chicago Stadium.

In spite of my many years in The League, and my experience in the business world, nothing prepared me for any of that. Despite the obvious tension, there were some amusing moments. In most cities, we had off-duty policemen guard Kareem. I remember one night my phone rang about 2 A.M. after we had played in Buffalo. It was Kareem. He was in the hotel and he was hungry. He wanted to go out and get something to eat, but there were no security guards outside his door. I got up and called the Buffalo police department, which sent over a couple of officers to accompany the big fellow on his quest for a midnight snack.

Our players did not know what to make of the whole thing, either. Most of them were no more familiar with the Muslim teachings than we were. Dandridge, who lived in the same apartment complex as Kareem, told us he was going to go home and nail a pork chop to his door, because the only thing he knew for sure about Muslims was that they did not eat pork and he wanted to make sure everybody knew he was not part of the religion. None of our players wanted to stand next to Kareem during the pre-game introductions in Chicago just in case some lunatic took a shot at him.

That was just one of several distractions off the court. On the court, a rash of injuries made our lack of depth even more obvious. Still, we won sixty games for the third year in a row. We seemed to be hitting on all cylinders, finishing the 1972–73 season by winning fourteen straight games. The play-offs were a different story. A Golden State team featuring Nate Thurmond and Rick Barry whipped us, four games to two, en route to the NBA championship. Our showing was disappointing and caused the skeptics to continue to question my ability as general manager.

If they only knew of the mounting off-court problems, many of which we did not want to make public.

Shortly after the season was over, I was at the Pfister Hotel's rooftop bar, the popular Crown Room, for the usual Friday cocktail hour when a man of color approached me and introduced himself as "Mack."

He had a reputation as one of Milwaukee's hustlers.

"Wayne, I respect your position and me and my partners want you to succeed," he said. Then he asked me to follow him to an isolated corner in the crowded bar. He told me he and some other hustlers who were engaged in illegal activities knew some of our players were involved in the same activities.

"I am pulling your coattail," he said, using a common black slang expression. "I hope that you can talk to them before they embarrass you and the franchise."

I cannot say this was the first time I had heard rumors of drug use by our players, but this was the first time the rumors were confirmed—or were at least being spread by sources closer to the action. My first inkling of trouble had come from the officers providing security for Kareem in Chicago. After staying on the same floor of the hotel as the players, the captain of the detail told me the smell of marijuana was overwhelming in the hallway. He wanted me to know before the players got busted.

I addressed the players the next day at practice, repeating what the police captain had told me. I added that this was a growing problem in The League. It was further proof that athletes were not immune from the activities on college campuses. I appealed to them to have more respect for themselves and their families and I implored anyone involved to stop.

After that, and my talk with Mack, I wondered if drug use had anything to do with our disappointing showing in the play-offs. We had beaten Golden State three out of four times in the regular season, and I thought we could beat them three out of four anytime—but we were unable to do so in the play-offs.

Our 60–22 record left us with the Number 18 pick in the draft, and selecting that low made it tough to get players who could provide immediate help. I decided to take a risk on Swen Nater, a back-up center to Bill Walton at UCLA under the great John Wooden. Walton may have been one of the best college centers ever, so Nater did not get much playing time. He would have been a starting center on any other college team in the country. He was six feet, eleven inches and built like a weight lifter, but I drafted him because I thought he was that talented. He had a great hook shot and could shoot facing the basket, too. Even though he played sparingly, I figured anybody who practiced against Walton every day had to be pretty good.

UCLA booster Sam Gilbert, who was referred to as "Papa Sam" by the UCLA players, represented him. Wes had a good relationship with Sam, so I thought we would have a good chance to sign him even though I had heard the ABA was interested. In fact, because the ABA was interested, I made it a priority to sign Nater.

Unlike the NBA, the ABA did not require players to finish their college eligibility, and more and more junior stars—and some even younger ones—were leaping to the rival league. Eventually, Spencer Haywood challenged the NBA's rule and the courts found that it violated antitrust law. As a result, players who could provide evidence of financial hardship were allowed to make themselves eligible for the draft, starting a trend that completely changed how we operated in pro basketball. Eventually the rule was relaxed enough so that high school players from well-to-do families could bypass college and enter the NBA.

But back then all I was worried about was keeping Nater. Immediately after the draft I called Sam to arrange a meeting to begin negotiations. He told me Swen was eager to talk and invited me to meet them at the Airport Marina Hotel in Los Angeles the next day at 4 P.M. The normally chatty Gilbert was all business during the conversation, which struck me as odd. Sam always liked to brag about his relationship with the UCLA players and how much he did for them.

On the four-hour flight from Milwaukee, I was confident I would come back with Nater's signature on a contract. Sam and Wes had all but agreed on the terms of the contract. Wes gave me a little more room to negotiate if I needed it. Wes would have had all of Papa Sam's players if he could have. Who could blame him? Just about every player from UCLA was a pro prospect.

I arrived at the hotel precisely at 4 P.M. There was no Sam or Swen. I wandered over to the newsstand and picked up a copy of the *Los Angeles Times,* then returned to the lobby where we had agreed to meet. I waited thirty minutes, then went to the front desk and asked if there was a meeting room in Sam's name. There was not. I called Sam's office and was told he had left at 1:30. That was more than enough time to get to the Airport Marina no matter how bad the traffic was.

Finally, about 6 P.M., Ralph Shapiro showed up. Ralph was Sam's lawyer who reviewed contracts before they were signed. This was not a good sign.

"Where in the hell is Sam?" I asked as he approached.

"Wayne, Sam told me to tell you that Swen has signed with the Virginia Squires in the ABA," he said. "I can't tell you any more than that."

I went crazy.

"What?" I screamed. "Why would he have me fly all the way out here if he was going to renege on our deal?"

I was fuming.

"Don't blame me," an embarrassed Ralph said as he began backing up. "Sam will call Wes tonight and call you tomorrow."

I stormed to the phone and called Wes, who was not happy about the news. He could not believe Sam would betray him.

"Welcome to the new world of the NBA," I said as I hung up the phone.

As I was calling United Airlines to book a flight back to Milwaukee, I saw Al Bianchi, the coach of the Squires, and Earl Forman, the owner of the club, climb into a cab. Not only had Sam betrayed us, he did it right under my nose. I took a red-eye flight back to Chicago. I drowned my frustrations in a bottle of red wine and finally got some sleep before landing at O'Hare.

Sam did call the next afternoon to apologize for my inconvenience.

He said he had had a conversation with Wes while I was en route to Los Angeles and Wes told him we could not match the ABA offer. That is not what Wes told me. Although I was jet-lagged and still mad, I held back my anger because I knew there would be more pro prospects coming out of UCLA.

The newspapers criticized me for not signing Nater, the second draft in a row that had not worked out as I had planned. The press and our fans were wondering how we were ever going to get back into contention. Each year Oscar was getting older, and each year The League was getting better and better. We did not have a second- or third-round pick in the 1973 draft, which meant Clyde Turner, our fourth-round pick, was the only draft choice we signed. The media had a good time with that. Barring any trade, we were heading into the 1973–74 season with the same team that got bumped out of the play-offs.

My off-season work was cut out for me. Dandridge wanted to renegotiate his contract. Of course, this was nothing new. He always wanted to renegotiate his contract. Whenever a player signed a contract for more than Bobby was making, I could expect a call from Bobby or his agent, Irwin Weiner, no matter how many years were left on his deal. Bobby felt, as did many other players, that we should just rip up his deal and give him a new one. He threatened to sit out the season if I did not do it. He challenged me to trade him if we did not want to renegotiate. Trying to explain the integrity of a contract did not mean anything. Bobby was persistent, which I respected, but I had to remain firm. If I did not, every player on the roster would have been at my door.

Bobby's reputation was well known throughout the league. I used this to calm him down for a while, but after several more demands, I invited him into my office to explore trade possibilities. Of course, I had no desire to trade him. He was a key to our team. In my opinion, he was one of the most underrated players in The League, even though he was highly regarded.

"We are not going to extend your contract," I told him.

"So why am I here?" he asked.

"You said you wanted to be traded if we did not do something, so I'm going to make some calls in your presence to see what we can do," I told him, praying that no one would take me up on my offer. I also let him know he was not going to dictate his destiny. I told him if I could not make a deal that would benefit the Bucks, he would have to remain with the team under his current contract.

I put on the speaker phone and called the teams he had listed as his preferences. Bobby did not like what he heard.

"I love Dandridge," we were told over and over, "but I don't need another malcontent."

It was an eye-opener for Dandridge. Players think every team covets them. I thought this when I played, as did others of my generation. Clearly, that was not the case. Dandridge left my office with his head down. I was not disappointed. I thought it would buy us some time. We loved Dandridge, too.

The summer of 1972, a representative from the State Department called to ask if I was interested in doing a USO tour of the military installations and hospitals in the Far East, and I jumped at the chance. With the antiwar protests continuing at home, and the end of the war seemingly nowhere in sight, the State Department sent celebrities from the sports and entertainment worlds to visit our soldiers stationed on bases close to the war zone. Morale sank as the casualties mounted.

Larry Costello, Lucius Allen, John Block, and their wives joined Terri and me for the four-week trip. I had gone on two previous State Department trips, one to foster relations in selected Iron Curtain countries and one to South America. On each of those trips we played against the national teams of those countries. This trip was different. We were not going to play. We were going to speak to the troops and try to lift their spirits.

We flew on Military Air Carriers with servicemen and their dependents. Our journey took us to bases in Japan, the Philippines, Taiwan, and Okinawa. Seeing severely wounded or drug dependent young men and women in their early twenties was a real eye-opener for us. It was an emotional experience engaging in conversations with bewildered GIs whose only concern was what was going on in the "world," which meant back home. We had a new appreciation for them as they lay in hospital cots wrapped in bandages and attached to machines. More casualties came in daily. It was a vivid reminder of the horrors of war. I often was overcome visiting with men and women who looked so much younger than nineteen and twenty. The nurses and doctors directed us toward patients who were not going to survive, and it was especially difficult to talk to them.

Despite the fact they were in the jungles of Vietnam, they still followed the NBA and were eager to know how their home teams or favorite teams were doing. There were Bucks fans who wanted to know how I was going to bring the championship back to Milwaukee. There were lots of questions about Kareem, who probably was the biggest name in the league at the time. I promised each one we would win the championship just for him or her. There were other questions about the homeboys who were in the league, players they had gone to high school with or lived near. So many had been high school or college athletes who had dreamed of playing in the NBA. Some asked for tryouts when they got out of the service, and I could not turn any of them down.

This was an important experience for all of us. We had an opportunity to bring joy to those who had sacrificed their lives for Americans, many of whom scorned them for going to war. It made all of us realize how fortunate we were to do what we did while hundreds of thousands of men and women our ages were being shot at in Vietnam. The hospital visits were inspirational for me, much like those I had had with Maurie Stokes, who never improved significantly and died of a heart attack in 1970.

I know I had a different outlook once training camp opened, but we still had some problems to correct. We had the same veterans and several rookies who had no chance of making the team. The fact that we had not acquired anyone to strengthen our bench was a concern to Kareem and Oscar, the media, and the fans. Nonetheless, we were regarded as the team to beat in the West, although the Warriors were the defending champion and the Bulls were stronger.

Wes still believed in me, as he reassured me in our nightly 2 A.M. chats. I promised that when an opportunity arose, I would go all out to get Oscar help in the backcourt. Wes, Larry, and I agreed this was our top priority. Oscar was thirty-four, and he was plagued by nagging injuries. We also needed size.

Larry hated to cut players and looked to me to do it. I did not much care for it, either. I found it difficult to tell an athlete who devoted so much time and energy pursuing his dream that he was not good enough to make the team. As a player, I hated it when another player got cut. Now I was doing the cutting. I always told them face-to-face, and I tried to show empathy. I always offered to help them catch on with another team. Players usually left with greater respect for the organization—and for me.

I say usually. In my second training camp, I had an experience I had never had before and have not had since—a player who refused to leave. Fred Warren had been granted a tryout for the team as a favor to Kareem, per Wes. Fred, who also had switched to the Islamic faith and adopted the name Abdul Monsuar, was a six-foot-four-inch guard with very few skills, although he was extremely strong. He had a build like former heavyweight champion Jack Johnson. The only basketball he played was in intramurals. I had never heard of him. The only reason he was in camp was because of his friendship with Kareem. He thought that was enough to allow him to make the team, but Larry and I thought differently. Not only were there players more deserving of making the team, but I also did not want to set a precedent of letting players dictate the composition of the squad. Plus, we had just acquired Fritz Williams.

When I told Fred he was cut, he stared at me defiantly. That look, and his physique, were enough to make me keep the conversation short. Thinking my job was done, I went home to Fox Point to spend the afternoon with my family and watch some football. Shortly after lunch the phone rang. It was Fred.

"I am not cut from the team," he insisted. "I talked to Kareem. You need to come to the Holiday Inn so we can talk."

My first reaction was to hang up on him, but I could not be that cold. Unable to reach either Wes or Kareem, I decided I would meet with Fred and assure him he had been cut. But as I drove downtown, I kept seeing that look in his eye, and I remembered reading in the paper that week about a football player with the Houston Oilers who had pulled a gun on the general manager who cut him.

When I got to the hotel, I called his room.

"Yeah," he answered.

"I'm in the lobby," I shouted, my anger plain. I declined his offer to meet in his room. I was no fool. I wanted as many witnesses as possible.

Fred finally met me in the coffee shop, and we had a heated discussion loud enough to arouse the curiosity of some other customers. He refused to accept that he had been cut. I had no idea how to deal with this. Nothing I had read or heard had prepared me for such an absurd situation. I tried everything, but nothing would placate him. The more I talked, the more he argued. The look of disdain was enough to intimidate most people, but I had never let anyone intimidate me and I was not about to start now.

"Fred, let's get out of here," I ordered, heading to the front desk. He stood with me wearing a puzzled look on his face. I introduced myself to the front desk clerk as the general manager of the Bucks, and I pointed at Fred.

"This is Fred Warren," I told the clerk. "He was trying out for the Bucks. He has been cut from the team and, beginning immediately, we are not paying for his room or incidentals."

Before I even finished talking, I walked out the door and got into my car. I could not get away from there fast enough. I was beginning to think being general manager was not going to be much fun.

I never saw Fred Warren again that preseason. But late in the regular season, he showed up at a game in Los Angeles. This big brute of a man with his shaved head threw his arms around me and gave me a big hug as we burst out laughing.

There was another "distraction" (if you want to call it that) during training camp that season. The rival ABA had come into existence in 1967, and the new league was signing young college stars before their classes graduated, scooping them up before they were eligible to play in the NBA. The ABA owners, coaches and players—and the agents who represented them and were becoming more of a factor in our business—believed their league was equal to the NBA. In their minds, the only difference was exposure. They were eager to prove their point, and in 1971 the NBA agreed to play preseason games against the ABA. It was not until 1973 that the Bucks did so. The ABA teams welcomed the move because it gave them a chance to prove their point, and they thought it might expedite a merger of the leagues. The NBA wanted to prove that the ABA was an inferior league and needed gimmicks to attract fans. With no television contract, survival was going to be impossible for the ABA, which was entering its seventh season.

I wanted to bury them. I was an NBA loyalist and hated everything about the ABA, including the red, white, and blue ball that looked as if it belonged in a circus act and the silly three-point shot. I thought they were making a mockery of the game. Even when I was still playing and the ABA was raiding the NBA for veterans to establish credibility, I had no desire to jump leagues as some of my colleagues did. Who knows? It might have meant a financial windfall for me. But with all the stories I had heard, this was no guarantee. Teams often struggled to make their payrolls as the NBA did in its infancy. I knew what it was like to rush to the bank to cash my check ahead of my teammates in case the money ran out. This was a common joke among players in The League during the 1950s.

I had another reason to dislike the ABA. My life would be easier if I did not have to compete for talent. I thought the ABA teams were paying players way too much. That made the agents the biggest beneficiaries. I also still dreamed of having Oscar and Kareem on the same team as Julius Erving, who had become an ABA star.

With the intent of proving the NBA's superiority, I scheduled three games against ABA teams during the 1973 preseason. One was against the defending ABA champion Indiana Pacers. Why not beat the best? What better way to prove our dominance? The other two games were scheduled against the Utah Stars and the Denver Nuggets.

After about a week, the team was ready for a break from the rigors of Larry's two-a-day practices. Despite the presence and influence of Hubie Brown, Larry had not eased up in his demands at all. In fact, he may have been more demanding. His teams were never going to lose by being out of shape or unprepared. My respect for Kareem continued to increase as he practiced as hard as, if not harder than, any rookie trying to make the team. Remembering how Red Auerbach and Bill Russell agreed to preserve Russ for the season, I approached Larry with the suggestion of doing the same thing with Kareem, Oscar, and Dandridge, but he did not want to hear it. He was a taskmaster, and he was totally inflexible when it came to preparation. He also was obsessed with winning another championship.

All this was starting to wear on the players. There was more grumbling and complaining than usual. Nagging injuries occurred more frequently. Some were legitimate; some were fake. When players start to fake injuries to get out of practice, it is a signal that things are starting to break down. While the players were complaining about Larry, Larry was complaining about the players. He was constantly coming to me asking me to trade whoever he was upset with at the moment. Of course, players upset with Larry asked to be traded, too. No one was really serious. The trade demands were just a way for both sides to relieve their frustrations.

From that standpoint, the games against the ABA came along just in time. The first game was against Indiana. Bobby Leonard, who played with the Lakers in the 1950s and 1960s, coached Indiana. Having graduated from Indiana University, he was very popular in the state and was a very good coach. To my amazement, Market Square Arena was sold out for the game. It was like a world championship environment. The crowd was loud, and the players were excited. We agreed to play the ABA rules, which meant that awful tri-colored ball and the three-point shot. The referees were two defectors from the NBA, Earl Strom and Norm Drucker. This eased my concerns about getting hammered.

I turned out to be more pumped than my players. I sat and watched a Pacer team that played as if it were in the seventh game of the NBA Finals. The Pacers outhustled us, outrebounded us, and flat-out outplayed us. Roger Brown, Darnell Hillman, Mel Daniels, Bob Netolicky, and Don Buse were too much for us. After the game, the players and fans celebrated as if they had won the world championship. Those Hoosiers sure love their basketball.

I was mad, and losing to the Pacers did not sit well with Oscar either, but that did not keep us from the post-game festivities at a bar owned by Netolicky. Our team was invited for free food and beer, which assured we would show up. We also wanted to show we were good sports. Quite frankly, it was enjoyable observing the camaraderie of players and listening to "Slick" Leonard tell us some crazy tales about surviving in the ABA. Terry Pluto's book, *Loose Balls,* does an excellent job describing the same sort of wacky goings-on in the league.

After regrouping and beating several NBA opponents, we traveled to Salt Lake City to play the Utah Stars. Ron Boone and Steve Jones were their best players, but the team lacked size. I thought there was no way they could beat us. But I was wrong again. The environment in the Salt Palace was much the same as it had been in Market Square Arena, and we lost another close game. Once again, we had been outhustled. In all my years as a player, and in my few years in the front office, the one thing I could not stand was a lack of effort. There was no excuse for not giving effort. I could not hold my emotions in check after the game. I could not handle losing to two ABA teams, and I decided to let my players know it.

I rose from my seat and practically sprinted to our locker room. I was there before the coaches and players arrived. The players came in, took their seats, and began undressing as the ballboys handed out beers, which was the custom. Dandridge opened a beer and was just about to take a drink when Larry yelled to the ballboys, "Take that beer away from him and the rest of the guys. They don't deserve anything to drink."

The players looked at him as if he was losing it. He very well may have been because, as an NBA diehard, he was as mad as I was. But I had gone in to deliver a message, and I did.

"Give back the beer," I ordered the ballboys. I turned to Larry and Hubie and yelled, "What makes you think you are doing such a good job? It's your job to prepare them for games, and they were not mentally or physically ready to play tonight."

I could see the players were feeling as if they were being treated as children, and I wanted to correct that, although this was in direct opposition to what I learned in "Administration 101," which was never to chew out a coach in front of his players. I went on to tell the players they had to get their acts together, too, and play the way I knew they could.

The episode helped bring our team together. Many of the players came up to me the next day in the airport and thanked me for recognizing a problem and having the courage to get on the coaches. It was not really courage, it was objectivity, but the players appreciated it regardless. To my surprise, Larry and Hubie expressed their appreciation, too. Progress was being made.

Our next stop was Denver. Our old friend Alex Hannum was the coach, and we knew he would have his team ready. I could not stand the thought of losing to another ABA team, but after spending some time with the players and coaches, I was starting to have an appreciation for the league. They were just trying to make a living, as we were.

We came and played like I knew we could and beat Denver. After the game, Larry asked me to join him and Alex for dinner. It was a reunion for the two of them. Larry had played for Alex in Syracuse and Philadelphia. Alex was a great NBA old-timer who had coached championship teams in St. Louis and Philadelphia. The ABA needed his credibility. He was successful in getting Rick Barry to jump to the Oakland Oaks and got other players and coaches to make the jump as well.

I had no idea what I was getting myself into. I figured it was going to be a long night from what I knew of Alex. In the NBA, he was known as "Shot-and-A-Beer Alex." We had a terrific dinner, exchanging war stories from the NBA and the ABA. Alex was a pioneer in both leagues, and his stories had me laughing hysterically. The evening lasted into the morning, and I enjoyed every minute of it. Alex confessed that he was shaking in his boots the time he challenged me to a fight in the semifinal series in which my Cincinnati team upset his Syracuse team. We laughed about that and many, many other things.

When I finally got back to my hotel room, I collapsed into bed and fell into a deep sleep. I do not know how long I was out before the phone rang. I thought it was my wake-up call and, considering the way I felt, it had come way too soon. Shaking the cobwebs out, I groggily said, "Hello."

A recognizable voice said, "Do you have any comment on Kareem and Lucius getting arrested last night for possession of drugs?"

I figured it was a prank, slammed down the phone and rolled over to go back to sleep. I did not do shots with Alex, but I had had my share of beers. I thought I was having a nightmare.

I was. Only I was not sleeping. The phone rang again a few minutes later. It was Larry.

"Kareem and Lucius have been arrested on drug charges and are in the county jail," he said.

After we spoke for a few minutes, I hung up the phone and sat on the edge of the bed, contemplating my next move. I said a prayer for the two of them before I got up and threw on some clothes. Then the phone started ringing off the hook. Because of the hour time difference, the news had hit back home before we knew what was happening in Denver. I just let the phone ring and left the room.

A myriad of thoughts went through my mind during my cab ride to the slam. One of them was the line from the old Johnny Paycheck song, "Take this job and shove it."

It was becoming clear to me that there was no glamour in being a general manager in major-league sports. The job was supposed to be fun, but it had not been much fun so far.

I had never been in a jail before, so I had no idea what I was doing. At 5 A.M., no one was friendly. Working the graveyard shift was no fun for anyone, let alone the desk clerks who had to book offenders all night. I could see the guy was not in a very good mood. Of course, neither was I.

"Do you have two guys in here from Milwaukee, Kareem Abdul-Jabbar and Lucius Allen?" I asked angrily.

"They're in there," he said in a similar voice, pointing to a metal door with a little barred window.

Both of them were wide awake, sitting with their chins in their hands, staring into space. I stood there dumbfounded. Looking at them, I realized I did not know what to say. Even though I was angry, I had to keep cool and try to be sympathetic. I kept reminding myself that people are innocent until proven guilty.

Finally, I spoke up. "Do you guys have bail money?" I asked them. I had learned from the not-so-friendly desk sergeant that the only way they could be released was if someone put up bail.

"No," they said in unison. Then they asked me if I could bail them out.

"Guys, I don't have enough money to get you out of here," I told them. But I did let them know that their problem was my problem and that I would get them out.

I did not want to wake Wes. I knew he probably had just gone to bed. So I decided to call Sam Gilbert, the booster known to UCLA players as "Papa Sam." He was used to these kinds of calls, he once told me.

Thank goodness he answered the phone. It was 6 A.M. in Denver, 5 A.M. in Los Angeles. I did not want to hear Rose Gilbert at that hour.

"Sam, two of your favorite sons are here in the Denver jail on drug charges, and between the three of us, we do not have enough money to post bail," I told him in one breath. "Got any suggestions?" I yelled into the phone. I wanted to make sure he heard every word I said clearly.

Because it was only 5 A.M. in Los Angeles, Sam was not able to come up with the money either. He suggested I call Arlen Preblood, an attorney who was the executive director of the ABA Players Association, who lived in Denver. By the time I reached Arlen, he already had heard the news, which was traveling fast. I wanted to get the guys out and be on our way to Milwaukee as soon as possible, but I had to wait until Arlen arrived. Waiting in the holding area, I thought about how to get all of us to Milwaukee without interference. There was no way I could disguise Kareem. Lucius maybe, but not Kareem. I envisioned a mob at the airport, and I needed a plan to get us through this.

I called team president Bill Alverson to keep him posted, and the two of us discussed our return. We decided the best way to deal with the media was to hold a press conference at the airport upon our return. Bill and public relations director John Steinmiller were going to handle that. All I had to do was get us home.

I called trainer Billy Bates and told him to call the Denver airport and ask about security and whether they had a room we could all wait in together until our flight departed. I also instructed him to change our tickets so we could fly to Chicago and then bus to Milwaukee. I thought that might cut down on the mob at the airport back home. Finally, I told him to get our gear packed up and loaded on the bus.

Mr. Preblood arrived and we got the players released. Lucius's two friends, Mordecai Cook III and Stephen Duncan, who had also been arrested, were on their own.

Kareem, Lucius, and I listened intently to Mr. Preblood's advice. He told us our only comments should be, "Per the advice of counsel, we are forbidden to comment." That seemed easy enough.

Mr. Preblood gave us a ride back to the hotel. Both players were anxious to tell me that they were innocent of any drug involvement. They insisted they were only passengers in the car. I assured them I had no reason to doubt their stories and would stand by them. Considering what they were about to face from their teammates, the media, and fans, they definitely needed a friend.

The team bus was quiet on the way to the airport. I briefed Larry and Hubie, double-checked our plans with Bates, and finally addressed the team about how to answer questions. As expected, the airport was a mob scene. Television trucks were parked curbside. Roving television reporters holding microphones eyed our bus while jostling for position with print reporters holding notebooks. The airport did a terrific job with security. Police and other uniformed officers formed a wedge and ushered our party through the media and curious onlookers and into a room near the United concourse.

Everything went perfectly, except for the paparazzi. They tried to break through the security barrier, and one closed in on Kareem, causing a little scuffle. No harm was done.

We flew home without incident and got on the bus for Milwaukee. I prepped everyone once more on the procedures we would follow and reiterated the "no comment" line. I promised to facilitate the process as much as possible. As we approached the Milwaukee airport, the bus slowed in traffic, and Kareem and Lucius shocked me by getting up, opening the front door of the bus, and bolting for the parking lot, where they jumped into their cars, drove over the curbs, and fled. That left me holding the bag, and I was furious.

After conferring with Steinmiller, we decided I had to face the press. All I could do was apologize and explain that the players had taken off. Rapid-fire questioning began. I had been up all night, and I wished I was anywhere else. They did not want to hear that our attorney had advised us not to comment. Finally, I threw up my hands and said, "Ladies and gentlemen. I did not get busted. No further questions."

Terri did a great job of screening calls that night, but it did not matter. I got very little sleep.

Once again, I had had no preparation for something like this happening under my watch. When I saw the headlines the next morning, I realized the magnitude of this story. Here was the best-known basketball player in the world being arrested for drugs. Now it was up to me to make things right.

Alverson set up a meeting with the board of Milwaukee Pro Sports the next day to discuss the issue. Although I was upset they had left me holding the bag, I met with Kareem and Lucius again to get their stories so I could report them to the board. Once again, they pleaded innocent and claimed they were passengers in the car when it was stopped by police for a minor infraction. While searching the car, the police found evidence of drugs and drug paraphernalia. I pledged my support and that of the organization.

Once the board heard their stories, it backed the players. Wes wanted to make sure we had the best attorney available in order to resolve the issue quickly. Within a matter of hours, the case against Kareem was dropped. It took a few months before the case against Lucius was dismissed, in part because it was the third narcotics arrest for Allen.

All of this served as more on-the-job training for me. I knew in the future I would have to warn players to be careful about their associates because they would be held accountable for their actions. Personally, I was desperate for something good to happen for the Bucks. In my short tenure as general manager, we had had far too many bad breaks. Of course, not much good was happening in society, either. Men and women were still dying in Vietnam and in the streets of our country. Watergate was dominating the news. In response, young people were holding peace rallies and concerts like the one at Woodstock.

When the 1973–74 regular season finally started, we won fifteen of our first sixteen games, with Kareem and Lucius leading the way. Both put the past behind them and stepped up to provide much needed leadership. We picked up Cornell Warner, a six-foot-nine-inch power forward/center to give Perry and Cunningham help up front. We were stronger than a year ago.

Ninety miles to the south, our old rivals, the Chicago Bulls, were threatening. Dick Motta was in his fourth season and had put together a superb team. If we were going to win the Western Conference we would have to go through them, which Motta knew better than anyone. Larry was the best prepared coach in The League. He was one of the first to scout the opponent and use film to prepare for the games, although the players were not much interested in two-hour film sessions.

Larry became obsessed with beating Chicago. He was an NBA loyalist and resented intruders like Motta coming from the college ranks and taking jobs he thought should go to NBA alums. I, however, always thought Motta, Cotton Fitzsimmons, Jack Ramsey, and other college coaches brought professionalism to The League. Larry could not stand losing to anyone, but losing to Chicago was out of the question. Because of our proximity to Chicago, he would go to Bulls games whenever we had a night off. He insisted Hubie or I go with him. He saw the Bulls play so much that he knew the Bulls offense as well as the Bulls players. That meant our players knew what would happen in the Bulls plays before it happened.

Nonetheless, Bulls general manager Pat Williams and Motta had put together an excellent team. They had acquired Chet Walker from Philadelphia to go with my old teammate Bob Love. That gave them one of the best scoring duos in The League up front. Jerry Sloan and Norm Van Lier were two of the toughest defenders in The League. Tom Boerwinkle was the center. The team played hard every night and was able to keep pace with us because Motta was almost as obsessed with beating us as Larry was obsessed with beating them. Motta was determined to find a way to stop Kareem.

Bucks fans remained enthusiastic. We continued to sell out the Milwaukee Arena, and there was the feeling that this would be our year again, despite the disappointment we had experienced since winning the championship. It seemed that everyone was talking about us in the streets and in the taverns that were the lifeblood of Milwaukee. In the Brew City, there was a bar on just about every corner, and the locals would gather after their work days to talk sports. The bars sponsored bus trips to our home games, and even to some road games. Major Goolsby's was located right across the street from the Arena and became a favorite hangout for players, coaches, the media, and our fans. Morry's and Saz's were two more of the earlier sports bars in Milwaukee. On any given night, you might find any number of our players or coaches bending their elbows and shooting the breeze with fans and/or reporters.

As the season progressed without any distractions, I was able to concentrate more on college scouting. I had not done well in this area to date, and I needed to focus on it. I used three regional scouts, and at the end of the season, I would hire Rick Sund, who had been an intern for us the previous season. Rick's basketball experience was limited to playing at Northwestern. But after graduation, he completed the Ohio University graduate program in sports management, the first of its kind, and received a master's degree.

I did not know many of my colleagues when I started scouting, but after a few weeks of scouting the same games, staying in the same hotels, and flying on the same flights, we became quite well acquainted. Pete Newell, the legendary coach who guided the University of California to the NCAA title in 1959 and coached the Olympic team the next season, adopted me. I also got to know Bob Feerick and Stu Inman while traveling with Pete. They coached against each other in the Bay Area and were good friends. Jerry Colangelo, the young general manager of the Suns, also joined our group.

Before long, we were scheduling trips together, making the travel much more fun and much less lonely. This was a great help to me early in my career because these great gentlemen had a great wealth of basketball knowledge that they would share with me. They also introduced me to many of their friends in the coaching fraternity, which also proved to be quite valuable. I was much more comfortable scouting games in the South when I was with them. There was safety in numbers.

Pete and I scheduled a trip to scout a game in Biloxi, Mississippi. I rented a car in New Orleans, picked Pete up at our hotel and drove the short distance to Biloxi. Pete was to be the navigator, although he was absolutely terrible at it. We got lost on our way to the Civic Center and found ourselves in a rural area somewhere outside of Biloxi. After several turns that took us nowhere, I suggested that we stop and ask directions. Pete pointed to a general store/gas station where several old men wearing bib overalls and red bandanas were sitting on a porch. All I kept thinking was "KKK."

"Wayne," Pete said, "why don't you get out and ask them how to get to the game?"

I stared at them, and they stared at me.

"Pete, they look a little red around the neck," I said. "I think you should ask them."

Pete grumbled, "They'll think I'm some carpetbagger." But he got out of the car. Then he turned around and looked at me, "You got my back."

We got the directions and lived to tell the story to our traveling buddies after the game. Pete could not wait to tell them our story. They got a big laugh out of it. None of us realized there would be a sequel.

To occupy our time during the days or on off days, we visited museums and historical sites, or went to the movies. Pete and I loved to go to the horse races. While having breakfast the day after our escapade in Biloxi, we noted that post time at the Fairgrounds was 1 P.M. The Fairgrounds was one of the top tracks in the country, and we did not want to come to New Orleans and not try our handicapping skills at one of the best, so we decided to go. We asked the bellman for directions, but we managed to get lost again. I was ready to fire Pete as a navigator, but that would mean he would have to drive, and that option was even worse. I was safer with him as a passenger.

I knew we were close, but we could not find the track. Our route took us right through the 'hood, and once again I suggested we stop for directions. As we approached a gas station, we observed a group of teens who looked like troublemakers hanging around the door. I told Pete to get out and find out where we were.

"Oh, no, Big Man," he said. "This is your territory. You go. I've got your back this time."

Turnabout is fair play, I thought as I got out of the car.

Obviously, we came through unscathed. But I always was happy to have company while scouting. I even scouted with my chief rival Pat Williams. He was a great storyteller and was quite entertaining. His post-game routine involved stopping at a Dunkin' Donuts, or a Krispy Kreme store if we were in the South. If I had traveled with him more, I would have doubled my weight, and goodness knows I did not need that.

What I did need was the camaraderie and the knowledge these trips afforded. All of us shared our philosophies. We talked about our common problems and discussed how current events were changing how we managed our players. We talked about these without breaching any confidences. Although we developed a great mutual trust and admiration, we were all serious about our jobs and remained competitive. Colangelo probably was the most competitive, whether playing basketball or gin, which we did well into the morning on some of our trips. He was a whale when it came to playing gin. I had had a fish before, but he was something much bigger and would not quit until he recovered at least some of his losses.

All of us discovered that post-season scouting was the best. There were several All-Star games that had to be scouted, and the weeklong Aloha Classic was Number 1. Red Rocha, a former NBA player and coach, was coaching at the University of Hawaii and founded the event, which featured the best thirty-two college seniors in the country, along with a ringer supplied by agent Ron Grinker. Ron and Red had become friends over the years, and he always kept a spot open for one of Ron's hopefuls who would be lucky to go as high as the second round. He usually was from the University of Cincinnati, where Grinker was the Bearcat mascot.

We were able to scout the best talent in the country and also had a chance to interview them. At the same time, we did take advantage of the great weather and the beaches of Waikiki. Trappers bar in the Hyatt Hotel became our post-game gathering spot to compare notes and trade stories. We figured this was a reward for all the trips we took through rain, snow, and sleet to the most remote spots in the country. One could truly understand how my experiences in twenty years of scouting could easily fill yet another book.

Back in Milwaukee, Kareem was vintage Kareem and Lucius was having the best year of his career. Oscar was steady and even though McGlocklin was slowing down, he was still making a contribution. We were on target to win sixty games for the fourth straight season when Lucius went down with torn knee cartilage. This was a devastating blow. Many thought our play-off hopes were gone. McGlocklin also was hampered with nagging injuries, which meant Fritz Williams and seldom-used Dick Garrett would have to step up if we were to have any chance at all in the play-offs.

We finished the season 59–23. Our opponents in the first round were the aging Los Angeles Lakers. Much to everyone's surprise, we beat them, four games to one, to advance to the conference finals against the pesky Bulls, who had won fifty-five games. We split the six-game season series, but with the injuries to Allen and McGlocklin, the Bulls were confident that they could beat us. With two coaching geniuses who had it in for each other, there was little doubt both teams would be ready. Larry had not made all those trips to Chicago Stadium for nothing. But Motta's offense was so disciplined it did not matter how much opponents scouted it. Love and Walker were going to get their shots, and Motta thought if his players executed the offense, it would work. That was always Red Auerbach's philosophy, too.

The games brought out the best in everyone, including the writers. The Chicago writers loved to come to Milwaukee for beers and brats as much as our writers loved to go to Chicago and hang out on Rush Street. There was nothing like sitting and listening to Bob Logan of the *Chicago Tribune* and Rel Bochat of the *Milwaukee Sentinel* exchange tales about their respective coach's quirks.

It was a great series for the fans, too. Lots of them took the opportunity to make the ninety-mile trip, even if they could not get tickets to the games. They found this to be almost as much fun hanging out in the bars, watching the games on television, and arguing with the locals.

We opened with a 101–85 victory at home and followed that with a 113–111 victory in Chicago that was even more intense. Game 3 was back at the Arena, and we continued to play well, leading most of the way in a 113–90 victory. Out of frustration, or maybe as part of his strategy, Motta got kicked out of the game early in the fourth quarter. He stormed onto the court to dispute a call made by referee Don Murphy. Earl Strom came running toward Motta signaling a technical foul. Without hesitation, Motta took off his jacket and flung it in the direction of Murphy. The jacket wrapped around his neck, and he called another technical on Motta, which meant an automatic ejection. Assistant coach Phil Johnson had to restrain Motta from any further hijinx. While he was doing that, Benny the Bull, clad in his red mascot outfit, charged onto the court looking as if he were about to gore the officials. He was tossed immediately, then took off his mascot head and tucked it under his arm as he stomped off the court with Motta to a mixed chorus of applause and boos. It was the first time I had ever seen a mascot get kicked out of a game, although there were not nearly as many mascots back then as there are today.

I knew there was no television in the Bulls locker room, and I knew not being able to watch the game would drive Dick nuts. So I invited him, and the mascot, to my office to watch the rest of the game on television. An extremely frustrated Motta sat there bemoaning the fact that he could not figure out a way to stop Kareem. Of course, no one else had been able to do so either.

Because Fritzie Williams and Dick Garrett came through for Allen and McGlocklin, we won the final game in Chicago to sweep the series. Bucks fans were thrilled as we returned to the Finals.

While we were winning the Western Conference, the revived Boston Celtics were winning the East. They had not been to the Finals since Russell retired in 1969. Auerbach and my friends, Jan Volk, the general manager, and Tommy Heinsohn, the coach, had put together a team of young stars to go along with some of the veterans left over from my era. Dave Cowens was an All-Star, and Don Chaney and JoJo White were emerging stars. Paul Silas, Don Nelson, and John Havlicek still were going strong.

We split the four-game season series with them. Under normal circumstances we would have been the favorites, but because of our injuries, the series was a toss-up, even though we had the homecourt advantage, if there was such a thing against the Celtics. No one ever really wanted to face the Celtics in a championship series. Still, our team and our fans were confident. After all, we did have Kareem and Oscar. Of course, the Celtics still had the lucky little leprechaun.

The city was primed for our opener in the Arena. Fans poured into Goolsby's and other bars to keep tabs on their beloved Bucks. Larry's popularity was at an all-time high after his undermanned squad knocked off the Bulls, and everybody expected good things against the Celtics as well.

The Celtics thought the only way to counter Kareem was to press. A full-court press would get the ball out of Oscar's hands, and it would also use up time on the 24-second clock, cutting down the time Kareem could get involved in the offense. That was crucial, given his five-inch height advantage on Cowens. Heinsohn also thought that pressing Oscar would wear him down. Don Chaney, their six-foot-five-inch guard and best defender, was assigned to Oscar. The Celtics knew that without the speedy Allen we were at a disadvantage because Williams was not a good ball handler.

The strategy proved to be effective, and the Celtics led the series, three games to two. Chaney pressured Oscar, White guarded Williams, and our backcourt really struggled, leaving Larry searching for an answer. He thought of moving Dandridge to the backcourt, which would have slowed us down up front. Plus, Bobby was effective against the aging Havlicek. So he left that matchup alone. But he did come up with a bold strategy—one of his greatest coaching decisions. In Game 6 at the Boston Garden, with the crowd poised to celebrate its first championship since 1969, Larry shocked everyone by starting Mickey Davis at guard instead of Williams. Mickey, the closest thing I had ever seen to a hippie basketball player, had played only garbage time all season. He was a good practice player, and his best attribute was his shooting. His lack of speed did not matter, because he was matched up against Chaney defensively. Larry wanted Mickey in the lineup for two reasons—to pull Chaney off Oscar so he could advance the ball against JoJo White, a weaker defender; and to give us another shooter, which would allow Kareem more room to operate inside. It worked. With his shoulder-length, blond hair flapping in the breeze, he nailed turnaround jumper after turnaround jumper in White's face all night.

The game will go down in history as one of the all-time classics because of the number of clutch plays by both teams, particularly in the closing minutes of regulation and the two overtimes. Dave Cowens dived after a loose ball that wound up in Havlicek's hands, and his mid-range jumper gave the Celtics a one-point lead late in the game. With seconds to go, Cowens fouled out, and Henry Finkel was called on to guard Kareem. Although Hank was taller, he did not have the physical strength Dave had.

Larry called a timeout to devise a play for the last shot. There was total bedlam in the Garden as fans were ready to rush the court. Everybody in the place knew the ball would go to Kareem when play resumed. Oscar took the inbounds pass and looked for Kareem in the post. But the Celtics pushed Kareem out onto the baseline, and he was about twenty feet from the basket when he got the ball. In one motion, he caught the ball and launched one of his famous skyhooks over an extended Finkel. As the ball swished through the basket, thousands of Boston fans stood in disbelief. Heinsohn called a timeout with five seconds left, but Havlicek's jumper was wide as the horn sounded on our 102–101 victory.

A weary but elated Bucks team rushed off the court, knowing that it was too soon to celebrate. We had to regroup for a Sunday afternoon game back at the Arena.

The city was wired for Game 7. The 1971 championship was won away from home, so taking one here would be a first for Milwaukee. There was a near-riot on North Fourth Street as fans filled the streets, trying to skip in front of those who had rushed downtown and slept out overnight in order to buy tickets for Game 7. Fans also poured into Goolsby's hoping Saz (popular bar manager and man-about-town Steve Sazama) or Goolsby's owner Jerry Cohen had tickets left from the allotment they bought from Bea. The police actually had to be called in to restore order.

The Celtics came in determined. They decided to move Chaney back on Oscar to pressure him full court and wear him down, figuring he had expended a lot of energy in Game 6. They were willing to let Mickey try to beat them. Mickey had another good game, but the Celtics prevailed, 102–87.

After the game, I made my way to the Celtics locker room to congratulate my old buddies. I fought my way through the media to see Red, Jan, Heinie, Nellie, and John. I noticed there was no champagne. Red had not changed. I told Jan that we had bought champagne, and I offered it to him. He checked with Red and, much to everyone's surprise, Red accepted it. My guess was because he did not have to buy it.

My team was dejected after losing a hard-fought series. We all felt that if Allen and McGlocklin were healthy, we would have been the ones drinking the champagne. But Mickey had done a tremendous job filling in for them, which was why, like Red, I always tried to convince each of my players to be ready because each was essential to the success of the team.

I sent Terri and the kids home after the game. They shared my disappointment and offered their support, but after all these years, Terri knew I wanted to be alone. I went to my office, closed the door, and quietly sat and stared off into space for hours. I reflected on the season. It was a year of controversy and adversity, but we were able to overcome both and nearly win the NBA title. Larry had done a great job of coaching, particularly after the injuries. He did a great job of keeping the team focused on basketball and not letting it get caught up in the distractions. Kareem and Lucius were able to recover from their problems and have spectacular seasons.

Normally, after all of this, one might say, "Wait until next year." But next year would bring changes for us. Oscar had announced he was going to retire, and we were facing expansion, meaning we could lose two players who had contributed to our success. There was no way we could replace Oscar, who, at the age of thirty-four, was still one of the top three players in the league. But we were not going to give up. I was determined to remain a contender. I was going to work to get talent to complement Kareem, either through the draft or trades or by picking up veteran players put on waivers by their teams. I had learned that from Red. Good players also were jumping from the ABA as more teams were folding or moving to new locations.

During the play-offs, I had asked Commissioner J. Walter Kennedy if I had to protect Oscar if he announced his retirement. I was told I did not have to protect him if he wrote a letter to The League stating his intentions.

But this was a touchy subject for me. What if he really did not want to retire? I did not want to seem presumptuous, even though it had been well-publicized that he was thinking about it. I called him in first thing Monday morning to explain my dilemma. After commending him for his gallant effort the past week, I asked him about his future.

"Big Fella, I don't know what I'm going to do yet," he told me.

I prodded him for an answer with no success. This did not make for an easy decision. In the end, we protected him. I was not going to allow an expansion team to draft him. It would have been an insult to one of the greatest players in the history of the game, who happened to be a good friend of mine.

Eventually, we lost Curtis Perry to New Orleans.

I decided to draft guards just in case Oscar decided to retire. Gary Brokaw, a lightning-quick six-foot-four-inch junior from Notre Dame, was our first-round pick. Later that spring, we signed former Marquette star George Thompson, who had played for the ABA's Pittsburgh Condors until they folded. The rest of the summer I kept my eye out for veteran players and kept an eye on what was happening in the rest of society.

Under extreme pressure as a result of the Watergate investigation, Richard Nixon resigned as president of the United States. The war in Vietnam was over, and it was a time to reunite the country. America cried out for honest leadership. Drug problems were still on the rise, which meant they were still a concern for the league. It was all part of the social revolution. The ABA was hanging on by a thread. Dr. J was still very much on our minds in Milwaukee. We kept thinking it would be great if the ABA folded and we could get him to play in Milwaukee with Kareem and, maybe, Oscar.

After Brokaw was signed, I took my family on vacation to San Francisco and then to Anaheim and Disneyland. I was feeling pretty good about our season, but many years in sports taught me we could not rest on our laurels. While in the Bay Area, I visited with my old friend Al Attles, coach of the Golden State Warriors. We talked about the changes in The League. He, too, was concerned about drugs and the emergence of the agents. Just like the rest of our country, the NBA cried out for honest representation, too. Most of the agents were legitimate, but there was a growing number who were downright dishonest. My eyes were opened in Hawaii, when I saw agents hustling players by using whatever worked—from prostitutes to payoffs to drugs. These guys were beginning to influence our decisions. Honest agents had the best interests of the players in mind and were easy to deal with. We therefore found ourselves steering away from players we knew were represented by sleazy guys.

I was hoping the rest of the summer would go along smoothly. I was becoming recognized as a leader among the general managers, who elected me chairman of our association. Later that summer, I was asked to serve as a trustee for the Basketball Hall of Fame. I really was feeling good about things. I thought all our problems were behind us, and I could continue having fun at the job I loved.

I was still waiting for Oscar's decision. I had several conversations with Jake Brown, Oscar's agent.

Finally, Jake called and said Oscar wanted to play another year. My stomach was tied in knots. After conferring with Wes and Alverson, I called Jake and told him we were not going to re-sign Oscar. We had signed Brokaw and Thompson, and they had to play. This was one of the toughest calls I ever made. In my heart, I knew Oscar was better than who we had, despite his age. I was telling my friend and former roommate that we no longer wanted him. Eventually he decided to retire.

Little did I know there was more controversy to come. One morning in late September, I awoke to the news that the Atlanta Hawks had signed Julius Erving. When I arrived at the office, Jean told me Richie Guerin had called. Richie was the coach and general manager of the Hawks. An ex-marine, Richie was a tough guy and his toughness carried over to the court, which caused many fights during his career. He nearly started World War III when the head of the Uruguay Basketball Federation asked him to throw a game while he was coaching a group of NBA players there. We literally had to fight our way through our final game. I called him back and unloaded with both barrels. If we had been in the same room, we would have come to blows. I was seething.

"What in the hell do you think you're doing?" I shouted over the phone, loud enough for the entire office to hear me.

"The Squires are about to fold, and we are prepared to fight in court to keep him," he yelled back.

"We'll see about that," I replied and slammed down the phone.

The NBA did not need someone to challenge our constitution and by-laws at this time, not with the ABA still hanging around. It was too early to call Wes, so my next call was to Alverson. He and I then called The League office to report what had happened. They were already aware of it and were as upset as we were. They, too, were prepared to take action. However, the lawyers in the league office were advised to go slowly for fear of opening up a can of worms. They did not want to defend any antitrust claims, but they were prepared to do so if necessary.

Julius, who had signed a secret five-year contract with the Hawks the day before we had drafted him, went to training camp and played in two exhibition games with the Hawks before the league got an injunction forbidding him from playing. That began an endless series of legal maneuvers that took the entire season to settle. On June 5, 1975, the NBA voided Erving's contract with Atlanta, ordered the Hawks to give the Bucks $150,000 and their two second-round draft choices in 1976, which we used to take Alex English and Scott Lloyd. The Hawks also had to pay $250,000 to the league. We retained Erving's NBA rights, but we lost them when the two leagues merged in 1976. No one will ever know how Erving's presence might have altered the future of either franchise.

Even without Dr. J, we opened training camp in 1974 optimistic that we would contend in the West. Bill Walton, the next great player from UCLA, was drafted by the Portland Trail Blazers and made them instant contenders. We were scheduled to play Portland in our first exhibition game at the Dayton Arena on October 4. I had given the game to my friend and former Celtic roommate, Don Nelson, to promote. He had some experience in promoting games on barnstorming tours of New England after the NBA season, and it was customary to give the games to a promoter because we did not have the staff to travel to the cities and work the markets. Nellie was prepared to give us a guarantee and split the gate. With the matchup between Kareem and Walton, the game was not going to fail, but Nellie moved to Dayton anyway and stayed there until he had to report for training camp.

About that time, I got a phone call from Sam Gilbert. I was not prepared for the bombshell that was about to be dropped. Sam told me Kareem wanted to meet with me, Wes, and Bill Alverson after the afternoon practice on October 3. I had no idea what this was about, but I figured he wanted to renegotiate his contract. I called Wes to tell him about the meeting, but he already knew about it. In fact, he knew what it was about. It seemed Kareem had called and asked to come out to the farm. While the two were fishing for trout in the pond near Wes's house, he told Wes he wanted out of Milwaukee. When I heard that, I immediately responded, "We have to change his mind."

I called Lou Zevertnik, the food and beverage manager at the Sheraton West Hotel, to reserve their biggest suite. I asked him personally to prepare all of Kareem's favorite foods, along with the finest wine. At 7 P.M. sharp, there was a knock on the door. We opened it to find Kareem and Sam. Flashes of the Nater episode entered my mind, but I knew I had to put that behind me and be on my best behavior. We talked over chateaubriand and expensive red wine. Finally, Kareem spoke his mind.

"I am unhappy in Milwaukee, and I want to be traded when the season is over," he said. "I am not culturally satisfied here. I'd like to go to New York, Washington, or Los Angeles. I am telling you now so you can get something for me, rather than sitting out my option year and then signing with one of those teams or the Nets of the ABA." Within minutes, he had eliminated Washington, after Sam reminded him of the shootings in the house he owned there. That left New York and Los Angeles.

My first response was to try to talk him into staying in Milwaukee. I asked a series of rapid-fire questions: "Do you want more money? Are you unhappy with the coach or with me? Are you dissatisfied with your teammates? What can we do?" He assured us none of those things was a problem, and he promised he was not going to change his mind. He wanted out. After three hours of trying to change his mind, we agreed to look into a trade, but we told him we could not guarantee a trade to New York or Los Angeles. We did agree to try. Furthermore, we agreed we would not tell anyone outside the room what was going on. We were afraid if it got out that we would lose our leverage, and that would hurt the franchise.

I left the meeting with mixed emotions. I kept thinking that if I did not have bad luck, I would not have any luck at all. Then I thought this might bring a solid foundation that we could build on. After all, it was difficult to draft quality players when we had the Number 18 pick every season. I did not have any idea the kind of year we would have without Oscar and with this hanging over our heads. Then again, it did not matter. The franchise was about to change. Only five of us knew it.

Chapter 11

A Tough Call

We beat the Trailblazers in a sold-out Dayton Arena. The matchup between Kareem and Bill Walton lived up to its billing and set the stage for classic encounters for years to come. It was obvious Portland was going to be a top contender in the West. I was happy for Nellie, because he made money and so did the Bucks.

Our second exhibition game was against the Celtics. Although it is usually hard to get an accurate picture of a team during a preseason game because there is so much experimentation going on with the line-up, we were playing against the team that had prevented us from winning the championship, and Larry was eager to see how the team would react without Oscar. Little did we realize what was in store for us. Late in the game, while fighting for a rebound, my old buddy Nellie accidentally poked a finger in Kareem's eye, causing severe damage. Kareem reacted by hitting the goal post with his fist, breaking his hand. (Much later, I found myself wishing he had hit Nelson with the punch.) The injury was going to keep Kareem out for six weeks, a devastating blow for a team already struggling to cope without Oscar.

In addition, it looked as if this would be Kareem's last season in Milwaukee. I kept trying to change his mind, and even told him Larry or I would go if we were part of the problem. He assured us we were not. Our board members tried to entice him with expensive gifts, including the Oriental rugs he collected. But none of this worked. I told the board I would examine trade options and report back when I had something significant to say. At some point, I knew I had to tell Larry, because this affected him, too. In fact, I had learned there was a faction of the board that wanted him fired regardless of where Kareem landed.

We started the 1974–75 season 1–13, which left us well back in the Midwest Division. The team took on a different personality, because most of our players had not experienced losing in college or the pros. We did not have Oscar to keep us together, and we missed him in other ways as well. We found out Lucius was not a point guard and that we needed one badly. The only time we saw Oscar was the day his jersey was retired, the first such honor bestowed on a Milwaukee Buck. Hundreds of Oscar's friends from sports and entertainment witnessed the ceremony, which proved to be the highlight of a season headed for disaster.

In an effort to get a point guard, we traded Lucius to the Lakers for Jim Price. The Lakers were looking for speed and quickness, and we needed ball handling and defense. The trade meant we were giving up Kareem's best friend, which worried some board members who still hoped Kareem would change his mind. Lucius was one of Wes's favorites, and one of Terri's as well. I got a lot of criticism from the media and fans about trading Lucius, until Jimmy scored 43 points and helped us beat the Suns in the Arena. He helped us win twenty of the next thirty games after Kareem returned to the lineup. He also joined Kareem and Dandridge on the West All-Star team.

With Kareem back and the players adjusting to each other, we fought our way back to .500. Our players and our fans showed new optimism. Then disaster struck again. Jim Price sustained a knee injury, which kept him out for the second half of the season. We struggled the rest of the way, finishing with a 38–44 record and losing a wild-card berth for the play-offs in the last week of the season. I felt bad for Dandridge and the other veterans. It was the first time they had missed the play-offs. Of course, a bigger issue loomed. It would not be long before they would find out Kareem had asked to be traded.

Word was beginning to circulate that Kareem wanted out. I was amazed that we were able to keep it a secret the entire season. None of my scouting buddies or any of the reporters had mentioned it. It was not until late March that I received calls from our beat writers, Rel Bochat and Bob Wolf. Staying true to one of my tenets was not easy, but I was not going to lie to them. They asked if Kareem was on the trading block.

"Who told you that?" I asked.

They told me a report had come out of New York that Kareem wanted to be traded to the Knicks. I was not surprised, since the Knicks would do anything to get Kareem back to New York. This was the same organization that signed George McGinnis when his NBA rights belonged to Philadelphia, causing the commissioner to revoke the contract and penalize the Knicks for their actions. I told both reporters we would trade anyone if it helped our team. I did not exactly answer their questions, but I did not lie to them and, in fact, indirectly I had told them Kareem was on the trading block.

With the news out, it was harder to try and make a deal that would allow the team to continue to prosper. But I convinced our board I could make a deal that would give us a solid foundation. I added that Kareem had given us six terrific years and a championship and that out of respect for him we should try to grant his wish. The thought of trading him did not sit well with one faction of the board. Jim Fitzgerald, a successful cable television operator from Janesville, Wisconsin, had been elected to the board in hopes that broadcasting Bucks games throughout the state would generate more revenue. Rumors were circulating that Fitzgerald was trying to keep Kareem. Rumors also were circulating that Larry should be fired because Kareem did not like him.

I thought this was absurd. Larry had done his best coaching when we made our championship run in 1974. He had no control over the injuries that plagued us the next season. But I later learned that several board members had secretly interviewed Hubie about the head coaching job. We really had a mess on our hands. With all this going on, I was charged with the responsibility of making the best possible trade for the Bucks while satisfying Kareem and protecting the future of the franchise. Nothing to it, I thought ironically.

I took a room at the Marc Plaza Hotel, away from the office and the telephones. I wanted to concentrate fully on what would be the most critical decision in the history of the franchise. This trade would be the biggest in the history of the NBA. Larry and I were going to be sequestered until we came up with a deal that made sense. We ranked players from other teams. We listed college players who would be available in the next several drafts. Besides these lists, we had our remaining players listed. I set the following criteria for moving forward, considering the chemistry of our team:

> I wanted young, talented players who would develop over the next couple of years because I was more concerned about how we would be in three years. This meant that age was a factor. We wanted either young players with promise in the league or college players. We needed to acquire assets to be part of our building process or as trade bait. We anticipated losing, which meant we would get high draft picks. We were prepared for that. I believed this was the best way to build.
>
> Since we were building from scratch, I wanted to place a big emphasis on character, both on and off the court. This was important because of the cultural changes in society, which had begun to affect athletes.
>
> I wanted players who would fit into the culture of Milwaukee and identify with the terrific Milwaukee fans . . . and not complain about the weather!

Once I got used to the idea that Kareem was going, I welcomed the opportunity to build a team the way I wanted, which included setting my own standards and codes of conduct. I would do something that had never before been done. I was going to interview prospects before the draft. I would also do extensive background checks on them. I would no longer take players for granted.

My first four years as general manager had been filled with damage control and crisis management. This was a valuable learning experience, and I figured I could handle just about anything as we moved forward. Through planning and proper choices I intended to minimize problems that would affect the performance of the team or discourage the fans, realizing that I would have to adapt to the changing culture without compromising the integrity of the game or the organization.

To no one's surprise, New York was the first team to call about Kareem. We had analyzed their team, and there was no way to work a deal with them. They figured they would be in the picture because Kareem was from New York and, strangely since we had been sworn to secrecy, they knew the Knicks were one of his preferences. Despite my discouragement, Eddie Donovan, the Knicks general manager, and Mike Burke, the president of Madison Square Garden and the Knicks, came to Milwaukee to meet with Bill Alverson and me. They offered a combination of players—including Willis Reed and Walt Frazier—and their draft pick. I rejected the offer of the aging Reed and Frazier, though both had been superstars in their prime. They may have provided instant success, but that was not what I wanted. I wanted high draft picks in the ensuing years.

The suave, polished Burke refused to take no for an answer and opened the Knicks' bottomless purse strings. He started by adding $1,000,000 to the offer and moved up from there. He tried to intimidate us, using some of the tactics I had witnessed at the Board of Governors meetings. Bill responded by telling him, "Who do you think we are? Some hicks from Milwaukee? Well, we are not." I loved hearing that. I finally told Burke money could not score or rebound, and we did not want the players they were offering. Finally, they got the message and the meeting ended.

We looked at Atlanta, because there were some young players on the roster we liked, but we thought it was a long shot that Kareem would go there. I was in constant communication with him, although with every progress report, I also tried to get him to reconsider.

Pete Newell finally called about ten o'clock on a Friday morning. I had been expecting to hear from him. Jack Kent Cooke, the owner of the Lakers, had instructed him to arrange a meeting as soon as possible and Pete suggested we get together at the airport in Denver that afternoon.

"I'll call Bill and have Jean check on flights and I'll get back to you," I told him.

"Mary Lou, my assistant, has already booked your flight," Pete told me.

"Damn, Pete, hold onto your britches," I said. "I'll call you right back."

Alverson was surprised when I called and asked if he could be ready to catch a noon flight to Denver to meet with Pete and Alan Rothenberg. Alverson was a lawyer by trade and a good one. He said he would drop everything and join me. We were ready for a little two-on-two with the boys from Los Angeles.

We did not have time to go home and pack, but it did not matter. We were prepared to return that night, no matter what the outcome. During the flight, I pulled out my file on the Lakers and defined what I would be willing to accept as a starting point for our negotiations. I told Alverson that David Meyers and Junior Bridgeman, recently drafted with the second and seventh selections, were musts. We needed a center, so Elmore Smith had to be a part of the deal. The other player we were prepared to accept was Brian Winters. Any cash add-ons were up to Alverson and the board.

With that settled, Bill filled me in on the emerging mutiny on the board. The boys from Janesville were trying to gain control, and he did not think that was a good thing, considering our circumstances.

We arrived at the United Airlines Red Carpet Club ahead of the Lakers contingent. But shortly after Pete and Alan arrived, a third man joined us. He was introduced as Jim Locker, Cooke's right-hand man. Suddenly our two-on-two was a three-on-two. But that did not matter. Bill and I knew what we wanted. After exchanging pleasantries, I started the negotiations by saying there was really nothing to negotiate as far as players were concerned. I told him I wanted the two picks, Elmore Smith and Brian Winters.

"No way can we give you all of that," Newell said. "We'll give you the picks and Elmore. Nothing else. You know you're going to lose him and you run the risk of getting nothing in return. You know how the ABA is."

He was trying to scare me, and I did not like it.

"Pete, I told you we were coming out here to make a deal and I told you to be prepared to do so," I said. "Should we turn around and go home?"

He told me they needed to caucus, and the three of them left the room. Moments later, Pete and Alan came back.

"Jack says we can throw in Gail Goodrich, but you're not getting Winters," Pete said.

"Peter, we must have Winters," Bill told him.

The discussion went back and forth.

"Goodrich."

"Winters."

"Goodrich."

"Winters."

Goodrich was an All-Star guard from UCLA and he would have helped us, but age was a factor and, like Reed and Frazier, he would be ready to retire when we were ready to contend.

Winters had played for Frank McGuire at South Carolina and we had loved him in the draft. My good friend Al McGuire had spoken highly of him, although he never did know his name. Al, the coach at Marquette University in Milwaukee, was from Rockaway Beach in Brooklyn, and so was Brian. Al frequently stopped in my office to hang out while his capable assistant, Hank Raymonds, was in charge during the Warriors practices in the Arena. As he stretched out on my couch with a floppy hat covering his face, he would talk about the great players who had played against his teams. He kept telling me to draft "that white kid who played for Frank."

"Which one?" I kept asking. There were several, including Brian Winters and Mike Dunleavy.

"You know, the shooter," Al would tell me.

Since he could not remember the names of his own players, the fact that he did not know anybody else's name should not have surprised me. Remember, he did not know who Dr. J was.

Brian had not played much as a rookie because of Goodrich, but I knew that if he got playing time he would become an All-Star. I told Pete I wanted Winters for the same reasons he did. I even tried to butter him up, calling him my mentor. But he was too smart to be flattered, even if it was true. After three hours, we were no closer to a deal. We decided to take a break and phone our offices. We returned to find out nothing had changed. They would not budge on Winters, and we would not concede.

For the rest of the afternoon and evening, Pete resorted to telling the kinds of long, rambling stories for which he was known. Naturally, he brought up our trip to Biloxi. Meanwhile, Rothenberg and Locker kept excusing themselves. I figured they had heard all of Pete's tales.

In a last-ditch effort, Pete turned to Bill and repeated, "You know, you'd better do this deal or he'll wind up in the ABA and you'll get nothing. You don't want that to happen, do you?"

I looked him right in the eye and said, "Pete, if he goes to the ABA, you won't have him either. You don't want that to happen, do you?"

After more caucuses and more stories, Alverson and I decided to take the red-eye flight back to Chicago and drive to Milwaukee. The Lakers contingent was bewildered as we left the Red Carpet Club. Then, just as we boarded the plane, we heard Rothenberg calling as he ran down the concourse, "Hold the door. Hold the door. I'm going with you." The astonished gate agent looked at his ticket and let him on board.

We ordered a bottle of wine and between sips the three of us continued to talk, despite the fact we were all physically and mentally tired. Bill and Alan were on a couple of the Board of Governors major committees, and they talked about some league problems while I tried to sleep.

But just before I dozed off, I repeated one more time, "No Winters, no deal."

It was 5 A.M. when three zombies walked off the plane in Chicago. Alverson and I bid Rothenberg farewell and proceeded to the car rental counter. We looked back to give him one last wave and saw he was on the phone again. We assumed he was explaining to his wife why he was not home.

Two hours later I was sound asleep in bed when the phone rang. "It's Alverson," said Terri, who had just gotten back to sleep. "Why on earth is he calling at this hour?"

I took the phone. "Guess who's in town?" he said.

It could only be Rothenberg. "We're going to meet at ten o'clock at the office," Bill said. "Be there. I think we have a deal. They've conceded on Winters. I will call a meeting of the board to decide the money issues."

Shortly after noon, the biggest trade in the history of the league was consummated. Post-trade dialogue revealed a couple of things. Locker and Rothenberg kept leaving the room to call Cooke, and Rothenberg had phoned Cooke from Chicago. Cooke had ordered them not to return to Los Angeles until they had a deal. Pete also revealed that Cooke had been negotiating with Portland for Walton, and when those talks broke off, he gave in on Winters.

The announcement at 1 P.M. Monday, June 16, 1975, was front-page news in that afternoon's the *Milwaukee Journal.* While fans had mixed emotions about the move, it was generally well received in the media. Wrote Bill Dwyre, then assistant sports editor of the *Journal*, "But putting loyalty and hero worship aside, the simple logic for many months has called for a trade. That Alverson and Embry were able to make the trade with minimal bargaining leverage and get what I consider a good return attests to their card-playing skill."

Wrote *Sentinel* columnist Bud Lea the next day, "Was it worth it for the Bucks? Probably not. But they made the best of a tough trade."

With that, the Milwaukee Bucks and I moved into a new era.

Timeout Number Three

Alex Haley's Pulitzer Prize winning book, *Roots,* which later became a television miniseries, inspired all Americans, particularly Afro-Americans, to trace their family histories. Tracing the Embry family roots back to Alabama brought some fascinating twists.

The Embrys were sharecroppers in rural Alabama near Talladega, in a township called Embry Crossroads. Growing up, whenever my grandparents, parents, aunts, and uncles talked about Embry Crossroads, my chest would swell with pride. I figured our family had to be pretty special to have a town named after it, and I always wondered what my ancestors had done to have a town incorporated in their names.

When I asked about it, my elders chuckled. "Don't be misled," they told me. "There were Embrys long before us, and they were white." Indeed, historical data revealed that we derived our name from the plantation owners who were our masters.

I did not really think about that much, until I had an unusual experience in the late 1970s. I was an owner-operator in the McDonald's restaurants. Terri and I were attending a McDonald's convention in Las Vegas. We had just checked in when a set of luggage was delivered to our room. The name on the luggage was David Embry. I have an Uncle David, but he was not with McDonald's. Instead of being angry, I was curious to find the owner of the luggage, because Embry is not that common a name.

Terri, on the other hand, was tired and was worried our luggage was lost. Luckily, a few moments later, a bellman arrived with our luggage. The problem was solved, but the mystery was not. I hoped I would have a chance to find the other Mr. Embry.

The next morning I did. Standing outside a meeting room, I glanced at the nametag of a man standing next to me. It read, "David Embry, St. Louis." Much to my surprise, the man was white.

"I guess our luggage got mixed up last night," I said to open a conversation.

He looked at the name tag pinned to my chest, which was considerably larger than his, and began to laugh.

"Man, I'm glad they finally got it right," he said. "You would have had a tough time getting into my medium-sized shirts, wouldn't you?"

I laughed, too. "You've got that right," I said. Then I asked if he was originally from St. Louis.

"No," he said. "My family is originally from Alabama. Outside of Talladega. A place called Embry Crossroads. What about you?"

I broke into a grin. "I hate to tell you this my man, but we're related. My folks are from the same place. Now, you don't suppose your ancestors had anything to do with my folks coming to America, do you?" I asked him, smiling. "Just don't expect me to call you master."

He was not quite sure what to think, but when I started to laugh, he did, too.

David Embry and I served on Op-Nad, an owner-operator committee, for several years and became good friends. We amused our associates by referring to each other as cousins.

Chapter 12

Laying a New Foundation

All summer long, I had to listen to post-trade analysis. Everybody had an opinion, and anywhere I went in the country I was asked how I could trade Kareem. By and large, Milwaukee fans were supportive, although there were those who thought if we had fired Costello, Kareem would have stayed in Milwaukee. That was the view of the Janesville connection on our board.

But none of this mattered. Kareem was a Laker. He was very grateful and complimentary to the Bucks organization and the Milwaukee fans and media. He handled the move with great dignity. In parting, he was careful to say that while Milwaukee had many good qualities, it just was not his bag.

Not many people got to know Kareem. I actually first met him when he was still Lew Alcindor, a lanky high school center who was the best player in New York City. One day I stopped in Harlem on my way to the Maurice Stokes memorial game, and Kareem needed a ride to the game. I was with Tom Thacker, so Kareem folded himself into the back seat and rode with us. We talked mostly about the game. He was reserved and quiet, but polite, and we had a nice chat. When he went to UCLA, of course, I knew he was a great player, but I did not really know anything about his personal life. I was not working for the Bucks when they drafted him. I was gone from Milwaukee for a year, and when I came back, Oscar Robertson had joined Kareem. The two respected each other, but they were not really friends. There was a bit of a generation gap between them. Oscar was a family man, and Kareem was a young, hip, single guy.

As a young general manager, I thought it was necessary to try to build a relationship with Kareem as well as the other players. I recognized his importance to the franchise, so I tried to respect his lifestyle and his privacy. I was always there to help. My door was always open. I think he appreciated that, and I know I appreciated what I learned from dealing with a nonconformist. He was an extremely private person. Many considered him aloof and unfriendly. A few took it so far as to call him rude. That was not true. A little man ran up to me in the Milwaukee airport and complained that Kareem was rude and would not sign an autograph. I knew that Kareem would sign if approached properly, so I wondered what the real story was.

Kareem watched the little snippet of a man complaining and then approached me while I was talking with some players in the boarding area. He nodded in the man's direction and said, "Can you believe that idiot asked me to sign an autograph while I was standing at the urinal?" Now who was rude and inconsiderate?

Just because Kareem was not an engaging person, this did not make him unfriendly. He was very intelligent, but he was his own person. I learned that if he wanted to talk, I would talk, and he could be very talkative when the subject interested him. If he did not want to talk, I left him alone. He enjoyed being by himself. I met his parents. He came from a very solid, two-parent home. He was very close to his parents. He was a jazz enthusiast and even did a radio show in Milwaukee. He collected fight films, too, a passion he shared with Wes. Wes had many of the old fights on tape, and he freely shared them with Kareem. Losing the big fellow was a tough loss for Wes, because the two had a special relationship.

But we had to move on.

David Meyers was a long, six-foot-nine-inch All-American from UCLA who was an excellent rebounder and a good shooter with decent range. He came from a family of good basketball players, and there were those who thought his sister, Ann, was the best player at UCLA at the time.

Junior Bridgeman was a six-foot-five-inch swingman from Louisville who led the Cardinals to the NCAA Final Four his senior year. He was a good all-around player who was just a fair shooter in college. I liked his character and Denny Crum, his college coach, told me Bridgeman would be better than most first-rounders in a couple of years because of his intelligence and tremendous work ethic. He told me he wanted to be great.

Elmore Smith was a good rebounder and shot blocker. Most of the NBA thought he was an underachiever who could be very good if someone lit a fire under him.

We thought Brian Winters would become an All-Star with playing time.

I had researched these players thoroughly and was certain they would be integral components of the Bucks' future. With the newcomers added to our veterans—Dandridge, McGlocklin, Price, Brokaw, and Jimmy Fox—we thought we would at least be competitive. We did not have our own first-round pick but we took Clyde Mayes in the second round, and he provided additional size.

Dandridge's contract was up, and I dreaded having to negotiate with my old friend Irwin Weiner, his new agent. Irwin was relatively new in the business, but he had two important clients, Walt (Clyde) Frazier and Dr. J. He thought Dandridge was in their league. Irwin was quite a character. He tried to emulate the flashy Frazier with his fine suits, fur coats, and limos. The only difference was that Clyde was younger and better looking. I always enjoyed Irwin, but he was a tough negotiator. He could be tough when discussing Walt and Julius, but I did not think Bobby had the same kind of leverage. I was wrong. The negotiation turned into a summer-long project. Bobby was an All-Star and much underrated, and Irwin wanted us to pay him what his other clients were making because he was our only remaining star. As much as I enjoyed the dinner meetings at famous New York eateries, including Dewey Wong's,

Irwin's favorite Chinese restaurant, I grew sick of negotiating with Irwin. Still, we needed Dandridge. Finally, Irwin called and suggested one more meeting. He suggested we drive from the city, get away from the distractions, and reach an agreement. He would never come to little ol' Milwaukee. There was just not enough pizzazz there, plus no one knew him.

He picked me up at LaGuardia in a big brown-and-tan limo. The first words out of his mouth were, "How do you like our new limo?" He meant it was his and Clyde's. By now he and Clyde had become partners. Players sharing other players' money did not seem right to me, but that was none of my business.

We crossed the George Washington bridge and headed north. An hour and a half later we were in the center of the Catskills. We pulled up to a lavish house overlooking the mountains.

"How do you like our retreat?" he asked, climbing out of the backseat of the limo.

Welcome to the big leagues, I thought to myself as I followed him into the house.

Sandwiches were made, wine was opened and cigars were plentiful. The houseboy had done his thing. We scarfed down the sandwiches and went to the deck. Irwin offered me a cigar and poured me another glass of wine. He was a connoisseur of cigars, and I had begun to smoke them occasionally.

"Ever smoke a Partages?" he asked. "Let me clip one for you."

I was not that sophisticated when it came to smoking anything. I did not smoke cigarettes and Billy Rohr would not be happy to know I was smoking cigars.

I was getting tired of the whole act.

"Let's get this thing done," I said.

"Pay us what we want and we can," he answered.

"We are not going higher than $250,000, Irwin," I told him.

He did not respond immediately. I looked over to see his red head propped up on the headrest of the lounge chair. He was sound asleep. I tried to wake him up several times, but I failed. So I decided to join him. I had nothing better to do while surrounded by trees, a hundred miles from the city. I woke up a short time later. He was still snoring.

It was several hours later that he woke up. He was not sure where he was. I demanded to be taken back to the city. On the way back, he rejected my offer again. The nap had not brought him to his senses.

We eventually got Dandridge signed for $250,000 and opened training camp with him as the leader of our young team. Larry and I did not know how he would take to that role. From our past experiences, we had learned that some veterans did not like to be on a team that was rebuilding. Veteran players can either be a help or a hindrance, depending on how they lead. Losing often brings out the worst of everyone on a team, which meant that Larry and Jack McKinney, his new assistant coach, had to communicate more than ever and give positive reinforcement to the veterans as well as the rookies.

But it was difficult for Larry to be positive after he learned that Hubie Brown, who had left after the 1973–74 season to coach the ABA's Kentucky Colonels, was being considered as his replacement. The board decided to delay extending his contract, and Larry was uneasy. What was unfortunate was that some board members had talked to some of the players about Larry and, as is usually the case, not all were supportive. Throughout my playing career and my short time in management, I never thought players should determine who coached the team. If that was the case, there would be coaching changes every week. I did, however, listen to their complaints with an open mind.

This was the situation as we headed into the 1975–76 preseason. Our second game was against the Lakers and Kareem. The sold-out crowd gave Kareem a long standing ovation as an expression of its appreciation for his six years with the Bucks. It was quite emotional.

It was obvious how much we missed him when we opened the season with five straight losses. Then we won five straight. Fans were not overly concerned about our won-lost record. Instead, they were focusing on the new players, each of whom made important contributions as the season progressed.

David Meyers proved he could score and rebound as we thought, and Brian Winters shot his way onto the All-Star team in his second season, averaging 18 points per game. Bridgeman showed his versatility, starting in nineteen games. Elmore Smith blocked shots and rebounded the way we had hoped. Elmore was talented, but he lacked a passion for the game, which presented a problem going forward. Dandridge finished the season in the top ten in scoring, and the Bucks finished the season 38–44, still good enough to win the Midwest Division. But our play-off run was short as we lost to Detroit, two games to one.

Larry did another great job of coaching and was rewarded with a two-year contract extension before the play-offs began. Alverson and I had lobbied hard for that to happen. Finally, we convinced the board that it was the wrong time not to extend him. But the anti-Costello faction still wanted him out.

With Larry signed, we directed our attention to the upcoming draft. We determined in our post-season assessment that we needed a true point guard. Our scouts and I ranked John Lucas and Quinn Buckner the two best in the country. Lucas was an All-American from Maryland, and Buckner was the quarterback of the NCAA champion Indiana Hoosiers, as well as a member of the Olympic team. We were confident we would get one of them, and it turned out to be Buckner. The Houston Rockets surprised everyone by making Lucas the Number 1 pick in the draft, so we took Buckner at Number 7. We also had the picks awarded to us by the league in the Julius Erving case, so we took Alex English and Scott Lloyd. We expected them to fit right in with our young team.

About this time, I also took my last shot at Erving. The ABA folded after the 1975–76 season, but it went out with a bang. Commissioner Mike Storen pulled out all the stops for the ABA All-Star Game, introducing the slam dunk contest, featuring high flyers like Erving and David Thompson, and the three-point shootout, featuring long-range bombers like Louis Dampier. Despite all that, and big-name entertainers performing, the league still could not generate enough support from television to cover its bad debts and some loosely run franchises. Four of the stronger teams—New Jersey, San Antonio, Indiana, and Denver—each paid $3.2 million to join the NBA. Players who had been drafted by the NBA reported to those teams, and there was a dispersal draft for the rest. In the end, this would make for a stronger league as players like Erving, Thompson, Dampier, George Gervin, George McGinnis, Artis Gilmore, and Moses Malone significantly increased the talent level. In the short term, there was much scrambling to add these superstars to the rosters.

In Milwaukee, we were thrilled with the merger. Although Julius was playing for the Nets, and the merger deal called for the surviving teams to keep their players, we had heard Julius was unhappy in New York and wanted out. Maybe there was still a chance. He certainly would expedite the rebuilding process.

Irwin Weiner called and told me to come to New York if we were interested in Erving. I dropped everything and flew out, arriving in his office at 11:00 A.M. for an 11:30 meeting. I was determined not to return without a deal. I still had visions of a storybook ending.

Irwin's assistant, Susan, directed me to an office so I could make some calls while waiting. I started to get nervous when noon came and I still had not seen Irwin. Surely, I was not going to get burned again, was I?

Torched was more like it. Susan had suggested I go across the street to get a bite to eat at a deli. I told her I was not hungry and I was not going anywhere. I did walk down the hall to the men's room and on my way back I thought I saw a familiar figure scooting out the side door. It was Pat Williams, now general manager of the Philadelphia 76ers.

"Hey, Pat," I said. "What the hell are you doing here?"

"I just signed Julius," he mumbled. "Sorry, Wayne."

I stormed into Irwin's office to find him puffing on one of his blasted cigars. How arrogant was that? I could have punched him.

"What the hell just happened here?" I demanded.

Irwin explained that Doc just was not interested in coming to Milwaukee. He wanted to stay on the East Coast, in close proximity to New York, and he wanted to play in a big market. He apologized for having me make the trip and bid me farewell after some further dialogue. As I said, he was extremely apologetic.

Because I had grown to love Milwaukee, I could not understand why some players would not give the city a chance. I later learned from Irwin that Erving, like most superstars, thought that playing in the big markets would bring more opportunities for commercial endorsements. This was another element in how we would manage in future years. We would now have to consider factors other than talent because agents and players wanted to maximize their earnings, and advertisers wanted these players in major markets.

At the time, however, I had to finally admit I was never going to get Julius Erving in a Bucks uniform. Wes always told me there was no way The League would let Julius come join Kareem and Oscar, creating a dynasty in a small market. He was not exactly right, though the outcome was the same. And it was clear that in order to win a championship now, we would have to go through Erving and the Sixers.

My disappointment was tapered somewhat by the fact that we were getting great reports on our youngsters who were playing in the Los Angeles summer league. We knew we were on to something when our West Coast scout, Dick Baker, called after the third game to tell me, "Wayne, you've got some players. Junior is good, Buckner is good and so is Meyers. But the player who is going to be great is Alex English. His shot doesn't look pretty when he releases it, but it goes in the basket and he can get it off against anyone. You've got to get out here."

I usually go to the summer league after the signings are done and things have quieted down. But this summer I lost another assistant coach. Jack McKinney resigned to join the Lakers, so I needed to hire another coach. Larry liked Rod Thorn, but Rod was a candidate for the Bulls vacant general manager spot, and he eventually was hired for that. I was receiving calls from my old roomie and friend Don Nelson, asking me to sign him as a player. The Celtics had released him, and no one else was interested. After several conversations, he realized his efforts were futile. He decided to try to become a referee, and he was working in the Los Angeles summer league under the watchful eye of top referee Darrell Garretson.

I finally made it out to the summer league in early August to check out our new juggernaut. It was readily apparent why everyone was raving about these guys. They were a joy to watch. I was more convinced than ever that there would be life after Kareem for the Bucks.

The biggest disappointment in the summer league was Nellie's performance as a ref. He struggled mightily, and he admitted to me over a couple of beers that he was failing in his bid to become the first ex-player to referee. After several hours of chitchat and laughs, and a few more beers, he asked me again about playing and again I told him no.

"Big Man, I'm scared," he said. "What am I going to do? The only thing I know is basketball. Can't you help ol' Nells?" he asked, slurring his words.

A lightbulb went off in my head. I was feeling sorry for him and really wanted to help my old roomie.

"We're looking for an assistant coach," I told him. "Would you be interested in that?"

I explained that one faction of our board thought Larry was out of touch with our players. I figured Nellie could help bridge that gap since he was fresh off the floor. I always regarded him as a good basketball man. I had observed his input when we were teammates under Russell. I knew he had a passion for the game.

Nellie jumped at the chance. I told him I had to talk to Larry, and I knew Larry would be concerned about Nellie's knowledge of the game, as well as his work ethic and loyalty. But I eased Larry's concerns and asked him to trust me. A week later, Nellie interviewed with Larry and passed all Larry's tests with flying colors. I hired Nellie, despite the fact that after we made our decision he jabbed me by saying the Kareem trade was the worst in the history of the NBA. I attributed that to ignorance.

Even though Larry was under contract, the rumors persisted and a cloud of doubt hung over the organization. The Janesville group, as I came to call Fitzgerald and his gang, was attempting to gain control of the board. Alverson kept me abreast of the situation. I tried to keep it from affecting Larry and the rebuilding job he was undertaking, but it was impossible. He constantly asked me to confirm the rumors on the street.

Finally it was announced that Jim Fitzgerald, Bill Blake, and JP Cullen and Son Corporation had made an offer to purchase 361,000 outstanding shares of Milwaukee Professional Sports and Service common stock. Fitzgerald became chairman of the board and president.

A short time later, Fitzgerald and Dan Finnane, a board member and longtime business associate of Fitzgerald's, came to my office to chat. I had met Fitzgerald when he involved himself in the Kareem saga. I had never met Finnane. It did not take them long to tell me they thought I was doing a terrible job of running the team and did not know anything about business. Of course I differed with their opinion. My grandfather's admonition to "remain humble" ran through the back of my mind. I told them we were winning and selling out the arena, as well as making a profit in a small market with limited income from radio, television, and sponsors.

Despite that, I could not help worrying about my future with the team. And all of this time I had been worried about Larry!

While this was going on the team got off to a horrible start, losing fifteen of eighteen games. We lost our fifteenth in Seattle, and I reached a decision. There was no way this team could develop under the present circumstances. Larry had lost his grip on the team. He was nervous about the new ownership and was coaching scared, which should never happen. He knew he was not "the man" in the eyes of the owners. The players were not responding, and a couple had even aligned themselves with the new owners. The dissension at the top permeated the entire organization. It was time for a change. I called Alverson and advised him of my decision. He was to confer with Wes, who was still reeling from what had just transpired on the board. I talked to Wes later and we agreed we would give Larry the option of resigning to preserve his dignity.

I called Larry in Seattle and laid out his options. He said he would prefer to resign when the team returned to Milwaukee. He actually sounded relieved.

Trading Kareem was well received, all things considered. Firing Larry was going to be the most controversial event in the team's history. He was very popular among the grass roots fans in Milwaukee. He was one of them. He represented all that was good in people—morality and integrity. So what if he was not a fashion plate? White socks with blue suits were accepted in Milwaukee. So what if he wore a crewcut when everybody else was wearing long hair? Under his leadership, the Bucks treated their fans to an NBA championship and a Western Conference title in six years. The team was a contender every year after the inaugural season. He was an excellent coach and human being, and he deserved a chance to rebuild. But I was not going to be able to give him that.

His critics pointed to his communications problems with players. They claimed Kareem and Oscar really won the title, without much input from Costello. Red Auerbach's critics said the same kind of things in Boston. Personally, I had found it tougher to manage superstars than average players. But this decision was being made by people who had not managed either one.

As the 4 P.M. press conference drew closer, I was examining my future with the team as well. The new owners had made it clear they were not too happy with me. I had no security, and Fitzgerald did nothing to offer any. In fact, he had confirmed the change in my status during a meeting at the Milwaukee Athletic Club. Team president Bill Alverson and I sat in a room with Fitzgerald and Milwaukee real estate investor Bill Blake discussing how the team was going to be run. They handed Alverson and me typewritten outlines of our job descriptions under the new regime. It was clear all of my power was being taken away. If I stayed, I would have tremendous responsibility with absolutely no power.

"You can take that paper and shove it," I said, handing it back to Fitzgerald. "I will not remain under those terms. I realize you may not like my response, but I don't care. At least I will be able to look myself in the mirror in the morning. I intend to maintain my dignity. This is important to me."

Several days later, on November 22, 1976, I stood in front of a room full of reporters and introduced Larry, who made his announcement. It was not a surprise. When Larry finished speaking, I announced I was resigning as general manager after the draft. This was a surprise. The questioning got tough. It was difficult for me to try to show support for Fitzgerald, who was seen as a villain, while being loyal to the people who hired me.

After some one-on-one interviews, Fitzgerald, Blake, and I caucused to discuss our next move. I promised to help during the transition and started by suggesting they name Nellie the coach. They did not know Nellie from Adam, so they had to take my word. The three of us and Nellie met in Fitzgerald's room at the Milwaukee Athletic Club. I turned to Nellie and said, "Congratulations. You are the next head coach of the Milwaukee Bucks." He had been a coach for all of two months.

"Whoa, Big Man, I'm not ready," he said.

"You are," I told him, and Fitzgerald echoed my sentiments. That seemed to ease Nellie's mind.

But after Nellie left the room, Blake said, "He's a little rough around the edges, isn't he?"

He was referring to the fact that Nellie was most comfortable in jeans and a denim shirt. He wore a coat and tie for the team picture and looked as if he was being tortured. Blake's observation was quite accurate for someone who had just met the guy.

Nellie and I met later to talk things over. He was still nervous, but I reassured him over a few beers. I thought he was going to be a good coach, and I told him I would be there to support him. I also told him he needed to hire an experienced assistant as soon as possible. I also suggested he meet with Al McGuire, Dean Smith, and Bobby Knight when the season was finished. I wanted him to learn from three of the best coaches in the country, each of whom had his own unique style.

Over the next several weeks, Nellie and I spent long hours together discussing my plan to rebuild the Bucks. Other than promoting games, he knew very little about front-office responsibilities. He also knew very little about coaching, which he readily admitted. It was a risk and I knew it, but I figured if he could impart his knowledge of the game to our young players and teach them the Celtic way to win, he had a chance of being successful. He was a Celtic much longer than I was and played on more championship teams, so he knew how to win. He followed my advice and hired another former Celtic, K. C. Jones, as his assistant. K. C. was out of work at the time, and I thought he would be a great complement to Nellie. He was one of the best defensive players to play in The League, and he knew how to teach defense.

Fitz and I eased the pressure by telling Nellie developing the young players was more important than winning for now. That was a good thing, because we did not win. We were building for the future by playing our youngsters and letting them play through their mistakes and learn from them.

While Nellie and K. C. coached, Rick Sund and I continued to scout college talent. The 1977 draft was months away, but it looked promising. We had scoped it out when we did our projections before the Kareem trade. Marques Johnson was a player we targeted back then. After watching the two of them at UCLA, we dreamed of having him and David Meyers as our forwards. We made another significant move when we traded Elmore Smith and Gary Brokaw to Cleveland for Rowland Garrett and first-round draft choices in 1977 and 1978, which gave us two first-round picks in 1977. We were well on our way to recovery. Of course, we had no way to go but up. We won thirty games in 1976–77, the worst in The League. But then we won the coin toss giving us the first pick in the draft.

This was my last official draft with the Bucks, and I wanted to make it a good one. When the season was over, I had to teach Nellie my process of preparing for the draft. Rick, the scouts and I had ranked the players. Nellie had not seen any of them except on television. We informed him and Fitz of our rankings, and Nellie was taken aback when we announced we were heading out to interview players.

"Why, Big Man?" he asked.

"Because we are hiring them for jobs, the same as IBM or accounting firms or law firms do," I told him. "We want to know their backgrounds, what their parents do, who had influenced their lives, what their aspirations were. We want to know if there is any history of drug use or any other problems or character flaws."

He was dumbfounded. "I never went through any of that," he said. "Did you?"

"No, but we're a different generation," I said. "The 1960s and 1970s brought a lot of cultural changes in society and The League. We can no longer take things for granted."

Cedric "Cornbread" Maxwell, an All-American from the University of North Carolina at Charlotte, was a player I wanted to interview. He was represented by my old friend Ron Grinker. I called Grinker to set up a meeting in Charlotte, and I insisted Nellie come with me. I told him I would pick him up on the way to the airport. When I pulled up in front of his apartment building, Nellie stood there dressed in jeans and a sport shirt.

"Get your bag, Nellie," I told him. "We don't have much time. You know we're staying overnight, don't you?"

He patted his shirt pocket. "I'm all set, Big Man," he said. "I've got my toothbrush." I should have remembered he was not worried about his appearance. After all, we had roomed together.

Both of us were surprised when we got to Charlotte and Maxwell was not there to meet us. I waited an hour before calling Grinker to ask him where Maxwell was.

"He should be there," Grinker shouted over the phone. "Call me back in fifteen minutes."

Cornbread finally showed up three hours later. After being introduced he asked us, "Why are you guys here anyway?"

"We want to interview you," I said, trying to control my temper.

We sat in the hotel lounge answering his questions and getting one word answers to ours. He did a better job interviewing us than we did interviewing him. Finally we parted, and Nellie and I headed to the car.

"Is it always like this?" he asked me over a beer.

"Nellie, it's just the beginning," I told him. "You'll see it all."

As the draft drew near, he was amazed at the amount of time Rick and I spent on the phone talking to coaches, trainers, and anyone else who might know the particular prospect. I explained to him that with the escalating salaries and guaranteed contracts it was crucial not to make a mistake. This was also one of the reasons I spent so much time on the road once the college season started. My feeling was that if I was responsible for the contracts, I wanted to see these players several times.

In this strong draft, we had decided Marques Johnson was our man. We never were able to get Julius Erving, but we thought Marques could be almost as exciting. Normally, in this situation, we would have taken a center, and Indiana's Kent Benson was the best available. But I did not think he would have as much impact as Marques. Besides, we also had the Number 11 pick and we thought maybe we could get a center there.

The night before the draft was filled with drama. It was Fitz and Nellie's first draft and they sat watching Rick and me "maneuver." This meant talking on the phones with teams about trades or with agents about how the draft might unfold. A trade possibility opened up. John Y. Brown, owner of the Buffalo Braves, called Fitz, who had me pick up the extension and listen in. What I got was a lesson in the changing complexion of The League.

"I need a white center," Brown said.

To my way of thinking, a team need a "good" center, whether he was white or black. But we had a guy who fit the bill—Swen Nater, who had actually joined us for the 1976–77 season after playing four years in the ABA. We found he was a good rebounder, but he did not really fit into Nellie's system.

"Have we got a guy for you," I told Brown.

We sent Nater to Buffalo for the third pick in the draft. With the first and third picks, we were almost assured of getting Marques and Benson in some order. As the evening passed with all of us reviewing the draft, talking about different scenarios and munching on junk food to calm our nerves, we settled on how to proceed. The only hitch was that rumors were circulating that Kansas City was going to take Benson at Number 2 if we did not take him at Number 1. I also was worried that if we took Benson at Number 1, Kansas City would take Marques at Number 2.

To ease our minds, I came up with a plan. We had also heard Kansas City was interested in Otis Birdsong. If that happened, we knew we would get the players we wanted with the Numbers 1 and 3 picks. I knew Birdsong was represented by Bob Woolf, the agent I had helped get established in the business years ago. I called Bob and told him we were thinking about drafting Birdsong and wanted to talk to him. He told me Otis had gone to Kansas City so the Kings could introduce him to their fans as soon as he was picked.

That was just the news I wanted to hear, although it did mean we would have to take Benson first.

"Gentlemen," I said to the roomful of people, "we are going to get the players we want at Numbers 1 and 3. Now let's focus on Number 11." That was the pick we had received from Cleveland.

The next day we added Benson, Johnson, and Ernie Grunfeld to the nucleus of Winters, Bridgeman, Buckner, and English, all All-Americans. I left my job as general manager of the Bucks, knowing I had left them with a bright future, as I had promised after the Kareem trade. Not only were there good young players, but there was a staff of dedicated, hard-working people, people who were nearly as responsible for our success as the coaches and I were. I was leaving a good friend and bright young executive in John Steinmiller, who, along with Rick Sund, served as alter egos and helped me get through some trying times. My instincts told me Nellie was going to be a good coach in The League. I was only sorry I was not going to be there to see it, or to finish the rebuilding job I had started. I thought I had become a good general manager. The biggest thing I had learned was that you did not manage basketball players. You managed people who happened to play basketball, people from different backgrounds with different needs. I learned the importance of communication. I learned how to turn adversity into opportunity. I had gained respect from our fans, the media, and the greater basketball community. After the 1976 Olympics, I was asked by USA basketball, the governing committee for our Olympic basketball teams, to serve on the selection committee for the next Olympiad. I had become quite active in the city of Milwaukee, sitting on several civic boards. But none of them would to be able to take the place of my Number 1 passion—basketball. I hated the thought of leaving it.

Despite his poor first season, Nellie's contract was extended and he also was given the title of director of player personnel, making the position of general manager obsolete. It was something I had advised Fitz against, because I thought it was too big a job for one person. I also explained coaches often made emotional personnel decisions that they regretted later. But Fitz disagreed. He wanted to hold the coach accountable for everything. Plus, as owner, he wanted to take a more active role in the operation of the franchise.

John Steinmiller became vice president of business operations, and Rick Sund remained as a scout. The rest of the front office stayed in place. Bill Alverson went back to practicing law, and Wes retreated to his farm in West Bend. A new board was elected, and several of the existing board members remained. I joined my partner, Sherman Claypool, as an owner-operator in the McDonald's restaurants, and we opened our third franchise behind the Milwaukee Arena in 1970. (Thank you David Danderand and Bob Beavers of McDonald's Corporation for presenting me with this opportunity in 1969.) One thing Nellie did that I did not like was letting our old teammate K. C. Jones go in favor of one of my former scouts, John Killilea, who was now Heinsohn's assistant in Boston.

To my surprise, that spring I received a call from Fitz asking me to meet him at a restaurant in the resort town of Lake Geneva, midway between his home in Janesville and Milwaukee. I had no idea what he wanted, but I had plenty of time to think about it on the hour drive. I had been rude to him in our meeting at the MAC, so I did not expect anything good to come out of our discussions.

We talked about the Bucks during lunch. He commended me on the draft, but he also expressed disappointment in how I handled the questions during the press conference announcing Larry's resignation. He thought I could have been more supportive of him. He did say he respected how I reacted to the job description that he had presented me. I again tried to explain there was no way I could be disloyal to Wes Pavalon, the man who had the courage to hire me. I assured him it was nothing against him or any of his partners. As we left the restaurant, he turned to me and asked me to stay on as a consultant with the title of vice president-consultant.

"Nellie and I need your experience and your knowledge of the game and the league," he said. "I also need your reputation locally and within the league and the college community. I can't pay you much at the start, but I will make you whole down the road. I can pay you $25,000, plus travel expenses and a reasonable expense account beyond that. I want you to continue scouting college players and help me with player negotiations when you have the time. Think about it and get back to me."

I thought about it all the way home and decided to accept the offer, which included some cable television stock options. It would allow me to stay involved in basketball and see the team develop from the inside.

There was no doubt in my mind they needed me. Nellie was best known as a player, and a rogue player at that. He did not always get along with his teammates. I spent many, many hours with him while we were teammates and roommates. Even after I moved to Milwaukee, we hung out when the Bucks played in Boston. I had been warned by some of my former Celtic teammates that I should not trust him, but I had no reason not to trust him at that point. I considered him one of my best friends. I wanted him to succeed for him and me and the fans.

There was another reason I accepted Fitz's offer. The money was not great, although it was not that much less than I had been making. And, considering that I had no responsibility other than consulting, it was not that bad. I remembered what my folks told me: Always seize the opportunity to learn from the people who have been places you have not been. I knew Fitz was a sharp businessman, as were the people around him, including Dan Nevaiser, another board member and real estate investor who became a good friend and business partner.

I watched with pride as the new Bucks recovered from the worst record since the expansion year. The talented rookies joined the second-year men and compiled a 44–38 record, finishing second in the Midwest Division in 1978. Nellie had grown as a coach, Winters was an All-Star again, Buckner was second-team All-Defense, and Marques made the All-Rookie team. When Seattle beat Golden State in the last game of the season, the Bucks were back in the play-offs. Fitzgerald got caught up in the excitement of the play-off race and arranged for a special feed of that game to be broadcast in Milwaukee to allow our fans a chance to listen to the game that decided our fate. It was a confident group of players and an excited group of fans that prepared for our opening-round series against the Phoenix Suns.

We swept the Suns, but we lost to Denver in a hard-fought series, four games to three. It was disappointing, but it established us as a team of the future. In fact, Fitz developed a marketing theme that incorporated the team's youth and its colors: Green and growing.

We suffered a relapse in the 1978–79 season. The Oscar Robertson lawsuit filed by the NBA Players Association against the owners had been settled, which removed oppressive "reserve" or "option" clauses in contracts that bound players to their teams even after the contracts expired. Thus, when free agent Alex English, whom we had drafted, signed with Indiana, we got nothing in return. Killilea had convinced Nellie that rookie George Johnson was going to be another George McGinnis so we did not really need Alex. Although I believed Alex was going to be something special, I was unable to convince Nellie otherwise. We also lost Dave Meyers for the entire season with a back injury. We dropped to fourth in the division and missed the play-offs. Marques Johnson continued to star, making the All-Star team and the All-NBA team as one of the best small forwards in The League.

The good news in our poor showing was that we had the fourth pick in the 1979 draft. Al McGuire, who had resigned as the Marquette coach and was now doing color commentary on television, told me about the "Three Amigos" who played for Eddie Sutton at Arkansas. He said they were really good and one could be a star, the tallest one, he said. As usual, he did not know their names. But we figured it out. He was talking about Sidney Moncrief.

Scout Garry St. Jean and I loved Moncrief and wanted to draft him. In doing our usual pre-draft preparation, we knew he would be there at Number 4. I learned that Detroit general manager and coach Dick Vitale wanted Michigan State star Greg Kelser at Number 5. As a matter of principle, we never told anyone who we were going to take, but Detroit wanted some kind of assurance we would not take Kelser. I suggested to Nellie that since we wanted Moncrief and we had the next pick, we should make a little money for Fitz. We asked for, and received, $50,000 from Detroit to switch picks. We each got our man. We would have done that anyway, but now we also had an extra $50,000. I had more than covered my salary.

Fitzgerald was very involved in the operation of the team, and I was pleased with our relationship. He involved me in key decisions, as well as recreational activities such as golf or high-stakes games of gin after dinner. I developed a greater comfort level when I was elected to the board of directors.

Nellie and I continued to be close. He stopped by my McDonald's nearly every morning to talk basketball. I talked him out of quitting a couple of times when he got down over the losing, and I even talked him out of leaving Milwaukee for Chicago when the Bulls made an overture. We relieved our frustrations by playing Pac Man at Major Goolsby's or Morrie's at cocktail hour. These encounters were very competitive and often went beyond my curfew, which did not sit well at home. There were many times I sat with him after games ended, replaying things, much as we had always done in Boston. Losses were particularly difficult. Nellie hated to lose as much as I did, whether it was basketball, Pac Man, golf, or gin. He kept me up all hours of the night trying to recoup his losses at gin, largely because of his affection for money. He was one of the cheapest people I have ever met.

Back on the court, we got off to a fast start with Marques and Bridgeman leading the way. As Denny Crum had predicted and I had hoped, Bridgeman worked hard and became one of the best pure shooters in the game and an effective sixth man. Midway through the season, we got another boost. Nellie called me and asked me to meet him at Dos Banditos, a Mexican restaurant owned by a mutual friend. It was near home, which was good because the margaritas were delicious. After a couple of them and a plate of nachos, Nellie started asking me questions about Leon Douglas, who was playing for the Pistons. I gave him my opinion and asked why he was so interested. He told me the Pistons had called and were interested in shaking up their team. They were offering anyone on their roster.

"We need a better center than Benson," Nellie told me. "He's driving me crazy."

I thought that was strange, because when we were talking about Benson before we drafted him, Nellie had thought he was going to be another Dave Cowens, although Indiana coach Bob Knight disagreed. I remembered telling Nellie at the time he should not be fooled by

Benson's red hair, which was the only resemblance I saw. However, I agreed we needed a better center. I thought Kent had become timid after Kareem decked him with one punch during his rookie year. The merger with the ABA brought an influx of quality centers, and we were not going to be a contender with Benson. But I did not think Douglas was the answer. I had seen Benson beat him in the NCAA regionals the year Indiana won the NCAA title.

After a few more margaritas, I asked Nellie if the Pistons were willing to part with Bob Lanier.

"Yes," he told me. "But we don't want him. He gets coaches fired."

Lanier was a premier center in The League who had the reputation of being difficult to coach.

"Nellie, there comes a time when you have to take a risk with a player, provided he has no issues off the court," I told him. "I trust your ability to handle him. You've done a tremendous job of relating to players. He will make you a better coach."

We debated the subject into the night, and I left thinking I had him convinced. Two days later we drove to Janesville for a meeting at JP Cullen's estate to get Fitz's approval. On the way there, I learned why Nellie was reluctant about the trade: Killilea and Steinmiller were adamantly against it. Still, I thought Nellie was 100 percent in favor. After discussing it with Fitz, Blake, and JP Cullen, I was feeling pretty good. I thought Nellie and I were united, and I had learned that Blake and Cullen usually did what Fitz wanted and Fitz always did what Nellie wanted. So imagine my surprise when Fitz went around the room asking our opinions and Nellie said he did not want to coach Lanier. The meeting ended.

The ride back to Milwaukee was quiet. I was not in a talkative mood after I had been hung out to dry. When we pulled into the parking lot at McDonald's, I pulled Nellie aside and asked him to have dinner with me—just the two of us. We went to Victor's for one of their great steaks. Nellie explained that Killilea had changed his mind and he did not want to tell me. By the end of the night, I had changed his mind again.

The next day, Nellie and I called Fitz and suggested we meet with Lanier and agent Larry Fleisher at the upcoming All-Star break so we could get to know Lanier a little better. Detroit granted us permission to talk to Lanier, and a lunch meeting was arranged in Fitz's suite. I had asked for permission to open the dialogue, which Fitz granted.

After lunch, we moved to more comfortable seating. Everyone sat but me. I wanted to stand and expose the full length of my six-foot-eight-inch frame and girth in order to take ownership of the situation and make a statement to the six-foot-eleven-inch, 260-pound Lanier and Fleisher. I hovered over them and asked Lanier in a firm, direct tone, "Do you want to play in Milwaukee?"

"Yes," he said. "I want out of Detroit."

We told him we were willing to help him get out of Detroit, but I laid down some ground rules.

"Mr. Fitzgerald is the owner, we don't need you to be the owner," I told him. "Nellie is the coach, and he's a pretty good one. We don't need you to coach. I am the vice president and I help in personnel decisions. We don't need you to do that, either. We need you to come and play basketball to the best of your ability and bring veteran leadership to a talented team of quality people.

"Do you understand that?"

Big Bob sat with his knees to his chest and looked sheepish. Finally he nodded and said, "I understand. I can do that."

The trade was made that day—February 4, 1980—and the Bucks went 20–6 the rest of the way and won the division title. We lost to a very good Seattle team in the semifinals of the play-offs, four games to three, but the fans were not overly disappointed because they could see the improvement of the youngsters and they knew the addition of a quality center like Lanier would make their home team a contender in years to come. The Bucks were, indeed, green and growing.

The next season, 1980–81, we won sixty games, regaining the form we had in the early 1970s. Our biggest problem was that with the addition of the expansion Dallas Mavericks, we had been moved into the

Eastern Conference, where the Sixers had put together a powerhouse, adding Moses Malone to a group that included Doc, Andrew Toney, Mo Cheeks, Lionel Hollins, and Bobby Jones. Billy Cunningham did a great job coaching them, and they beat us in the conference semifinals, four games to three.

We won more than fifty games the next three seasons but we could not beat the Sixers. We also had to worry about an emerging Celtics team. It was only a matter of time before they resurfaced. Red had pulled off two more shrewd deals in order to acquire Robert Parish and Kevin McHale to go with Larry Bird, who was eligible for the 1978 draft although he had chosen to remain at Indiana State another year to finish college. The Celtics were contenders again, making the Eastern Conference stronger than it had been in years. In fact, The League was experiencing a resurgence.

My relationship with Nellie started to change when I would not support him on his trade for Dave Cowens before the 1982–83 season. Nellie was searching for a power forward, and he thought Dave could fit the bill if he was healthy. Tom Sanders and Nellie ran a camp at New Hampshire College, which was twenty miles north of my basketball camp in Nashua, New Hampshire. Our camps ran at the same time, so Nellie arranged for Dave to come up and visit with me in an effort to persuade me. Dave had been sidelined with a chronic hip problem. I rented a car for the week and made several trips to Nellie's camp to spend time with Dave. A healthy Cowens would have been just what we needed, but a healthy Cowens would not have been available. When we returned to Milwaukee, I repeated to Fitz what Dave had told me: "I don't know if I'll hold up, but I'd like to try." I opposed Nellie and told Fitz not to guarantee Cowens's one million dollar asking price. But Nellie convinced Fitz to trade Buckner to Boston for the rights to Cowens and then guaranteed the one million dollars. Nellie did not like the fact I had disagreed.

Still, he was there for me when Terri required emergency surgery in the middle of that season. I was on my way home from a scouting trip just before Christmas. One afternoon, Terri told our daughter Jill that she had a terrible headache and wanted to lie down. Jill insisted she call an ambulance. Thank God. It saved her life. She had an aneurism that required surgery. Naturally I was shaken. I spent all my time at the hospital, and we celebrated the holidays there. But Nellie would come by to sit with me, or play cards. One night he brought us a feast of soul food. It was quite a gesture, and we were genuinely touched.

We had barely recovered from Terri's illness when my mother had a heart attack and died in January of 1983. I was devastated. I realized how much of her personality I shared. She had been such a great inspiration to me, overcoming so many difficulties but remaining a sweet and gentle woman. She was tough on Ruthie and me, but she really would not harm a fly. I realized almost everything I had accomplished was to win her praise. All I wanted was for her to be proud of me.

Nellie and Fitz were supportive through that time, too. But as time went on, Nellie and I seemed to drift apart. We still would meet for coffee, but not as frequently. Then one morning when we were having breakfast he stunned me.

I was scanning the newspaper and read aloud that Paul Silas had been fired as coach of the San Diego Clippers after the 1982–83 season. "That's too bad," I mused, thinking Nellie would agree since he and Paul were teammates in Boston. "I doubt he'll get another chance. There has not been lateral mobility for blacks."

There was a pause in the conversation and then Nellie said, "They're not qualified."

I was shocked. I pointed out that Al Attles and Lenny Wilkens had won championships. "Don't forget Russ," I said. "And what about me? I hired you, and it was my reputation that allowed me to keep you out of the gutters in the streets of Boston."

He stuttered a bit before saying, "You are the exception."

"No, Nellie, I am not an exception," I shouted. "I was given an opportunity. Everybody should have the opportunity to fail. Most coaches in The League have, you know."

The final blowout came during the 1984 draft. As usual, I gave my report on each of the players. UCLA's Kenny Fields was high on our list, but I did not think we should draft him because I did not like what I had heard during our two-hour interview in Hawaii. I did not think he was sincere and I thought he had an overinflated opinion of himself. When I left to go home the night before the draft, I thought St. Jean and I had convinced Nellie to take Fresno State's Ron Anderson. But between then and draft time, Nellie changed his mind. When Fitz went around the room to ask each of our opinions right before we selected, Garry and I stuck to our guns. But Nellie belted out, "We're taking Kenny Fields."

"Nellie, I don't . . . ," I started. But before I could finish the sentence, he yelled, "I'm sick of your shit." I sat there dumbfounded, wondering what the hell I had done to make him come down on me like that. Afterward, Fitz could not give me any explanation, but he said he had to support Nellie. Nellie could do no wrong as far as Fitz was concerned. He had adopted Nellie as a surrogate son, and Nellie knew it. I referred to Fitz as Nellie's Sugar Daddy.

The Bucks were one of the elite teams in The League, along with the Sixers and Celtics in the East and the Lakers in the West. David Stern had become the commissioner in 1984 at a time when The League was on the rise, thanks to the arrival of Bird and Magic Johnson in 1979 and Michael Jordan in 1984. Bird and Johnson thrilled the country with their meeting in the Final Four the previous year, and their additions to the Celtics and Lakers, respectively, put a new spark in that old rivalry.

Meanwhile, in Milwaukee, Fitz was struggling to make a profit. Fitz always said two things were essential to running a business: making a profit and paying yourself. Cable television was not the answer. He determined he had to be in a large market to make money. He had taken the company private in order to set up the move. There was no doubt making money was why he was in business, which is the way it should be. Many owners think differently. He scheduled a board meeting to disclose his plan to sell the Bucks, or trade them for a bigger market. He wanted to stay in the NBA. He liked being around the players almost as much as making money. He enjoyed the limelight, too.

At a meeting at The Abbey in Lake Geneva, he spelled out his plan to me, Nellie, and Steinmiller. He said keeping the Bucks in Milwaukee was his first option. He swore us to secrecy because he did not want to alarm the fans and start an auction. He said he would announce his plan to the public at the appropriate time. He had his sights on Chicago. Marv Fishman, the Milwaukee real estate investor who was the original owner of the Bucks, was in litigation with one of the owners of the Bulls for a right to buy. Fitz would have loved to work out a deal with Marv. If he was successful, he would have taken Nellie, Steinmiller, and other key personnel with him. I was hoping to remain as a consultant. When it finally became public that the team was for sale, Fitz advised the board that all inquiries should be directed to him or Dan Finnane.

My relationship with Nellie had polarized, and we had very little contact. I also had very little contact with Fitz that spring. I did not know what was going on with the team. Rumors would circulate once in a while. One rumor was that heiress Jane Pettit was negotiating to buy the team, although she denied that in the newspapers. She was an heir to the Allen Bradley manufacturing fortune, and when the company was sold to Rockwell, she came into a lot of money. She already owned a minor league hockey team in the city, and with part of the money from the sale, she agreed to build a new arena in downtown Milwaukee.

I received a call from Fran Croak, who was a lawyer in the firm that represented the Pettits.

"Contrary to what you've read," he said, "we are interested in buying the team. Can you come over to our office?"

Fran and I were old friends, and I knew he was serious. But I told him he had to call Fitz or Finnane.

"We will do that," he said. "But we need to know more about how the salary cap works, and we thought you could help us. If we decide to go forward, we would want you in a prominent role."

"I'll be right over," I said.

I was not there fifteen minutes when a secretary opened the door and told us there was a news bulletin that the Bucks had been sold to U.S. Senator and Milwaukee businessman Herb Kohl. Attorney Joe Tierney immediately left the room to call his daughter Mary Alice, who worked for a local television station. Moments later he returned and confirmed the news. It was March 15, 1985. I was shocked and wondered why, as a board member, I was not informed. I bid Fran and Joe farewell and went back to the office to share the news with my assistant, Judy Berger. I called my former assistant, Jean, and asked her what was going on. She said a press conference had been called for 4 P.M.

The next day Herb announced that he had entered into a new contract with Nellie. I was shocked to hear this because of Fitz's plan. Had Fitz changed his mind? Perhaps he was not sure he would get another franchise? Or was that deal part of the sale? I knew he was involved with Franklin Mueli, who owned the Warriors. He had loaned Franklin some money to help his cash flow with some kind of stipulation that he could buy that team after a certain period of time.

I waited a couple of days before I called Herb to discuss my role with the team. I had no right to be presumptuous, I guess, but I was hoping to continue as a consultant. Herb was very vague during our short meeting. He suggested I talk to Nellie about my future with the team, explaining that Nellie had complete control over hiring team personnel.

Nellie and I agreed to have lunch the next day. When I walked into Sally's restaurant, Nellie was waiting at a table away from everyone else. He seemed aloof and reticent. He said very little as we ordered and waited for our food. When we finished eating, he looked into space and said, "Big Man, I am hiring some other people, and I told Herb that I did not want you around any more. You'll have to talk to him to see if he wants you."

I knew Nellie had nothing good to say, because he would not look me in the eye. While driving back to my office, I had flashbacks. For a guy who had been a failure as a referee and begged me for a job when he had no place to go, he had come a long way. And he did not need me any more.

Later that evening, Herb and I met again. He said maybe he would hire me to be a consultant to him, with no involvement in basketball. He said he could not give me a raise. I left the short meeting and told him I would have to think about it and would get back to him.

Meanwhile, I was prepared to exit my two passions—basketball and the NBA. I had expanded my businesses, and I had been elected to the board of the G. Heilmann Brewing Company. At this moment, I was preparing for life after basketball. My only involvement with the game now would be my positions on committees of USA Basketball and the Basketball Hall of Fame.

Several weeks passed before I heard anything about Nellie and the new ownership. I stopped by Major Goolsby's for a beer one night before facing the traffic I knew I would encounter on my way home. Goolsby's was a popular place in those days, and it was unusual to go in and not know anyone there, even if it was only the bartenders and waitresses. Sure enough, there were a couple of familiar faces at the bar. Both worked for the *Journal.*

"What's going on with you, Big Man?" one asked me.

"Oh, I'm making it," I said. "We are getting another McDonald's and I'm doing some consulting."

"Anything in basketball?"

"Not at the moment."

Then one of them said, "I know why Nellie and the Bucks did not want you," he said. "Nellie told us it was because you cheated on your expense account."

I nearly fell off the stool. "Are you sure he said that?" I asked.

"Absolutely," he said.

I drove home in a rage, and as soon as I walked through the door, Terri asked what was wrong. I told her what I had just learned.

"I told you not to trust him, Wayne," she said, releasing all the pent-up anger she felt for all the late nights I had spent with Nellie in Boston and in Milwaukee. She never did like Nellie.

The next morning I called Fitz. Dispensing with the pleasantries, I asked his assistant to speak with him.

"Wayno," he said, using a nickname he had given me.

"Fitz, let me be direct," I said. "Did you or any of your financial people question my expenses?"

"No," he said. "Why do you ask?"

"Because Nellie is saying the reason the Bucks did not retain me was because I cheated on my expense account," I said, trying to hold back my anger. "Why the vicious attack on my character?"

"I don't know why he would do that, Wayne," Fitz whispered.

I hung up and asked Judy to get Dan Finnane on the phone.

"Dan, did you ever question my expenses?" I asked, making no attempt at small talk.

I got the same denial from him.

"Call Nellie," was my next command to Judy.

Now that I knew Nellie had fabricated this story, I calmly suggested we meet for coffee at the Hyatt Hotel coffee shop across the street from the Arena. I was surprised he accepted, since we had not talked in weeks.

I took giant strides while walking from my office. I was ready for a fight. Rage consumed my 300-pound frame. I had never been this angry.

Nellie could tell it was not going to be a friendly meeting when I approached him with my slightly raised right hand balled up in a fist. Given the size of my hands, my fist looked like the head of a sledge-hammer.

"What's wrong, Big Man?" the startled Nellie said.

I am not sure how I controlled my temper, but I managed to spit out, "Why did you tell people the reason you did not want me around was because I cheated on my expenses?"

He was shocked and vehemently denied it.

"Nellie, you're lying," I yelled. "I have this from reliable sources. My reputation is my most valuable asset. I've worked hard to build it. And I will not let you take it from me."

He recovered enough to claim that when we were at our camps in New Hampshire, I had rented a car and charged the Bucks. "You should not have done that," he said.

I asked if he was referring to the time I had driven up to interview Cowens and reminded him that was official business. "How did you expect me to get there?" I asked.

"You could have borrowed a car," he said, weakly.

"Why do you have to destroy my credibility?" I roared.

Nellie clammed up. "I've got to go," he said and left.

"You are the bottom of the barrel, the scum of the earth," I shouted as he hurried through the tables and out of the coffee shop.

Walking back to my office, I tried to find some sort of rationale for his actions. I thought about our times together as roommates and teammates and all I had tried to teach him during our years together in Milwaukee. I wondered where he would be if I had not hired him, and I wished he was there, wherever that was. But I also remembered something else my parents told me: When you get too big, evil people will try to tear you down. This holds true no matter who you are or what you do and no matter how much you ultimately accomplish in life.

Nellie had used me up and tossed me away.

It took me some time to overcome the disappointment and hurt. My pastor must have been thinking of me the Sunday morning he recited scriptures from Exodus. His sermon was about Moses and his flight into Egypt to free the Israelites. "Some of the elders turned on Moses," he preached. "Quite often, those you help are those who hurt you the most. Often those you help resent the fact that you are in a position to help them," he continued. The message was so true.

Chapter 13

Moving On

I had to move on. I could not fret over the past. My college coach, Bill Rohr, always said that I had to be prepared for life after basketball. That life started now.

I thought back on the day he had come to The Hill and dwelled on the importance of academics. I had just been through another learning experience in human relations. This was a lesson in how people changed because of greed or the need for power, although I have often wondered if I had read Nellie right from the start. I remember someone telling me people were the most enjoyable things in life and people were also the most disappointing things in life. What a true statement that is.

I left the Bucks, rented an office downtown, and devoted all my time to developing my businesses. I sold my interest in McDonald's and became president of MALCO, a company I helped create that fabricated parts for the auto industry. I also became more involved in civic organizations. I was on the board of Summerfest, the popular annual event on the shores of Lake Michigan that became a world famous stop for entertainers and artists. I was elected to the board of Children's Hospital and the Medical College of Wisconsin. I increased my speaking to various groups, particularly youth groups. I talked to them about the importance of education and character as the keys to success. I liked sharing my experiences. My most recent personal experience led me to emphasize the subject of trust. I kept my basketball camp in New

Hampshire. I still enjoyed working with our staff and the kids. And I stayed involved with Special Olympics.

I also was able to attend more of Wayne Jr.'s sporting events and Debbi's and Jill's activities. Basketball had consumed so much of my time that I had missed out on much of their early childhood.

One morning, my assistant Judy Berger came into my office and told me there was a Mr. Salyers on the phone. I had met Bob Salyers, president of the Indiana Pacers, when I attended a fund-raiser for USA Basketball in Indianapolis in 1984. Though I was seated at his table, we spoke only briefly, so I was somewhat surprised to hear from him and even more surprised when he suggested we meet to discuss an opening he had for an experienced person to help the Pacers rebuild. He told me the owners, Herb and Mel Simon, had spoken to Red Auerbach, Pete Newell, and Stu Inman about me and now Bob was inviting me to Indianapolis for a meeting.

The Simons were commercial real estate developers and had malls around the country. They had saved the Pacers franchise and promised to bring the city a winner. Bob was the president, George Irvine was the coach, Donnie Walsh was an assistant coach, and Mel Daniels and Tom Newell were scouts. George and Mel played in the ABA, where Mel was a perennial All-Star. Donnie had coached with his North Carolina roommate Larry Brown with the Denver Nuggets and was an assistant to Frank McGuire at the University of South Carolina.

Herb offered me a two-year consulting contract worth five times more than I had made with the Bucks. I did not have to move, and I could continue working in my businesses. I jumped at the opportunity to rekindle my passion, though I knew I was facing a huge job. The Pacers had decent talent but they constantly finished in the cellar. My first task was to evaluate the coaching staff and players.

I got there in time to participate in the draft lottery. Bob, George Irvine, and I went to New York in hopes of winning the first pick, which was sure to be Georgetown center Patrick Ewing. That certainly would have sped up our rebuilding efforts. While we were in New York, Herb and the rest of the Pacers staff were back in Indianapolis at a lottery party, but there was not much partying when we wound up with the Number 2 pick and the New York Knicks got the Number 1 selection.

After the lottery, there were allegations that the Knicks' envelope had a folded edge, which allowed Commissioner David Stern an opportunity to make sure New York got the big prize during the televised proceedings. In fact, there was so much complaining that the process was changed, and it has been modified several more times until the current system using ping-pong balls was developed. And to think we had gotten the rights to draft Lew Alcindor (later Kareem Abdul-Jabbar) by winning a coin toss between the two teams that finished last in each conference. But we had gone away from that in order to discourage bad teams from tanking it late in the season. Houston was accused of doing that when it won the Number 1 pick in back-to-back seasons and took Ralph Sampson and Hakeem Olajuwon. However, I still believed losing could serve a purpose—if you were able to get a high enough draft choice the following season to get a shot at a player who could turn your team around.

The week after the lottery, I got my first glimpse at how the marketing types were starting to influence decision making. As the draft approached, we were not sure which player we would take. Even with a week to go, we had not decided between Waymon Tisdale, an All-American from Oklahoma who had decided to enter the draft after his junior year, and Karl Malone, a lesser-known player from Louisiana Tech. At a draft meeting with the owners and board on the Sunday before the draft, Mel Daniels was adamant we take Malone. But we were told that the Simons' marketing department was conducting a survey in the newspaper, asking fans who they thought we should draft. This was a first for me. After endless hours of scouting and conducting interviews and background checks, this was going to be a popularity contest.

The results of the survey came out overwhelmingly in favor of Tisdale. So on Tuesday morning, we drafted Wayman Tisdale with the Number 2 pick. The marketing department was not satisfied with just determining who we drafted. Now it was in total control. Before the basketball staff even got to welcome our newest addition, the marketing people arranged for him to tool around the track during the Indianapolis 500 trials before thousands of fans. That is how Wayman Tisdale was welcomed to Indianapolis. Now he had to live up to that billing. It was totally unfair to him and only set him up to disappoint the fans.

I spent the summer in Milwaukee and talked to Bob Salyers periodically. The week before training camp, I joined Bob and his staff at a retreat south of the city. They asked me what I thought about their team. I told them I liked Clark Kellogg, Herb Williams, and Vern Fleming, although I realized Clark's future was questionable because of his chronic knee problems. All of us were hoping Wayman would give the team a boost. But there was a problem. Wayman still was not signed.

Bob had been negotiating all summer and was frustrated by his inability to reach a deal. It was an unusual situation. Ted Steinberg was the lead agent, but in order to represent Wayman, he had to help Wayman's brother Weldon and his friend, Paul Samuels, get into the business of representing athletes.

Wayman, of course, was their first client. With camp approaching, Bob and Herb asked me to get involved. After several phone conversations, we were invited to Los Angeles to meet with Ted face-to-face, which I thought would be the only way to get something done.

When we walked into the conference room at Ted's office, we were surprised to be greeted by Ted and the entire Tisdale family, along with Paul. After the introductions and some chitchat, I asked Ted if there was a room we could use to negotiate. I was shocked when Reverend Tisdale, Wayman's father, told us they were all there to participate in the negotiations, so there was no need to move. I looked at Bob and we both looked at Ted for a response. With none forthcoming, I turned to the family and said, "Shall we begin by reviewing where we are?"

Then Reverend Tisdale spoke.

"Let us join hands and pray," he said, bowing his head.

I had never seen anything like this. Believe me, I have no objection to prayer, but I figured the deck was stacked against us when he ended the prayer by saying, "Let all go well for Wayman."

We talked for a couple of hours and made no progress. Bob and I stepped outside to collaborate on a different strategy. We agreed this was going to be difficult for a number of reasons, including the fact we were leery about saying anything derogatory about Wayman's game because we did not want to offend his family. It was one of the calmest negotiations I had ever conducted. I raised my voice only once and was reprimanded by Reverend Tisdale, who said, "Now, Wayne, there is no point getting excited, is there?"

After four hours, we had gotten nowhere, so we took a break for dinner.

As I stood to leave, Reverend Tisdale stopped me, saying, "Let us join hands and pray."

Bob and I headed for the Chinese restaurant in the Century Plaza Hotel.

"I think we're in over our heads," I said between bites. Bob agreed. "We will have to have faith that God will mediate," I added.

About 9 P.M., we decided we were at an impasse, and Bob and I returned to our room and called Herb. The next day we headed back to Indiana. We kept replaying the experience of the previous day. We were impressed with Wayman's family, and with Paul. They were class people. But we were worried we might not get an equitable deal done. The only other time I negotiated with a family member was when Quinn Buckner's father took over from agent Steve Ferguson. I will never forget the Sunday morning shouting match I had with Mr. Buckner. It is only natural for family members to hold their loved ones in high regard, but it makes for tough negotiating.

Several days into training camp, we finally got Wayman signed. Despite that, it was going to be a long year. Kellogg's knee problems continued. Steve Stipanovich, the seven-foot center from Missouri, had back problems. The team was young and inexperienced, and so were the coaches. I spent a great deal of time with Bob and scout Tommy Newell because the coaches preferred to spend time away from us. There did not seem to be a lot of solidarity in the organization. I sensed that the coaches felt threatened by my presence. I was an intruder. They were very guarded whenever we met, regardless of how much I tried to ease their concerns. Bob and I had periodic meetings with the owners and board to address the needs of the team, and they always asked my opinion of the situations. Midway through the season, we met to discuss the team. I reviewed each player and summarized my feelings by saying, "Herb, we are not very good."

Herb did not like hearing that. "What about George?" he asked. "Don't you think he's a great coach?

"He's inexperienced and insecure," I replied. "Time will tell."

He stunned me when he said, "I brought you here to make him a better coach."

After that meeting, I started to examine the culture of the Pacers. I felt as if the only guys I really knew were Bob Salyers and Tommy Newell, and I sometimes thought they were the only two receptive to my being there. I wanted to learn more about Herb and Mel. I wanted to get to know George better. I tried to be at all the home games, and I suggested Herb and I have dinner before the games. Bob and Mel joined us sometimes.

One night, we were meeting at Herb's favorite Italian restaurant, Maxie's.

"What do we need to do with this team?" he asked me for the umpteenth time.

"We need shooting, rebounding, experience, and patience," I told him, repeating my stock answer.

It was as if he had not heard me.

"You should know George is a dear friend of my family's," he said. "His wife and my wife are friends. We have Chinese food at my house just about every Sunday."

I could not help but think of Fitz and Nellie. It did not matter what I thought then, and I realized it did not matter what I thought now.

Late in the season, Herb brought in Billy Cunningham, an old friend of Donnie's, to ask him about the state of the franchise. Bob and I saw the writing on the wall. They were circumventing us. Although Herb had given me a token raise in appreciation of my efforts, I knew my time here was limited. I just did not realize how limited.

But on the Saturday before I was to leave for the Aloha Classic, Herb called to tell me he was sending Donnie to Hawaii, too.

"He's been coaching and doesn't know the college players," he told me. Then, almost as an afterthought, he added, "I'm thinking of making him president."

I told Herb I had no problem with that. Furthermore, I said, "It's your team. It's wise to build your organization with people you're comfortable with."

Several weeks later, the appointment became official. During a lunch meeting, Herb asked me if I had any problem reporting to Donnie.

"No, I don't," I said, and I meant it. "But I have to ask. Why wasn't I considered for the GM job?"

I got no answer.

Chapter 14

Another New Start

I put the Pacers behind me and charged into Cleveland in the summer of 1986. But The League had changed significantly since my rebuilding years in Milwaukee. Thanks to players like Larry Bird and Magic Johnson, the 1980s had ushered in a new era for the NBA. Drug scandals had marred the 1970s, but The League reformed and when David Stern became commissioner in 1984, he broadened its marketing efforts with an eye toward the international market. Brian McIntyre, the director of media relations for The League, organized the public relations departments of the franchises and, under the direction of Stern, they set about generating publicity globally. Basketball was becoming an international sport, and the NBA had the best players in the world. The security department of The League also grew in an attempt to police drug activity and any other illegal activities that would hurt The League's image. They also were on hand to protect the players, who were becoming increasingly more high-profile.

The League expanded to twenty-three teams, and actually would reach twenty-seven by the end of the decade. But at the start of the 1980s, the dominant teams were still the Celtics and the Lakers. Boston featured Larry Bird, Kevin McHale, Robert Parish, and Dennis Johnson and was billed as the team to beat in the East. The Lakers' style of play had become known as "Showtime," primarily because of flashy point guard Magic Johnson, and they were the team to beat in the West because of Johnson, Kareem Abdul-Jabbar, and James Worthy. At this point, the team was still greater than its individual players.

Other teams were on the rise: Chuck Daly's Detroit Pistons, with Isiah Thomas, Joe Dumars, Rick Mahorn, Dennis Rodman, and former Cav Bill Laimbeer; and the Chicago Bulls with a young Michael Jordan. We were confident we would be in the company of those teams if we were patient. We figured eventually the Celtics and Lakers would age, and we wanted to be at our peak as they inched over the hill.

Despite the rocky start of the interviewing process and the uncomfortable developments in the 1986 draft, we finished my first Cavs season strong, winning fourteen of the last twenty games and finishing with thirty-one victories, two more than the year before. Fans took to the team, and attendance increased as the season progressed. There definitely was optimism and hope for the future.

Harper led the team in scoring, averaging almost 23 points a game. He proved to be the exciting player we always thought he would be. Williams and Daugherty also had good rookie years, joining Harper on the 1987 NBA All-Rookie team. It was the first time three players from the same team had received the honor since Maurice Stokes, Jack Twyman, and Ed Fleming did it for the Rochester Royals in 1956.

Ron Harper grew up on the west side of Dayton. After he finished high school, he was recruited by Miami University and became the best player in the history of the school, and it does not even pain me to admit that. He eclipsed all the scoring records. Most scouting reports described him as a fair outside shooter, but because of his speed and quickness, his ball-handling ability and his size, he was able to score. In NBA scouting terms, he was labeled a scorer. At six-foot-six-inches, he was the perfect size to play guard in The League. His greatest attribute was that he had a great passion for the game. He loved to play.

Brad Daugherty showed he was going to be one of the best centers in The League. He quickly shed the "soft" label some scouts had given him. He could shoot the ball facing the basket, and he was able to shoot the seldom-used hook shot effectively with either hand. His size and strength made him an effective rebounder and a presence inside. He was a great passer and did something that was near and dear to my heart—he set a great pick and rolled to the basket or stepped back for a short-range jumper. He and Mark Price ran the pick-and-roll to perfection. Playing for Dean Smith at North Carolina, one of the best college programs in the country, Brad had been well schooled in the fundamentals.

Hot Rod, which was what everybody called John Williams, was a six-foot-eleven-inch power forward who was as agile as a small forward. He also was able to shoot the ball facing the basket and put it on the floor. His long body made him an effective rebounder and shot blocker. He, too, was fundamentally sound.

Mark Price was sidelined by an appendicitis attack for part of the season, but when he did play, he showed signs of greatness. Being the son of Denny Price, a longtime coach in college and the pros, he knew the game. Scouts passed on him, thinking he was too small at six feet tall, but his tenacity and competitiveness made up for his lack of size. Although he split playing time with the veteran John Bagley at point guard, we knew he was our point guard of the future. Having Brad and Mark gave us key players at the two most important positions to build around.

Johnny Newman showed signs of becoming a good player. Unfortunately, he was involved in a car accident that set him back. Phil Hubbard gave us the veteran leadership that we wanted. He was a blue-collar worker on the court, but he was great for us in the locker room. He helped teach our guys how to become pros.

We had a solid foundation. They were all going to be better players two or three years out. They were smart and possessed the character that coach Lenny Wilkens and I sought. Lenny was a great teacher, and they were eager to learn. We just needed to be patient with this group. They reminded me of the "green and growing" group we rebuilt the Bucks with in 1975–76.

The coaches, player personnel director Gary Fitzsimmons, and I were enthusiastic when we sat down to review the season with our owners. We told them we wanted to keep the rookies, along with Hubbard, Mark West, and Craig Ehlo, who showed signs of becoming a good backup guard or small forward. The rest were expendable, as far as we were concerned.

When assessing our needs, I told owner Gordon Gund we had to figure out what we had before we could figure out what we needed. That said, we knew we needed some shooters to protect Brad. Mark Price was our only pure perimeter shooter, although he shot just 41 percent as a rookie. We knew he would improve on that.

We also knew we could get a good player in the 1987 draft with our Number 7 pick. We were looking for a small forward, but only if a good one were available. We identified four players we thought would be there at Number 7, and we would have been happy with any of them, but Scottie Pippen, from Central Arkansas, was the guy we wanted. We had done extensive background checks on all of them, and they all passed our character test.

It got tense the night before the draft—my first with new ownership. I was not sure how much they wanted to participate. My previous owners were satisfied that my staff and I had done our homework, and they did not interfere. So I was a little surprised when team attorney Dick Watson appeared at my door on the eve of the draft. "Here's how we're going to do this," he told me, holding up some sort of matrix on a large piece of paper. I remembered that during my interview he had boasted about how he and Gordon orchestrated last year's draft, and I had heard from other staff members how he liked to be involved and take credit for things.

But I took the draft as seriously as I did the play-offs. I put on my game face and concentrated on getting the best possible player. In fact, those around me were always glad when the draft was over. So I curtly told him, "Dick, we've got it covered. We don't need your help. All of us have done this before, and pretty successfully. We will be prepared to present our decisions to Gordon." I also reminded him of the terms of my contract, which spelled out that I reported to Gordon. He did not take this well.

As it happened, we were talking to Seattle about switching picks, which would give us Number 5. Seattle also was talking with Chicago, which had Number 8. We did not want to part with our rookies, so all we had to offer were future picks or cash. I talked with Seattle general manager Bob Whitsitt continuously throughout the day and into the night. While I was talking to him, Gary Fitzsimmons was talking to Jimmy Sexton, Pippen's agent. We were trying to get him in for an interview. We had been unsuccessful in getting him to come in earlier. Sexton told Gary that Scottie was in Chicago, and that Chicago and Seattle were making a trade. (Agents often were our best sources of information.) Despite several denials, I was convinced we were out of the picture and I told Gordon and the rest of our ownership. Everybody took it well except Watson. To this day, he contends that we could have had Pippen. Nothing I have said since has convinced him otherwise.

In fact, Whitsitt and Chicago general manager Jerry Krause confessed to me that they were using us to find out who we were going to draft. Chicago wanted Pippen and Kevin Johnson. Seattle wanted Olden Polynice. We told Gordon we would be happy with Pippen, Johnson, Horace Grant or Kenny Smith. But Pippen went to Chicago at Number 5, and Kenny Smith went to Sacramento at Number 6. To the boos of our fans at our draft night party, we took Johnson, the lightning-quick point guard from California. Fans and reporters were shocked when we announced we were taking another point guard. Harper, who attended the draft party, showed his dismay by covering his face with his hands as the announcement was made.

I have always believed that point guards were hard to come by and if we did not need both of them there would be a market for one. Both were going to be stars, which meant they both needed to play. It was not a popular choice. Little did I realize that my first draft as the Cavs general manager would haunt me for the rest of my tenure in Cleveland.

But there was a new excitement in Cleveland. Season ticket sales were

My first press conference in Cleveland (Courtesy of Paul Tepley)

surging, and our marketing department generated revenues from other sources, which brought about a new challenge for me. The League's marketing efforts had increased, and teams were adding more and more marketing people in an effort to promote marquee players in much the same way the entertainment industry promoted its stars. Team staffs had nearly quadrupled since my days in Milwaukee when we ran the Bucks with fewer than fifteen people. I thought this was good. It helped expose The League to more fans. But it also created conflicts between the marketing departments and the coaches and general managers, who were responsible for managing the egos of the players.

Our marketing people wanted to promote Harper much as they had promoted World B. Free. It appeared the Cavs were going to be Ron Harper's team, and the marketing department wanted to bill him as the Cavs' Michael Jordan, who was emerging as a superstar in Chicago. I had to put my foot down there. I did not want to put pressure on Ron to be somebody other than he was. In fact, Lenny and I would be satisfied if he was just himself, which was going to be good. Also, we had other talented players, and we did not want their egos bruised. I thought our marketing department could achieve its goals by marketing the entire team, as the old Celtics, Lakers, and Pistons did. Gordon agreed. Those teams won with cohesion. Larry Bird and Magic Johnson emerged as stars because their teams were winning.

But we had problems outside our offices. Despite the rapidly increasing salaries available to players, overzealous agents had begun marketing their clients with shoe companies and other businesses. Agents received 25 percent fees for endorsement dollars as opposed to the 4 percent fees they got for negotiating contracts. They, too, were trying to capitalize on the growing popularity of The League. But this kind of marketing started to create other problems. Because advertisers wanted maximum exposure for their clients, they liked to see the players in the biggest markets, which meant smaller market teams had trouble attracting and keeping their stars. Players started worrying about endorsements and exposure, which translated into selfishness, which in turn created another whole set of problems for coaches and general managers.

I wanted our players to stay focused on becoming a contender. I remember Ray Kroc, founder of McDonald's, telling us at my first convention, "Give me a quality product in a clean environment with excellent service . . . and then market the hell out of it. If you don't have a quality product with good service in a clean restaurant, save your marketing dollars. Never expose your customers to a bad experience." That is why McDonald's is one of the best marketers in history.

We were on our way toward building a quality product, one that projected a positive image and one to which our fans could relate. But

Harper severely sprained his ankle in the second game of the 1987–88 season, and Hot Rod missed the first five games with a sore left foot. When everybody got healthy, we returned to the level we had left at the end of our first season together. We could see definite improvement. Brad was vastly improved and became the first All-Star with the franchise since Mike Mitchell in 1981. Mark Price had emerged to become the starting point guard. He recovered from a so-so rookie year and began shooting the ball and passing the way he did at Georgia Tech. Harper was establishing himself as one of the top guards in the East. Harper, Daugherty, Price, and Williams were playing like veterans. But Kevin Johnson was emerging as well and was demanding playing time. His presence would give us depth, if he could handle coming off the bench, which was becoming more difficult for talented young players to do if they thought they were going to be stars. Agents also were getting involved, trying to make sure their players got playing time to maximize earnings and exposure.

On October 9, 1987, we were able to consummate a three-team deal that enabled us to trade players who did not fit into our future plans. Lenny kept asking me when we were going to get rid of the deadwood. He wanted to go forward with the young kids. I had promised Lenny I would do everything possible to trade Turpin. Because he was not playing, his weight had ballooned to more than three hundred pounds and reporters were calling him "Dinner Bell Mel." Trading him was not going to be easy because of his contract, which had several years left for quite a bit of money. With Mark emerging and Kevin backing him up, we also did not need John Bagley. He was a good player and a terrific person, but he, too, needed to play to keep his weight down, and he was not going to play in Cleveland. There also was no place for Keith Lee, who was often hurt. I worked overtime on the phones, trying to find a place for them. I discovered that former general manager of the Cavs, Harry Weltman, now with New Jersey, had interest in Bagley and Lee, two players he had drafted for Cleveland. Then I was able to convince the Utah Jazz they needed Turpin. I had made previous attempts to pry

Dell Curry from the Jazz. In 1986, he was the player I would have liked had Harper not been available. Although he was not playing much in Utah, I knew with playing time he would develop into a premier guard because he was a great shooter. We needed shooters on our team to keep the defenses from sagging on Brad, who was quickly becoming a dominant center who demanded a double team in order to stop him from scoring on the block. Mark Price was the only legitimate shooter we had.

The complicated deal took hours to make. Negotiations went well into the night and way beyond the working hours of the lawyers in the league office. I asked Gary Fitzsimmons to call Joel Litvin in the commissioner's office to inform him that a deal was in the works and to ask him to stay put until it was done. When Gary told league officials who was involved, they laughed. They were sure we would never unload Turpin's contract.

Finally, at 10 P.M., Watson, Gary, and I put the deal together. Thank goodness Joel and Dan Shorr-Rube stayed to accept the conference call to go over the contracts and the other issues that would make the deal official. The deal sent Turpin to Utah and Lee and Bagley to New Jersey. We got Curry and Kent Benson from Utah and James Bailey from New Jersey. That was a lot of bodies to move. Old pro Phil Hubbard was the only player remaining from the group that was here when we took over, and we liked him as a player as well as a leader.

We really liked our team now. We had a good young backcourt in Harper, Price, Johnson, Curry, and Craig Ehlo. Now we just had to get them enough playing time to develop and keep them happy.

In late February, we were three games above .500 and playing well. The team seemed to have jelled and was getting better each game. However, we were about to go on the dreaded West Coast trip. We were in the play-off hunt and needed to sustain our good play if we were to make the play-offs for the first time since 1985. Fitzsimmons strolled into my office about mid-morning as he usually did. Most of the time we just talked basketball, whether we were discussing our team, The

League or some college player we had noticed. Simmie loved to talk basketball.

"What if we could add Larry Nance to our team?" he asked, seemingly out of nowhere. "Would you do it?"

"At what price?" I asked. "Why?"

"I talked to my father (Phoenix's Cotton Fitzsimmons) last night and the Suns want to shake their team up," he told me. "They would trade Larry in the right deal. They would want Kevin from us in some kind of package."

I liked Larry. I had scouted him as a college player at Clemson and I liked him as an NBA player. But I was curious about why Phoenix would trade its best player. He was averaging 22 points a game in his best season as a pro. I remembered the drug scandal that decimated the Suns and wondered if there had been a recurrence, although I had never heard anything but positives about Larry. I also was worried about the aftershocks of a trade with a young team, especially since we were in a play-off run. Over the years, as a player and executive, I had seen the remaining players shaken after a trade. Our guys were young and would not understand what we were doing, even though Lenny and I tried to prepare them for these kinds of events.

"I need to check it out," I told Simmie.

I was intrigued enough to begin my due diligence. My first call was to John MacLeod, who was Larry's coach when he came into The League. John and I had become friends over the years, and I knew he would be straight with me. I was able to track him down within hours.

"John, I've got to ask you some questions in confidence," I told him. "What can you tell me about Larry Nance."

John did not hesitate. "Wayne, if you can get Larry Nance, he will take your team to another level," he said. "He is top notch, someone you would like your son to grow up like."

"Thanks, John," I said. "That's good enough for me."

Gary Fitzsimmons and I thought that even though Larry was six feet, ten inches tall, he could play small forward. With Hot Rod at power forward, we envisioned a front line of six-foot-ten, seven-foot, six-foot-eleven. Our backcourt was Harper, at six foot, six inches, and Price, who was barely six-foot tall but played bigger because of his great heart. We had the size to match Boston, and the quickness as well.

Lenny had the same initial concerns I had. He, too, had seen young teams fall apart after a significant trade. He did like Larry, but he was not sure he could play small forward in his system. I used the Celtic philosophy in my debate. Bird was six-foot-nine, Parish seven-foot-one and McHale six-foot-ten. Red believed you should play your best players and let the other team worry about matchups. At the end of the day, Lenny was on board. We both had reservations about trading Kevin. He had stardom written all over him, but with Price's improvement, particularly his shooting, we felt comfortable.

"What's the deal, Jerry?" I said to Phoenix general manager Jerry Colangelo after Ruthie, his assistant, chased him down.

"Here's the deal," he said. "We will trade you Nance for Kevin Johnson, Tyrone Corbin, and Mark West, and a first-round pick."

We were giving up a small forward with toughness in Corbin, and I did not like that. I also did not like giving up "The Hammer," the nickname we had given Mark West. He was a solid backup for Brad and had the best work ethic of any player we had had. We thought Hot Rod could back up Brad for short minutes, at least until we found someone else. The pick, which we had had picked up from Detroit in an earlier transaction, did not bother me at all, since it was going to be a late first-round selection.

To replace Corbin, we needed Mike Sanders back because they were similar players. Jerry agreed to that, and we had a deal. Now I had to run down Gordon and Dick Watson and try to sell them on the deal. Gordon wanted to know about all trades. His concern was not about the talent, because he trusted my judgment. He wanted to know the type of person we were getting and he wanted to know the economics. All that was fine with me. The problem was that we tracked Gordon to some remote location that did not have phones, which made it tough to communicate. Jerry was becoming impatient, and we nearly lost the deal. But, using intermediaries, we were able to get Gordon's consent.

Ironically, we were on the way to play the Suns, and Lenny had to pull Kevin, Mark, and Tyrone off the team bus so I could tell them they had been traded. It was tough, as always, but I had been through this before. All of them were shaken, despite my reassurance that their careers would flourish because they were going to have an opportunity to play. I made it clear Phoenix really wanted them, and it was not because we did not. I had the hardest time convincing Kevin's mother, who had just moved to Akron to be near Kevin.

Larry was shaken as well. He never thought he would get traded from Phoenix. We had to convince him that we really wanted him and that it was not because Phoenix did not. We tried to explain he was traded because the Suns were rebuilding and he was too far along in his career to go through that.

After all the players passed the required physicals, we were each different teams. We had a proven star to go along with our young stars. The trade was similar to the one we made for Lanier when I was with the Bucks. I hoped it would have the same effect. Leaving the Valley of the Sun to come to Cleveland was not going to be easy, so I did not know what to expect from Larry. He was very subdued when I called him after the conference call with The League confirming the trade. It took quite a selling job from Lenny and me to make him feel comfortable. We wanted to make sure he did not lose his self-esteem.

Larry and Mike joined the team on the road, but we were completely out of sync. We lost twelve of the next fifteen, and the media and fans let us have it. Even some members of our organization were critical. Then Lenny made a brilliant coaching decision. He inserted Sanders into the starting lineup and we went on a tear, closing the 1987–88 season with eleven wins in our last fourteen games to get back into the playoffs after a two-year absence. Finishing above .500 had been one of our objectives, and we went 42–40, the first time we had been over .500 since 1977–78.

A radio interview with the voice of the Cavaliers, Joe Tait (Courtesy of Paul Tepley)

Excitement had returned to the Coliseum. The day we put play-off tickets on sale brought thousands of fans to the building, and the line snaked around the parking lot. It was quite a sight to see. I rounded up Gary Fitzsimmons and my assistant, Judy, and we went out to greet them and thank them for their support. We served coffee and doughnuts. I shook so many hands that my arms were sore, but the fans appreciated the gesture.

To create a family environment, I asked Gordon if he would host the players' parents for our home games. Jim Fitzgerald had done this in Milwaukee. All of the players' parents came to Cleveland and were made to feel part of the Cavs family.

We took the Bulls to the fifth and deciding game before losing in the first round. We jumped out early in Game 5 and held our own in the first half, but Michael Jordan scored 21 of his 39 points in the second half. He averaged a five-game play-off record 45.2 points a game in the series.

We were encouraged by what we saw. For the young team to experience play-off intensity was important. We learned a lot. We learned our guys could raise it up a notch. We were particularly pleased with Harper's performance, and we learned that Ehlo was to be more than an adequate backup. Daugherty and Price were good as well, and we were really excited about the future of the team after watching Nance and Sanders. We were not the only ones who were excited. The fans were excited as well. Season ticket sales were on the rise. People were talking about the Cavs.

Shortly after the season ended, Judy walked into my office with my daily stack of correspondence.

"Hey, Big Man, you're not going to believe this," she said, handing over the mail. "Guess who sent you a letter?"

The answer was right on top of the pile—a handwritten, two-page letter from the one and only Don Nelson. We had not spoken since our confrontation at the Milwaukee Hyatt two years earlier. We had no communication in all that time, despite efforts from several mutual acquaintances to bring us back together.

Imagine my surprise then at seeing a letter of apology. Nellie admitted he was wrong in his attempt to discredit me and said he just did not want to answer questions about why he did not want me to continue with the Bucks.

"What do you think he's up to, Big Man?" Judy asked.

"No telling," I said. But I knew he was up to something. Still, he had apologized and asked for forgiveness. I believe in forgiveness. We patched things up enough that I actually stood up in his wedding a few years later. But I would not forget what had happened.

At that time, I had other concerns. My biggest problem was trying to put together a list of the eight players league rules allowed us to protect in the upcoming expansion draft for the new teams in Charlotte and Miami, who would get to select players off the other team's rosters. As soon as The League announced it was expanding, we knew we would be hurt because we were in the process of rebuilding. We liked all our young players, and we knew it was unlikely an aging player like Phil Hubbard would be very attractive to the new teams. The coaches and scouts and Gary and I debated from the time expansion was announced until the deadline for submitting our list, and the names on our list changed daily.

Protecting Price, Daugherty, Nance, Harper, Williams, and Ehlo was a no-brainer. We decided to expose Hubbard, but deciding on the other two players was tough. We loved Curry's upside. He was one of the best pure shooters in The League. His demeanor made it seem as though he was not playing hard, and we gave him the nickname "Cruise Control" because that is how he appeared to be playing. But, in fact, he was very intense. Sanders was a big part of our winning chemistry, plus he was the starting small forward when we went on our late-season surge. Chris Dudley, a six-foot-eleven center from Yale who was a fourth-round draft choice, was a promising backup for Daugherty.

Finally, we decided to keep Sanders, so our decision was between Curry and Dudley. I exhausted every possible means to make a deal with the new teams to take one our other players. I offered cash, draft picks, or both. When I could not make a deal, I had to make a decision. Did I go against one of my main tenets and give up shooting, quickly becoming a lost art in The League, or size and rebounding, which were equally tough to replace?

Reluctantly, we exposed Curry, which was a mistake. The Charlotte Hornets jumped at the chance to take him, and we lost a promising young player without getting anything in return.

The following week we tried to replace Curry's shooting by drafting Randolph Keys, a six-foot-seven-inch small forward from Southern Mississippi, with the twenty-second pick in the first round. We took Winston Bennett, another small forward from Kentucky, in the second round. We still had work to do. Our promising backcourt of Price, Harper, Ehlo, Curry, and Johnson was down to Price, Harper and Ehlo, but our nucleus was intact and getting better. We needed to improve our depth, though, and that was my task for the summer.

It was going to be an especially busy time. I had to negotiate new contracts for Lenny, Brad, and Mark; and Larry was entering the option year of his contract. In addition, I got involved in as many civic activities as I could, repeating a process I had adopted wherever I lived. It was a great time to be in Cleveland. Through a great public and private partnership, Cleveland was being billed as "The Comeback City." It was crucial for the Cavs to be an integral part of the renaissance. I spent the summer speaking about the Cavs all over Northeast Ohio, trying to build trust and support. I found people receptive and enthusiastic. Being an engaging person, I would talk to anyone and everyone about the Cavs—or anything else for that matter. If I met people who were not Cavs fans, I would try to convert them, and I usually succeeded.

Back in the office, I found I had little leverage in any of my major contract dealings. Lenny, Brad, Mark, and Larry were vital pieces of our team, and all of them continued to improve. Doing Lenny's deal was fairly painless, but player salaries were escalating at an alarming rate. I found that Cleveland was much like Milwaukee or any other team in a small market. We had a limited budget. Player payroll was the bulk of our operating budget, so we had to stay within it. Gordon did not hesitate to pay fair market value, but he also did not want to lose money. We had to advance in the play-offs in order to make money, so there was no question we had to sign the players. We also had to be fair to the players in order to avoid internal problems.

There were other things that came into play, too, or at least things agents tried to bring into play, although I wanted no part of them. Some agents who represented white players thought white players should be paid more; some agents who represented black players thought black players should be paid more—especially by me. In all my days, I never thought those things would become issues and, luckily, it was not often that they did.

The deals for Brad and Larry came together fairly easily. Brad was an

All-Star who was represented by Lee Fentress, who also represented Moses Malone, David Robinson, and Hakeem Olajuwon. Lee considered Brad to be in their class, and I did not disagree. Larry was a proven star who had had a tremendous impact on our success since coming over from Phoenix. He also was a veteran with a track record. We signed Brad to an extension with a good-sized raise and picked up Larry's option and extended his contract, too.

That left Mark, and that was a challenge.

Mark was represented by Richard Howell. Howell was coach Bobby Cremins's attorney, and he represented most of Cremins's players from Georgia Tech. Howell really stood up for his players, and if you were a general manager, he would wear you out. He was the toughest negotiator I ever faced.

Howell already was upset with us because he was unhappy with the first contract Mark signed, which reflected the fact that Mark was a second-round draft choice. Richard told us we should be prepared to pay the next time around because Mark would prove he should have been selected higher. Mark had done that, and we were prepared to pay—but not enough to satisfy Howell.

Richard wanted to reestablish the pay scale for point guards. His contention was that Mark was the most valuable player on the team and should be paid accordingly. Every agent wants his player to be the highest-paid player on a team. That makes it so much easier to recruit clients. But I had other players to sign, and I had to make sure I kept our salaries in line.

Richard tried everything. He accused me of not liking Mark, because I was not physically in Cleveland for the 1986 draft. I reminded him I had tried to trade for Mark while participating in Indiana's draft. So then he accused me of being partial toward centers because I had been one. Each time we talked, he used a different angle. When he got frustrated talking to me, he would call Watson. When he got tired of Dick, he came back to me. He even wanted to call Gordon, though that was strictly forbidden. Dick and I started comparing gray hairs. Though the three of us talked through the summer, we remained in a stalemate, which angered Richard even more.

In the meantime, we strengthened our bench by signing seven-foot Tree Rollins from Atlanta and added Darnell Valentine to back up Mark at point guard. Of course, we still had not signed Mark. On September 14, Washington general manager Bob Ferry called to tell me they had signed Mark to an offer sheet. We had fifteen days to match the offer or lose Mark. Ironically, the offer of $8 million for four years was only slightly higher than what we had offered. I called Mark and told him we very much wanted him back and were going to match the offer, although we took the full fifteen days to do so. In the end, the contract was reasonable and in line with the rest of the team. I called Ferry and thanked him for doing my job—and congratulated him for surviving the negotiations with Howell.

Lenny really liked his team and thanked me for keeping it intact. He knew it had been a difficult summer. Most coaches do not care about the difficulties of signing players. They just want them signed, no matter what the cost. Lenny was different because he was once a general manager.

Training camp was fun. The players were having fun, and they exuded confidence. The coaches were having fun watching the young players respond. The media was having fun because our team was going to be a good story, and there was nothing reporters enjoyed more than having a good story to write.

It was fun to be around that season, and everybody got along so well that after practice the reporters often faced off against the staff in games of H-O-R-S-E. Though I seldom attended practice, occasionally I played, too, using my baby hook to win because, like modern players, the reporters had never seen a real hook shot. I sat out the full-court games of five-on-five, but Lenny and Gary Fitzsimmons often joined our public relations guys, Bob Price and Bob Zink, and whichever intern was available. Price and Zink did a tremendous job of facilitating access for interviews, but I secretly believed the real attraction in attend

Saying goodbye to a retiring Kareem Abdul-Jabbar on his last visit to Cleveland
(Courtesy of Paul Tepley)

ing practice in those days was the post-practice workout. Sometimes Simmie and I would scout the games. I sure hope none of those guys was waiting for a call from us. They were good writers, but they could not play a lick. Burt Graeff, Terry Pluto, JoJo Menzer, Bob Dolgan, and Bill Livingston . . . not one of them had a decent jump shot. Livingston barely got off the ground. Dolgan still shot free throws underhanded. It was quite a crew.

Fortunately the crew I was paying looked a lot better and, after an 8–0 preseason, expectations were sky-high. We opened the 1988–89 season with a 133–93 victory over the expansion Hornets. We were off and running and established ourselves as contenders in the Eastern Conference. Although the rough-and-tough Bad Boys were the defending conference champions and the favorites, any one of eight teams looked as if it could win the East. We finished December with a 21–5 record and kept pace with Detroit in our division.

Off the court, Gordon named John Graham president of Cavs coliseum management company, and I was promoted to executive vice president in addition to general manager. Gordon was thrilled with our progress. We were off to the best start in the history of the franchise, drawing sellout crowds to our home games. It never fails. When a team wins, the fans come out.

I occasionally traveled with the team, and I went to Milwaukee for a game against the Bucks because I wanted to be at the ceremony when they retired Sidney Moncrief's number. Lenny, Dick Helm, and I were having lunch in the coffee shop at the Hyatt. Jim Fitzgerald and several other Bucks people were seated a few tables away. After I finished, I headed for the elevator. Fitz approached me and asked me to have a cup of coffee. The last thing I needed was more coffee, but I wondered what he wanted. The last time we had talked, he kept asking me why I got back into the NBA. He seemed troubled that I took the position in Cleveland. I kept telling him I thought I was good at the job and I still had a passion for my work.

After the usual pleasantries, he got to the point. "What's going on with you and Nellie?" he asked me.

"You know the NBA is like a fraternity. You and Nellie need to communicate."

I could not believe what I was hearing. I asked him if I needed to remind him what happened during my last days in Milwaukee, and I reminded him how hurt and upset I had been.

"Wayne, you have to put that behind you," he told me. "Didn't Nellie apologize?"

I wondered if Fitz had put him up to it.

"Yes, he apologized, and I accepted his apology," I said. "But you can't expect us to be friends. How could I ever trust him? And by the way, don't refer to the NBA as a fraternity. You should say it's a good ol' boys network. And I don't belong."

I probably should have stopped there. But I kept going.

"You know, Fitz, you are a good person," I said. "But Terri thinks you live vicariously through Nellie."

"We don't understand why you adopted him as you did."

"He's made me a lot of money," Fitzgerald said.

That was true, but in the back of my mind I could not help thinking that I deserved some of the credit for the success of the Bucks, although I had been completely ignored when Fitzgerald gave out bonuses after selling the team. Nellie later told me Fitz was upset because he thought I withheld information about prospective buyers (like Jane Pettit), which I had not.

I decided our conversation was over. "See you later," I said to a bewildered Fitzgerald as we parted company. "Good luck the rest of the season."

I headed to my room, shaking my head and wondering, "What next?"

Chapter 15
The Shot

By the middle of the 1988–89 season, we were earning recognition for our accomplishments.

Lenny was the coach of the East All-Stars, and Mark, Brad, and Larry had been selected for the team. Ron Harper also was having an All-Star year.

In addition to great talent, we had great chemistry. It is a tough term to explain completely, but part of my definition of great chemistry is everyone understanding and accepting their roles in order to contribute to a winning effort.

Teams should have at least three primary scorers, and we had four in Nance, Price, Daugherty, and Harper. We had a terrific role player in small forward Mike Sanders. Hot Rod would have started for any other team, but he was content to come off the bench for us, along with Ehlo and Tree. Lenny was right to start Sanders in place of Nance. Mike was what we called a "dirt worker." He rebounded, hit an open seventeen-footer, and defended opposing small forwards. He might not have started on any other team, but he was perfect for us. On the other hand, Lenny recognized Larry's shot-blocking ability and by playing him at big forward, he was able to roam and help Brad protect the basket. Big forwards usually are not primary scorers. Kevin McHale, Karl Malone, and Nance were the exceptions.

Larry's shot-blocking skills helped make us one of the best defensive teams in The League. He once blocked eleven shots in a game against

Honoring Lenny Wilkens for his 600th victory (Courtesy of Ron Kuntz)

New York, and the team blocked twenty-one shots to set an NBA record. We finished third in The League in team defense that season and won fifty games for the first time in franchise history. We were in the play-offs for the second straight season and only the sixth time in the twenty-year history of the franchise.

Once again, our opponents were Jordan and the Bulls. Little did we know that their fate and our fate would be inextricably linked as the result of the upcoming series.

We had beaten the Bulls six times in the regular season, but Lenny and I knew that this made no difference once the play-offs started. The slate was wiped clean in the post-season. Plus, Price, Daugherty, Nance, and Ehlo were hobbled with a variety of injuries, while Jordan was emerging as one of the more dominant players in The League. He had raised his game several notches in last year's play-offs, and there was no reason to believe he would not do it again. Yes, we had the home-court advantage, but it was only an advantage if we won at home.

In fact, without an injured Mark Price, we lost Game 1 as Jordan scored 31 points. We won Game 2 behind Harper's 31 points. Chicago took Game 3, but we hung on and won Game 4 in overtime to set up a fifth and deciding game, perhaps the biggest in the history of the franchise.

The coaches were confident. The players were confident. I was confident, but cautious . . . and moody.

In fact, my attitude was exactly the same as it had been when I was playing. Over the years I realized it was much tougher to be the general manager because, unlike the coaches and players, there was nothing I could do then to affect the outcome.

All I could do was watch, like the 20,273 fans who crammed into the Coliseum on May 7. The game would go down as one of the best-played and best-coached games in the history of The League, and it very well may have been the game that launched Jordan to legendary status.

The game was everything we had expected. Michael was unstoppable, but we were able to stay with him. The Bulls held a 99–98 lead with seven seconds to go. Lenny called time. While Judy, Simmie, and I paced in the tunnel behind our bench, Lenny devised one of the best plays I had ever seen. Ehlo inbounded the ball and got it back for a layup gave us a 100–99 lead with three seconds to go.

The Bulls took a timeout as the twenty thousand fans went absolutely bananas. I knew better. I knew one second was enough time for Jordan to get off one more shot. It was not just a shot.

It was The Shot.

Lenny always refused to double-team Jordan as a matter of principle, but he assigned Nance and Ehlo to guard him on the inbounds play. As Brad Sellers searched for someone to inbound to, Jordan made a hard cut and Nance, who had played the whole series with a bad Achilles tendon that required surgery after the season, stumbled. Jordan caught the ball, took a dribble at the top of the key, went up, and shot. Ehlo went with him.

This moment is frozen in my mind. I am sure it is frozen in Michael's and Craig's, too. It has been featured on a million posters and highlight reels.

"He went up and I went up," Ehlo told the *Cleveland Plain Dealer*. "I came down and he was still up there. I still can't believe how he hung up there."

The shot drained through the net as the buzzer sounded. It seemed to go on forever, or maybe it just sounded that way because there did not seem to be another noise in the building. There were twenty thousand hearts in twenty thousand throats, and twenty thousand dreams in forty thousand pieces.

The 101–100 victory was the coming of age for Jordan and the Bulls.

"That was how we won the city [of Chicago] over to believe," Jordan later told the *Akron Beacon Journal*.

Former Bulls assistant John Bach told the *Beacon Journal*, "Joe Dumars used to have a saying that a clutch shot was a dagger. That was not just a dagger. That tore their hearts out. That remained long after the game, season after season. It took the city [of Cleveland] a long time to get over it. That sent [the Cavs] reeling. They have never really recovered from that."

It took me a long time to recover that day. Somehow I dragged myself toward the locker room to congratulate Lenny and the players on a gutty performance and a wonderful season. Marilyn Wilkens was walking toward me. I was about to offer some words of comfort when she screamed at me, "You had better get my husband some players to coach so that we can win. You can't expect . . ."

Judy and Simmie jumped between us and ushered her away, telling her now was not the time for that discussion.

I was stunned by the outburst. I felt bad for the coaches, the players, and even Marilyn. They deserved to win the game. I felt bad for Gordon and the fans. Terri sat with the wives and tried to console them, as she had done many times before.

After commiserating with Lenny and the coaches, I took the long walk to congratulate the jubilant Bulls and wish them good luck in the next series. Then I went to find Terri. I told her that I just wanted to be alone for a while and that I would meet her at home later. I went to my office and closed the door and replayed the game, over and over.

I also reflected on Marilyn. I knew she and Lenny had a close relationship and I knew she was his biggest fan. I knew when I hired him, she was part of the package, and I was fine with that. She was very supportive, as a wife should be. But I was still stunned by her actions. I had only witnessed one other outburst like that. When I was a broadcaster in Boston, I went into Red Auerbach's office to do an interview before a game. Jim Barnes's wife burst into Red's office to complain about her seats. Needless to say, Barnes's tenure as a backup center in Boston did not last long. But I did not know what to make of Marilyn's blowup. Was she just venting her anger and frustration over the loss, or was she giving voice to concerns Lenny had been keeping to himself? Was she saying what any other fan would say?

After a few hours of staring into space, I headed home. The Shot was still on my mind, so much so that I was stopped by the police while heading up Harper Road. The officer recognized me as he approached the car.

"Mr. Embry," the kind man said gently, "you were exceeding the 35 mph speed limit."

I was too numb to respond, and he seemed almost embarrassed to have stopped me.

"I'm just going to give you a warning this time," he said. "You've had a rough day. I saw The Shot."

It was going to be a long summer waiting until next year. We had our team meetings, our post-season press conferences, and our breakup dinner, all too soon. The Bulls went on to beat the Knicks but lost to the Pistons, who beat the Lakers for their first NBA title. Their physical play set the standard for the NBA in the 1990s. Every team wants to follow the champion. Back in Cleveland, we were trying to come to terms with the fact that it was not going to be us.

Chapter 16

The Trade

Our players could not wait for the 1989–90 season to begin. No one was ready to concede that the Bulls were better than we were. The list of "what ifs" was way too long: What if Mark had not missed Game 1? What if Brad and Larry were healthy? What if Larry had not slipped on that last play? The questions remained with all of us during the off-season and we could not help but wonder: Was this going to be our year?

It was encouraging to see most of the players working on their individual skills and playing pickup games throughout the summer. They rarely took any breaks. I thought it meant they knew how close we were and they wanted to be ready for the season. We were still young enough to show improvement individually and collectively. We were not even close to peaking. And because of the character of our players, they were committed to work hard in an effort to get better. We never had to worry about that.

Unlike many pro athletes, our guys bought homes in the Akron area and lived there most of the year. Having the practice court and weight room at the Coliseum was convenient. As an added bonus for the organization, the players became active in the community. Mark was active in his church, and the others did camps and worked with youth groups. The players made an effort to reach out to our fans, and our fans related to them.

As the summer passed, Larry's Achilles tendon did not get better and our medical staff recommended surgery to repair it. The operation was done in June, and Larry was expected to miss training camp and the start of the season. More bad news came in August. Brad continued to experience pain in his right foot. Trainer Gary Briggs took him to The Cleveland Clinic, where Dr. John Bergfeld had arranged for a specialist to examine Brad. Surgery was recommended for Brad, too. His operation was performed on August 30, and Brad was going to be out indefinitely.

To improve our depth, we acquired seven-foot Paul Mokeski and six-foot-three Steve Kerr, the great outside shooter who starred at the University of Arizona. Paul was a veteran who was with me in Milwaukee, where he backed up Bob Lanier. We were hoping Paul, Tree, and Chris Dudley could fill the void until Brad came back, but even collectively they would not give us the scoring, rebounds, assists, and picks Brad gave us. Mokeski was big and a decent outside shooter. Tree was a defensive specialist. Chris could rebound and waste fouls. Hot Rod also could play center, although he hated to play there. He was going to start at power forward until Larry got back.

Despite being without Brad and Larry, training camp was spirited. We finished the preseason 4–4, but we got more bad news as the season neared. Dudley broke his wrist and was going to be out six to eight weeks. We opened our twentieth season with Brad, Larry, and Dudley on the injured list. Erasing memories of "The Shot" was going to be harder than we thought.

As luck would have it, we opened the season in Chicago and lost in overtime. After losing four in a row, we won five in a row and seemed to turn things around on the court. Off the court, we had some problems.

I was receiving calls from security officers for the other local pro teams. While keeping an eye on their own players, they had received information that Ron Harper was spending time at some places that were under surveillance for drug activity, although there was no indication he was involved. It was a case of being in the wrong place at the wrong time. I had heard reports from the street before that call, but I chalked them up to the rumor mill and hoped they were not true. I should have known better because of my experiences in Milwaukee.

As The League increased in popularity, the Board of Governors and the commissioner's office had taken steps to prevent a repeat of the problems in the 1970s, when several franchises were decimated by players using drugs. The League appointed a vice president of security and hired representatives in each NBA city to provide security for the players and team officials and to ward off drug dealers, who took a look at NBA salaries and wanted a piece of the action. Yes, it was still a problem in The League, just as it was still a problem in society. The security officials usually were former law enforcement officers who collaborated with local, state, and federal law enforcement agencies to assure safety and protection for our players. They were well connected and knew everything that was going on with the players, especially with regard to illicit activities.

So when the rumors about Harper persisted, Lenny and I confronted Ron. He denied the rumors, and we had every reason to believe him. He was having an outstanding year. There was absolutely no indication he was using drugs. He was never late for anything—usually one of the first indications of drug usage. Plus, Ron loved to play basketball, and it was hard for us to believe that he would do anything to impair his ability to play.

Still, I felt it imperative that I keep owner Gordon Gund up to date about what was happening.

While the team was struggling, the rumors persisted. Finally I received a phone call I wish had never come. It was Horace Balmer, The League's vice president of security.

"Wayne, I received a call from the regional office of the Drug Enforcement Agency with instructions for Ron Harper," Balmer said firmly. "He is to be at the federal building in Cleveland at ten o'clock Monday morning. Please tell him to be there. A drug enforcement agent from Cincinnati is driving to Cleveland to interview him.

"Tell him not to be late. These guys don't play."

I was dumbfounded for a minute, but then I asked, "What in the hell is going on here? Is he in some kind of trouble?"

Balmer told me they wanted to talk to Ron about a friend of his from Dayton who had been under surveillance for drug trafficking. He told me Ron was not the focus of the investigation, but he suggested I tell Ron to pull away from his friends.

After talking with Gordon, I called Lenny into my office and we decided we needed to talk to Ron again. After a home game that Saturday night, we approached Ron, who once again told us he was clean. I gave him the typewritten details of his Monday morning meeting.

When I went up to the practice court as Monday's practice was ending, I was surprised to see Ron there. Lenny told me Ron's agent, Mark Termini, had taken care of things.

Lenny, Simmie, and I went to lunch to discuss the situation. We decided to keep things to ourselves, figuring that the fewer people in the loop on this, the lesser chance there was of a leak to the press or to the rest of The League. It was important to protect Ron and the franchise. We did not even tell our assistant coaches or the rest of the team.

Tuesday morning, I called Horace to see if he had gotten a report of the meeting. He told me to call the DEA agent, who confirmed that Ron still was not the focus of the investigation. The agent told me Ron should be careful, though, because the investigation was intensifying.

Lenny passed that along to Ron, and we all hoped he would comply. At the same time we knew how tough it was to give up friends. We all had gone through similar experiences with friends involved in unsavory activities. And when I was in Milwaukee, Kareem and Lucius Allen got arrested because they happened to be with the wrong people.

A week passed before I got a call from a local security officer asking to meet with Lenny and me as soon as possible. After that morning's practice, we drove to the airport hotel for a lunch meeting. It was more of the same. Another friend of Ron's who lived in Cleveland was under investigation. He advised us to convince Ron to stay away because an arrest was coming any day.

Driving back to the Coliseum, Lenny and I discussed our options. He was committed to continue talking to Ron, hoping he would understand the gravity of the situation. I told him I had to start thinking about trading Harper, something none of us wanted to do. I called Gordon to pass on the latest development and raised the issue of a trade, pointing out that, in addition to everything else, Harper's contract would be up at the end of the season and it likely would cost us a lot to keep him.

We were in the middle of a winning streak at the time, and Ron was averaging more than 20 points per game. We were encouraged, thinking that when we got healthy we would be able to contend. Then again, I was worried that if we got more unfavorable information, I would have to make a move and tear the team apart.

It was not long before that information came.

Horace Balmer called again. "Wayne, I know you don't want to hear any more about Harper, but I have to tell you he is going to be subpoenaed to appear before the grand jury on December 19," he said. "Let's keep our fingers crossed. This is still about his friends."

I had started investigating trade possibilities, and I was talking with the Clippers about Danny Ferry, who had been taken Number 2 in the draft. Before the draft, Ferry told the Clippers he would not sign with them and they drafted him anyway. He did not sign and went to play in the Italian professional league. I was intrigued, but I was still hoping we would not have to make a trade. I really hoped we could ride this out, and it would go away. I should have known better.

Gordon came to town a couple of days later, and his brother George happened to be in town as well. Gordon, George, Lenny, and I sat in my office and deliberated for an hour or so. Team attorney Dick Watson was on the phone. The Clippers were serious about obtaining Ron and, against my better judgment, I recommended we trade him. There still had not been one shred of evidence implicating Ron in drug use, but I was tired of the distractions. Ron was a likeable guy, and a good leader, and I was worried some of our younger players might want to follow in his footsteps. We knew one of Ron's friends who frequented our games was being investigated. I did not want anybody who was involved with anyone who was around drugs to be anywhere near our players. I did not want law enforcement agencies constantly snooping around. Neither did The League.

Gordon turned to Lenny and said, "Lenny, none of us want to move Ron. Do you think you can turn him around?"

Lenny whispered, "I don't want to, but we have to move him."

That was all Gordon needed. "GET HIM OUT OF HERE," he roared, his voice loud enough to be heard throughout our offices.

After Gordon and George left, Lenny and I sat and agonized. We were worried how the trade would affect the other players. They would never forgive us for trading their leading scorer. Neither would the fans. And Ron loved Cleveland. He was a perfect complement to Mark. He was great defensively. Craig Ehlo would have to move into the starting lineup, but he had played a lot in the play-offs and looked good. Steve Kerr would have to back him up. But more than any of those individual concerns, we worried about upsetting the chemistry we had worked so hard to create.

That night I went home and agonized some more. I had had many sleepless nights in my career, and this would be another. It really was a twenty-four-hour-a-day job. I had not told any of our scouts, but it was time to at least talk to one of them, Darrell Hedric, who had recruited Ron to Miami, where he had coached him for two years. Darrell said it would be hard for him to believe Ron would have anything to do with using drugs. He told me what I already knew: Ron loved to play the game, and he would not do anything to jeopardize being the best player he could be.

I continued talking to Gordon and to the Clippers. It was important we protect the integrity of our franchise, one we hoped was going to be a contender in the Eastern Conference for years to come. More than one publication called us the "team of the nineties." We did not know if anything ever would come out of the investigations, but none of us wanted to be in the position of having to decide whether to tell an owner or general manager about the probes or withhold information, which none of us could do in good conscience. And if something did break and Ron was implicated, we were afraid his value would go down, regardless of his innocence. This was one of those cases in which perception could become reality.

After days of negotiating, we acquired the rights to Danny Ferry and Reggie Williams. We sent Harper and our 1990 and 1992 first-round picks to the Clippers, although they were protected if they were lottery picks. Still, it was a lot to give up, particularly if we were wrong in projecting we would be drafting in the late first round.

Danny Ferry was the leading scorer at Duke and led them to three NCAA Final Four appearances in his four seasons. He won the Naismith Award as a senior, given to the best collegiate player in the country, and was the Atlantic Coast Conference Player of the Year as a junior and senior. He played center/forward and was a very good perimeter shooter. He also was a good passer. In fact, he was the first player in ACC history to finish with more than 2,000 points, 1,000 rebounds, and 500 assists. He was not fast, but we thought his shooting would be a real asset. Reggie Williams was an impressive guard/forward who was the leading scorer at Georgetown, and he was a good outsider shooter, too, something our team needed. We thought he could back up Ehlo, along with Kerr.

The hard part came after the deal was done. I had to tell Harper, and we had to figure out how we were going to address the press and our fans. This was going to be an unpopular move, one that was going to be hard to explain for several reasons. First of all, we were not going to be able to announce the real reason for the move—the ongoing investigations into Ron's friends. Second, we had traded a popular player approaching the peak of his potential for one who would not come to the NBA until next season.

Calling Ron to tell him we were trading him to the Clippers was the hardest call I have ever made in my management career. I needed strength from God and all the courage I had learned back on The Hill to endure the next several hours. When I finally reached him, we did not have much of a conversation. I wished him well. There did not seem to be much else to say. He was very cold, which was understandable. I was sending him from a young, hot team to the Siberia of the NBA. No wonder he had nothing to say.

While I called Ron, Lenny called the other players. We did not want them hearing about it on television or reading it in the paper the next day. And what were we going to tell the media? Bob Price, Lenny, and I struggled trying to put a positive spin on the move and not incriminate Ron. It was important to protect his integrity, since, to our knowledge, he had done nothing wrong. But it was going to be extremely difficult to answer the questions that were sure to come.

Finally, we turned the information over to our public relations firm, which put out a press release. The release said Ferry would be worth the wait and recalled how the Boston Celtics had waited a year for Larry Bird after drafting him as a junior. I insisted that reference be taken out. Larry Bird became one of the best players in the history of The League. I was not sure how good Ferry was going to be, but he was not going to be Larry Bird, of that I was certain. After a caucus before the press conference, I was overruled and the sentence remained. To this day, I think it was a mistake, created unrealistic expectations, and set Ferry up to fail. I often wonder how his career might have been different without the pressure created by an irresponsible flack.

The room at the University Club was crammed with reporters. In addition to the usual beat writers, all the columnists and television and radio types showed up. Gordon, Lenny, and I were seated on a dais as the reporters entered the room and picked up the release. Bob Price interrupted the shocked whispers to introduce me for the official announcement. It was November 16, 1989.

As expected, it went over like a lead balloon. The questions came hard and fast, tough questions, good questions, ones we were asking ourselves. Of course, we could not answer most of them. After saying, "No comment," for what seemed like an hour, the press conference broke up. We knew no one believed a word we had said. They all knew there was more to the story. It was the toughest press conference I have ever been through, much tougher than the ones after the Kareem arrest and the Kareem trade. I hoped I would never have to go through anything like it again.

When it was all over, Simmie and I went up to the bar to try to get the bad taste out of our mouths. We were not alone for long. Bill Livingston, the savvy columnist from the *Plain Dealer*, came in, and we invited him to join us. Bill was a well-respected NBA writer for the *Philadelphia Inquirer*, where he covered the great 76ers teams in the 1980s when I was still with the Bucks and our teams met in a great playoff series. He loved the NBA and was very knowledgeable. Gary and I did our best to convince him the trade would be good for the franchise, but he knew there was more to it. He had been around too long to be fooled by us.

When I got home, Terri handed me a long list of messages. As I expected, Terry Pluto, the beat writer from the *Akron Beacon Journal*, had called, as had Burt Graeff of the *Plain Dealer* and Joe Menzer of the *News Herald*. They were all good reporters, and they were trying to get to the bottom of this. They quizzed me long into the morning.

When I woke up, I found the newspapers had killed us. The television guys killed us. The radio guys killed us. Fans were angry. The meeting with the team was difficult. We were unable to tell them any more than we told the reporters. But it was a done deal. This was our destiny. We had to rally the players and get them to focus on the season. We really had to wait a year for the outcome of the trade.

I probably have been asked about that trade almost every day since and, believe me, I have asked myself about it, too. It has been a true test of my conviction. I cannot help but wonder what I could have done differently. Maybe I should have talked to agent Mark Termini, although I did not know him as well then as I do know. I have grown to respect him a great deal, and maybe I should have tried to press him to influence Ron. I am often asked, and I have asked myself, if I had it to do over again, would I have made the same decision? I know fans want me to say no, and I will admit it was a bad basketball decision. But if I had to do it over again I would, because I believe it was the best thing for everyone. Given that nothing ever came of the investigations as far as Ron was concerned, maybe we should have held firm. Of course, we did not know that would be the outcome. None of us could see into the future. If I could have, I would not have believed the turns my career would take in the next ten years.

"The Trade" would be another test of the character of this young team. Lenny and I were concerned they would quit on us, using the excuse that management destroyed the chemistry and no one expected them to win now anyway. The mood was not good. Despite our attempts to reassure them that the Cavs would survive after losing Harper, there remained a cloud of doubt. Lenny and I tried to tell them similar things happened when we played. I told them how upset Oscar and I were after Cincinnati traded Bob Boozer.

No matter how much anyone complained, it was not going to change what happened. As pros, it is necessary to move on and fulfill your obligation, which is to play to the best of your ability. We had to ignore the comments of friends, reporters, and fans and stay focused on winning. Lenny did a great job of getting the players to put the trade behind them. At the end of the day, management, not the players, would be held accountable.

Ehlo welcomed the opportunity to start at shooting guard. He had been a key player off the bench and proved that he belonged in The League with his stellar performance in the play-offs, when he was still sharing minutes with Harper. In his first start, he responded by scoring 31 points in an overtime victory in Atlanta. But our lack of depth at shooting guard became a problem. We hoped the newly acquired Reggie Williams would do that job, but it was the undersized Steve Kerr who stepped up to be Craig's backup. He also was backup at the point. He gave us one more three-point threat to go with Price and Ehlo, something Brad would welcome when he returned after his foot surgery.

We struggled after winning five in a row, losing to the expansion Minnesota Timberwolves and to Harper's L.A. Clippers. Larry returned on December 9, and we won four in a row. We were losing more than we were winning, but Lenny was able to keep them focused, reminding them that Brad would return. The objective was to keep on improving, and there were many pluses to dwell on, in spite of the losing. Mark was named to the All-Star team. Hot Rod was having a great year, and Ehlo was doing quite nicely as a starter. Kerr also remained consistent.

Brad was activated on January 30, and our core was back together. But our play was still inconsistent. It was like a mid-season training camp as players got used to playing with Brad again.

In February, we traded for the seldom-used Derrick Chevious, a slasher who could cut to the basket. We were hoping we could replace the aspect of the game that we had lost by trading Harper. We also traded Dudley and Keys to clean up our roster in the wake of Brad's return. And we ended up waiving Reggie Williams, who never quite fit in with us. Lenny never did seem to want to play him, and I wondered privately if it was his way of protesting the trade. Eventually, Lenny suggested we move him.

On the other hand, Reggie never recovered from being traded the first time. I was reluctant, but I realized that if he were to succeed, he was not going to do it with us. Reggie was a quiet, sensitive person and never gained the confidence to realize his potential. No matter how much Lenny and I tried to build his confidence and make him feel wanted, he could not overcome his rejection complex. I had several conversations with John Thompson, Reggie's coach at Georgetown, hoping he could help us find the right button to push. John was as surprised as anyone that Reggie had not lived up to what the scouts had projected. He did say he still believed Reggie would be a good player in The League, which he had told me at the time of the draft. Of course I wanted him to do it with us. If he had showed progress, he could have fit into our rotation, giving us depth and, yes, helping shut up those who remained relentless in criticizing "The Trade." After all, he was the fourth player taken in the 1987 draft, behind David Robinson, Armon Gilliam, and Dennis Hopson. He did go on to become a starter with Denver, where he became the player I thought he could be.

After the roster moves, we seemed to jell. Our timing was back, as was our chemistry We won eight of the next eleven after Brad returned to the starting lineup. We won seventeen of the final twenty-three games to make the play-offs for the third straight year. Our character surfaced again.

Although we finally were healthy, redeeming ourselves for our 1989 finish was going to be difficult because we had to go through Charles Barkley and the 76ers. We did not make it. We lost in five games, largely because of the heroics of Barkley and Hersey Hawkins. Our players did learn something from that series. They realized how physical playoff competition was. They found that if we were ever to advance, we were going to have to respond better to physical play. That was the way it was in the play-offs. Barkley bullied the Sixers to victory in Game 5 in Philadelphia.

Philadephia lost to Chicago in the next round, then Chicago lost to Detroit, which went on to beat Portland for its second straight NBA title. Star players set the standards for the next generation of players to follow. Champions set the standards for teams to follow. Detroit's "Bad Boys" set the stage for how the game was going to be played in the 1990s, and that meant the more physical, the better. Rick Mahorn, Bill Laimbeer, and Dennis Rodman, who became the league's best rebounder, punished those who played the inside game or even thought about driving to the basket. Superstar Isiah Thomas, plus Joe Dumars and Vinnie "The Microwave" Johnson, were skilled players, but they also were physically tough. They were well coached by my old neighbor Chuck Daly.

Though I admired their tenacity, I thought they took it too far. I vividly remembered Mahorn nearly decapitating Mark Price with a shot to the temple the previous season. It took Mark a long time to recover from that. During a game in Detroit the next season, I was so upset by the way the referees allowed the Pistons to beat up on us that I jumped up from my seat in the stands and ran down ten rows onto the court to help break up a fight between Daugherty and Laimbeer. At the age of fifty-five, I should have known better than to run onto the court and I also should have known better than to challenge someone twenty years younger. But secretly, I was hoping Mahorn or Laimbeer would take a shot at me. Before that could happen, referee Billy Oates tossed me out of the game, and I was rightfully fined $10,000 the next day by The League's vice president of operations Rod Thorn. I did not care, though. I needed to make a point to my players that I was behind them.

While talking with Rod about the fine, I vented my frustrations about the way The League and the Pistons were glorifying their "Bad Boys" image. My fear was that other teams would emulate the Pistons' style of play, causing a trend. That was exactly what happened. Teams began drafting or recruiting brutes to enable them to compete, and the ensuing years were the most physical in league history. Players were spending more time in the weight rooms than on the court refining their dribbling, shooting, and passing skills. I did not want young people thinking this was the way the game had to be played.

Believe me, I know the pro game has always been physical. I was a physical player. But now we were taking physical play to the extreme, at the expense of the other beautiful parts of the game. The game became so ugly that the competition committee had to take action. The fans were not enjoying the wrestling for position on the court or the cheap shots on the way to the basket. The commissioner became so concerned, he ordered Rod to have his officials clean up the game.

Despite my disdain for their style, I would come to realize that like all championship teams, the Pistons had talent, character, and some luck—just like the best teams I played on. Isiah Thomas and I had been friends since former Indiana University coach Bobby Knight invited me to spend an evening with Isiah and his family during the recruiting process. Much later, Isiah and I sat next to each other on a flight from Los Angeles to Detroit. He told me he and Laimbeer called a meeting as the play-offs approached and reinforced the team rules regarding curfews and drinking policies. In a different conversation with Laimbeer, he told me that after every game in the Coliseum, as a sign of unity, each of the Pistons would spit on my car, which they passed en route to their bus. He stepped away from me as he told the story, not quite sure how I would react, and he seemed genuinely surprised when I said, "Good for them. It probably needed to be washed anyway."

When I told Terri the story later, she was not as understanding. "That was my side," she complained. I must admit, I had not thought of that.

Anyway, after Laimbeer saw my reaction to his revelation, he asked me why I was so hard on their team. I told him I liked his team and the fact that the Pistons played hard, but I did not like the way the marketing types exploited it. He agreed with me.

Our teams had developed a heated rivalry, and we thought we were ready to join the Bulls in dethroning the Pistons. Our guys were once again committed to a summer of hard work because, for us, the 1989–90 season ended with the same kinds of questions the 1988–89 season did: What if we had been healthy and earned the homecourt advantage? Hot Rod was the only player to play all eighty-two games. Brad missed forty-one, Larry missed seventeen at the start of the season and Mark missed eight of the first fifteen. But the overriding question was: What if we had not traded Harper?

I had gotten used to this question. I think I was asked it every day. My answer was that we might have won a few more games, but probably not enough to make a difference. There also was a follow-up question: Why did we not keep Reggie Williams?

As soon as the play-offs were over, we began planning for the next year. We had our usual staff meetings to review the season and analyze our players individually and collectively. We assessed our needs. Our biggest need was to be patient and let the team continue to grow. We were gaining valuable experience with each practice and each game. Our players continued to learn from a great teacher in Lenny. We concluded we were still a contending team if we could stay healthy. We were fundamentally sound and a good shooting team. We were an intelligent team. Our players were unselfish. We had good team speed and individual speed. Our players competed every night, which was another indication of their character. Our players liked each other and had great respect for the coaches, key components of winning. Nance emerged as a team leader, something else every good team needs. Larry was a consummate pro and commanded respect from the rest of the players, making it easy to impart his professionalism to them. Most important, we had not begun to peak. So, despite our record, we were not ready to make any radical changes. We did not have our first-round draft pick. It had gone to the Clippers in the Harper deal. We searched other team rosters and inquired about some small forwards. That was to be one of my objectives over the summer.

First, though, I had to sign Danny Ferry. The process started by resuming my relationship with David Falk, Ferry's agent. I had not seen him since he was working with Donald Dell when I interviewed a player by the name of John Lucas, who was represented by Dell.

Ferry welcomed the chance to play in The League, having grown up watching his dad's teams in Washington. Bob and Rita Ferry were excited for their son, and they were glad he was coming to play in Cleveland. But signing Danny was not easy. Falk had become one of the best negotiators in the business with a growing stable of clients that included Michael Jordan and Patrick Ewing. After several tough negotiating sessions over Chinese food, we finally reached an agreement. Although I opposed it at first, we ended up signing Ferry to a ten-year deal. I had been holding out for a four-year deal. I always figured that a player had a good year in the first year of the deal to prove he was worth of the contract. I figured they would show improvement in the second and third seasons and then would work their tails off in the fourth year to get another good deal. If the player was exceptional before the fourth season, we could always extend him. I thought a long-term deal offered too much security to a player and took away his incentive to perform, although I did not really think this would be a problem with Danny because of his character.

Agents were demanding long-term contracts for their clients, and because of the threat of losing players through free agency, it made sense for teams to agree. Plus, long-term contracts were like annuities for agents, who received 4 percent of the annual contract. Danny's deal was for $40 million. There was an escape clause after seven years that could be exercised by either Danny or the Cavs. The contract was back-loaded so that the present value was much lower, but expectations were that salaries would soon escalate to that level. Plus, we thought Danny would eventually prove his worth. We also paid $3 million for his marketing rights, although that was beyond my authority. I was not responsible for marketing him, and I did not think it would be in the best interests of the team. Because of his outstanding career in college, Danny was already a poster boy, and so much had been made about the trade that expectations were high. I did not want to raise them any higher by promoting him, and I did not want the established All-Stars and the nucleus of our team to wonder just what we were doing. I did not want him portrayed as "The Great White Hope." I wanted to stay consistent and promote the team, not the individuals.

There was great anticipation for the press conference to announce the signing. No matter how hard I tried to play down the introduction to the local media, and thus to the fans, there was no way I could do it. The media came out in full force. Danny was asked about snubbing the Clippers, about playing in Italy, about fitting in on the Cavs. Even though he handled it well, both of us were glad when the press conference was over and we could get on with the business of basketball, which meant rookie camp and the Los Angeles Summer Camp. Danny participated willingly, despite sore knees, which eventually required surgery.

With Ferry in the fold, my next priority was to get Hot Rod signed. He was still on his rookie contract, which meant he was considerably underpaid. He had been paid for the year he sat out waiting for the commissioner's ruling on his appeal to be cleared of the alleged gambling charge while at Tulane. He had had a tremendous season, and I knew we were in for a tough negotiation.

When we met with Gordon and the ownership group to review the team, we all agreed signing Williams was our top priority. We did our salary projections, and it was our intent to sign him to a contract similar to what the starters were making, even though he was our sixth man. Watson and I immediately began negotiations with Mark Bartlestein, Hot Rod's agent. We soon found out we were in for a long summer of negotiating. Other power forwards were signing for far in excess of where we were. Bartlestein used that as the bar. There was no doubt salaries were escalating at a rapid rate, despite the fact that players were restricted free agents.

The 1980s may have been the best decade in the history of The League. There was greater television exposure with TNT and NBC, meaning greater revenues. NBA basketball had become a global sport. For years, The League had been courting fans overseas. Commissioner Walter Kennedy arranged the exhibition tours in Europe and South America in the 1960s. My old friend Pete Newell started doing clinics in Japan in 1962, and he took an All-Star team to Japan to play in the 1970s. But David Stern took things to another level. He found ways to grow revenues and increase popularity of The League, although he did it by promoting the best players in The League—Michael Jordan, Larry Bird and Magic Johnson—instead of the best teams. Playing in the McDonald's Classic, which pitted an NBA team against the best teams from Europe, gave The League exposure in Europe. After the inaugural game in Milwaukee in 1987, the games were played in major European cities. This opened up a global market for NBA Properties, the licensing arm of The League, which sold replica jerseys, caps, T-shirts, and anything else with an NBA logo on it.

Another monumental decision was made in 1990, when the international governing body of basketball ruled that pro players were eligible to play in the Olympics. Contrary to popular opinion, the move actually was pushed by the Europeans because many of their best players were competing in the pro leagues in Italy and Greece. As a member of the selection committee, initially I was opposed to our Olympic team being made up of pros. I thought the Olympics remained a goal for college players, which encouraged them to stay in school. But my opinion did not matter. We intended to send our best players, regardless of where they played. That meant Jordan, Bird, and Johnson would headline what became known as "The Dream Team" for the 1992 Summer Olympic Games in Barcelona.

NBA popularity skyrocketed. The staffs of The League office and the franchises grew at a rapid rate. Revenues grew, but so did player salaries. We had to alter our thinking as to how much agents were going to demand in the 1990s.

Negotiations with Bartlestein continued through the summer. He was relentless. He kept telling me he was confident he could get Hot Rod for more than we were offering but that Hot Rod wanted to stay in Cleveland. Finally, Watson and I went to Chicago to make a deal. We got authorization from Gordon to increase our offer. When we presented it, Bartlestein was receptive. We just needed to tinker with the language a little. Watson was a genius when it came to making the arithmetic work, and we reached an agreement, contingent on the league approving a pay-out concept. We were close to agreeing on a dollar amount.

While awaiting word from The League, I received a call from Billy Cunningham, part owner and president of the Heat, telling me they had signed Hot Rod to an offer sheet calling for a six-year contract for an amount slightly over $24 million. He went on to say he hoped the offer sheet was more than we could afford. This took us by surprise, since we thought we were close to signing Hot Rod.

We had fifteen days to match the offer. There was no doubt we would, but we planned to take all the time we were allowed. Why not make them wait? Waiting on our decision would keep them from making any more decisions. I was mad. Billy knew our salary structure and gambled we would not pay Hot Rod more than our starters. The Heat was willing to overpay him to get him away from us.

Yes, it was more than we were offering. It was slightly more in dollars on an average and it was for more years. Nevertheless, we were prepared to match. The media was taking shots at us for not being responsive when news of the Heat's offer leaked out. Hot Rod was being quoted everywhere as saying, "I'm a Heat. They did not want me. I'm a Heat."

The fact of the matter was that we did want him. Before we responded to Miami, Gordon, Watson, and I met to discuss our payroll again. Hot Rod's contract would have been considerably more than Brad's, Mark's, and Larry's. From my experiences as a player and general manager, I knew this was not going to be well received. Human nature takes over, and soon the other players' agents would be calling. Because of that, I recommended we make adjustments to their contracts. Normally, I would not recommend renegotiating a player's contract, particularly with multiple years remaining. But I wanted to keep harmony in the locker room and keep the players from complaining or causing dissension.

In the old days, we might have been able to get away with this for a year. Players were able to keep their contracts confidential. But now every contract became public knowledge. The agents liked everybody to know what a good job they were doing, and by making sure the numbers were out in the media, it drove up the costs for other players, which in turn made more money for the agents. In Hot Rod's case, it would have been tough to justify a bench player making more than a starter. It would not have been long before those calls started. I also thought it would be nice to demonstrate that we wanted to be fair. So we surprised Richard Howell and Mark by offering and eventually signing Mark to a contract extension. Indeed, Richard jumped at the opportunity to make up for Mark's rookie year. But he was happy we respected Mark enough to make the adjustment. We also made modifications to Brad's and Larry's contracts. When all of this was done, we matched Miami's offer sheet. Our key players were now signed for about the same dollars, plus or minus the $4 million Hot Rod was making.

But this was just the beginning. Salaries were going to continue to escalate as a result of free agency and teams irresponsibly throwing huge amounts of money at players to lure them away. Before we knew it, things were going to get completely out of hand.

Timeout Number Four

The 1990s began with more hope and prosperity for nearly everyone in the world. The Cold War was over. The Berlin Wall came down. The world became a smaller place, and The League welcomed foreign players with open arms. Of course, with the different languages and cultures, communication skills became more important than ever.

The United States experienced an economic boom with the increasing popularity of computers and the Internet. Unemployment reached an all-time low. Wall Street indexes reached an all-time high, giving birth to a growing number of millionaires.

But not everyone shared in the economic explosion. There was a wider gap between the haves and the have-nots. More Americans were living on the streets than ever before. Although the black middle class had grown, the inner cities remained a war zone. Black youths seeking an identity or a sense of belonging joined gangs, and the gangs were active in the drug trade. Crack and cocaine became the drugs of choice, not just in the inner cities but the suburbs, too.

The sports world also experienced an economic resurgence. With inflation under control in most areas of our economy, sports franchises started charging more for tickets, luxury suites, and sponsorships. Bigger and more modern arenas were built to take advantage of the growth of the economy and the increasing popularity of the NBA. The average ticket price in the league was in the $65 range, and the average player salary topped $4,000,000 dollars.

The economic, social, cultural, and moral changes in our society caused us to adapt our management philosophies. Younger and younger athletes were entering our league as a way to escape the poverty and hard life of the streets. Some came right from high school; some after a year or two of college. Because they were so young, their games were immature, and many were underdeveloped physically, intellectually, emotionally, and socially. The Amateur Athletic Union teams and the shoe companies behind many of those teams gained prominence and exerted more influence on the players than high school or college coaches, who were much better prepared to teach the fundamentals of the game. Unlike the sport of baseball, which had a well-established farm system in the minor leagues, basketball players were getting their on-the-job training in the NBA. With no education to fall back on, I wonder what they will do when they are done playing basketball, and I wonder who will be in charge of our league if our young people are not adequately prepared to replace us old-timers.

The kids brought the symbols of the street into The League—rap music, tattoos, gaudy gold jewelry, corn rows, and punk haircuts. They were products of their environments, which they did not create. Many came from single-parent homes, which they did not cause. Many craved discipline from a male influence they could trust. They wanted someone who was not there to rip them off. But there often was nowhere for them to turn. There was so much moral decay in our country. Yes, there was crime in the streets, but there also was crime in the boardrooms and scandal in the White House.

All of this spilled over into sports. There was increased drug abuse, weapons charges, sexual abuse, domestic abuse, and even murder.

As we crossed into the new millennium, we faced many challenges in society and in sports. We need to manage growth as we look to the future. History tells us the three basic reasons for the collapse of the Roman Empire were economic, social, and moral changes.

Sound familiar? Stay tuned.

Chapter 17

New Faces

When training camp opened for the 1990–91 season, the focus was clearly on Danny Ferry. He came in ready for training camp, and our veterans welcomed him with open arms. I was curious to see how he would be greeted. He had been working out with some of our guys for weeks, and Brad, Mark, and Chucky Brown had played against him in the Atlantic Coast Conference. Although we tried to diffuse the attention, he was very much the focal point when camp began. I tried desperately to downplay his arrival. We did not want it to appear that we saw him as a savior, and we did not want to bruise the egos of any of our established stars. Plus, Danny just wanted to be one of the guys. He did not want any fanfare. He did not need any extra pressure. In the end, it did not matter what he wanted or what we wanted. The media made him the story, and all of Ohio was waiting to see how it would play out.

If there ever was a kid who was used to the NBA life, it was Ferry. His father, Bob, played from 1959 to 1969 for the St. Louis Hawks, the Detroit Pistons, and the Baltimore Bullets before becoming general manager of the Bullets, who later moved to Washington and much later changed their name to the Wizards. Like most general managers, Bob brought the game home with him, so from a young age, Danny learned about the business side of the game.

On the court, Danny was exposed to outstanding coaches. He watched K. C. Jones and Dick Motta coach the Bullets. In high school, he played for the legendary Morgan Wooten at DeMatha before moving on to Duke under the equally legendary Mike Krzyzewski. Although he actually grew up near Annapolis, he spent his summers in Washington, D.C., playing against some of the best high school, college, and pro players in the country. He had the credentials and the pedigree to be a good NBA player. Our scouting reports said he would be a good player on a good team. His strengths were his outside shooting, passing, and his knowledge of the game. His weaknesses were lack of speed and quickness. He was a fair rebounder in college, where he played forward and center, but mostly on the perimeter. He did not really have a position in the pros, although we were hoping he could play small forward for us. Basically, we regarded him as a basketball player who could contribute to a team's winning effort.

I had scouted Danny often. All of us enjoyed going to Tobacco Road to scout. The University of North Carolina had outstanding teams and prospects, and it was a pleasure to go to Smith Center, the House that Dean built. But it was a real treat to scout games at Duke's Cameron Indoor Stadium. The place is a throwback to the old gyms. It is one of the few buildings that still has bleacher seats, and the fans are right on top of the court. There is no other gym in the country where the fans are as entertaining. Dressed in outlandish costumes and body paint, the students sit in a special section and from the introductions to the final horn, they harass the opposing coach and players with clever remarks and chants. Though they would never admit it publicly, the visiting teams cannot help but be amused.

When Ferry got to Cleveland, the fans were less supportive. That is an understatement. He came into his first training camp competing for the small forward spot with second-round picks Winston Bennett and Chucky Brown. (We had lost Mike Sanders to the Indiana Pacers, who offered him more money than we were willing to pay.) By the end of the pre-season, Lenny did not think Ferry could play small forward in his system, and the starting spot went to Bennett. Needless to say, the owners and I were disappointed, but I could not fault Lenny's decision.

Danny had been so-so in training camp. He had struggled in the preseason games. It was apparent players around The League were going to make his transition difficult. Unfortunately for Danny, long before the trade we had scheduled an exhibition game against the Clippers in Los Angeles. There were not many fans there, but those in attendance booed loud enough to make the crowd sound ten times larger.

Danny's lack of competition during his year in Italy showed. Somewhere between Duke and Cleveland, he lost his jump shot and his confidence. Lenny was good at restoring confidence, and I expected him to be able to help Danny, but Danny continued to struggle on the court. Off the court, he blended in well with our team. As he always did with new players, Larry embraced Danny and the other players followed Larry's lead and made Danny feel part of the team. Danny did not regard himself as anyone special. He realized he had to earn his way. That made him likable. Because of his background, he could have been a prima donna, but he was just a good guy and the other players appreciated that.

The focus shifted from Ferry when Hot Rod went down with a strained left foot. Our record was 6–4 when he went on the injured list on November 21. At that point we activated Milos Babich, one of the first foreign players to play in the NBA. By no means was he going to be Hot Rod's replacement. Was Ferry going to be able to step in?

With Hot Rod out, we were playing .500 basketball. Then things got worse. I was at home watching our game at Atlanta on November 30 when Mark Price chased down a loose ball in front of the scorer's table in the third quarter, stepped on a board that anchored the signage, and fell to the floor clutching his left knee. I could tell he was in great pain. I tried desperately to reach our trainer, Gary Briggs, in the dressing room but got no response. A few minutes later, my phone rang.

"We think Mark has a torn ligament," a forlorn Briggs said, adding a few choice words about the board anchoring the signage. He told me he had already called John Bergfeld, our orthopedic surgeon, who was going to see Mark at the Cleveland Clinic the next day. On December

3, we put Price on the injured list and signed journeyman Darnell Valentine. On December 4, Mark had surgery to repair the anterior cruciate ligament in his left knee. He was done for the season.

We quickly learned how valuable Mark was to the team. Valentine was not an outside shooter, and John Morton was not a point guard. Ehlo was better at the shooting guard, although he liked to consider himself a point guard. He was a decent ball handler, which allowed him to get the ball up the court. But his decision making needed work. I loved to watch Lenny's face as Craig tried to copy Mark's specialty and throw a lob pass to Larry for a dunk. This was a thing of beauty when Mark and Larry connected. Mark's passes were precise and Larry's timing was perfect. But Craig never quite got a handle on Larry's jumping ability. Craig's lobs always ended up on top of the backboard and out-of-bounds, a turnover.

Craig was determined to get this right. His determination and hard work enabled him to make a career in the NBA, so every time he got a chance in practice, he would nod at Larry and let it fly. One unfortunate day when he nodded and lobbed, the ball hit the top of the backboard, caromed off through the open door to the practice court, and bounced down four flights of stairs to the bottom floor of the Coliseum. Players were weeping with laughter. Only Craig could have pulled off a stunt like that.

"Eggs," Lenny yelled, using Craig's nickname. "No more &@# lob passes."

This confirmed Ehlo was not a point guard, so we went with Darnell, who did not have Mark's outside shot, and Steve Kerr, who did not have Mark's quickness. Just about the time we thought we had seen it all, Winston Bennett, who Lenny insisted on starting at small forward, went down with a strained lower back. Ferry was nursing bad knees, but he, Derrick Chevious, John Morton, Henry James, and Chucky Brown had to help make up for the injured players. They were not up to it. We went on a six-game losing streak, won a game, then lost the next eleven. Hot

Rod and Winston came back in February, but we still struggled. We finished the 1990–91 season 33–49.

The loss of Mark was too much to overcome. It was a disappointing year for everyone—owners, players, coaches, staff, and fans. Our attendance dropped from the previous season. Danny's popularity did not improve. He played tight and with little confidence. We had projected that he had average between 12 and 15 points per game. He averaged a little over 8.5 points and less than four rebounds. He continued to be booed at home and on the road. I continued to be criticized for the trade. My response was always the same: "Be patient. He will improve. He is a determined person and he will work to get better. He is more disappointed than you are with his first year."

Time would tell whether we would recover. Lenny and I had set different objectives for the team. We asked them to play hard every day in practice and every night in the games. Losing is never fun, but we thought if the players continued to play hard and worked to improve something could be accomplished. We convinced them to work on the things they could control and not be upset or worry about the things that were out of their control. And yet here we were again, two years after "The Shot," still using the battle cry, "Wait until next year."

At least something positive came out of the injury-plagued year. We were drafting in the lottery. Theoretically, we had a chance at the Number 1 pick, but I knew it was the longest of long shots. In fact, we wound up with the Number 11 pick, which was what we would have had even without all the rigmarole. I hated the lottery. The only good thing about it was the food. Commissioner David Stern and NBC found a way to glorify losers by featuring the drawing at halftime of a nationally televised play-off game. Nobody on that television stage wanted to be there, and only one guy left happy—the guy whose team got the Number 1 pick. Depending on how good that player was, you could turn around your franchise, like Orlando did when it earned the Number 1 pick and took Shaquille O'Neal. Good centers were rare, and they often became the top picks. We thought we were lucky because we already had Brad.

So I came home with the Number 11 pick. We were not sure we could get a good player there, but the odds were better than if we were drafting in the twenties. That pick became the focus of our usual post-season review with our ownership. We repeated much of what we had said the previous season. We thought our team was good, but we were not sure how good because injuries had prevented us from being able to properly evaluate it. Some of the players who did play, like Hot Rod and Brad, had shown improvement, and Larry showed no signs of slowing down, even though he was a year older.

When Simmie reported on the upcoming draft, our owners were surprised to hear him say the player we liked at Number 11 was Terrell Brandon, a five-foot-eleven sophomore point guard from Oregon who had declared he was entering the draft. The coaches, scouts, and I supported his opinion, but the owners wanted to know why we wanted to draft another point guard when we already had Mark. I thought the answer was obvious.

"Look where we finished without Mark," I told them. "You have to have two positions covered in this league—center and point guard. No one knows how Mark will recover, and we want to protect ourselves. When you have a center as good as Brad, you have to make sure you have a point guard to complement him. Furthermore, a quality point guard always will be marketable. Remember, we got Larry Nance for Kevin Johnson."

Pete Newell lived in Los Angeles and had seen Terrell Brandon play several times. Pete's handwriting on his scouting reports was terrible, but his message was clear: He thought Brandon would be a star. He could pass and shoot with range. He was quick and could stop and pull up off the dribble and hit the fifteen-foot jump shot. He had a strong body even though he was small. He could defend from baseline to baseline. He could run a team and make a play. I sent Simmie to see him play, and Simmie came back raving about him. After studying a film, I decided Simmie and I should go visit him for an interview and a workout. We went to Oakland, home of his agents Billy Duffy and Aaron Goodwin, and worked out Terrell. We had dinner with him later, and we were convinced he was the right fit for us.

Our draft preparation continued without interference from team attorney Dick Watson. No matter what kind of information Watson came up with on his computer, Gordon still trusted us and the integrity of our process. He did not appear to have lost any confidence in us despite the fact that late first-round picks John Morton and Randolph Keys had not panned out and fans and the media often criticized us for taking them.

Naturally, we considered some other players if only to protect ourselves in case someone else took Brandon. But when our turn came, we took Brandon. I was told the selection was booed by the fans attending our draft night party, and it was hard to convince the media it was a good idea to draft another small point guard they did not know. As was the case with the University of California's Kevin Johnson, because of the time difference between Cleveland and the West Coast, our fans did not stay up late enough to see either Johnson or Brandon play. Fans always like teams to pick players they have seen play.

With the 1991 draft completed, I was looking to a busy off-season. Actually, I had been busy since April with my commitment to the USA Basketball Council. That organization was sanctioned by the U.S. Olympic Committee to govern American participation in all international competitions for men and women. USA Basketball then appointed a Games Committee to select the coaches and players who would represent our country in the Olympics, World Championships, the World University Games, and other junior tournaments. While American fans tended to focus on the Olympics, the rest of the world regarded the World Championships as the ultimate competition to determine a world champion. Until 1988, the United States had dominated international competition, but by the 1988 Olympics, the rest of the world had caught up. In fact, Russia beat John Thompson's squad of college kids for the gold medal in the 1988 Summer Olympics in Seoul, South Korea. Of course, many of the Russian players were older and had been playing for years in the European leagues. But the 1992 Summer Olympics were going to be different.

I had been a member of the Games Committee since 1978, back when the official title of the parent organization was the Amateur Basketball Association United States of America Basketball Council. It was an honor and a privilege to serve. Pete Newell, who had coached the United States to a gold medal in 1960, and I were the only representatives from the NBA. It gave us a great opportunity to network with the college and high school coaches and administrators who also were on the committee. College coaches had always coached the U.S. Olympic teams, and the teams were made up of amateur players from colleges, junior colleges, the military academies, or the Amateur Athletic Union. That had always been the rule in the Olympics; that competition was for amateurs only. No pros allowed. Traditionally, the head coach and his staff were selected before the trials, and then we invited sixty-four aspiring Olympians to Colorado Springs, home of the U.S. Olympic Committee. After watching the players go through drills and scrimmage for four days, we picked the team.

While it was fun to watch the players, what I really enjoyed was visiting with legendary coaches like Hank Iba, Bobby Knight, Dean Smith, John Thompson, Big House Gaines, John McClendon, David Gavitt, Gene Keady, Eddie Sutton, Marv Harshman, Jack Hartman, and Denny Crum, along with young coaches like Mike Krzyzewski, Rick Majerus, Kelvin Sampson, Lon Kruger, Roy Williams, Bob Huggins, and P. J. Carlesimo. We would talk basketball at breakfast, lunch, and dinner, and well into the night. We talked about recruiting experiences and the changes between different generations of athletes. I was fortunate to be able to increase my knowledge of the game and learn about managing people from those who had contributed so much to the game. In addition, I was able to observe and talk to the players during the workouts. This allowed me to gain valuable information that helped me rate the players. The college coaches had great insights into the players they had known since high school. These players eventually would be NBA prospects, and all this knowledge would come in handy at draft time.

But when the international basketball federation changed the rules to allow professionals to play in the Olympics, the composition of the Games Committee changed. NBA executives such as Rod Thorn, Russ Granik, Ernie Grunfeld, Wes Unseld, and Pete Babcock were added. Selecting the coach of the team was going to be the same, but selecting the team was going to be different. There was no way we could expect NBA players to come to Colorado Springs and try out. With the pool of talent we had to choose from, there was no need for that.

At a meeting at the Hyatt Grand Cypress at Disney World, we selected Chuck Daly to coach the team. Although Lenny and Don Nelson also had been mentioned, Chuck was a unanimous selection after winning back-to-back NBA championships. Chuck submitted a list of candidates for his assistants, including Lenny. I lobbied to make Lenny the first assistant, figuring that would make him the favorite to coach the 1996 team. George Raveling nominated Lenny, and I quickly moved that the nominations be closed. We also wanted to add some college coaches as assistants, because they were more familiar with the international rules and style of play. Duke's Mike Krzyzewski and Seton Hall's P. J. Carlesimo filled the other spots. I thought we had a dream coaching staff to coach what would be known as the Dream Team that would represent our country in the 1992 Summer Olympics in Barcelona. Michael Jordan, Magic Johnson, Larry Bird, Karl Malone, John Stockton, Patrick Ewing, Chris Mullin, Charles Barkley, Clyde Drexler, Scottie Pippen, and David Robinson, plus Duke's Christian Laettner, were indeed a dream team.

There were other developments for me during the off-season. I was reappointed by the Governor to serve a nine-year term as a member of the Board of Trustees at Miami University, part of the state university system. I had served four years after replacing a trustee who had resigned. How ironic to be serving as a trustee for a school that would not hire me as an assistant coach! Many years had passed, and attitudes had changed. I also was elected to two corporate boards, along with two civic boards. Gordon encouraged me to get involved in the community. It was good for the franchise for people to know me. He just did not want me to spread myself too thin. But, like the various basketball committees I served on, these were valuable experiences for me. Many of the people I served with were CEOs of companies that were season ticket holders or suite holders at our games. It was good they got to know me and develop confidence in my management. Sure, I had to answer a lot of questions about the team, but that did not hurt. In fact, I thought it helped for people to know where I stood and why we had done things they way we had.

Gordon also extended my contract four more years, which was a nice expression of confidence, especially after two straight disappointing seasons. Of course, there was not much I could do about the injuries.

I signed John Battle, a six-foot-two guard who was instant offense off the bench for Atlanta. He gave us more offensive punch. All that was left was to sign Terrell Brandon and then pray that Mark came back healthy. I hoped the added depth would allow us to withstand any more injuries. I had learned something the past two seasons—injuries to key players could devastate a franchise.

I was able to get Brandon signed after a dinner meeting with his family and his agent in Portland, Oregon, Terrell's hometown. Terrell was only twenty years old, so his mother was concerned about her son moving so far away. They had had the pleasure of watching Terrell play while at the University of Oregon in Eugene, about ninety minutes from Portland. Charles and Charlotte Brandon were delightful people. I developed a rapport with them immediately. But Terrell and his parents also wondered why we drafted another point guard when we had an All-Star point guard. They were worried about Terrell's playing time. After spending two hours at dinner, I was able to get them to trust me, and when I told them I thought Terrell would benefit in being brought along slowly behind Mark, they believed me and concluded their son was headed for the right place.

We started the 1991–92 season by losing four of five on the dreaded West Coast trip. But when Mark was activated and inserted into the starting lineup, we went on a tear, winning six in a row. Mark had not lost a step. He was shooting the ball better than ever, he seemed quicker, and he was stronger. He spent a lot of time in the weight room during his rehabilitation, and his added strength made him more effective from three-point range. He had even developed a little attitude. Never a flashy guy, I will never forget the time he went on a three-point tear in New York, much to the dismay of director Spike Lee, the Knicks Number 1 fan who trash-talked opponents from his seat in the front row. After hitting yet another shot, Price flipped the brim of Lee's cap as he turned and ran down the court. It was hard to know who was more surprised, Lee or Mark's teammates.

We were on our way toward establishing ourselves as contenders. We had a winning record every month en route to a fifty-seven-win season, and with twenty-four more victories over 1990–91, we were the most improved team in The League. The team was exciting to watch. We were playing great basketball. Brad looked as if he were going to develop into the best all-around center in The League. He and Mark were running the pick-and-roll with improved precision. Larry was scoring and blocking shots at a record-breaking pace. Ehlo was becoming a better than average shooting guard and was making clutch three-pointers to win games. Hot Rod was effective as our sixth man. Our reserves responded when inserted into the game. Everyone was having fun, and it was great coming to work. Even the reporters had improved their basketball skills. Pluto was not turning the ball over as much, Livingston got off the ground on his jump shot, and Joe Menzer committed fewer fouls. Burt, the best golfer in the bunch, challenged me to a round "after you win the championship." Dolgan even started making his underhanded free throws to win an occasional game of H-O-R-S-E, a shooting game where players have to make shots from certain spots on the floor. Our fans were enjoying themselves, and we were selling out the Coliseum again. It seemed as if everyone who worked for or with the Cavs organization was having fun. It is amazing what winning will do.

Okay, maybe not everybody was having such a good time. Danny's minutes were sporadic. He had arthroscopic knee surgery over the summer but he had fully recovered. Still, Lenny chose to start Winston Bennett at small forward, with Chucky Brown playing behind him. When Mike Sanders was released by Indiana, we quickly signed him for the rest of the season. Danny's minutes decreased, but he was a team player and he was happy we were winning, even if he did feel as though he could contribute more. He was still getting booed by some of our fans as he struggled, and I thought he pressed even more when he continued to be vilified by our fans and the press.

We had some injuries, but our depth allowed us to play through them. We finished the season 57–25, which was a miraculous turnaround. But we still were not good enough to win our division. We finished in second place, ten games behind the Bulls, who replaced the Pistons as division champs. We finished with the second-best record in The League, tied with Portland. In our conference, the Bulls beat us three times in five games during the regular season, and the Celtics, who won the Atlantic Division, beat us three of four times.

We were healthy and confident going into the play-offs. We disposed of New Jersey in four games in the first round and moved on to face the Celtics. Boston's superstar front line of Larry Bird, Kevin McHale, and Robert Parish was aging, but the team was still experienced and confident and it still carried the Celtic mystic. The Celtics also had an emerging star in Reggie Lewis. It seemed a long time since The Shot, but it was never far from our minds, and if we were going to redeem ourselves this year, we were going to have to go through the Celtics.

Lenny had our guys ready. We opened with a victory before a sold-out Coliseum. But we lost the next game, and the series was tied as we headed to Boston. Bird was nursing a bad back, but he put on a clinic at our expense in Game 3. He shot. He passed. He was vintage Larry

Bird. Reggie Lewis was shooting the ball better than ever and posed a tremendous problem defensively for Ehlo and Battle.

After practice on Saturday, the reporters let me have it again. "Don't you think you'd have a better chance to beat the Celtics if you still had Ron Harper?" I was asked again and again. All I could say was, "It's not over yet."

And it wasn't. Game 4 was a classic play-off game. Ehlo went crazy, scoring 27 points. Price and Nance made clutch shots to get us to overtime and we went on to win and tie the series. We won Game 5 and they took Game 6, setting the stage for Game 7 back in the Coliseum. There is nothing like a Game 7. Of course, a sweep is better. Winning a series as soon as possible is better. But that does not happen often in a competitive series, and nothing can match a final game for intensity and thrills.

Our guys were confident and loose during Saturday's light practice. I was sure we would win Game 7. Yes, I knew it was the Celtics, and I had some flashbacks to my playing days there. I also remembered how they had denied my Bucks in Game 7 of the 1974 Finals. I knew they thought they would win Game 7. But I also knew it was not going to happen.

I went to the Coliseum early Sunday morning. I needed to get out of the house, and Terri needed me to go. I was a mess. I went to the office and tried to keep my mind off the game by watching films of college games, focusing on the players who would be available in the draft this summer. Forty-five minutes before the game, Simmie and Judy came in and told me to go out and look at the crowd. As soon as I stepped outside my office, I could hear the fans. The noise kept increasing as I got closer to the arena, and when I looked in, it was already three-quarters full. Incredible. I walked into the locker room to wish our players and coaches well. They were loose and joking, but they also were focusing on a tape of Game 6 shown while they got dressed.

When Simmie and I got off the elevator on the suite level, you could not hear yourself think. Employees and fans wished us well as we made our way to our suite. At least I think they wished us well. I could not hear a word. The noise was exhilarating, and the team had not even come out to warm up yet. I remembered that when I first came to Cleveland, there were more Celtics fans than Cavs fans. That sure was not the case any more. In fact, I could not spot one shamrock in the sea of orange and blue.

As the team ran onto the court, the noise increased, which I did not think was possible. It continued through the introductions, making it impossible to hear Howie Chesak, our public address announcer. The only time it was quiet was during the singing of our national anthem by recording artist Regina Belle, who was married to John Battle.

We jumped on the Celtics early, despite the hot hand of Reggie Lewis. Mike Sanders got after the taller Larry Bird and denied him the ball early, making it difficult for him to get going. Brad was having his way with Robert Parish, and Nance was handling McHale. We were on fire as we set a team play-off record by shooting 59 percent and set another record with 42 assists. We won easily, 122–94, marking the first time a Cavs team won two playoff series in a season. It was the second time the team advanced to the conference finals.

I firmly believed it was our fans who pushed us past the Celtics. Yes, the Celtics were older, but they were still fine representatives of the dynasty. We played great and were a better team. Now it was on to the Bulls, who had finally beaten Detroit. The Bulls were primed, but so were we. How could we help it? Every promotional ad for the play-offs showed The Shot, as if we needed to be reminded. The worst thing for us was that Jordan and the Bulls were more confident now than they were then.

We exchanged blowout victories in Chicago before coming home to split two close games. It was great to see how our fans stayed in the games. We had developed real fans, and they deserved to be rewarded. We needed to find a way to beat the Bulls. But we were going to have to wait another season. Chicago won Game 5 in Chicago and then took a hard-fought Game 6 in Richfield. Still, we were unable to gain revenge for The Shot. The Bulls went on to win their first championship, and Jordan took another step toward greatness. As devastated as we were, this loss did not sting as much as the one after The Shot. We had had a great year. Nance was selected to the NBA's All-Defensive Second Team and Brandon was named to the All-Rookie Second Team. I was named NBA Executive of the Year and Lenny was heading off to be the assistant coach of the gold-medal-winning Dream Team.

Our post-season review was fun. It was fun to talk about this team. We were going to get better because we were still young. But we needed help. We figured our top priority would be size in the backcourt. We thought that was what we would need to beat Jordan and Reggie Lewis. We found we were in trouble in that area when Ehlo got into foul trouble. At six-foot-two, Battle just was not tall enough to defend those two. Of course, I was told over and over, we would not have that problem if we still had Harper.

I was rewarded with another contract extension in April, and I was ready to get on with building the Cavs into a championship team. We did not have a first- or second-round draft pick, so we were looking for a free agent. Gerald Wilkins fit the bill perfectly. His game was similar to Harper's. He was a fair outside shooter, but he could run on the break and he could slash to the basket. I courted him all summer and finally signed him as training camp approached.

The last season had been relatively injury free, but then something unexpected happened before the 1992–93 season. Coach Lenny Wilkens injured an Achilles tendon playing in an informal pickup game in Barcelona during the Olympics. He ended up having surgery in August and remained bedridden as he developed life-threatening blood clots. Lenny had to stay off his feet for most of training camp and eventually used a golf cart to get him to and from the practice court.

Brad went down in November with tendinitis and bursitis in his right knee, and we struggled to win three of our first nine games. We got back on track in December and were keeping pace with our record from last season. Hot Rod missed the entire month of January with a sprained right hand, and Mike Sanders missed twenty-nine games with a knee injury as injuries continued to hex our franchise. But we were able to play through them and win fifty-four games, finishing three games behind the Central Division champion Bulls. It was the third-best record in the East as the improving Knicks won sixty games. We needed all five games to win the first-round playoff series against New Jersey and, once again, faced our nemesis, Michael Jordan and the Chicago Bulls. This time, they swept us unceremoniously out of the second round of the play-offs. I began to wonder if we would ever be able to get past the Bulls.

The Danny Ferry saga continued throughout the season. Even with Sanders out, Danny still played fewer than twenty minutes per game. Ehlo and Wilkins played small forward, and late in the season we picked up six-foot-five-inch Bobby Phills, who played guard and small forward. Ferry's lack of playing time was causing problems. We had a lot of money invested in him. The heckling continued and his confidence continued to plummet. He never openly complained but he was convinced he could make a greater contribution if given more minutes. As athletes, we should be mentally tough enough to take the criticism. We get paid to perform, and criticism comes with our jobs. But athletes also are human. With positive reinforcement from me and his teammates, especially Larry Nance, Danny's spirit never changed. He became more determined. He was the first player at practice and the last to leave. He came back in the evenings to shoot and brought his girlfriend, Tiffany, to rebound. Without compromising my relationship with Lenny, I had many heart-to-heart conversations with Danny during his struggles. He really needed a friend. I tried to assure him that we were behind him. I told him to let me take the flak, because I was responsible for him being in this mess. I encouraged him to concentrate on basketball and told him good things would happen for him and the team. But it was tough for him. He had tremendous pride and felt that he could overcome his weaknesses and be a productive player.

I also was concerned about Lenny. He still was feeling the aftereffects of his surgery. Lenny was a fighter, and he was not going to let his condition slow him down. But all season, his energy level seemed low. He seemed mentally and physically drained. At times, he was irritable. We had never had a conflict in our entire working relationship until this season. We had just lost a game in which we were badly outrebounded. I made a comment about our rebounding to assistant coach Dick Helm. Lenny snapped that there was nothing wrong with our rebounding, and I exploded. He later confronted me, and we had another heated discussion about rebounding. The next day we had lunch and talked about how we could improve our team.

From time to time, we had meetings with our owners. During these meetings, we were to report on Danny's progress. Lenny had to explain why he was not playing Danny. I knew better than to tell him to play Danny. A general manager does not have that authority. But I did ask about Danny's progress and what he had to do in order to earn more playing time. Since I was accountable to ownership, I felt I had a right to ask. Lenny was respectful, but he was adamant about who played and who did not.

I was not convinced that Danny could not play in The League. I recognized his weaknesses, but I remembered Red Auerbach's philosophy: Do what you do best, and I will determine how to use it. Danny could shoot the ball. I still thought he could complement Brad. But I was also beginning to think he was in the wrong place at the wrong time. Expectations were just too high for him in Cleveland, and they were expectations that he might never be able to meet. But trading Danny was impossible because of his salary and because he really had not distinguished himself. I was not sure that was the way to go. We let Reggie Williams go, and he went on to become a starting small forward for the Denver Nuggets, averaging 17 points per game. That did not sit well with our ownership. We had to continue to be patient with Danny. Eventually his hard work and dedication were going to pay off. I knew he did not want to fail.

I was thinking about all these things when my phone rang. It was Gordon.

"Lenny called a few minutes ago to tell me he was resigning as coach," Gordon said.

I was speechless. After a moment or two I finally was able to ask, "Did he give a reason?"

"He said he just felt the team wasn't listening to him anymore," Gordon replied.

I had to calm down before I could call Lenny. Then I picked up the phone. "Lenny, Gordon told me about your decision," I said. "Are you sure?"

His voice was firm. "Wayne," he said. "I've had it." We talked for a few minutes and I was convinced that he was serious and that he would not change his mind. It was May 24, 1993.

Naturally, this decision preempted our regular post-season review of the team with our owners, or "the suits" as one of our coaches called them. I had mixed feelings about Lenny's decision. I also felt the players had heard the same voice too long. I knew a person could overstay his welcome. When this happens, it becomes difficult to motivate. But our players were veterans, and I did not think it took much to motivate them. Still, this obviously played into Lenny's thinking. I also thought he was frustrated that we had not been able to overcome "The Shot." It was not the coaches' faults that we could not beat the Bulls. You needed talent, which we had. You needed character, which we had. And you needed luck, which we did not have. No team in the history of the NBA suffered as many injuries to key players as we did. Dating back to when the Celtics lost to the Hawks in 1958, when Bill Russell missed the final game with a sprained ankle, no team had won an NBA title without its key people. Lenny Wilkens had done a great job of building the Cavaliers into a contending team. What more could you ask? We just had the misfortune to come along at the same time as the dynasty in Chicago. A lot of other teams could not get past Jordan's Bulls, either.

I once read where great coaches or leaders leave a piece of themselves with the people they manage. They always put the players ahead of themselves. Lenny left a piece of himself with each of our players, and he always put the team first. He believed that the game belonged to the players, and he did what was necessary to create the environment and the leadership for them to succeed. He was an effective, quiet leader, despite his relaxed personality. He was a great bench coach. He had a great understanding of what was happening on the floor. He never embarrassed players by shouting at them in front of people during games. He always waited until he got to the locker room or until emotions had subsided. He never talked negatively about a player to the press, the way so many coaches do today. I will never understand how coaches can ridicule players publicly and then expect them to perform for them.

Gordon, Watson, and I had not yet decided to extend Lenny's contract, and maybe he sensed there was some question about doing that. Perhaps that played into his thinking. There were some innuendoes, and Lenny was a proud person.

I was going to miss Lenny. I could not have asked for a better working relationship. The mutual respect we had as players had carried over into our professional lives. He trusted Fitzsimmons and the scouts and my recommendations on draft picks and NBA players, and he respected my opinions about the game and occasionally would ask my opinions, especially about the inside game. We were always able to work through our differences. He never wanted my job. He just wanted open communication. He wanted to be heard. Yes, we differed on how to use Ferry, but I respected his position and tried not to force the issue. It was a great seven years, but it was the end of an era. With the end came the inevitable questions: What would have happened if I had not traded Harper? Would we have beaten the Bulls and won a championship? Did "The Shot" destroy our confidence? What if we had remained healthy? Why did Michael Jordan have to come along now?

Personally, I was grappling with another question: How was I ever going to replace Lenny Wilkens? Gordon asked for a list of candidates, and I started what I liked to call the "Stu Inman Drill." Back when Stu was general manager of Portland, one of the things we did to pass time on the road scouting was rate coaching candidates, just in case we had to replace a coach. We would exhaust every possible option, pro and college. I had not done this in quite some time, but I quickly prepared a short list to review with Gordon.

As the news of Lenny's resignation was made public, I expected calls from every unemployed coach in the country. I was not surprised the first call came from Mike Fratello, who had been fired in Atlanta three seasons earlier. He had stayed involved as a television commentator, joining Marv Albert to form a popular duo on NBC's broadcasts of NBA games. I was sound asleep when the phone rang. It was just after midnight, and Lenny's resignation had just been broadcast on ESPN's SportsCenter, which had become mandatory viewing in the sports world.

"Wayne, Mike Fratello," he said. "I'm your man."

I informed him he was on my short list, then I hung up the phone and tried to go back to sleep. But before I did, I went through the "Stu Inman Drill" a few more times.

The next day I met with Gordon to review candidates. We wanted an experienced coach because we had an experienced team. We preferred a coach with NBA experience, but we did not rule out college coaches. Within a day, I started making calls to the coaches on my short list, and I received calls from hordes of interested parties. Some called to express their interest in the job. Others called to make recommendations.

There were three college coaches on the list: Roy Williams at the University of Kansas, who had been Dean Smith's assistant at North Carolina when Brad was there; Bob Huggins at the University of Cincinnati; and John MacLeod of the University of Notre Dame. MacLeod was the only one of the three with NBA experience, having been a successful head coach at Phoenix, New York, and Dallas. All three were committed to their college programs.

In addition to Fratello, the other former NBA coach on my short list was Paul Silas, the same Paul Silas who had sparked that argument with Nellie all those years ago. As I had feared, he had not gotten another chance to be a head coach after the Clippers fired him in 1983.

I had preliminary discussions with Fratello and Silas and was prepared to set up follow-up interviews with Gordon and Watson. This was our usual practice, and Gordon and I remained in constant communication. At least I thought we were in constant communication. I was to learn that he was not satisfied with how we had communicated over the past several years.

Less than a week after Lenny resigned in the spring of 1993, Gordon and I had a conversation about our communications. He wanted assurances that our lines of communication would remain open. We talked about how we needed to stay focused on common objectives, and we talked about our mission and strategic goals. I agreed with most of it, as long as I retained the authority I insisted upon when I took the job in 1986. A few days later, I received a six-page letter from Gordon reviewing our conversation. The letter outlined the responsibilities of the key people in the organization. Upon careful examination, I realized that the letter was an attempt to override the contract extension I signed in 1992.

Certain passages stood out to me:

> Ownership . . . has final authority over all decisions that involve significant assets. These assets include capital assets, player personnel and other key people in the organization . . . I will have final approval over the hiring of the coach, based upon your recommendation and after conversations (alone and together with you) with candidates you present to me . . . I would like you to develop policies for my approval which can be presented to the new coach when he comes aboard, in order to minimize the number of administrative issues that will need ongoing negotiation between you and the coach . . . I will have final approval on the hiring of assistant coaches, bench coaches, off-court coach and trainer, based solely on the joint recommendation of you and the coach . . .

> Should it become necessary, I will have final approval on the hiring of a new Director of Player Personnel, solely based on your recommendation . . . On medical matters of significance, the team physicians will be expected to report to me directly, as well as being obligated to report to you and the coach.

With regard to the draft, Gordon was asking for my recommendation, but before making the selection, he wanted to talk to the coach about his plans for developing the player. He clearly was not going to have another situation like the one we had gone through with Danny Ferry.

I sent the letter to my attorney, who agreed that it was an attempt to dilute my authority. He composed a response, which I signed and sent to Gordon, stating that I would continue to comply with my 1992 employment agreement. That contract was binding; the letter was not.

Each subsequent contract that I had signed since my original contract was an extension of my original deal. All those contracts empowered me to hire, fire, and determine the terms of employment for all coaches, scouts, and trainers, although the owner did have to approve the hiring of the head coach.

The letter made it obvious to me that Gordon had lost faith in my ability and was taking a more hands-on approach to running the team. With costs escalating the way they were, many owners were doing the same thing, and with the Cavaliers about to move from the Coliseum to the new Gund Arena in downtown Cleveland, perhaps I should not have been surprised at Gordon's increased involvement.

But, looking back, it was this letter that marked the beginning of my end in Cleveland.

Was it the Harper trade? I will take the blame, but I thought we were all on the same page when we made that decision. I have come to realize that Lenny did not really say what he meant. Still, anyone who was in our offices that day remembered Gordon bellowing about Harper, "Get him out of here." That did not leave much room for interpretation.

The deal had not worked out. I could not deny that. I certainly understood his disappointment and his desire to avoid having it happen again. Believe me, I did not want it to happen again either.

But the trade had been more than three years ago. Why send the letter now? Was he unhappy with the people I had hired? Remember that when I was hired, a board member asked me whether I would hire a black coach. I had hired Lenny. Now I was in the process of hiring another coach. Were they trying to make sure I would not hire another black coach?

Although I was still puzzled by what was going on, I continued the coaching search. I met with Mike Fratello at the O'Hare Westin Hotel. He was in Chicago to broadcast a play-off game between the Bulls and the Knicks. Mike fit most of our criteria. He had been a head coach, and he had some success with the Hawks featuring Moses Malone, Dominique Wilkins, and Doc Rivers. He coached them to the Eastern Conference Finals in 1986, when they were beaten by the Celtics. I had recommended to Gordon that we try to find someone whose personality was different from Lenny's, and Mike's personality definitely was different. He was an energetic, animated coach, and I thought perhaps his coaching style might be enough to get our veteran team over the hump. From my observations and interviews with those who had worked with him and played for him, I had some reservations. But in assessing his strengths and weaknesses, I thought his strengths outweighed his weaknesses. I was confident I could manage his weaknesses, as long as there was open communication.

Mike and I went to Princeton for an interview with Gordon and his group of advisers. Gordon seemed pleased. Watson interviewed Mike a week later in Chicago, and he was pleased, too. I was not completely convinced, and I spent a lot of time talking to Mike about my concerns. He told me that he had learned a lot in the time he had been out of coaching and that he had also learned from his mistakes.

I recommended that we hire Mike, but I cautioned Gordon that he might have a short shelf life and that we would have to manage him and keep his ego under control. Do not get me wrong. We all have egos. I have one, too. But the players' egos are what count. The team should always come first.

After negotiating with agent Lonnie Cooper, who seemed to represent every coach in the country, we agreed to a contract, and on June 17, 1993, Mike Fratello became the eleventh coach in Cavaliers history.

Chapter 18

The Czar

Mike Fratello was a protégé of Hubie Brown. Some say he was a clone of Hubie Brown. Both emerged from the fabled Five-Star Camps. These camps are held in the Pocono Mountains every summer and attract the best high school basketball players in the country. Hubie, thanks to me, was the first Five-Star coach to come to the pros when I hired him in Milwaukee. Mike was an assistant to Hubie with the New York Knicks and, later, the Atlanta Hawks. When Hubie was released in Atlanta, Mike became a head coach for the first time. He also had been an assistant coach at the college level.

Hubie went on to become one of basketball's best television analysts after leaving Atlanta, and when Mike was fired in Atlanta, he followed in Hubie's footsteps again. He had been out of coaching for three years and was working with Marv Albert on the NBC broadcasts of the NBA games. Marv gave him the nickname "Czar of the Telestrator," referring to the electronic chalkboard Mike used to diagram and explain plays on television. Mike loved to be called "The Czar." When he gave me a "Czar" baseball cap early in our relationship, I became a bit concerned. He was selling other merchandise that also carried "The Czar" label on it. Why did this concern me? The dictionary defines a czar as being a dictator, a despot, much like Caesar . . . maybe that is not the best analogy. Anyway, history tells us that most dictators were overthrown, like the Russian czars of the nineteenth century. History also tells us that

Nicholas II, the last Russian czar, was a charming fellow. But I bet he had nothing on Mike. He is a true charmer.

In putting together his staff, Mike picked Five-Star guys. Ron Rothstein had been fired in Detroit, and Richie Adubato had been fired in Dallas. All of our coaches had been head coaches in the league, so I thought we had an experienced staff for our veteran team.

The biggest question in my mind was how the players would adjust to Mike's confrontational style. I thought our guys would be able to handle it because they were professionals. In fact, several of our players told me they welcomed a change in leadership style. It was not meant as an affront to Lenny. But they were searching for a way to win a championship. What we had been doing was not working, and time was growing shorter with each passing year.

Mike, his staff, Simmie, and I spent many hours together talking about our team. It also was a way for us to get to know each other's philosophies. Mike and I spent additional hours getting to know each other, and I certainly got my fill of Italian food that summer. But if our team was going to win a title, it would be because of our leadership. He and I came from entirely different backgrounds and had different basketball experiences. We covered some of his philosophy during our interviews, and he also shared his opinions of most of our players. Naturally, he said he liked our team and was looking forward to coaching it. I went through what I saw as each player's strengths and weaknesses, and we talked in depth about their personalities, their moods, and their sensitivities. We talked about their families, since most of them were married. To ease the transition, I wanted Mike to know as much about our players as possible. He specifically wanted to know about recently acquired players like Bobby Phills, who earned a contract for the rest of the season after I originally signed him to a ten-day deal, and Terrell Brandon, who had had a great year as Mark Price's backup. We had traded for Tyrone Hill to give us rebounding and depth. Hill was the strongman selected by Golden State in exchange for our 1994 draft pick.

Despite being confused by the letter from Gordon, I continued functioning as I had been. But I felt like a fired man walking. It was imperative that I spend time with the entire staff, the coaches, trainer Gary Briggs, and our scouts. We needed to become a team if we were going to win a championship. Through my entire career, teamwork had been important to me. I had been elected or appointed captain of each of the teams I played on, except the Celtics. Each player on the team has a role, and my role with this team was to develop and manage the team I had put together, including the coaches.

Even though the core of our team was getting older, especially Larry, I was optimistic about the 1993–94 season. I thought we would be better than last year because Brad, Mark, and Hot Rod were just reaching their primes. One problem was that we had lost Craig Ehlo. After Craig developed into a reliable shooting guard with us, his agent, Ron Grinker, took advantage of the opportunity and demanded an outrageous salary. We were not prepared to pay it, but Lenny, who had signed to coach the Atlanta Hawks, persuaded them to sign Craig as a free agent. I hated to see Craig go. He was a good player for us, and he had a way of keeping his teammates loose. I was glad to see someone paying him that kind of money. But with Gerald Wilkins and an emerging Bobby Phills, we were covered at the shooting guard position. We also were excited about drafting Chris Mills, a six-foot-seven-inch swingman who was the Pacific Ten Conference Player of the Year. We were amazed Chris lasted until the twenty-second pick.

My first impressions of Mike and his staff were good ones. He was well organized for training camp. He had every minute of the two-a-day practices detailed. After practice, he and his staff met over lunch and dinner to evaluate each player and the team. He often solicited my opinion and the opinions of Simmie and the scouts. I also was impressed with his team-building methods. To watch our talented players demonstrate their skills at karaoke was a treat. Mike made it mandatory that each of us do some singing at the team dinners during camp. Everyone participated, and everyone shared in the laughter. It was a good thing God blessed each of us with other talents.

We started the season 6–6. Brandon missed the first nine games with mononucleosis, and Gerald Madkins, our third point guard, was put on the injured list with a broken hand. After playing the first nine games, Larry had arthroscopic surgery on his right knee. We struggled through December and January with injuries, but it gave us an opportunity to see how our bench would respond. Tyrone Hill stepped into a starting role to replace Larry, and scored and rebounded as we had hoped he would. John Battle and Bobby Phills stepped up their play, and we were able to fight our way back to .500. In February, we even got above .500. The team was responding to Mike. The players seemed to be having fun and feeling good about the future. Brandon stepped in when Mark was injured, and we did not miss a beat. We were glad we had that five-foot-eleven-inch point guard everyone was concerned about when we made him our draft pick. Terrell was good enough to start on most teams, and several teams inquired about his availability. But I was not going to let him go anywhere.

We had climbed to ten games over .500 when Brad complained about an excruciating pain in his lower back. He was diagnosed as having a herniated lumbar disc. Our doctors prescribed rest to see how he would respond. Brad went on the injured list, joining Battle, who was already on the list with a knee injury. There were more problems. We found out Larry Nance had torn some lateral meniscus cartilage. He joined Battle and Daugherty on the injured list and had his second arthroscopic surgery of the season. This was not a good sign for an aging player. We were hoping to get a championship ring before Larry retired.

"We've got problems," I told my staff as we huddled to go over the names of players who were available to help us try to salvage the season. I had used that phrase often throughout the years, but it was never truer than it was this season. It was March, and three of our key players were out, probably for the season. Jay Guidinger was Brad's backup at center, although Mike used Hot Rod there most of the time. With Larry out, we needed Hot Rod and Tyrone at power forward. As usual, we turned to Simmie to work his magic. Simmie was the best at finding players. This time he found Tim Kempton, a six-foot-ten-inch center from Notre Dame who had just returned from Europe. Tim played a few seasons in The League before going overseas. We signed him for the rest of the season.

One of the highlights of the regular season, our last after twenty years in Richfield, was the Cavalier Classic Weekend to mark our last regular-season games in the Coliseum before moving to the new Gund Arena downtown. We played the Washington Bullets. Both teams wore replicas of the uniforms they had worn during the Miracle of Richfield in 1976, when the Cavs upset the Bullets to advance to the Eastern Conference Finals. We beat the Bullets again, and then the Celtics, to close out the regular season.

Despite missing 223 games to injury, we managed to hold on and make the play-offs. Brad had missed thirty-two games and Larry forty-nine. We used a total of seventeen players to get through the season. We were 7–5 in April and finished the season 47–35, winning our last eight home games, thanks to the improved play of Brandon, Mills, and veteran Rod Higgins. Danny's minutes stayed the same, but his determination grew. He hoped the coaching change would revive his career.

Mike did a good job of keeping the team focused on winning, and our players remained determined. There were no excuses. It would have been easy to toss in the towel, especially when we found ourselves matched up against Jordan and the world champion Bulls in the play-offs. Chicago clearly was becoming a dynasty and disposed of us in three games. There was no way a Cavs team without Daugherty and Nance was going to challenge, much less upset, Jordan and the Bulls.

I had mixed emotions leaving the Coliseum, and many fond memories. Although I was not with the team at the time, I had come to appreciate Austin Carr and Bill Fitch and that Miracle of Richfield team with Bingo Smith, Campy Russell, Jim Chones, Dick Snyder, Foots Walker, and Nate Thurmond. I had watched the resurgence of the Cavs under

Harry Weltman and George Karl with World B. Free, and I had been privileged to work with Lenny Wilkens and our current squad. I would never forget the 1992 play-offs against the Celtics.

Now there was Mike Fratello and a world of uncertainty as we prepared to move to our new home. A group of community leaders had banded together in an effort to revitalize downtown Cleveland. Indians owner Dick Jacobs had built a beautiful new ballpark, and Gordon, who prided himself on his community involvement, had put up an equally beautiful arena next door in the area that became known as "Gateway." We had just set a franchise record for attendance, averaging more than eighteen thousand fans per game. We hoped they would move downtown with us, although those who lived north of the Coliseum were more excited about the move than those who lived in the Akron-Canton area. It was a dirty shame we were not able to hang a championship banner in the Coliseum for all of them before we left.

Like every other team, the Cavs had appreciated in value, and Gateway was a great opportunity to further increase that value. There would be twice as many suites and other premium seating, as well as increased ticket prices for other seats. The entire organization had been involved in the design of the new arena. Much time was spent picking out the colors, tiles, locker room amenities, and other accessories that were going to make the building a state-of-the-art facility. Gordon spent a great deal of time in Cleveland during the construction of the building, and he joined Mike and me for dinner a number of times in an effort to get to know Mike better.

I called frequent meetings with my staff so we would be well-prepared for our end-of-the-season review with Gordon. With the injuries to Brad and Larry, and with other key players aging, we were facing many tough decisions. It was critical that we have a state-of-the-art team to open our state-of-the-art building. On the other hand, we had been pleased with the young players who were able to play. Brandon continued to improve. Hill and Phills gave solid efforts, and Mills had surprised us as a rookie. The big questions, though, concerned Brad and Larry.

There were no questions about our new home. The Gateway complex was a welcome addition to downtown Cleveland. The baseball complex and the arena were adjacent, which was wonderful for me. I could walk across the street to watch the Indians, who had been my favorite baseball team since childhood.

Our new quarters were definitely state-of-the-art. Our offices were six stories above ground level, quite a change from our subterranean offices at the Coliseum. One of the biggest benefits was that bands doing sound checks or monster trucks practicing no longer drowned out our discussions about the team.

In our war room, we had charts that listed the entire rosters of every team. We could check these for free agents or trade possibilities. We had modern video equipment to review game films or films of college prospects.

We were going to spend much time in the war room over the summer. Nance underwent two operations on his troubled knee and his future looked bleak, which was a shame because I always thought if we were going to win a championship he had to be a key player. I could not help but wonder if we would be able to leave the injury jinx behind when we moved from the Coliseum. We desperately needed to change our luck.

I was happy to sign Bobby Phills, who was coming off a good year as a backup, but our primary need was to find a veteran big man because of the uncertainties with Larry and Brad. We decided to pursue unrestricted free agent Michael Cage, a perennial rebounding leader who could play power forward or center. Cage came into The League with the Clippers and moved on to the Sonics. I learned he did not want to return to Seattle. Other clubs were after him, but his agent, George Kalifidis, was from Cleveland and was able to convince him to join us.

In another surprise, given the letter he had sent, Gordon added the title of president and chief operating officer to my general manager title. My job description remained the same, and I continued to function in the same way. There were frequent meetings of the board and the officers to make sure we were successful in launching our first season in the new arena, now called Gund Arena. Gordon wrote a mission statement that we signed, and we posted it in the lobby of the main entrance to the building. It guaranteed our patrons a satisfactory experience. My contribution to the statement had to do with winning games.

Mike and I continued to bond throughout the summer. I had not eaten as much Italian food since I left Boston, where I frequently dined with my friends Freddy Carangelo and Teddy Tomasone at Mother Anna's and other fine Italian restaurants in the North End. It was not doing my waistline any good, but we were developing a relationship of trust. At least I thought we were. Mike even surprised me and agreed to travel to New Hampshire and be a guest lecturer at my camp. Of course, first he made sure there was an Italian restaurant in Nashua. We spent hours talking about the team and the what-ifs: What if Larry cannot come back? What if Brad's back keeps him out? Even though we still had Hot Rod, Tyrone, and Danny, we needed our All-Stars. Tyrone was an unrestricted free agent, but we were able to sign him. We certainly did not need him to leave.

John Battle was another concern. We knew when we signed him that his knees eventually would be a problem. We hoped to get four years from him, and that is what we got. We were still okay at the guards, with Terrell and Mark at point and Bobby and Gerald at the shooting guard.

Our worst fears were confirmed when Larry Nance announced his retirement on September 24, 1994. He was with the Cavs for six and a half years and made a tremendous impact. He was our leader, our inspiration. He was what the doctor ordered for a young team. His contributions were going to be missed. He scored more than 15,000 points in his thirteen-year NBA career. He would be remembered in Cleveland for his shot-blocking records. In fact, he would be remembered as the best shot-blocking forward to play the game. For his contributions on and off the floor, we retired his Number 22. This was a quite an honor for a player who had not been here all that long. But it was an indication of what he meant to our team.

Assistant coach Richie Adubato left us to join Brian Hill with the Orlando Magic, and Mike submitted the names of several candidates for me to consider. There were no Five-Star guys on the list, because most of them were employed. But Sidney Lowe, best known for being on Jimmy Valvano's NCAA championship team, had been fired as Minnesota's head coach and was looking for work. I wanted at least one person on the staff who had played in The League and recommended him to Mike. Mike liked Sid, so we hired him on October 3, just before training camp. We learned at training camp that Sid was going to be terrific as a coach. He also brought some talent to the karaoke party.

We experimented with several different lineups. We remained desperate for another big man, so we signed seven-foot-one Greg Dreiling, who had played for the Mavericks. But we were going to rely on Hot Rod, Hill, Cage, and Ferry. Yes, Ferry. Danny shot the lights out during training camp, and Mike promised him that if he continued to shoot like that he would be a part of the rotation. Danny's hard work was beginning to show. His confidence was at an all-time high and he was feeling wanted, which contributes to one's success.

We had barely started training camp when we got more bad news. On October 18, Gerald Wilkins ruptured his right Achilles tendon in an exhibition game against the Celtics. He was operated on three days later and was going to miss the entire season. Apparently the injury jinx had followed us downtown. With Larry retired, Brad out indefinitely, and Wilkins out for the season, we had lost more than 50 points from our lineup. How do you replace that? In an attempt to gain some of the scoring we lost, we signed Tony Campbell, a journeyman small forward who had played at Ohio State and in Europe.

We opened the season with brand new uniforms designed by a company out of California. It featured a slash of baby blue on the front of the jersey, replacing our old orange-and-blue color scheme. We had come a long way from my days in Milwaukee, where I would go visit my old friend Jack Shlicht at Milwaukee Sporting Goods to order uniforms. It usually meant a trip to Berlin, Wisconsin, for a round of golf, dinner, and a visit the next morning to Sand Knit, the manufacturer. All I wanted was something traditional and durable. Now getting new uniforms was a big deal. You had to go through NBA Properties. You had to apply a year in advance to change a design or color. It was important that the design be marketable. The marketing people determined the color and design of the uniforms, although they did consult the coaches, players, and me.

We broke out the new uniforms at the start of the 1994–95 season, and Phills scored the first two points in Gund Arena. However, we lost to the World Champion Houston Rockets, 100–98. With the new arena as a draw, we played before sellout crowds as we were able to stay around .500, which was remarkable given our injury situation. Our players did not buckle under the adversity and gave an all-out effort every night. We thought if we could just hang in there until Brad returned, we would be okay.

But Brad was not going to return. After nearly a year of suffering and treatments, Brad traveled the country to get different opinions. He was looking for relief. He often could not reach down to tie his shoes because of the pain. He was very frustrated because at the age of twenty eight, he was just reaching his prime, although he had already had a productive career. Finally, he decided to have surgery at University Hospital in Cleveland to remove two herniated discs in the lower portion of his back. He was expected to miss the entire season.

Under Mike's leadership and with the whole team giving everything it had, we went on an eleven-game winning streak in December, despite losing thirty-nine games to injury. This was quite impressive given the circumstances, and watching the young players develop was a good sign for the future of the franchise. Everyone was having fun. We played like a contender. Mike, who prided himself on being a fashion plate, was strutting the sidelines with his colorful ties and impeccable suits. I have never known a coach to pay so much attention to his attire. His shoes had to match his suit. I heard that once when he had brought the wrong shoes, he wanted a police escort so the proper ones could be retrieved.

His suits had to be wrinkle free. His ties had to be just right. Part of the assistant coach's duties was to pick out the right tie from an array of ties that was in his locker (or his valise, if we were on the road) after the team had gone out for pre-game warm-ups. There was an evening that I needed to tell Mike something before a home game. I walked into the coaches office, tripped over an ironing board, and felt the hot vapors from an upright steamer. I just shook my head. I figured it was a habit he got into when he was at NBC. Television has makeup artists and valets. We had not quite gotten there in The League.

We were 23–11 when Mark hurt his wrist in a game against Golden State. It was diagnosed as a fracture of the scaphoid (navicular) bone in his right wrist. I dreaded the calls from Briggs. He never had good news. Mark underwent surgery to place a pin in his wrist and was put on the injured list. We signed point guard Elmer Bennett to a ten-day contract to back up Terrell.

Tyrone was selected to play in the All-Star Game in Phoenix. He was having an All-Star year and deserved to be there. However, his playing time was limited because of a hand injury. When he returned from Phoenix, he underwent surgery on his right hand to place a screw in a small chip fracture of his right ring finger. Once more old Simmie had to search the board to find a healthy body, who turned out to be veteran Fred Roberts.

It was amazing that we were trailing the Charlotte Hornets by only a half game at the end of January. And we were only a game and half behind the surging Pacers and Charlotte at the end of February. Price missed twenty seven games; Hill and Battle missed most of the month. Price returned in early March, and Battle went back on the injured list with inflamed knees.

"I know you are bored with the injury report," I said to Gordon in one of our frequent phone calls. "But I've got some more bad news. Terrell has a stress fracture of the tibia in his right leg and will be out the rest of the season."

Terrell had surgery to place a rod in his tibia and the prognosis was good.

We finished the 1994–95 season 43–39 and made the play-offs for the seventh time in eight seasons. Patrick Ewing and the Knicks beat us, three games to one, but we were competitive, losing the third game at the buzzer as Danny missed a three-point attempt. Danny was terrific in the play-offs, scoring a career-high 20 points in Game 1.

The encouraging thing about this team was that the players never gave up. Mike would not let them give up. Mike did a great job coaching, and the character of the team was apparent. Once again this team could have given up and quit. Mike was runner-up to Del Harris, coach of the Lakers, as coach of the year.

We drew an average of 20,338 fans in our first year in the Gund Arena. The fans deserved better. Even though we were making the play-offs, with all the injuries we had no hope of advancing toward the championship as long we played without Brad. Hot Rod and Mark were aging, but with the added experience and improvement of Brandon, Phills, Mills and, yes, Ferry, I thought we could be in the thick of things next year if Brad returned.

How many years did we have to say wait until next year? It was getting old. Our fans were getting impatient.

Changes were inevitable. First, we lost Gerald Wilkins to Vancouver in the expansion draft. He had never really recovered from the Achilles tendon surgery. But losing Gerald meant we were able to protect our key people. In an effort to get a third guard who could play point or shooting guard, we drafted Bobby Sura from Florida State.

We were hoping Brad would return, but we had no such luck. In late September, we announced that Brad would miss at least half of the season. This caused me to think that maybe we should retool. Mark was another year older and was having more and more nagging injuries, as was Hot Rod.

In one of our staff meetings, I raised the subject of trading them if there was an opportunity that made sense. In a subsequent meeting with

Gordon, I again suggested that we should think about it. Trading players who contributed so much to the tradition of the franchise was tough for me. The Celtics would never trade a player who had been loyal to the franchise. But we were in a different era. Plus, the Celtics won championships. We had not won any.

Washington had inquired about Mark. The Bullets always liked Price. Wes Unseld, their Hall of Fame player who had become their general manager, became persistent and was willing to give us their first-round draft choice. I projected the Bullets to be a lottery team, so it made sense for us to think about it. Gordon was willing, but before I agreed, I wanted to extend to Mark the courtesy of letting him know what was up. I explained to him that we probably were going to be in a rebuilding mode, and I asked if he wanted to be a part of it. Being the professional he was, Mark said, "Wayne, this a business. I would do the same thing if I were you."

Once I heard that, I got back to Wes, and we traded Mark to the Bullets for an unconditional first-round pick in the 1996 draft. This was a sad moment for all of us. Mark had meant so much to our franchise—so much so that Gordon decided to retire his Number 25. Mark excited our fans with his gutsy play and his three-point shots. He was one of those unique players who would not let you lose. He was going to be missed for more than his basketball. He was also very active in the community.

We were not finished. Phoenix wanted Hot Rod. We were able to negotiate a trade that would bring Dan Majerle, Antonio Lang, and a first-round pick in either 1996, 1997, or 1998. Before I made the deal, out of respect to Hot Rod, I called him, as I had done with Mark. Hot Rod was a little more reluctant. But after I explained our rebuilding situation to him, he was more receptive. Phoenix general manager Jerry Colangelo called him to tell him how much they wanted him. Once Hot Rod was comfortable, we made the trade. Hot Rod was popular in the locker room, and he, too, was active in the community. He was going to be missed as well.

All of a sudden, our old gang was gone. The team that Magic Johnson had called "The Team of the Nineties" had disbanded—without winning a single championship. Coach Lenny (which was what the players called him), Coach Helm, and Coach Winters were gone. Phil Hubbard, nicknamed "Hubs," who was our team leader during the transition years, was gone. Larry, the leader and consummate pro, was gone. Hot Rod, also called "Wood," was gone. Mark, nicknamed "Lil' Bit" by Larry, was gone. Eggs was gone. Doug E was gone. He was known as Gerald Wilkins. In addition, all their wives were gone, and we'd miss them, too. We always had two occasions when the players and their wives got together with ownership, management, and the coaching staff in a relaxed atmosphere—our annual Christmas party and the breakup dinner at the end of the season.

Breaking up that team was one of the hardest things I had ever done. Those players had given Northeast Ohio so many thrills. It was a shame they were defeated by all those injuries—and by coming along at the same time as Michael Jordan. I know I was often criticized for acquiring players with character. My critics on sports talk radio accused me of wanting a team full of Boy Scouts or choir boys. What is wrong with having good players who were good guys? I would never take a player just because he was a good guy. I valued talent. I was not that talented a player, so I appreciated the skills of others. But I was a hard worker and I believed in that. I believed in character above all else. Most players drafted into the NBA were talented. We could help them maximize their talents if they were men of character. It is quite an indictment of our society when we disregard citizenship and tolerate all sorts of bad behavior from those that some have set up as role models. I did not agree with outspoken NBA superstar Charles Barkley when he said parents, not athletes, should be role models. We cannot assume everyone has a positive role model. Sometimes, parents need role models, too. Those Cavs players were real role models. They put the team above all else. They played for each other. That is what a "team" is all about, having people depend on each other. Those guys did that every night. The fans could depend on them, too.

Another part of our "team" was gone, too—the beat writers, Plutes, JoJo, and Burt. Though they did not care for the notion, they had become part of the Cavs family, too. They traveled with us on many of the road trips, which allowed them to get to know the players and coaches. Of course, that was before we got our private jet and left them behind. They had shared our frustrations over the years. They gave way to younger journalists—Bob Finnan, Mike Holley, Chris Broussard, L.C. Johnson, and Chris Tomasson.

There were very few injuries that season, and the Cavs finished the 1995–96 season with a 47–35 record, another terrific job by Mike and his staff. These Cavs played and conducted themselves with the same character as the previous group. This time we lost to the Knicks in three straight games in the play-offs. There were bright spots, though. Danny Ferry continued to perform well, averaging 13 points per game. He finally found his way into an eight-man rotation.

The pick that we acquired from Washington for Mark ended up being Number 12. Our own pick was Number 20. We definitely wanted a center if we were convinced he could develop into an NBA player in three or four years. Gary, our scouts, and I spent a lot of time on the road looking for a center. We deduced that there were four, though we rated them just fair. Three of them were undersized at six-foot-ten inches. The other was seven-foot-three inches tall but sat out the year with a bad foot. We brought all four in for interviews and drills. The centers were Todd Fuller, Erick Dampier, Vitaly Potapenko, a sophomore from Wright State, and Zydrunas Ilgauskas, a talented Lithuanian who missed the season with an injured foot. Everybody agreed junior Tim Duncan was the premier center in college, but he opted to stay at Wake Forest for his senior year.

Kobe Bryant, the son of our friend, former NBA player Joe Bryant, entered the draft right out of high school. Kobe was six feet seven inches tall, and was going to be a guard in the NBA. He was on the board at

Number 12, and, although I always had been a proponent of players staying in school or going to school in this case, we were tempted to draft him. But with the uncertainty surrounding Brad, we wanted to protect ourselves in case he could not come back, so we drafted Potapenko. Dampier and Fuller were taken just before him. If we were more confident about Brad's return, we definitely would have taken Bryant. Or, if we were sure Ilgauskas would be there at Number 20, we would have drafted Bryant. We had a relatively young guard in Phills. We had no center. Even Jordan needed Bill Cartwright, Will Perdue, and Luc Longley.

As it turned out Ilgauskas was available at Number 20. Even though his injuries made him a risk, we took him. We thought if we could ever get him healthy he would be a very good center. My scouting report said he had a great touch, great hands, and a great understanding of the game. And he could play with his back to the basket, which very few centers can do.

It looked as if drafting the two big men was a good decision in July, when Brad announced his retirement at the tender young age of thirty, after two years of intense rehabilitation on his back. This was a devastating blow to the franchise. Brad was going to be hard to replace. His 20 points, 10 rebounds, and 5 assists per game were going to be missed. Losing Brad was not like losing Mark or Hot Rod. We had an All-Star point guard in Brandon to step in, plus we got something in return. We had forwards in Hill and an improving Ferry. We got nothing in return for Brad, and we had no center to replace him. There were few good centers in college, and the centers in the league were not available—at least none that would come close to replacing Brad.

Our original group was gone now. I had considered not extending my contract when it was up at the end of the 1996–97 season. There was great joy, but there were many frustrations. I had never been associated with a team that had suffered so many debilitating injuries. I felt bad for Gordon and the entire organization. I felt bad for the fans. I felt bad for the players. I wanted them to experience what I had experienced by playing on a world championship team.

Yes, I always will wonder what would happened if we had not traded Harper—one way or the other, good or bad. He may have separated himself from the friends whose lifestyles we did not want around our team. Ron went on to join the Bulls and, later, the Lakers and became an important part of the their dynasties. I was happy he was so successful.

I changed my mind about retiring. I was too young, and when I looked at the young players left on our roster, I was encouraged. There was a nucleus there, and I was confident that with a plan we could become a contender again in two or three years. I wanted to leave the game on top.

Phills worked on his shooting every summer. He already was a second-team All-NBA defensive player. Terrell was an All-Star, Tyrone was one of the league's best rebounders, and Chris was a solid small forward. If we were able to add a couple of players with the draft picks that we acquired and sign a free agent, it might not take us three years to get back. In fact, looking at the age of the contending teams in our conference, I thought that if our players continued to improve and we added the right pieces, we would be peaking just as other teams in our conference were aging. This was the template I used in Milwaukee and when I came to Cleveland.

But I had questions about whether it would work again. Would our owners—and our fans—be patient? Could Mike implement this plan as Nellie and Lenny did? The coach has to buy into the plan. Making the play-offs as we had done in the past two years and being eliminated in the first round was never satisfactory for me. Winning fifty games during the season and not advancing in the play-offs was getting us nowhere. We really had not won anything. It just got us a lower draft pick and kept us in mediocrity. That was not what I wanted. Sometimes a team had to go all the way to the bottom if was going to build itself back up.

Dick Watson and I continued our post-game "chats," as he would call them. We would meet either in his office, which was located on the second level of Gund Arena, or in his luxury suite. Dick was quite proud of the arena because he was a driving force behind the decision to move to downtown. We spent many hours in his suite at the Sheraton Airport Hotel, another one of his investments. Many deals were made in Suite 999.

I enjoyed most of our conversations. We talked about a broad range of subjects. He liked to talk about the days when he attended college and law school at the same time. We would argue about which of us had been poorer or more deprived as a kid. He would tell me stories about his days as a covert agent for the government. He would also put in his two cents' worth about basketball. As time passed, he began to give his opinions on basketball, which were still only worth two cents to me. We talked about the salary cap, his forte, and where it was going. We talked about the social changes taking place in society and the NBA.

Occasionally, we would meet for dinner at one of Cleveland's great restaurants. It was at one of those dinners that we discussed the controversial book, *The Bell Curve*, by Richard Herrnstein and Charles Murray. Their theory, widely debunked as racist or elitist, explored what they called a "cognitive elite" they claimed was based on high intelligence. According to them, the common denominator of the underclass was low intelligence, rather than racial or social disadvantage. He asked me if I had read the book. It so happened that I did buy the book but put it down after reading less than a chapter because I disagreed with the content. Much to my surprise, Dick said he thought the authors were onto something. I left the dinner completely baffled and wondering what would be next. But I was getting the feeling that there were going to be many more "nexts" in the ensuing months.

Mike and I continued to talk frequently about the team and its progress. I was adamant about playing the young players. He was adamant about trying to win the game. This usually causes a feud between the coach and general manager. General managers are responsible for the long-term stability of a franchise. Coaches want to win today because of the insecurities that come with the job. I tried to assure Mike that he had job security, but there was another element. Mike's contract was up at the end of the season. Naturally he wanted a good record going into negotiations.

We talked about the economic and social changes in the NBA, particularly the contractual demands and changes in coaching and managing players. We talked about the growing external influences and demands on the players. I tried to convince him that he had to play our young guys so they could learn to play through their mistakes. We needed to know if a player could play or not in order to determine his worth when we entered into contract negotiations. I loved to win as much as Mike. Winning to me was winning a championship, or at least being a contender to win a championship. We were not good enough to do that. We needed help, and rather than supplement our team with aging veterans who would be gone when we got good, I wanted to go with youth. Also in the back of my mind was Wake Forest center Tim Duncan. We needed ping-pong balls in the upcoming lottery if we were going to get a shot at him. Duncan would have expedited our development.

I was told by ownership during one of our discussions that I could not tell the coach to lose. I would never tell anyone to lose. Players should compete to win every time they step on to the floor. Young players need to learn to win. But you could not expect them to win against veteran teams. That was the rub. I was reflecting on my experience in my playing days in Cincinnati, where we played rookies and lost for two years and then Oscar joined us and we won for several years. We did the same in Milwaukee, and in Cleveland. There is such a thing as losing with a purpose.

We were plugging along in the 1996–97 season with a 25–22 record, but we had played a couple of real stinkers, scoring 65 and 66 points in back-to-back home losses to New York and Miami shortly before the All-Star Game. Our entire staff had been gearing up for that game, which was to be played in Gund Arena. It was the fiftieth anniversary of

The League, and the highlight of the weekend was going to be honoring the fifty greatest players in the history of The League. All the legends who were still living were expected to be in Cleveland. Another highlight of the weekend for me was the chance to talk about the direction of the game. It was customary to have meetings during the All-Star break. To me, the most critical item on the agenda in 1997 was the slow-down style of play that was becoming prevalent in The League. Attendance was dropping, and NBA writers were bashing the style of play. NBA executives Russ Granik and Rod Thorn had been directed by the commissioner to discuss changes.

Because my host duties kept me busy, I was late to the meeting. But as I walked in and took a seat, I realized the topic had generated an intense conversation. Finally, several of the committee members looked at me, waiting for a comment.

"I agree we must do something to speed up the game," I said. "I don't think our fans like a deliberate, controlled, slow-down game. Yes, I know that is our style. As a matter of fact, we played a game here against the Knicks that was one of the worst games I had seen in my forty-some years in The League. It may have been an aberration, but it was symptomatic of the problem. For the preservation of the game of basketball we need to change."

I have always put the game first. And I have always been willing to express my opinions on the play and conduct of the players on and off the court. I have been outspoken on various subjects in an effort to protect the integrity of the game, the NBA, and the image of the teams that I played for or worked with. I have been outspoken against the interlopers who preyed on the wealth and notoriety of our athletes and led many of them to adopt lifestyles detrimental to the image of The League. Sometimes my speaking out caused problems with the commissioner, though I did not find that out until later.

I found out sooner that my speaking out caused friction between Mike and me. One of my colleagues told the press that I criticized Mike in the meeting. The new breed of aspiring general managers talking to the media about our private meetings was an evolving problem. I guess these guys figured that was the way to get reporters to like them—or at least write about them. Anyway, Mike did not like the comments, and he felt that I should have supported him. He took the comments personally. I was not attacking him as a person or a coach. But it was no secret that we played controlled basketball. Everybody wrote about it, and our stats proved it.

Reports of a feud between Mike and me started to spread, and people seemed to be taking sides. I was reminded of an incident in November, when assistant coach Ron Rothstein, a longtime friend of Mike's, approached me as we were leaving a brief meeting with Gordon and Watson after the tipoff luncheon in Akron. Ronnie told me he had suggested Mike get closer to Gordon. I saw this as an attempt to bypass my authority. This was the same Ronnie who had called me shortly after we hired Mike to suggest that I needed to hire him to help manage Mike. "You know Mikey, Wayne," I recalled him saying. "He can be tough to manage, and no one knows him as I do."

I guess he thought Gordon could better manage Mike. Or not manage Mike. It was becoming a trend in the NBA for owners to hire high-profile coaches and give them complete authority over the basketball operation. The coaches would then hire a general manager who reported to them. Miami did it with Pat Riley. Boston did it with Rick Pitino. These coaches were being paid salaries in excess of $5 million a year, while the general managers were getting a fraction of that. Furthermore, now the coaches were responsible only to the owners.

A few weeks after the All-Star Game, Gordon sent me a copy of that troubling letter I had received in 1993, apparently to remind me that my authority over Mike and the coaches was diminished. However, for his part, Mike remained respectful, and we continued to talk about the team and its needs. I was beginning to think we were on the same page.

A dinner meeting was arranged with Gordon and the board. I was not sure what the agenda was, but when I arrived, I discovered we were seated in a private room. I realized this was not to be a social meeting. After we were all served, the waiters were asked to refrain from returning to the room until further notice. Out came the cigars, and we engaged in discussions about the team, including Mike's contract extension. What I thought was going to be an objective discussion about Mike turned into a tribunal. Every person in the room took turns attacking my management style and my handling of Mike. They took turns throwing darts, and I was the dart board. They thought I had an axe to grind with Mike, which was not true. I wanted Mike to succeed. If Mike succeeded, I succeeded, and we all succeeded. It was clear Mike was their man, and they were ready to commit to him for several years. Finally, Gordon asked my recommendation.

"I recommend that we extend Mike for two years and an option year," I stated.

Without hesitation, Gordon responded, "You know that he is not going to accept that."

"Let's try it," I said. "He might not accept it, but I believe you should be conservative with your offer."

If I heard it said once, I heard it a half a dozen times: Mike was an entertainer, and he was a key part of the in-game entertainment package we were trying to sell. Every time I heard that, I shuddered. I just wanted him to coach. I would rather he not be as animated on the sideline, parading and gesturing like a contortionist as he shouted plays to the players. He tried to control every play. I often told him I could not have played for him because it would have been too hard for me to concentrate on the game while looking to him on the sidelines for instructions on every play. On the other hand, the marketing people loved his act. He had them convinced people paid to see him coach.

I was glad when the evening was over. I had been caught off guard from start to finish. But it was a defining evening for me. It was further verification that my days with the Cavs were over. If I had any doubts, they were erased in a conversation I had with Watson as we waited for the valet to bring our cars.

"We can get rid of you and the players, but we cannot get rid of

Mike," Watson said. "You may be popular in the business community, but Mike is popular in places like Parma and just about everywhere else. All you have to do is listen to the talk shows."

I was fuming. "Dick, I don't listen to the talk shows," I said of the medium that had become the bane of our existence with guys spouting opinions based on little or no information or research. "I am working. I'm on the phones. I'm on the road scouting. When do I have time to listen to talk radio?"

I was deep in thought on my drive home. I did not need an expert in the demography of the region to translate the meaning of Watson's statement. Parma was a working-class, primarily white suburb where integration had been a slow and painful process. I did not think it was an accident Watson had singled out that area. I had no idea why my relationship with the Cavs had gone sour. I sat up most of the night wondering what had gone wrong. I knew one thing for sure: If they thought Mike was more important than the players, they were in for some tough times. It was the last thing Mike needed. Even Red Auerbach knew it was the players who won the games.

I was still ruminating over the night before when I got to work the next day. I passed Gordon in the hallway leading to my to my office and asked if he had a couple of minutes so that we could talk alone. He obliged.

"Gordon, you seemed extremely upset last night," I said. "May I ask why."

He said, "You seem hesitant on Mike. We have to move forward and get him signed."

Later that day, we met again with Mike to discuss our relationship, which I thought was normal. After a short discussion Mike excused himself, leaving Gordon, Dick, and me.

"My contract is up also at the end of the year," I said. "Are you going to extend my contract?"

"We thought that you wanted to retire," Gordon responded. "We'll talk about it later."

We were playing .500 ball when this was happening. Attendance was starting to drop. I resigned myself to the fact that maybe I had been here too long. As Lenny had discovered, there is a time to leave.

A few days later I was encouraged by a call from Gordon. He told me the Milwaukee Bucks were looking for a general manager, and their owner, U.S. Senator Herb Kohl, had called and asked permission to talk to me. It was customary and legally correct to follow this protocol if a team was interested in interviewing someone under contract with another team. This was the second time Herb had sought permission. Both times, Gordon refused to grant permission. This gave me the feeling that my contract would be extended, which was fine with me. Despite what I had been through the past few months, I wanted to stay in Cleveland and continue rebuilding the Cavs. I was more confident than ever, if a bit surprised given the tone of our previous meetings.

I thought there were some good signs ahead. It appeared that we would be in the lottery again. Plus, Phoenix was not having a good year, which meant we probably would opt to take their first-round draft choice. That would give us two high draft choices. We would add two more young players to a team whose average age was less than twenty-six. Also Ilgauskas, who sat out the year after surgery on his foot, was coming along and his prognosis was good for next season.

The college scouting season was reaching its peak, and I was glad. I needed to be on the road. I needed a break from all the controversy in the office. That was a trick I learned from my old friend Stu Inman. When things were going bad in the office, head out on the road. More important, since it appeared we were headed for the lottery, I needed to see the top players as many times as possible. So it was on to the NCAA tournament and the Final Four. I always enjoy the Final Four. I like the college atmosphere and the competition, and it is a chance to network with the thousands of coaches and athletic directors in attendance. It allowed me to quiz coaches about basketball trends in general and players in particular.

The Final Four is followed by the Portsmouth Invitational tournament in Portsmouth, Virginia, the Desert Classic in Phoenix, and the NBA pre-draft camp in Chicago. These tournaments gave us a chance to see the top prospects in the upcoming draft compete against each other, although, in recent years, agents kept the best players out of these competitions for fear that they would get hurt or see their value drop. Since every general manager or player personnel director is there, it gives us the opportunity to interview prospects, talk trades, do mock drafts, and confirm rumors. When these post-season tournaments are over, we have a pretty good handle on what teams are going to do in the draft.

This spring, Simmie, the scouts, and I were required to do double duty. It was to be the inaugural season for the Women's National Basketball Association. Cleveland was granted a franchise, so we had to get acquainted with women's basketball in a hurry. Women's basketball had been growing in popularity, and the performance by our gold-medal winning women's Olympic team generated many fans. I must admit that the Rockers provided a refreshing departure from all the backbiting going on with the Cavs.

After three weeks on the road scouting NBA prospects—or "suspects" as scouting guru Marty Blake would say—I was glad to get home. The post-season routine was difficult but necessary. Now it was time to focus on the draft.

We finished the 1996–97 season 42–40 and were eliminated from the play-offs with a loss to Washington in the last game of the regular season. This meant that we had the thirteenth pick in the draft, unless a miracle happened at the lottery. There was no way Tim Duncan would be there at Number 13. He was going to be the first player taken. Whoever was lucky enough to get the first pick was not going to trade it.

Monday morning I walked into the office and was faced with yet another surprise. The coaches were sequestered in the assistant coaches' office most of the morning. When I asked what they were doing, I was told they were working on their post-season evaluations. I wondered why they were not in the small conference room where they usually met. The coaches would do their evaluations before they met with Simmie and me, then we would all go over our strengths and weaknesses and our needs before we met with our owners.

Mike came out of the assistant coaches' office and told me Watson had called him and asked him to prepare two lists. Watson wanted our players ranked against the rest of The League and he wanted a list of NBA stars in order of preference. Mike told me this was to preempt our usual meeting when we talked about our team and our needs.

"I'm just doing what I was told to do," Mike said, heading back into the assistant coaches' office.

Simmie later came to my office wondering what was going on. He, too, had noticed that the coaches were acting secretly. There was very little communication with Gary and me, as if they were hiding something from us. At any rate, we definitely were not invited to participate.

That afternoon I received a call from Gordon advising me of a meeting with the ownership group on Thursday afternoon. This, too, was unusual, since Gary and I had just returned from scouting and did not have time to do our customary post-season reports. Something was up.

The coaches, Simmie, scout Darrell Hedrick, and I sat waiting for the board to assemble. Mike brought a flip chart and an easel into the board room. The pages were hidden until Gordon opened the meeting by asking us what we had. Gary and I looked at each other while Mike leaped up to uncover his charts. It was like unveiling a piece of art. He began tearing pages from the flip chart and pasting them to the walls. He had enough sheets to cover three walls. Gary and I tried to figure out what was before us. Gordon and the suits sat eagerly awaiting commentary. Watson was checking the screen on his laptop computer to make sure it was ready.

"Let's see what you've got, Mike," Gordon said. "We need a plan."

My heart dropped into my stomach as I realized I was no longer in charge of the team. When I was in charge, Gordon always asked me to begin the meeting. When I was in charge, it was my plan we considered—and I always had a plan. When I was in charge, I knew going in what we would discuss. Now I sat anxiously, waiting to see what kind of plan the coaches would present.

Mike began explaining the charts. He started with the ranking of our players against the rest of The League. He started with point guards. There were three levels with five players in each. Terrell was in the third- or worst-tier. Bobby Phills was in the third tier of shooting guards. Chris Mills was in the third class of small forwards. Hill was in the third class of power forwards.

As we wordlessly perused the wall, every so often we got an editorial comment from Ronnie.

"Mike did a hell of a job coaching for this bunch to win forty-two games," he would say.

Then Mike unveiled the "star list." To no one's surprise, Michael Jordan was at the top of that list, followed by Shawn Kemp, Karl Malone, David Robinson, Antoine Walker, and on and on.

When Mike finished talking, Gordon turned to me. "Do you agree with this list, Wayne?" he asked.

All eyes were focused on me for my reaction.

"I was not a part of the process," I muttered. "This the first time I've seen the lists. Give me a minute to digest them."

Gordon seemed surprised and said, "This the first time that you have seen this?"

I thought I had better speak up before Ronnie told us again what a wonderful job of coaching Mike had done with such an inferior bunch of athletes.

"I think that our guys are ranked too low," I said, and I should have added that I had not signed or extended any contracts without checking to see how the players fit into Mike's plans. "Terrell Brandon is one of the top point guards in The League. *Sports Illustrated* did a rating of all facets of the game pertaining to a point guard, and he was ranked Number 1. And he is only twenty-six years old. He has not reached his peak yet. I'd rank Bobby higher. He was second team NBA All-Defensive team. His scoring is improving, and he is still young. I'd rank

Chris and Tyrone, who was an All-Star in 1995, higher than the coaches have them."

Gordon listened to me, but then he took the floor.

"The reason for this drill is that we have to get out of mediocrity, and these guys aren't going to do it for us," he said. "We must be aggressive in securing a star. We need at least two stars if we expect to win a championship. What about the star list? I expect each of you to be aggressive calling coaches and GMs in an effort to find a trade for one of the stars on the list. It doesn't matter who calls."

I realized this would lead to chaos and would make us the laughingstock of The League.

"I disagree with some of the players that are on the star list," I said. "I know that Jordan is not available, and most of the others are not either. Those who might be available have character deficits or are aging and their skills are deteriorating and I wouldn't recommend them for the Cavs.

"I agree that superstars and stars can facilitate winning, but we may have them in the players we have on our roster if we remain patient."

As I spoke I could feel every eye in the room on me. David Prescott, who had asked the infamous question in my first interview, had been staring me down from the moment I entered the room.

"How do you know?" Watson asked. Then, speaking like an accountant, not a general manager, he said, "Anyone is available for the right price."

I tried to bring them back to reality.

"I talk to GMs about availability of players often, either by phone or when we are together on the road," I said. "Other teams aren't anxious to trade their stars. They aren't here to make us better. Furthermore, Bobby and Chris are free agents, so they have no value. A team can wait until July and sign them. They're not going to give us anything for them."

I took a deep breath. "I would like to talk about plan B," I said.

"There will be no plan B," Gordon shouted from the head of the table.

As I tried to get over my shock, Gordon announced that we were going to meet weekly for the next several weeks so that we could give progress reports.

I continued to believe that if we were lucky in the lottery and our young veterans continued to improve and remain healthy, we would again contend in the Eastern Conference. We would peak as aging Miami and New York declined. Our key guys would have played together for several years. An experienced lineup of Hill, Ilgauskas, Phills, Brandon, Mills, Potopenko, and Ferry, along with whomever we could get in the draft and a free agent or two, would go beyond the first round of the play-offs in a couple of years. The perception was that none of these guys were stars or had fan appeal. We were experiencing attrition in season ticket sales, and our marketing department insisted that we needed a star to sell to the fans. I knew better. I knew winning was what would attract fans.

But the star syndrome was the new trend in the NBA. If you did not have one, you created one by over-promoting a given player, even if his best attribute was his hairstyle, his tattoo, or his slam dunks on SportsCenter. Michael's superstardom created this phenomenon. The League has had superstars since its inception. Each generation had them. These players were legitimate superstars who were team players and led their teams to championships. They emerged off of winning teams. They had substance to their game. Only a few stars are born. You can draft potential stars, and drafting in the top three enhances the chance of getting a potential star. Seldom can you trade for a star, and seldom does a star become a free agent. Players will become free agents if they are unhappy in an environment, which was a concern that I had. Players also will become free agents to go to a more desirable market.

Amid all this, we went on to the lottery—and we came back with the Number 13 pick. What did you expect with all the bad karma going around our offices?

Oddly enough, the thing that most surprised me that weekend had nothing to do with the lottery, or the trade rumors that inevitably followed. It was a comment that Commissioner David Stern made. We were discussing some of the problems facing The League, such as the trash talking, which I hated. During the conversation, I mentioned that I was feeling a bit insecure in Cleveland. David and I had an open relationship over the years and I was waiting for a reaction. He surprised me by saying, "I would like to see you in Milwaukee." The conversation ended there.

The entire team division was in Chicago for the NBA pre-draft camp, which is always held in early June. We had meetings over lunch or dinner daily to discuss the players we were watching or the draft in general. We also discussed any trade possibilities, since every general manager and coach was there. We also reviewed our roster again. I told Mike I still believed our players were better than he and his staff rated them. I asked him if he had changed his mind about any of them, and he said he had changed his mind on Mills.

In keeping with their quest for a superstar, Gordon and the board flew to Chicago to meet with us. But, as I had predicted, we were not having much luck in pursuing a trade for anyone on the so-called "star list." The responses varied between, "Are you crazy?" and "You know better than that."

There was no better news when we met the next week back in Cleveland. We eliminated the definite nos and dwelled on some maybes, although in my opinion, the maybes were dubious stars. I still thought our guys were better. But it did not matter. We spent several hours rehashing the same thing.

One thing we did agree on was how much we would spend on two free agents. I thought that Phills and Mills could be signed in the $3–$4 million range even though they were going to demand more.

We were bringing players in for interviews as we prepared for the 1997 draft. We opted to take the Phoenix pick that we got in the John Williams trade. We had the Numbers 13 and 16 picks and were able to get the two players we wanted. We drafted Kentucky's Derek Anderson with the first pick and came back and drafted Stanford's Brevin Knight with the second. Gary and I thought that Derek could become a star in time. He was a six-foot-five-inch guard with blazing speed. He would give us depth behind Phills. The five-foot-ten-inch Knight would give us depth at point. We were pleased.

Gordon and I met once more to discuss a contract extension. Dick had negotiated a new contract for Mike and the assistant coaches, giving them sizable raises. Gordon was hoping to make a joint announcement, but I would not accept the offer they made me because it was much less than what some of my less experienced peers were making. We agreed to disagree. They made the announcement that Mike and the coaches had signed contract extensions. With that out of the way, we went back to work trying to acquire a star.

It had been several weeks and nothing was even close to happening. Gordon was not going to give up. I understood that. He was committed to trying to get a star on this team. He scheduled a meeting for the following week so that we could continue the process. It was early evening when the meeting ended, and I went to my office to see if I had any messages. As I scanned the pink message slips that Karen had neatly placed near my phone, Dick entered my office and closed the door.

"You need to do something about your body language, young man," he shouted. "You are like a linebacker."

I was startled by his unexpected entry and none-too-pleased with how he addressed me.

"What do you mean?" I asked him.

"If you disagree with something you dig in like a linebacker," he said.

Then he said something I will never forget.

"We wish there were a graceful way out of this relationship," he told me. "Gordon wants to do your job."

Frankly, by this point, I was not surprised. The dynamics of the organization had changed, and my power was diminishing.

"Then why didn't you give Milwaukee permission to talk to me?" I asked.

"That would have been a disaster," he said.

I was not sure what he meant. Was he worried about having to compete against me if I left? If he feared I would be successful elsewhere, why did he not believe I would be successful with the Cavs? He knew how rejection inspired me. He and I had many talks about that, and he knew enough about my childhood to understand how I had used rejection as a springboard to success. Was he worried about the reaction of the fans and the business community, particularly the African Americans in each group? He did not have to worry about that. Blacks have come to realize that if we deserve to be hired, we must accept being fired if there is just cause or if a relationship ceases to work, which was what seemed to be happening here. Equal opportunity works both ways. It is only a disaster if discrimination is involved. If the Cavs did not want me, I did not understand Gordon refusing to give Milwaukee owner Herb Kohl permission to talk to me about a job with that organization. It is a common practice in sports. I will say Gordon was consistent. He refused to give the New Jersey owners permission to talk to Mike about their vacant coaching job. The difference was that Gordon wanted to keep Mike and signed him to a twenty-million dollar contract extension. In my case, the Cavs did not want me and did not want anyone else to have me, either. It seemed they wanted to control my destiny and force me to resign or retire, two options that did not interest me.

I did not know what to say to Dick, but I finally managed to tell him, "I am leaving at the end of the June anyway, Dick. I don't want to be any place I'm not wanted."

He said, "You can't leave. We've got you as a consultant for two more years."

As I got up to leave the room, I said, "We'll see."

It got worse. Dick presided over our next meeting in Gordon's absence. Mike and Ronnie were not at the meeting, either. Mike was off doing television, and I had no idea where Ronnie was. We again gave progress reports. Still nothing.

Finally, Dick asked Gary and me if we would trade Hill and Brandon for Shawn Kemp.

"If . . . ," Gary began.

But before he could finish, Watson interrupted.

"If you two don't do something you have failed," he yelled. "YOU . . . HAVE . . . FAILED. Do you understand me?"

I slammed my notebook shut, causing board member John Graham, who was seated next to me, to nearly jump from his seat.

"Wayne, calm down," John whispered.

"Let's get out of here, Gary," I said to Simmie. "We are gone at the end of the year anyway."

With Sid Lowe and John looking on, I left the room.

Dick called me from his car several minutes later to tell me that what he said was not meant for me.

Yeah, sure, I thought.

Timeout Number Five

When the Women's National Basketball Association came into existence in 1997, I was no stranger to women's basketball, because I had been running a basketball camp for girls for fifteen years. I ran the camp with Kathy Delaney-Smith, the coach at Harvard, and Ron Spinney, a high school coach in the Boston area. Like the camp I ran for boys, the staff was made up of college and high school coaches in the region. College coaches also would come in and lecture.

To prepare for the inaugural WNBA draft, I hired as a consultant Alfreda Harris, who was my assistant recreation director when I was director of recreation in Boston. Alfie was well known in women's basketball. I also asked Gordon Gund's permission to hire Gayle Bibby-Crème to oversee the team that we eventually named the Rockers. Gayle had had many duties as a Cavs employee. Gordon agreed that Gayle was the right person to get our team launched. We had learned over the years that if we wanted something done right, we would put Gayle on it. So in the spring of 1997, Gayle and Alfie joined Gary Fitzsimmons, the scouts, and me in Orlando to scout the players for the WNBA. Gayle and I hired Linda Hill-McDonald as head coach and Susan Yow and Mike Wilhelm as her assistants. We then had a dispersal draft of the pros playing elsewhere and a college draft. We now had a staff and a team, and we were ready to embark on a new challenge. Gayle was in charge, and I was ready to get back to the rebuilding of the Cavs.

It was great to watch the Rockers come together as a team. The squad was composed of veteran players who had been playing in Europe. Lynette Woodard, the first female member of the Harlem Globetrotters and one of the best players to play the game, Janice Braxton, Michelle Edwards, Isabelle Fijalkowski, and Eva Nemcova were the veteran players. We were able to supplement them with our draft picks, Rushia Brown, Merlakia Jones, Jenny Boucek, and some free agents. Team building was the first thing we had to do. Gayle and I had to have several sessions with the coaches and players individually and collectively to establish a winning attitude, but because we had drafted players of character for this team, just as I had done throughout my career, I knew we would be fine. We struggled early in the season but turned it around and we began to win. At least this part of my job was fun. Being a part of their enthusiasm was uplifting for me.

CHAPTER 19

The Reignman Cometh

I was still trying to acquire that "star" player for the Cavs. As the summer progressed, the "star" list grew smaller as we crossed off the names of players who were unavailable. The one player who was high on Mike's list was Seattle's All-Star power forward Shawn Kemp. Because Mike liked him, Watson liked him. Shawn never played college basketball and came into the NBA at the age of nineteen. He was nicknamed "The Reignman." At first he was known for his thunderous dunks, but as his game broadened, he became a perennial All-Star and was one of the most gifted athletes to play in The League. He was absolutely magnificent during the NBA Finals against the Chicago Bulls in 1996. Despite all that, I had reservations about him. I was concerned that his body might be breaking down. He had played a lot of games the past eight years. I also had concerns about his character, and we did not need that on a young team. After the World Championships or the Olympics, the selection committee always had a debriefing, and I had heard a lot of negative things about Shawn after the 1994 World Championships. Still, every time I called Seattle general manager Wally Walker over the summer, he denied Shawn was on the market.

I felt it would only be a matter of time until Shawn was available. His feud with management and coach George Karl had been well publicized. Part of the problem was his salary. All-Star point guard Gary Payton had just received a monster contract, and my old friend Ron Grinker had gotten an outrageous amount of money from the Sonics for unproductive free agent center Jim McIlvaine. (Thank goodness they made that mistake. We were negotiating for McIlvaine, too. I have always said the best trades are the ones that you do not make, and the best signings are the ones that you do not get.) Once McIlvaine came on board, Shawn wanted to renegotiate the remaining years on his contract so that he would remain the Sonics' highest-paid player. But because of salary cap rules, Seattle was stuck and could not give Kemp any more money. Seattle's options were to trade him or let him remain there as a malcontent and destroy the morale of the team.

With that melodrama going on in Seattle, unrestricted free agents Chris Mills and Bobby Phills left Cleveland, as I had expected they would. Mills went to Boston and Phills to Charlotte for slightly above the salaries Gordon was willing to pay. Gordon based his offers on the coaches' rankings and perceptions, which I thought undervalued both players. In fact, neither thought we were sincere in our attempt to sign them, plus both were tired of Mike's constant haranguing. Gordon did bend a little because of our lack of success in making a deal for a "star," but it was too late. Man, I was sad to see those two good guys go. Bobby was mentally and physically tough, and he guarded Jordan as well as any one person could. He also was a leader, something every team needs. Chris was just a solid player and would play in any team's eight-man rotation. Neither had yet reached his peak. With them gone, we were really going to be young at the guards. And, again, we let two good players go without getting anything in return. That was no way to rebuild a franchise.

We also lost another key person who shared the responsibility for the Cavs' rise in the 1980s and 1990s. Gary Fitzsimmons did a great job of supervising our scouting efforts. Whenever we needed a player for a ten-day contract, he immediately had the right person. He found Craig Ehlo and Bobby Phills, both of whom became key players for us. Gordon, in keeping with the infamous letter he had sent me, negotiated with Gary and failed to reach an agreement. Meanwhile, former Milwaukee assistant coach Garry St. Jean had become general manager of Golden State and was looking for a personnel director. He snapped up Gary, leaving me in a void in many ways. In addition to Simmie's duties as director of player personnel, he was a great friend and an alter ego for me. He and I spent many hours talking about our team and players in The League and in college who could make us better. I would miss him tremendously.

I headed for The League meetings in Orlando intent on continuing our "star search" but knowing that trades were rarely made at these meetings. There were many meetings over breakfast or lunch and lots of conversations on the golf course, but usually nothing happened. I approached Wally in the hallway on the first day of the meetings, but he was not interested in anything I had to say. I decided that I was going to be persistent, so I sat next to him during the meeting. He was going to get tired of me over the next several days, but, just as in any challenge I had undertaken, I was determined not to fail. And even though I did not completely believe in this plan of action, Gordon and Watson had made it clear that not pulling this off constituted failure.

One of the main topics of conversation at these meetings was the salary cap. Commissioner David Stern, Deputy Commissioner Russ Granik, along with league executives Rod Thorn and Matt Winick, plus every lawyer in The League office, were there to explain the cap for the umpteenth time and scold those who tried to circumvent it. We also discussed the image of The League and what we could do to protect it. Presentations were made by the television networks and merchandise manufacturers. Matt, the schedule maker, talked to us about dates in our buildings. Rule changes and the state of the game were discussed at the competition committee meeting with far fewer people in attendance.

The image of The League was high on everyone's mind. Trash talking and excessive physical play were at an all-time high, and a number of players had been arrested in off-court incidents. Given that trend, maybe we should not have been surprised the next season when Golden State's Latrell Sprewell tried to choke Coach P. J. Carlesimo in an altercation during practice in one of the most notorious incidents in league history. But even before that, I was adamantly opposed to the direction The League was headed and often expressed my opinions during these meetings.

With the many problems in society, particularly problems facing the young people who were so often victims of their environments, I wanted to suggest something that we had done at our conventions when I was a McDonald's owner-operator. In an effort to improve communications between different cultures, we invited experts to hold workshops on various changes taking place in society and offer suggestions on how to deal with those changes. I raised my hand to ask a question of the commissioner.

"Would it be worthwhile to invite a social scientist to our meetings to give us a refresher course in sociology, so that we can better manage our product, which is our players?" I respectfully asked. My thinking was that in order to manage anyone you had to understand where they came from and what they had been through. That was the theory behind all the diversity and sensitivity training sessions that were becoming mandatory in the business world. I thought that if the NBA sponsored the sessions, rather than the individual teams, all of us would benefit from the same message.

The response was a cold one. "That is not appropriate for these meetings," the commissioner said.

End of conversation.

An incident at the competition committee meeting the next morning confirmed my suspicions that I was all but finished in the NBA. We were talking about drafting high school players. I was curious as to whether this would encourage more high school players to bypass college. I raised my hand to ask the question. As soon as the commissioner saw my hand go up, he stopped in mid-sentence and said, "Here goes Wayne picking on me again."

"Okay, I won't ask the question," I quickly responded. I was appalled by his statement. All I wanted to do was ask a question and offer a constructive comment.

The meeting continued with a discussion about officiating. Still perplexed about Stern's comment, I decided to take a break. I removed myself from the U-shaped table where the other twenty-eight members of the committee were sitting and took a seat in a chair against the wall on the far side of the room. I was trying to figure out what to say to the commissioner when I confronted him after the meeting. I needed to know what the problem was.

I did not have to wait until the meeting was finished. A few minutes later, David Stern came over and sat down next to me.

"Wayne, you should think about retiring," he said.

I had no response. After a few minutes passed, the commissioner continued, "What makes you think Milwaukee will pay you a lot of money?"

I was angry, and offended, but I kept my cool. I still did not respond. I could not believe what I was hearing. Why should I retire at the age of sixty-two? Was this age discrimination? Or was this some other type of discrimination? Was I being blackballed? The last I knew there were general managers and coaches in The League older than I. And what did money have to do with anything? Was I not entitled to make money? All the salaries in the NBA had escalated, even the commissioner's. I thought back to those odd jobs I had done with my uncles and my friends growing up back in Springfield. I thought of my first contract as general manager of the Bucks. Being paid less than whites for equal work had been a fact of life for my generation, but I thought those days were past. I could not help but think of Jim Fitzgerald's question ten years ago when he asked me why I got back into the NBA with Cleveland? I could not help but wonder whether there was a conspiracy to get me to retire. If they wanted me out, why not just fire me? It remains a mystery to me why they collaborated and handled my dismissal in this manner. On the other hand, if they could make it seem as if I was retiring as opposed to resigning, it would look as if I would not be interested in any other jobs.

When we were at the lottery a few months earlier, the commissioner had volunteered that he would like to see me in Milwaukee. I always thought he and I had a good relationship. I had held many leadership posts in The League, and he had never given me any indication he did not like me or my ideas. I wondered what had changed in the past few months and why I was being driven out of the league. Was the commissioner sorry he had named me to those leadership positions? Did he resent the fact others saw me as a leader? I had heard many times about Watson's relationship with the commissioner. Watson loved to boast that he was the commissioner's lawyer, and Gordon was chairman of the NBA's Board of Governors, so he had a close relationship with Stern. It seemed now those relationships were taking precedence.

Whatever was going on made me more determined to make the deal Gordon and Watson wanted me to make. After the competition committee meeting, I approached Wally Walker as we were walking to lunch. This time he was receptive to talking. He said he was working on something with Milwaukee involving Shawn and Vin Baker. Seattle wanted Baker, but Milwaukee was not keen on Kemp. Bob Weinhauer, Milwaukee's general manager, suggested Walker talk to me about Brandon and Hill. The stage was set. I called Gordon to inform him of the conversation, and he was excited. I forced myself to show some enthusiasm then and in the ensuing days of working on the deal. I did not feel good about it, but it did not matter. I was following instructions.

While working out the details of the trade and reviewing the contracts, I continued to do my due diligence. I talked to everyone I knew who had anything to do with Shawn. I talked to his former coaches and players. I came up with three pages of notes, most of which were not good. I was most concerned about rumors of drug usage. I read my notes to the group during a break in the negotiations hoping to discourage Gordon. There was quiet in the room until Gordon turned toward me and asked, "Should we make this trade?"

I hesitated for a moment before responding. I could not help but remember Watson's declaration months earlier: "If you two don't do something, you have failed."

I swallowed. "Yes, I think so," I softly responded in words I would live to regret. I still did not think Gordon would go through with it after I presented my report.

There was a big risk in making this trade. Watson insisted that we had to take a risk if we were going to get a "star." The bigger the risk, the bigger the reward, was his theory. Gordon, Watson, and I got back on the phone with Herb Kohl and Bob Weinhauer to work out the details, which included Brandon, Hill, and a first-round draft pick for Kemp. With the proper lottery protection on the pick, we had a deal.

In some ways, this was not fair to Shawn, who had been in the Finals two years earlier. Now he was going to be twenty-eight years old, and the rest of our players were in their early twenties. By the time they peaked, Shawn would be approaching retirement. I did not like the chemistry. With this group, the players would look to Shawn to be a leader. I was not sure that was in his nature. In fact, given the rumors I had heard, I did not want him to influence our young players. We were going to have at least four rookies on the team.

But I had done my job. We had a "star." Still, I was mad at myself. I always said what I meant, and that time I did not. I compromised. Grandpa would not have been proud. I should have told Gordon I could not make the deal and resigned right there and then. I thought about it. I do not think it would have mattered. Kemp was the only "star" available, and they were determined to have him. They would have made the deal with me or without me. At this stage in my career, I was trying to survive, just as many other coaches and general managers had done. So I went along with the program, kept my mouth shut, and did as I was told. I have no one to blame but myself.

Mike and his staff were meeting in a suite at the Renaissance Hotel. I had called Mike periodically during the negotiations to keep him informed of our progress and, when the deal was consummated, I went over to the hotel to personally deliver the news. I walked into the room and sat by a flip chart that contained a list of our players by position. I took a marker and added the name of Shawn Kemp to the power forwards.

"The deal is done, I got your man," I said.

"Great job, Big Man," each of the coaches said as they extended their hands upward for high-fives. They were happy. I had gotten the player they had ranked second behind Jordan on their star list.

Now came the hard part. Calling players to tell them that they had been traded had not gotten easier over the years. Tyrone was hurt. A Cincinnati native who liked being close to home, he thought he was going to retire a Cavalier. It took us a season to earn his trust. He was an extremely sensitive person and demanded a lot of attention, but most players of his generation needed a lot of attention. Probably the most memorable exchange between Tyrone and me came during the 1995 play-offs, after I had learned he had taken a limo from Cleveland to New York for the opening of the post-season. A nervous flier, he refused to get back on the team plane after it had flown through terrifying turbulence while returning to Cleveland from a road game at the end of the season. "We are a team," I barked at him in the locker room while ordering him to resume traveling with our party. Now he was no longer part of that team.

Terrell was more nonchalant about it. He was grateful to the Cavs for the opportunity to develop into a solid player. Both had served the Cavs well. We also were going to miss Charlotte Brandon and the work that she was doing to create an organization for the mothers of the players.

That evening Mike and I joined Gordon, Watson, and the board members for dinner in a private room at a downtown restaurant. The mood was joyous as we talked about our recent transaction. My mood was ambivalent. It became more so as I was talking to John Graham, who was sitting to my right. Watson and Mike were having a separate conversation at the far end of the table. I overheard one comment that certainly caught my attention.

"Finally," Watson told Mike, "the line of authority flows from Gordon to me to you and then Wayne."

Later, after they had all left, our waitress came up to me and said, "I hope those weren't your friends. They cut you up pretty good."

I did not talk to anyone about what I heard. I filed those statements along with the rest. I was a lame duck. My efforts in getting them a "star" did not matter after all. And it had cost me my self-respect.

Shawn was excited about coming to Cleveland. Of course, he would have been pleased to go to any team that had room to satisfy his salary needs. We had the room under the salary cap to adjust his contract. Although he still had two years left on his existing contract, we knew we would have to restructure it to make him happy.

The hastily called press conference was well attended, despite the fact that it was at 8 P.M. on September 25, 1997. Gordon, Mike, Shawn, and his mother sat at the dais, and as I introduced Shawn to a room filled with reporters and Cavs and Gund Arena employees, I could sense the excitement. That was not to say that the media took it easy on the newest Cav. Reporters asked tough questions about what had happened in Seattle. They asked about his rift with George Karl, the coach. They asked about rumors of alcoholism. They asked whether he expected a new contract. To his credit, Shawn handled all the questions like a pro. He was candid and seemed to be truthful. He talked about being from Indiana and wanting to get back to the Midwest to be closer to his family. He was very complimentary of our organization, and particularly me.

After the press conference Tony Dutt, Shawn's agent, told me how happy they were to have Shawn in Cleveland. "Shawn needs a person who will be honest and direct, and that's what we have heard about you," Tony said with Shawn looking on.

I thanked them, but I told Shawn I had had two big reservations about making the trade.

"The first reason is your age and where you have been in your career," I said. "Our team is young and inexperienced. It may be frustrating for you living with rookie mistakes. And I have heard that there are character issues. But you are a Cavalier now and we are starting anew, and I am looking forward to working with you."

I shared my comments with Barbara, Shawn's mother, and she was happy to know that I was prepared to be the father influence that I had heard Shawn never had. In another conversation, Tony told me Shawn really needed some tough love and I was the one person that could do it. Little did I know that Tony and I were going to become good friends over the next couple of years. And little did they know I was on my way out.

Gordon, Watson, and I had a get-acquainted meeting with Tony Dutt in New York to listen to his contract demands. To no one's surprise, he wanted every penny of cap room that we had—and more. There was no question that Shawn was about to become the highest-paid Cavalier ever and one of the highest-paid players in The League. Watson, who had taken over contract negotiations, had his work cut out for him. I was beginning to realize that Mike and I had our work cut out for us, too. Every time Tony and I were alone, he would reiterate how much Shawn needed me and how much he needed my help.

"We'll be talking a lot," he said to me as we departed the New York meeting.

I turned my attention back to our team. Ilgauskas had come back from foot surgery and looked good in the summer league and our informal workouts before training camp starters. With him healthy, and a great insider player like Shawn, I needed another shooter on the team. Mike and I talked about how the defense would sag on the two if we did not get one. I had liked Wes Person in the 1994 draft because he was one of the premier shooters available. He was playing sparingly in Phoenix, and I happened to know that the Colangelos, my friend Jerry and his son Bryan, who was the new general manager, were looking to clear some cap room. So we traded a future first-round pick to get Wes.

"The Big Man is on a roll," Mike said at the press conference to introduce Wes.

While I was busy making the Person deal, Watson was busy trying to get Shawn signed. Watson and Dutt agreed on a contract the day training camp was to begin. Dick found a way to make the numbers work by back-loading the contract. Shawn would be paid $20 million and $25 million in the last two years of the contract. With the dollars agreed upon, Watson called Gordon to report on the progress. There was one hitch. The Seattle contract had a weight clause in it. The contract had a clause that gave the team the right to fine Shawn $150,000 if he reported to training camp weighing over 265 pounds. Dutt wanted that clause stricken from the contract or at least raised to 275. Gordon asked me what I thought, and I adamantly recommended it stay at 265. I knew that as players aged it became more difficult to get into shape, and I knew Shawn had to be in shape because of his body structure. He had tiny ankles and legs for his size, and the more weight he carried, the more likely he was to sustain injuries. Watson told Gordon that Shawn would never sign the contract if the weight clause was not changed. Gordon came to our training camp at the University of Dayton, and the contract was signed under Dutt's terms, with a weight limit of 275.

Shawn became a $100 million man, and he was all ours. I remembered what Red always said, "As long as a player is on your team he is part of your family. Treat him accordingly. Make him feel wanted and important."

I did not know exactly what Tony Dutt had in mind for me, but I was going to take on the challenge of being a positive influence on Shawn. I had learned the past couple of years that communication was going to be more important than ever with the players. We were well into the hip-hop generation, and this group of athletes had different needs. They had been coddled and exploited their entire lives by the Amateur Athletic Union coaches in the summers, by unscrupulous college recruiters and by agents. Many came from single-parent homes that lacked a father figure, and they craved discipline. They needed someone to care about them as people, not just as conduits to the lavish lifestyles awaiting young, talented basketball players. Shawn needed this love and attention more than many of them, because he had literally grown up in The League. A variety of circumstances prevented him from playing college basketball, so he had gone from the arms of his family into the NBA. As a result, the circle of those he trusted was extremely small. Everyone knew who he was, but no one really knew him. As our relationship grew, I was amazed that someone so talented had so little self-confidence. As I would soon find out, that was at the root of many of his problems.

Chapter 20

Trouble on All Fronts

Shawn Kemp was welcomed to Cleveland with great enthusiasm that fall of 1997. Of course, our marketing department wasted no time collaborating with Shawn's agent and Reebok to increase his visibility. Billboards went up around the city. Most of our print and video advertising featured Shawn. Receptions were held to introduce the new Reignman shoe. Much of this occurred before we played a game in the 1997–98 season.

While all of this was going on, I was hoping Shawn was all right. I was worried we were making him so big that if any of his character flaws were ever exposed, it would deflate his image and that of the franchise and The League.

I was thinking that this would be my last season as president and general manager, and I was inspired by recent events to leave the franchise a winner. Despite Shawn's presence, creating a winning environment was going to take time because of the number of rookies and young players on our roster. Danny Ferry and Shawn were the only true veterans. Managing the different cultures in our locker room was going to be a challenge. But the biggest challenge was going to be managing Shawn. In one of our last meetings, Tony Dutt told me, "Wayne, I really need your assistance in helping Shawn to get his life in order." I kept hoping he was exaggerating.

I had put a contract extension out of mind and was preparing myself to conquer other challenges outside the game and The League I loved and had been involved with for forty years. But then one day I received an unexpected call from Gordon wanting to open dialogue about an extension. I refused to talk directly with him and suggested that he and I remove our emotions from the negotiations. I told him that I was going to be represented by an attorney, George Andrews, and his brother, Paul, a financial adviser. I told Gordon to have Watson call George. This took Gordon by surprise. I had never used an agent. But I decided to use one this time because things had gotten so adversarial in our last talks, and I wanted to preserve the mutual respect that we had for each other.

Dick and George initiated negotiations, but it was not until we met in good old Suite 999 at Dick's Airport Sheraton that we agreed on a deal. It was where I had signed my first contract. Now I was back to sign my last. George and I met Gordon, Dick, and John Graham there. Gordon spoke first. "We would like to extend your contract for two years as president/general manager and two years as a consultant. I would like you to submit a list of potential successors to replace you in two years. We will pay you in a competitive range of the other general managers with your experience."

Ignoring my many years in business, Gordon felt he had to explain to me how major companies liked to have an executive succession plan in place. Dick and John reiterated that the contract would be for only two years. It was clear to me that I really was not wanted beyond the two years. I was not sure that I was even wanted at all. I remembered Watson's words when he burst into my office several months earlier, "We wish there was a graceful way out of this relationship."

George opened his mouth to respond, but I interrupted him.

"I do not, let me repeat, do not want to be anywhere I'm not wanted," I said. "I was taught as a boy to stay away from places I wasn't wanted. I was taught never to engage in a pseudorelationship. There is no way a person could keep their dignity."

"Furthermore, you don't need to explain executive succession to me.

I am quite familiar with the process. Remember, I sit on four corporate boards."

George made a counter offer, which Gordon accepted. Then he ordered Dick to write the contract, which would pay me $2.5 million over the two years. When I received a copy of the contract to review, I called George right away.

"George, I can't accept the paragraph that says I must do as directed by ownership," I told him. "That means I have no authority."

George sounded as if he knew what my reaction would be before he sent me the contract.

"Wayne, it's all right," he said. "You must understand they don't want you. If you had not pursued the Kemp trade as you were instructed, they would not have offered you this contract. This is a nice severance package for you. Just sign it. You deserve it for all that you have done for the franchise."

So I signed the contract, put it all behind me, and focused on my job, attempting to carry on as I always had done. My dedication and commitment to the game and my desire to succeed in rebuilding the team was as strong as ever. I also submitted a list of possible successors to Gordon. From that list, we interviewed two prospects: Billy Knight, a great NBA player who had become vice president of basketball for the Indiana Pacers; and Jim Paxson, another former NBA player who was assistant general manager in Portland. Paxson was briefly a Cavalier until a trade that sent Keith Lee to Portland for Paxson was overturned when Lee did not pass the physical. After the interviews, Gordon hired Paxson as vice president of basketball operation for the Cavs. We also hired former Philadelphia center Marc Iavaroni to work with Vitaly and Zydrunas. I finally had a coach more than six-feet tall.

The new-look 1997–98 edition of the Cavaliers with superstar Shawn Kemp started the season with much enthusiasm. Shawn was every bit the exciting player everybody thought he would be. But it was the play of Ilgauskas and the rookies that caught the attention of everyone. Mike did a good job of creating a competitive chemistry. Wes Person was shooting well and starting at two guard, backed up by the lightning quick Derek Anderson. Mike tried starting Bobby Sura at the point, but Sura gave way to another rookie, Brevin Knight. Sura was better coming off the bench, playing either guard position. Brevin was the son of a high school coach and, like Mark Price, grew up in the game. Pete Newell, the basketball legend who was now a consultant for the Cavs, said Knight was one of the best leaders he had ever seen. The surprise starter at the small forward was another rookie, Cedric Henderson, a late second-round pick. We were winning, and things were going well. Shawn was voted a starter for the All-Star Game, the first time the fans had voted a Cavalier into the starting lineup. We became the first team to have four rookies selected for the Rookie Game that had become a part of the All-Star weekend, and Ilgauskas was voted the MVP of the game.

Publicly, everything seemed to be going great. But behind the scenes, things were not running so smoothly. In fact, after one month with Shawn, Mike wanted me to trade him away. The coach said he could not handle his tardiness and his lackadaisical practice and workout habits. A few weeks before the All-Star Game, Tony Dutt called and asked if we could meet to talk about Shawn. He was coming to Cleveland to meet with Shawn to go over some personal business. When Tony and I met, Tony had not met with Shawn. He had not been able to locate him. We spent a good portion of the day together sharing some mutual concerns about Shawn. Mike had fined Shawn several times for being late for practices, flights, and buses. This habitual tardiness was not a good sign. I had learned from my experiences in Milwaukee that tardiness was the first sign of drug abuse.

I asked Tony whether Shawn was using drugs. He confirmed there were problems and pleaded for my assistance in helping Shawn. He also had other problems. He had several pending paternity suits, and Tony was concerned about how Shawn would cope with the stress caused by this. The more I talked to Tony, the more empathy I had for Shawn, his mother, his girlfriend Mervina, and even Tony. I also was worried about our franchise and our fans. It would not be long before his problems, which were now our problems, would be public knowledge. I started my career doing damage control and crisis management in Milwaukee, and it appeared as if I was going to end my career the same way. I finally understood what Tony meant when he said Shawn needed a father figure to help him get straightened out, and I understood I was it.

It was while we were in New York for the All-Star Weekend that we learned it was about to hit the fan. A national magazine had been tipped off about Shawn's paternity suits and was ready to break the story. I got so many calls in my hotel room that eventually I had to have my phone blocked. I decided to stay in my room and not go to the games. I did not want to have to comment on something I knew so little about. Plus, I wanted to confer with Gordon, Watson, and Mike to determine how we would handle the inevitable publicity. I approached Shawn at the Sunday morning brunch Gordon traditionally hosted for our All-Star Weekend participants and told him what was about to happen. I then got our public relations men, Bob Price and Bob Zink, involved to help Shawn deal with it. While we were preparing Shawn to face the media, we also were trying to dissuade the magazine from releasing the story. But it did not matter what any of us said. The story was going to be written. The reporter had done too much research. He had talked to the mothers of the children.

The story appeared the next week, and our newspapers all carried stories, even though Shawn declined to comment. When I was asked to comment, I said only, "This is a personal matter. Shawn will deal with it."

That is what I was hoping, but I was not sure. I was there to offer support, but I still did not know him well enough to know how he would react. General managers and coaches always have lived with the problems of their players, but those problems had become more complex in recent years and we were busy trying to keep them from becoming public knowledge. It was not included in our job descriptions, but we were really social scientists, psychologists, and counselors, along with being managers and leaders. I always had made it a practice not to interfere with the personal lives of my players unless I was invited. I was invited in many times during my career, though I was still able to maintain enough objectivity to make some tough decisions. Still, in all my years I had not dealt with anything like this.

Amazingly, the furor died down quickly, and there did not seem to be much effect on the team. We won the last five games of the season to finish fifth in the Central Division with a 47–35 record. Shawn led the team in scoring and rebounding. Wes Person had his best year as a pro. Ilgauskas, Anderson, and Henderson scored in double figures. Brevin Knight led the team in scoring and steals. Potopenko, Ferry and Sura gave added support off the bench. Even though we were beaten by Indiana in the 1998 play-offs, we were excited about the future of the team. The rookies, along with Sura and Person, were going to get better. There were two questions: Would we be patient enough to let things come together? Would Shawn implode?

Mike did a terrific job coaching under some difficult circumstances. Shawn's tardiness continued. It drove Mike crazy, which was ironic since Mike was sometimes late himself, and it also was distracting for the young guys. Shawn could have been a leader for our band of rookies, but instead they looked at his actions in wonderment. Still, they made the NBA All-Rookie Team, which was a first in the history of the NBA. Brevin and Zydrunas were first team, and Derek and Cedric were second team. Later in the spring I was elected Executive of the Year by my colleagues. How ironic was that? If it was based on making the Kemp trade, I did not think I deserved it. On the other hand, if it was based on putting together our group of rookies, well, I would take credit for that. But my colleagues who voted for me had no idea of what was going on in our organization. And they did not know, as I did, that it was going to get worse.

Actually, things were going to get worse for everyone in The League. The Collective Bargaining Agreement between the owners and the players was going to expire on June 30, 1998, and the parties were unable to reach a new agreement. There were several issues the owners wanted changed. Salaries had escalated far beyond the established salary cap of 52 percent of basketball revenue, making it difficult to make profits. Salaries were closer to 60 percent. The salary cap only partially served its purpose, since most teams operated above the cap. Larger markets could afford to pay more, thus attracting the better players. The smaller markets were challenged. Obviously this caused a competitive imbalance.

The NBA Players Association was a strong, viable union under the leadership of Billy Hunter, a very bright lawyer who was tough and diligent. Through the efforts of the union's leadership over the years, player benefits had come a long way from the night I sat with twenty-three other scared but courageous souls who voted not to play the 1964 All-Star Game in Boston if the owners did not recognize our union and agree to a pension plan for the players. Now the average salary for players was $3 million. Meal money was $82 per day. All teams either owned planes or chartered planes. With all of this, how could there be any problems? The union questioned the validity of reported revenues, especially that from suite sales, a big source of income.

The owners had other concerns. The salary cap was put in place to protect the owners from themselves. It was necessary to protect the integrity of the cap. A drug enforcement initiative was imperative, because of the increased number of players being busted for drugs. Player conduct in general was an issue. There was far too much trash talking and taunting.

The objective of the union has always been to get the best deal for the players. The objective of the owners was to get the best deal for the owners. I was hoping that they would get the best deal for the NBA and basketball and, most important, the fans. Gordon asked for my input. I had the same economic concerns as he did. To keep the games affordable for the fans, there had to be some constraints on salaries. Player conduct on and off the court and drug testing were high on my list, and I had long been an advocate of a player code of conduct for just those reasons. I had heard too many fans and sponsors complaining about paying high ticket prices to watch overpaid athletes who, in their opinions, showed little respect for the game and the law. All parties needed to be reminded of their respective responsibilities to the game and the fans. I thought the system should be overhauled to bring costs under control. Players were overpaid; coaches were overpaid. Yes, general managers were overpaid, too. Coaches were beginning to be paid more than players, which became a problem with the union.

The lack of trust between the players and owners was a reflection of the social and cultural changes in The League and in society in general. By now The League's players were 93 percent black. Most of the players came from urban environments and urban schools where the faculties and student bodies were predominantly black. Owners and general managers and most of the coaches came from an entirely different background, and I would contend that the only contact that most of them had with black people was through The League. This meant there was a fundamental lack of communication and understanding between races and classes. No wonder there was no trust. Gordon once asked me during the negotiations if I thought there was racism involved. I told him it was more of a lack of sensitivity. No matter how much progress we had made in race relations, separatism still existed.

The parties failed to reach an agreement before the deadline, and, as predicted, the owners locked out the players and ceased all basketball-related activities. This meant we were restricted from having any contact with the players. We could not talk to them. We could not talk to their agents. We could not pay them. They were not allowed to even come into the building to work out. All our summer programs were put on hold. Not being able to be involved in basketball activity during the summer was not good for our team. Although the coaches gave the players workout regimens to follow all summer, we had no way of checking up on their progress. There was no bending the rules. Since Gordon was chairman of the Board of Governors, he was very much involved in the decisions governing the lockout.

Despite several meetings between the owners and the union, the lockout continued into the fall with no hope of an end in sight. This was a classic battle between wealthy owners and wealthy players. I think the owners underestimated the staying power of the players. They were negotiating with an intelligent union head in Billy Hunter who had the support of an intelligent and empowered group of players on the executive committee. I was surprised at the willingness of the players to hold firm. I did not know too many players who liked missing those checks on the first and the fifteenth of the month. As usual, the agents got involved and stayed abreast of the negotiations in order to advise their clients on whether to ratify a deal. Of course, the agents also wanted to protect their stakes in the future of the gold rush they had experienced over the last several years.

October came with no agreement. As a matter of fact, very little progress was made. November came and the start of the season was officially delayed. There was still a big gap. The players were as determined as ever, as were the owners. There was no end in sight. Gordon kept us well informed on the lack of progress and warned that we could very well lose the whole season. If things continued, it would be a lose-lose proposition for everyone.

As we got into December, the owners relaxed the no-contact rule, although this did not sit well with the union. A designated member of each team—for the Cavs, that was me—was allowed to talk to the player representative to the union, within limits prescribed by The League. Danny Ferry was our player representative. I liked this because of Danny's background. He could be objective because although he was a player, his father had been in management. Danny also recognized that I had been a player and he knew of my part in the creation of the union. Relatively speaking, they were making a similar stand now, even though the owners initiated the lockout. On each occasion that we spoke, I finished by saying the most important things were the game and the fans who supported the game. The great players and teams of the 1980s and early 1990s raised our fans' expectations. They expected well-conditioned athletes to provide the best competition in sports for the dollars that we charged. Together, we had the responsibility to make that happen.

Just before the deadline to cancel the season, the parties reached an agreement. It was mid-January and the fifty-game season was to start February 5, 1999. There was a little over a week to get the team in shape for the abbreviated season. We also had to do major damage control because many fans were turned off by the lockout. To their way of thinking, both sides had gotten so greedy that neither side could see how good they had it. Bringing the fans back into the fold was going to be a huge challenge.

In Cleveland, it was going to be a gigantic challenge, because our star player had gotten gigantic. Trainer Gary Briggs called Mike and me to inform us that Shawn had reported in at 315 pounds.

There was very little time for him to get in shape. Strength and conditioning coach Stan Kellers had a big, big task in front of him. Literally. The other players were in shape but rusty. The rest of The League was experiencing the same thing. Whatever teams were in the best shape would definitely have an advantage in the short schedule. We were not one of them. We were all disappointed in Shawn's physical condition. With the money we were paying him, we had every reason to expect him to stay in shape. It was not as if he could not afford to hire people to help him do that. The Cleveland Clinic nutritionist put him on a diet, but Shawn did not have the discipline to adhere to it. We even offered to have a chef go to his house and prepare meals for him. I tried my darndest to help him, having had to fight the weight problem as a player, particularly as I got older. I told Shawn the same thing I told Mel Turpin years ago: "I don't want anyone playing for me that weighs more than me." That did not work either.

Because the season was delayed in starting and because we were not allowed to have contact with the players, we did not impose the fine that we were contractually allowed to do. The consensus of ownership, management, and the coaches was to let Kemp slide and hope that he would get in shape as quickly as possible. Despite his weight, he was producing. Actually, his scoring was up. His rebounding was surprisingly good. He was doing it differently. He was using his body more to get position. He could because it was so big. But he had no lift on his jump, which always had separated him from most players his size. As the season progressed, we were worried he would break down because of the fatigue caused by carrying too much weight.

We were playing .500 basketball throughout most of the season. This was disappointing because the kids had played so well the year before. Not being able to work with our young players over the summer cost us continuity. The team actually regressed. The biggest blow came five games into the season when Zydrunas re-injured his foot and was out for the remainder of the season. He had impressed the NBA and our fans by his play as a rookie. With "Z" and Vitaly, we thought that our center position was secure. But after trying to extend Vitaly's contract, we realized we could not afford to keep both of them. So we traded Vitaly to Boston for a first-round draft pick and Andrew DeClerq.

Shawn did not come close to getting into shape. He continued to be late, Mike became more adamant about trading him. Shawn was the topic of most of our meetings with ownership. Gordon was more involved with team policies and joined us in trying to establish a system of fines designed specifically for Shawn, the one hundred-million-dollar man. If he was not going to hold up his end of the bargain, we wanted our money back in whatever increments we could get it. We spent hours debating the composition of the team rule book. This time could have been devoted to finding ways to improve the team or restoring the support of our fans. Our attendance continued to decline as the season progressed. Some dropoff was expected because of the lockout, but we were losing fans, and the fans who did show up began to boo and heckle Shawn. He was a disappointment, and I had to face the fact that his persistent tardiness indicated drug usage.

I had warned Gordon of this before the trade when I presented the results of my due diligence. But my report also said Shawn was a good guy. I had found him to be a good guy, too. I liked Shawn, but I did not like his lifestyle. As a matter of fact, I decided that in my final days with the Cavs I was going to do all I could to change his lifestyle for the good of Shawn Kemp, his family, the franchise, and the fans. As I mentioned previously, for a person who had accomplished so much, he had very low self-esteem. I talked with a psychologist and a psychiatrist for advice. I was determined to change him. I agreed with Mike that if we could trade him, we should. However, there was not much of a market for a $100-million, overweight, fading superstar. My only option was to try to get him back on track. Gordon and I were consumed by this idea.

While dealing with Shawn and our young players, I also was dealing with my own survival. I do not know why I was concerned about the franchise because I was leaving anyway. I was getting much more input from members of the board, something that had not happened for most of my tenure. In addition to all the unsolicited advice, I was being questioned by board members, some of whom were neophytes in the industry. One day I received a letter from Warren Thaler, a bright young man Gordon had recently hired. Accompanying the note was a copy of an article about Red Auerbach. The note suggested that I read the article because I might learn something from it.

I called Warren. "Warren, I received your note," I said. "You should know I played for Red Auerbach."

"Oh," was all he could say.

This was the same person who once told Lenny he wanted to sit down with him someday and learn everything he knew about basketball. "Son," Lenny said to chuckles from the rest of us, "there is not enough time left in our lives to do that."

Anyway, Shawn held up until late in the season, when a rash of injuries kept us out of the play-offs for just the second time in the last eight years. It was going to be a long spring. I could not wait to get back out on the scouting circuit to be away from the growing controversy in Cleveland. We had two draft picks, both of which were going to be in the lottery, so I wanted to make sure we got the right players to complement our group.

The one community event I looked forward to each spring was the Court of Nisi Prisis. Nisi Prisis was a fraternity of local lawyers, and every year they entertained clients and guests with an evening of great food, song, and skits. It is a night of fun and laughter as the guests watched the lawyers who represented them so well perform on an entirely different stage. The musical and humorous skits usually were spoofs of local or national current events. At the close of the evening, a notable local civic or corporate leader was surprised by being selected to stand before the twelve hundred-plus attendees and be roasted. Terri had called me several times while I was on the road scouting to tell me that Dick Watson had called several times to make sure that I would be back in time to attend this year's event. I usually was his guest and had not missed one of these nights in thirteen years. I looked forward to putting on my tuxedo and meeting Dick and his other guests.

The evening was as entertaining as ever, right up to the moment everyone had been waiting for. While we all sat in suspense, the judge of the court bellowed out to the bailiff, "Deliver the body of Wayne Richard Embry." I nearly sank to the floor. I wanted to crawl under the table. Dick and John Graham sat with sheepish grins as I made my way to stand before the judge.

"Will the reader of the scroll read the claims before this body?" the judge commanded.

I stood next to a lawyer about half my size and listened to a hilarious roast that amused all of those in attendance. I went from being roasted to being toasted for all the trades and drafts of my career. I was more amused by the lawyer who was visibly shaking as he was reading the scroll. I could have easily been humiliated by the content of the text, but it was just too funny for that to happen.

What I did not know was what was in store for me later. After the roast, the bar stayed open and the lawyers and guests sang and socialized well into the evening. I remained in a celebratory mood. I considered it a distinct honor to be among those well-respected leaders in Cleveland who had been roasted by this distinguished group. My spirits were further lifted by the rousing applause I received. I was so happy I even tried to sing, and I cannot carry a tune in a bucket.

It was late when Dick approached me and suggested that we retire to his suite for a nightcap, as was our usual custom. We would review the evening, critique the skits and argue about his thespian talents, or lack of them. I always told him to keep his day job.

When we got to his hotel room, Dick opened the minibar, took out two small bottles of vodka, and asked, "Care to join me?"

But his mood was different than it had been in years past, and it did not take long to realize what was bothering him.

"You know Gordon and I are jealous that you were honored this evening," he said. "Gordon's father was honored by the group years ago."

I did not know exactly what to say for a moment. Then I told him, "Dick, I had nothing to do with being selected for this honor. I figured that you had something to do with my being selected, and I was going to thank you."

Dick continued as if I had not spoken.

"You should know that I told those people downstairs that the deal between you and I is that I make all of the deals and you take the credit for them," he said. "We have been doing things your way for the first nine years. Now we are doing things my way."

I was shocked. Here I was in my tuxedo being verbally dressed down by Dick. I felt as if I was back on Hill, wearing my raggedy overalls, about to get a whipping. I cannot tell you how close I came to punching him. Then I decided I would not dignify his comments.

"Dick, it's late. I'm leaving." Refusing to be drawn into an argument made me feel good.

During my forty-five-minute drive home, my mind wandered. I wondered if he had been trying to provoke me into some sort of hostile exchange that would have provided the Cavs with a way to end our relationship. I knew Dick was unhappy with me. The exchange confirmed something that general managers and coaches have known for years:

Beware of the five percenters. Five percenters are people who own five percent of the team. These people are usually legal or financial advisors to the majority owner. Sometimes they are business associates or just friends. They boast about their involvement to their friends at cocktail parties and country clubs, and they usually exaggerate their roles. When times are good, they sit in courtside seats and high-five anyone they can reach. When times are bad, they go underground. I have always thought they were responsible for most of the leaks of classified information to the press. If you listen to them, they have hired and fired all of the coaches. I am sure, in their minds, that is how they think things are done.

Chapter 21

On My Way Out

I had to put the uncomfortable exchange with Watson behind me as we began a series of meetings geared toward assessing the needs of our team. Once again, Mike had been asked to rate his players against the rest of The League. He posted the results on the walls of the boardroom and began to speak to each position. There were several conspicuous revelations. Our former players, Bobby Phills, Chris Mills, Tyrone Hill, and Terrell Brandon, who had moved on and played well for their new teams, had moved up in the rankings, while most of our guys were ranked way below them. This did not go unnoticed.

"Mike, our former players have moved up in your ratings," Gordon said. "You rate them ahead of our current players."

We all sat waiting for a response.

"Oops," I said under my breath as I looked across the table at scout Darrell Hedrick and smiled.

While having dinner that evening, I said to Darrell, "I think Mike just trapped himself. I think everyone realizes now that we got rid of some pretty good players."

We would have a good team with Derek and Bobby Sura backing up Bobby Phills and Brevin backing up Terrell. That would have been our backcourt. Our front court was also adequate with Danny, Tyrone, Chris, and a healthy Ilgauskas. I was also confident that we could have picked up a solid veteran, either through a trade or by signing a free agent. With an aging Eastern Conference, we would have been very competitive.

"That was my plan and no one bought it," I continued. "I guess I did a terrible job of convincing my bosses and our fans. They said we were stuck in mediocrity. I could not convince them that a mediocre team with players whose average age was twenty-five left plenty of room for growth. If our average age was thirty and we were mediocre, then we would have had problems."

Because of the drastic decline in attendance, the marketing department brought in several consulting firms to poll our market to determine the reasons. There definitely was growing apathy. I do not think anyone anticipated that our fans from Richfield and Summit County would not make the move with us. The marketing people held focus groups, they asked season-ticket holders to respond to questionnaires. We held additional meetings with the marketing department to learn the results of the polls and to determine a countermarketing strategy. I sat in on most of those meetings with other senior managers. It was a good thing that I had a thick skin, because there was much criticism of management, which meant me. The style of play also was criticized, which meant Mike.

No one could fault Gordon for doing a market study to find out why the attendance had declined. He had just moved into a state-of-the-art building. He had just paid a large sum money for what he thought was a star. He had just signed his coach to a contract that could have been worth twenty million dollars. He needed to know what was wrong. I had no choice but to assume that I was part of the problem.

Perhaps to check up on me or perhaps just to protect his investment, Gordon joined me as I continued to meet with Shawn in an effort to correct his lifestyle. Gordon learned firsthand what it was like to manage athletes. Shawn was pleasant enough. He was great at telling you what you wanted to hear. He was not so great at following through on his promises.

Gordon also wanted to meet with the players individually. I was removed from that process, which I thought was unusual. Then again, the unusual had become the usual. Gordon asked Jim Paxson to accompany each player to a room on the lower level of the arena. I have no idea what was discussed in the meetings. Did they vent their frustrations with Mike? Did they have an axe to grind with me? Something must have come out of those meetings that Gordon did not like.

A few days passed, and Gordon called to ask me where I was going to be Memorial Day weekend. He was prepared to meet me anywhere. On the Saturday before Memorial Day, Gordon flew to Martha's Vineyard, where I had a summer home, and we met on his plane. Gordon has a place on Nantucket, the neighboring island. We started the conversation talking about fishing in the waters surrounding both islands. We both loved fishing for striped bass. But I knew he was not there to talk about fishing. I was prepared to be told that he was terminating me and making Mike general manager. Instead he shocked me.

"I have decided not to pick up the option on Mike's contract," he said in announcing the overthrow of The Czar. "I plan to tell him Tuesday that he is terminated, so I want you to keep it quiet until then. And by the way, I am moving up the timetable for Jim Paxson to take over your job. I want you to stick around as a mentor to Jim, and I want you to announce his promotion at the press conference when we announce Mike's termination. You will be president and general manager until June 30, so I expect you to run the draft and help Jim in searching for a new coach."

It was not until later that I realized that I was being fired a year early as general manager along with Mike. I was absolutely shocked that he was firing Mike. I thought Mike had secured his relationship with Gordon as Ronnie had told him to do. Maybe getting closer to Gordon in order to circumvent my authority allowed Gordon to know Mike better, and he did not like what he saw. Something must have come out of the meetings with the players that Gordon did not like.

"Can you believe Gordon is going to fire Mike on Tuesday"? I said to Terri as I climbed into our Jeep Cherokee.

"What did you say?" she asked. "I don't believe it."

"And by the way, I was fired too," I added.

She was not surprised by that, having lived through the past couple of years. She was angry, but relieved that I would be leaving this negative environment.

Mike showed up at the office on Tuesday and did not have a clue as to what was about to happen. Gordon and his public relations people were there bright and early. We had to rehearse for the press conference that was called for that afternoon. We were to go over questions that might be asked by reporters sure to be shocked by the announcement of Mike's firing.

Mike was even late for his meeting with Gordon. But it did not matter at this point. The meeting lasted about forty-five minutes and Mike was gone. Mike was shocked. He thought he had done a credible coaching job, considering the injuries and youth of our team. I think he went into the meeting expecting to be named general manager in addition to coach. Gordon also had decided to fire the assistant coaches. He wanted to clear the slate for Paxson to hire his own coaches. The assistants were even more surprised than Mike was.

The press conference was well orchestrated. Gordon was to announce Mike's firing, and he was then to turn the podium over to me to announce Paxson's promotion. I knew why they wanted me to make that announcement. They wanted to make it look as if I was the one who wanted to step aside. In many ways, this was the ultimate compliment to me, although it did avoid the public relations backlash that might have resulted from the business or black communities, and the players, had I been fired outright. Gordon was willing to take the blame for firing the coach, and he was allowing me to protect my dignity by making it appear as if I were retiring. To be honest, I would have preferred to have been fired. It would have given me more options and kept my name out there in basketball circles. As a matter of fact, on the way to the press conference, I jokingly told Davis Young of our public relations firm and Jim Boland of our staff that I was not going to make the announcement of Paxson's promotion because I did not think it was my place to do so. It did cause quite a stir when I threatened not to participate. But I was not about to burst their bubble. After all, I was still president of the team division, even if I did not have any authority.

The media was as shocked as Mike was. After listening to the announcement, they bombarded Gordon with questions and then rushed out to find Mike. He made himself scarce. The only newspaper he talked to was the *Plain Dealer*. I could only imagine how devastated he was.

Mike and I had lunch a couple days after that and rehashed our experiences. He never really got to coach the team I hired him to coach. Career-ending injuries and retirements prevented that. Then he had to coach an injury-riddled young team. The lockout also impeded our progress. We talked about why and how our relationship had deteriorated over the years. I am sure there were things in my management style he did not like, but there was more to it. Others also contributed to our difficulties. I remember Ronnie Rothstein entering my office and coming around behind my desk to tell me they were throwing a surprise fiftieth birthday party for Mike and that I should stay away from it. He was trying to make a point, and I got it. I think that if Mike and I had been left alone, we could have worked through our differences and built a competitive team. It did not matter now. We were both gone, and the Cavs were heading in a different direction. In all, nearly twenty people from my regime would be fired. Even Danny Ferry, such a prominent figure in my tenure, opted to leave as a free agent and signed with San Antonio for the 2000–01 season.

As for Mike, I think he was in the wrong place at the wrong time after the composition of the team changed. Some coaches are better coaching veteran teams. In today's NBA, I questioned whether Mike had the patience to build a young team and let the youngsters work through their mistakes. I knew it would pay off in the long run. After all, the San Antonio Spurs' record dropped off dramatically when David Robinson was hurt. They got the Number 1 pick in the draft, Tim Duncan, and won the NBA title two years later.

As for me, I stayed with the Cavs too long. I will never understand why an organization looking for a graceful way out of a relationship would forbid another team from talking to me. I do not understand why Watson thought that would be "a disaster." I do not understand why anyone would want to continue a false relationship. I do not understand why a person with my credentials was forced to retire at the age of sixty-two.

When the commissioner suggested that I retire, I knew my days in the NBA were numbered. He controlled so much that happened in his NBA, and I had the feeling he did not like to be questioned about how The League was run. I always believed that when it came to basketball, the commissioner was a style-over-substance person who thought the best way to sell the NBA was to promote stars or individuals as opposed to teams. The more slam dunks on ESPN, the better. I was greatly distressed when one of my favorite authors, John Edgar Wideman, described the NBA as a modern-day minstrel show. John loves the game, as does his daughter, Jamila, a Stanford graduate who played for our Rockers.

I agreed with Wideman. Stern converted the players into entertainers rather than competitors. If entertainment is the goal, winning is not that important. And if winning is not the goal, character is not that important. As a result, many of the so-called "stars" of The League came from terrible teams, and many of them were complete fabrications. He rode the backs of superstars Magic, Bird, Isiah, and Jordan to prominence. They entertained the fans because they were exceptional talents and because they made their teams great. They won championships. They followed in the footsteps of Russell, Cousy, Havlicek, and the Jones on the famed Boston teams, and Chamberlain, Cunningham, Greer, and Walker on the awesome Philadelphia teams. There was West and Baylor, Kareem and Oscar, Barry and Thurmond, Dr. J and Moses. All of these great players were parts of teams that won the hearts of NBA fans because of the way they competed and won championships. I am not sure he realized that is why fans loved the Showtime Lakers or the legendary Celtics.

The job of a commissioner in all sports is very challenging, and David Stern's job has become more difficult. He has been able to grow revenues through television contracts, merchandising the NBA brand, and attracting sponsors. The value of the franchises has appreciated immensely. However, diminishing skill levels (caused in part by younger and younger players entering The League), stagnant play, and conduct on and off the court threaten the future growth of The League as television ratings and attendance in many cities are declining. Stern failed to listen to the dedicated basketball people in the trenches whose jobs were to protect the integrity of the the game. Whenever we talked about the way the game was being played or made comments about the image of The League, I felt as though we were held in contempt. It was not Stern, but rather my good friend Jerry Colangelo who insisted we needed a blue-ribbon panel to address the problems plaguing the game in the late 1990s. Colangelo had gone from a gofer and scout with the Chicago Bulls to the general manager and then owner of the Phoenix Suns and powerful chairman of the NBA's Board of Governors. I was honored when he asked me to join the panel, along with several former NBA coaches and general managers, including Jerry West, Rod Thorn, Jack Ramsey, and Dick Motta. I had long been an advocate of changing the rules to allow a zone defense in the NBA, which, I thought, would prevent the one-on-ones and force players to learn to shoot better. This would reward the kids who practiced until dark on the playgrounds and driveways. Many of those kids were white. As an advocate for diversity, I knew we needed to find spots for those kids in The League. Of course, the panel was not concerned with that, but it did recommend ending the ban on zone defenses and changing a few other minor rules that the Board of Governors ultimately adopted. Stern was on board with us at the end, but it was Colangelo's initiative that may have saved the game of basketball.

Neither Jerry nor I tried to upstage the commissioner. We respected his authority and acknowledged his many contributions. But, in my opinion, Stern has little respect for intellectual capacity of the veteran players, coaches, and general managers who saw the many changes coming and tried to warn him about how they would impact The League. Like many of my colleagues, I wanted to take care of the game and have a positive influence on those young men playing the game, which he could not appreciate. There are some of us who do what we do for the passion of the game. I was not doing it for the money, Mr. Commissioner. I do not know if Milwaukee would have hired me or what they would have paid me. I just wanted to continue my contribution to the game and your NBA.

The first nine years of my tenure with the Cavs was enjoyable. The last four years made it difficult for me to enjoy the game that I love. Our organization became fragmented. We were dysfunctional. Decisions were being made by committee, and we did whatever the consensus wanted. We were a blueprint for failure. There were too many bosses. Management 101 taught me that no organization could succeed without solidarity. Without solidarity at the top, there can be no solidarity in the rest of the organization. Our actions permeated the organization. There must be vertical reporting. I was doing my best to rebuild the franchise into one that met the fans satisfaction while protecting the security of the people who reported to me. Gordon often said to me that he was the only boss, but I was reporting to Watson and a host of others. In a private meeting, Gordon told me Watson did not speak for him.

"You should tell him that," I replied. "All of us spent more time competing against each other than competing against The League. No team will ever win under those circumstances. My contract reads that I do as ownership directs, and Dick has part ownership in the franchise."

Gordon did the right thing by getting rid of us. If Gordon thought Mike was the problem, he did the right thing by getting rid of him. I knew he could not get rid of Mike and not get rid of me. It would have been a public relations blunder. I also assumed the responsibility of hiring Mike. However, I maintained that if we had continued with my plan we would have been a contender in a couple of years. But it did not matter what I thought. I did not own the team.

I still had the Chicago pre-draft camp and the 1999 draft as my last official duties with the Cavs. I wanted to make the draft a good one. Gordon told me to let Jim sit on the stage during the televised lottery to change our luck. We still did not move up. We were to have the eighth and eleventh picks. It did not matter because I felt the player that Pete and I loved would be there at Number 8. I called a lunch meeting while in Chicago to review the draft. After talking about the players we saw at the morning session, I said, "Fellows, I think our work is done. If Andre Miller is there at Number 8, we will take him, and if Trajan Langdon is there at Number 11, we will take him." Andre was the best guard I had seen in college ball the past two years. And I liked Trajan as a shooter off the bench. Draft day came and we drafted the two players I wanted. We had added two good players to an already young nucleus.

I finished the last year as president making myself available for consultation and cleaning out my office. Jim Paxson was the general manager now and needed to establish his authority. I sensed discomfort in our relationship. Very seldom did he talk to me or seek advice. When Gordon was in, they would go into Jim's office and close the door. I felt like an outsider. There was no doubt that I was estranged from the front office, although I was called upon to deal with Shawn, who again reported to camp for the 1999–2000 season well above three hundred pounds. This time Gordon decided to fine him in accordance with the clause in his contract. I was the one who had to deliver the letter to him informing him of the fine.

After a game I asked Shawn to come into a private office adjacent to the training room.

"Shawn, this is a letter informing you that we are exercising the right to fine you $150,000 pursuant to your contract," I told him. "I am really disappointed in you."

Shawn acted as if nothing had happened. Of course, $150,000 was

A historic photo featuring (clockwise from left) the first black player in the league, Earl Lloyd; the first black coach, Bill Russell; the first black president and general manager, Wayne Embry; and the first black owner, Robert Johnson (Courtesy of NBA)

not that much money to him. In fact, that was the first chunk of what would amount to nearly $300,000 in fines that season.

"Wayne, you are just doing what you are told to do," he said after I handed him the letter. "I won't hold any grudges toward you."

I said, "Shawn, I don't care whether you do or not. You can hate me forever. If you get your life in order, I will be happy."

I tried to take my own advice. I tried to get on with my life outside of basketball, and I was finding I could be happy, even though I tremendously missed the day-to-day involvement with the game. I had little to do with the team the rest of the season, and they even took away my locker downstairs. On my last day with the Cavs, Gordon invited me to lunch in his office in the Gund.

I told him my only regret was not winning a championship for him and the franchise and for the fans. It was my desire to leave the game on top. In a way, I was leaving on top because of the many personal honors and citations that I received. But I always put the teams first, so leaving on top for me really meant winning a championship, or at least being a contender.

Gordon was very complimentary and grateful for my contributions toward making the Cavs one of the most respected franchises in The League. He went on to say that I was the hallmark of the franchise, which made me feel good even if I was still out of a job. I asked Gordon if there was anything I could have done differently and better. I thought it was a typical exit interview. But I asked the question because I wanted to satisfy myself that I did the best I could, remembering the advice given me at an early age by my parents and particularly my grandfather, who wanted all his children and grandchildren to be the best we could be.

I was thinking of them as I returned to my office to begin packing up many years worth of files and personal belongings. There were many mementos, awards, and citations that I received over the years. As a mat-

Sharing a laugh with Bill Russell during a panel discussion on the pioneers of the NBA (Courtesy of NBA)

ter of fact, I was still being honored by organizations that appreciated my contributions to the city of Cleveland and the state of Ohio. I was deeply touched to receive the highest honor given by my alma mater, the Distinguished Achievement Award. I was proud of what I had done in Cleveland. The Cavaliers were better because I had been with them. If success is measured by winning championships, I failed, but so did twenty-seven other teams every year. If success is measured by being a contender and having a classy organization, I succeeded. My two executive of the year awards were proof of that.

I never tooted my own horn while doing my job, so I never thought I really got the credit I deserved for what I had done, especially in Milwaukee. As I watched others promote themselves and receive credit for and benefit from work I had done, I figured there were those who recognized my efforts. I was right. But more important to me was that I knew and was satisfied with what I had done. There were times when I am angry about things that happened to me. But the anger is fleeting because when I think about where I came from, I realized I have been blessed. I think I followed the script that was written for me. I often reflect on the days spent on the Hill and the values instilled in me. My folks wanted me to make a difference.

Have I done that? I think that I have. I know I tried. Pioneers open the doors for others to follow. I believe that the door is open. As those pioneers who went before me did, I believe I set an example for future generations of young men and women. I can say that I am proud of my accomplishments. I have proven that I belonged, although, as my parents warned me, belonging does not always mean that you will be welcomed or accepted. In many respects and in many arenas, I have been accepted. My folks would be proud, and that, for me, is the greatest victory I have registered in The Inside Game.

Timeout Number Six

I cannot believe what I just saw. Then again, maybe I can.

I just took a break from writing to watch the last few minutes of the Cavs game against Michael Jordan and the Washington Wizards. That still does not sound right, does it? But Jordan, president of the Wizards since 2000, had come out of his second retirement to play for the team in the 2001–02 and 2002–03 seasons.

In their second game against Jordan's Wizards on January 31, 2002, the Cavs outscored the Wizards, 33–6, to overcome a big deficit, and they had a five-point lead with less than two minutes to go. I flipped the channel momentarily, and when I came back to the game, the Wizards were up one. After a timeout the Cavs went inside, missed a shot, got the rebound, and scored for a one-point lead with 1.6 seconds left. The Wizards called timeout.

Surely this was not happening again. There were more than twenty thousand people in the arena and an unknown number watching on television who knew exactly where the ball was going when the clock started.

When play resumed, Jordan broke to the baseline and doubled back to the free-throw line, where he was, inexplicably, wide open. He received the inbounds pass, turned, and shot.

You got it. SWISH. The Cavs lost, 93–92. It was déjà vu all over again, an instant replay of "The Shot."

The nearest defenders were about as close as Ehlo was when he defended Jordan on "The Shot" in 1989. I have a message for Ricky Davis, the boastful young forward for the Cavs who was carrying on a feud with Michael: Respect your elders, son.

Two Cavs chased Chris Whitney, who had made several threes during the game, and left Michael alone. Unbelievable. Where had they been the past ten years?

Injuries cut short Jordan's season. All I know is he was back long enough to beat the Cavs again.

Epilogue

Early in the summer of 2003, I drove to Cincinnati to discuss some Hall of Fame business with Oscar Robertson and Dave Cowens, two of the greatest players in the history of the game. But before we got down to business, we talked about what everyone else was talking about—or, rather, whom everyone else was talking about—young phenomenon, LeBron James. It was before the NBA draft, but after the Cavaliers won the lottery, which gave them the Number 1 pick and the chance to draft the most famous graduate of Akron's St. Vincent-St. Mary High School.

None of us had seen anything like the hype surrounding this eighteen-year-old kid who was being called the best high school player in history. Of course, many of those making those pronouncements were in their thirties with a fairly narrow view of "history." The one thing I know for sure is that James is the most publicized high school player in history. But Oscar was a pretty darn good high school player, too.

I have seen James play, and it looks as if he is the real thing. I am happy for him, happy for the Cavaliers and Gordon Gund, and happy for the city of Cleveland. I sent a note of congratulations to Gordon after the lottery, and I meant it sincerely. I wish James and the team well. I think he will resurrect a dying franchise. He certainly gives the Cavs hope.

But I do worry about the pressure being put on him. The Cavs were desperate to have him. The League was desperate to have him. Nike, which signed him to a $90 million deal before he graduated from high school, was desperate to have him. The city of Cleveland was desperate to have him, and the downtown business community is looking to him to turn around a stagnant economy. That is an awful lot of responsibility for anyone.

Of course, I do not really have to worry about this. Although I still love the game and The League, I am on the outside looking in. I have had little official contact with anyone from the team since I left, though I have chatted with Gordon, Jim Paxson, and team president Jim Boland about a variety of topics. Still, I have to believe I was the highest-paid, least-used consultant in The League. I no longer have my box in Gund Arena. Gordon told me to call him anytime I wanted to come to a game, but I do not like to ask for tickets.

Being forced into retirement is the equivalent of being fired, and it is not the way I would have chosen to end my career in the NBA. No matter how hard I have tried, I cannot seem to convince anybody that "retiring" was not my idea. But every time a job opens up and I am not contacted (despite inquiries to the appropriate parties by my agent), the point is driven home again.

At the age of sixty-six, I am trying to get over it and take advantage of the fact that I no longer have to work, although I do still serve on a number of corporate boards. Terri and I are living a passive, almost reclusive, existence, splitting our time between Cleveland and Martha's Vineyard. There are so many things I love about the Vineyard—the casual lifestyle, fishing, golf, and the opportunity to escape to the beach. No one cares who you are or what you look like. I do not have to defend the Ron Harper trade. No one asks what Shawn Kemp was really like. There are some attendants on the ferry from Wood's Hole who remember me from my days with the Celtics. They are always surprised I have so little news to share about The League.

That is not to say I am not in touch with old friends and colleagues. In fact, I often feel like an unofficial consultant to the masses. Hardly a day goes by when I do not get a call from a former classmate, player, coach, executive, or business associate. Bobby Dandridge called to thank me for my guidance. So did Lucius Allen. Reuben Britt, one of the more than ten thousand youngsters who attended the camps I ran with the assistance of many coaches at Daniel Webster College in Nashua, New Hampshire, for twenty-seven years, survived the streets of Boston, went on to become an administrator at a small college in New Jersey, and acknowledged me in the book he published recently. I had lunch with Danny Ferry after he won the 2003 NBA title with the San Antonio Spurs. Those are the kind of rewards that make it all worthwhile.

One of the greatest advantages of slowing down is that I have so much time to think and reflect on my life and my career. Whether sitting on my favorite boulder, Cracked Rock, lodged in the sand near the water, or walking the beach near my home on a hill near Makonikey, the NBA

Who'd have thought a shy kid from Springfield, Ohio, would grow up to introduce the President of the United States, George Bush, during a Cleveland Growth Association luncheon? (Courtesy of Embry family)

is never far from my mind. It works its way to the forefront whether I am sitting on the porch watching the sailboats pass through the Vineyard Sound or trolling for striped bass on my boat, the "Pk'n'roll IV." I cannot imagine what my life would have been like without basketball.

The best thing about the Vineyard is that it reminds me so much of The Hill. I still get back there a couple of times a year. All the surviving family members get together for a reunion every year to reminisce about the good old days and to celebrate the love, strength, and conviction of those who raised us. We have formed a trust fund to make sure The Hill remains taken care of and in the family, and I guess we will have to trust each other that the values we learned there will be passed on to future generations.

As if to reinforce those values, whenever I am back home, I take a ride out US 40 to the Glen Haven Memorial Garden, about ten miles outside town. In the far southwest corner of the cemetery rest the bodies of those who went before us. My dad is there now, along with Grandpa and Grandma, and many aunts, uncles, and cousins. Memories flood my mind and, sometimes, if the light is just right and a gentle breeze is blowing, I can almost hear Grandpa's voice telling me that everything is all right. On my worst days with the Cavaliers, I used to tell Dick Watson, "I don't care what you do to me. I can always go back to The Hill and be content. It doesn't take much to make me happy."

Ironically, this part of the cemetery is on a hill, too, and I cannot help but think that it completes a grand circle of life. My life has taken some twists and turns, and there have been some bumps in the road. But I am who I am because of all that and because of the people who loved me enough to teach me right from wrong. As I make a silent prayer of thanks to them, I realize that all I ever wanted or needed was ten miles away on The Hill, my home, my heart, my history.

Appendix 1

Wayne Embry's Playing Career

Year	Team	Record	Avg. Pts.	Avg. Rebs.
1955–56	Miami University (varsity)	12–8	7.5	9.9
1956–57	Miami University (varsity)	17–8	23.1	17.2
1957–58	Miami University (varsity)	18–9	24.9	18.0
1958–59	Cincinnati Royals	19–53	11.4	9.0
1959–60	Cincinnati Royals	19–56	10.6	9.5
1960–61	Cincinnati Royals	33–46	14.4	10.9*
1961–62	Cincinnati Royals	43–37	19.8	13.0*
1962–63	Cincinnati Royals	42–38	18.6	12.3*
1963–64	Cincinnati Royals	55–25	17.3	11.6*
1964–65	Cincinnati Royals	48–32	12.7	10*
1965–66	Cincinnati Royals	45–35	7.6	6.6
1966–67	Boston Celtics	60–21	5.2	4.1
1967–68	Boston Celtics	54–28	6.3	4.1**
1968–69	Milwaukee Bucks	27–55	13.1	8.6

*Selected as an All-Star
**NBA champions

Appendix 2

Wayne Embry's Executive Career

Draft Choices (while serving as president, vice president, general manager, or consultant)

1972: Milwaukee: 1. Russell Lee (No. 6 overall), Marshall; 1. Julius Erving (No. 12 overall), Massachusetts; 2. Chuck Terry, Long Beach State; 3, George Adams, Gardner-Webb; 4, Art White, Georgetown; 5. Ron Harris, Wichita State; 7. Mickey Davis, Duquesne; 8. Charles Kirkland, Cheney State; 9. Jim Regenold, Ball State; 10. Jolley Spight, Santa Clara.

1973: Milwaukee: 1. Swen Nater (No. 16 overall), UCLA; 4. Clyde Turner, Minnesota; 4. Harry Rogers, St. Louis; 5. Larry Jackson, Northern Illinois; 6. Jim Floyd, Shaw College; 7. Ed Childress, Austin Peay; 8. Walt McGary, Tennessee-Chattanooga; 9. Bob Vacca, Quinnipiac; 10. Ron Battle, Sam Houston State.

1974: Milwaukee: 1. Gary Brokaw (No. 18 overall), Notre Dame; 3. Greg McDougald, Oral Roberts; 4. Lionel Billingy, Duquesne; 5. John Johnson, Denver; 6. Larry Williams, Kansas State; 7. Bob Hornstein, West Virginia; 8. Ralph Talamar, Cameron; 9. Mike Deane, Potsdam State; 10. Bruce Fetherston, Southwest Texas State.

1975: Milwaukee: 2. Clyde Mayes, Furman; 2. Cornelius Cash, Bowling Green; 3. Brian Hammel, Bentley; 4. Bill Campion, Manhattan; 6. Oliver Purnell, Old Dominion; 7. Wilbur Thomas, American; 8. Bob McCurdy, Richmond; 9. Eric Hays, Montana; 10. Romie Thomas, Wisconsin-Eau Claire.

1976: Milwaukee: 1. Quinn Buckner (No. 7 overall), Indiana; 2. Alex English, South Carolina; 2. Scott Lloyd, Arizona; 3, Lloyd Walton, Marquette; 4. Dan Frost, Iowa; 5. Tom Lockhart, Manhattan; 5. Jim Rappis, Arizona; 6. Phil Spence, North Carolina State; 7. Ron Barrow, Southern University; 8. Bob Warner, Maine; 9. Bennie Shaw, Florida Tech; 10. Hugo Cabrera, East Texas State.

1977: Milwaukee: 1. Kent Benson (No. 1 overall), Indiana; 1. Marques Johnson (No. 3 overall), UCLA; 1. Ernie Grunfeld (No. 11 overall), Tennessee; 2. Glen Williams, St. John's; 3. Gary Yoder, Cincinnati; 4. Lewis Brown, Nevada-Las Vegas; 5. Ron Norwood, DePaul; 6. Chuck Goodyear, Miami (Ohio); 7. Ron Bostic, Detroit; 8. Larry Pikes, Wisconsin-Milwaukee.

1978: Milwaukee: 1. George Johnson (No. 12 overall), St. John's; 3. Pat Cummings, Cincinnati; 4. Otis Howard, Austin Peay; 5. Russ Coleman, Pacific; 6. Dave Kyle, Cleveland State; 7. Kim Anderson, Missouri; 8. Tom Zaliageris, North Carolina; 9. Gary Rosenberger, Marquette; 10. Tom Anderson, Wisconsin-Green Bay.

1979: Milwaukee: 1. Sidney Moncrief (No. 5 overall), Arkansas; 2. Edgar Jones, Nevada-Reno; 3. Larry Gibson, Maryland; 4. Eugene Robinson, Northeast Louisiana; 5. James Tillman, Eastern Kentucky; 6. Derrick Mayes, Illinois; 7. Stan Ray, California Fullerton; 8. Larry Spicer, Alabama-Birmingham; 9. Roger Lapham, Maine; 10. Chris Fahrbach, North Dakota.

1980: Milwaukee: 3. Al Beal, Oklahoma; 4. Jeff Wolf, North Carolina; 5. Ken Jones, Virginia Commonwealth; 6. Alex Gilbert, Indiana State; 7. Ron White, Furman; 8. Keith Valentine, Virginia Union; 9. Del Yarbrough, Illinois State; 10. Melvin Crayton, Alabama State.

1981: Milwaukee: 1. Alton Lister (No. 21 overall), Arizona State; 3.

Mark Smith, Illinois; 4. Kris Anderson, Florida State; 5. Kelvin Troy, Rutgers; 6. Jo Jo Hunter, Colorado; 7. Lewis Latimore, Virginia; 8. Mike Brkovich, Michigan State; 9. Chip Rucker, Northeastern; 10. Artie Green, Marquette.

1982: Milwaukee: 1. Paul Pressey (No. 20 overall), Tulsa; 2. Fred Roberts, Brigham Young; 4. Jerry Beck, Middle Tennessee State; 6. Tony Carr, Wisconsin-Eau Claire; 7. Bobby Austin, Cincinnati; 8. Bryan Leonard, Illinois; 9. Robert Tate, Idaho State; 10. Bob Coenen, Wisconsin-Eau Claire.

1983: Milwaukee: 1. Randy Breuer (No. 18 overall), Minnesota; 2. Ted Kitchel, Indiana; 2. Mike Davis, Alabama; 3. Billy Goodwin, St. John's; 4. Mark Nickens, American; 5. Mark Petteway, New Orleans; 6. Russell Todd, West Virginia; 6. Charles Hurt, Kentucky; 7. Anthony Hicks, Xavier; 8. Brett Burkholder, DePaul; 9. Billy Vamer, Notre Dame; 10. Bob Kelly, St. John's.

1984: Milwaukee: 1. Kenny Fields (No. 21 overall), UCLA; 3. Vernon Delancy, Florida; 5. Ernie Floyd, Holy Cross; 6. McKinley Singleton, Alabama-Birmingham; 6. Mike Reddick, Stetson; 7. Tony Williams, Florida State; 8. Brad Jergenson, South Carolina; 9. Edwin Green, Massachusetts; 10. Mike Toomer, Florida A&M.

1986: Indiana (consultant): 1. Chuck Person (No. 4 overall), Auburn; 2. Greg Dreiling, Kansas; 4. Derrick Taylor, Louisiana State; 5. Richard Rellford, Michigan; 6. Jeff Hall, Louisville; 7. Steve Woodside, Oregon State.

1987: Cleveland: 1. Kevin Johnson (No. 7 overall), California; 2. Kannard Johnson, Western Kentucky; 3. Donald Royal, Notre Dame; 4. Chris Dudley, Yale; 4. Carven Holcombe, Texas Christian; 5. Carl Lott, Texas Christian; 6, Harold Jensen, Villanova; 7, Michael Foster, South Carolina.

1988: Cleveland: 1, Randolph Keys (No. 22 overall), Southern Mississippi; 3. Winston Bennett, Kentucky.

1989: Cleveland: 1, John Morton (No. 25 overall), Seton Hall; 2. Chucky Brown, N.C. State.

1990: Cleveland: 2. Stefano Rusconi, Ranger Varese.

1991: Cleveland: 1. Terrell Brandon (No.11 overall), Oregon; 2. Jimmy Oliver, Purdue.

1992*: Cleveland: No selections.

1993: Cleveland: 1. Chris Mills (No. 22 overall), Arizona.

1994: Cleveland: 2. Gary Collier, Tulsa.

1995: Cleveland: 1. Bob Sura (No. 17 overall), Florida State; 2. Donny Marshall, Connecticut.

1996: Cleveland: 1. Vitaly Potapenko (No. 12 overall), Wright State; 1. Zydrunas Ilgauskas (No. 20 overall), Lithuania; 2. Reggie Geary, Arizona.

1997: Cleveland: 1. Derek Anderson (No. 13 overall), Kentucky; 1. Brevin Knight (No. 16 overall), Stanford; 2. Cedric Henderson, Memphis.

1998*: Cleveland: 2. Ryan Stack, South Carolina.

1999: Cleveland: 1. Andre Miller (No. 8 overall), Utah; 1. Trajan Langdon (No. 11 overall), Duke; 2. A.J. Bramlett, Arizona.

*Executive of the Year

Major Trades

June 16, 1975 Milwaukee traded Kareem Abdul-Jabbar and Walt Wesley to Lakers for Elmore Smith, Brian Winters, David Meyers, Junior Bridgeman, and future considerations.

Feb. 4, 1980 Milwaukee acquired Bob Lanier from Detroit for Kent Benson and a first-round draft choice in 1980.

Feb. 25, 1988 Cleveland acquired Larry Nance and Mike Sanders from Phoenix for Mark West, Kevin Johnson, Tyrone Corbin, a first-round pick in 1988 and two second-round picks.

Nov. 16, 1989 Cleveland acquired the rights to Danny Ferry, along with Reggie Williams, from the Los Angeles Clippers for Ron Harper, first-round draft choices in 1990 and 1992 and a second-round pick in 1991.

Sept. 25, 1997 In a three-way trade, Cleveland acquired Shawn Kemp from Seattle and Sherman Douglas from Milwaukee, while sending Terrell Brandon, Tyrone Hill, and future considerations to Milwaukee. Seattle acquired Vin Baker from Milwaukee to complete the deal.

Index

Index

Index